Charles Wells

# The Literature of the Turks.

A Turkish Chrestomathy

Charles Wells

**The Literature of the Turks.**
*A Turkish Chrestomathy*

ISBN/EAN: 9783337015442

Printed in Europe, USA, Canada, Australia, Japan

Cover: Foto ©Thomas Meinert / pixelio.de

More available books at **www.hansebooks.com**

THE

# LITERATURE OF THE TURKS.

A

## TURKISH CHRESTOMATHY,

*CONSISTING OF EXTRACTS IN TURKISH FROM THE BEST TURKISH
AUTHORS (HISTORIANS, NOVELISTS, DRAMATISTS, &c.), WITH
INTERLINEAR AND FREE TRANSLATIONS IN ENGLISH,
BIOGRAPHICAL AND GRAMMATICAL NOTES,
AND FACSIMILES OF MS. LETTERS AND DOCUMENTS.*

BY

### CHARLES WELLS, Ph.D.,

PROFESSOR OF TURKISH AT KING'S COLLEGE, LONDON;
FORMERLY PROFESSOR AT THE IMPERIAL NAVAL COLLEGE, CONSTANTINOPLE;
AUTHOR OF "A PRACTICAL GRAMMAR OF THE TURKISH LANGUAGE," ETC., ETC.

London:
BERNARD QUARITCH,
15, PICCADILLY.
1891.

TO THE RIGHT HONOURABLE

# LORD STANLEY OF ALDERLEY,

A WELL-KNOWN ORIENTALIST,

WHO HAS PROMOTED THE STUDY OF ORIENTAL LANGUAGES BY HIS

EXAMPLE AND SUPPORT,

AND A STATESMAN WHO HAS IMPARTIALLY UPHELD THE

RIGHTS OF THE NATIONS OF THE EAST,

THIS VOLUME IS DEDICATED AS A TOKEN OF RESPECT

BY

## THE AUTHOR.

# PREFACE.

THE Turkish dominions are about four times as large as France, and the Turkish language is spoken not only in them, but it is the Court language of Persia and Egypt, and is more or less used from the Danube to the Nile, and from Constantinople to the confines of China. It is the language of millions of Mussulmans who hold some of the most important strategic positions in the world, which, if occupied by a more aggressive power, might threaten the liberty of the world. Friendly intercourse between Turks and Englishmen, and a good understanding between their governments, which have many interests in common, would be greatly promoted by Englishmen being able to talk to Turks in their own language. The trade which England now carries on with Turkey might be immensely developed and extended, if English merchants in the Levant, or their *employés*, could speak and write the language of the country, which at present, with exceedingly rare exceptions, they cannot do. Our political and commercial interests in Turkey are, therefore, at the mercy of Levantine interpreters, who cannot be expected to have the good of Turkey or England very much at heart; as they are, properly speaking, neither Englishmen nor Turks, and they are most often men who possess only a colloquial and imperfect knowledge of Turkish. Their sympathies are generally not with the Turks, and the Turks would much prefer dealing directly with Englishmen, if Englishmen could understand them. Yet, until quite lately, the number of Englishmen who knew Turkish was exceedingly small, and even now there is a wide-spread belief in Europe that the Turkish language is scarcely worth learning, and that the Turks have no literature, or no literature worth perusing. A few years ago the War Office having seen, I suppose, during the war in Egypt, the difficulties and evils which arose from our officers not being acquainted with Arabic or Turkish (which latter language is very useful for a military man in Egypt), very wisely offered rewards to induce them to study Turkish and Arabic. The result has been that numerous English officers have studied those languages, and many successfully. If some inducement to study Turkish were also offered to civilians by the Government and the London Chamber of Commerce, no doubt English Civil servants in the East would, in a few years, be able to do business directly with the Turks; and English merchants would find English representatives competent to transact their business and extend it by direct communication with the Osmanlis. Englishmen are quite capable of acquiring Oriental languages, but one can hardly expect them to learn them without some object in view. The Germans, who have perceived the importance of having the Turks as their allies in the event of a war with Russia, and the splendid field for commercial enterprise in the Turkish dominions, have lately established an Oriental Academy with a view to teaching not only diplomatic and consular officials, but mercantile men, Turkish, Arabic, and other Oriental languages.* The German merchants in Turkey have already begun to take the trade out of the hands of the English; and if the Oriental Academy in Berlin send out men conversant with Turkish to extend German trade, and the English do not take a lesson from them in time and turn their attention to Oriental languages, they will not only not obtain the enormous trade which might be done between the Levant and England, if intercourse were easier, but lose that portion of it which has for many years been almost a monopoly in their hands —and they will deserve to lose it if they do not bestir themselves and take warning in time.

The Imperial Institute has done England a great service by

---

* The Correspondent of the *Morning Post* at Constantinople wrote in November last:—"The Imperial visit will increase the tendency which already exists among Germans to find a field for commercial enterprise and an opening for military and civil official careers in the dominions of the Sultan. It is somewhat humiliating for an Englishman to observe with what persistency the Germans are asserting their commercial position in Constantinople. Already people are beginning to ask if Germany is to become the commercial mistress of the Levant."

starting a School of Oriental languages, where our countrymen have now an opportunity of acquiring Turkish and other Eastern tongues. In the excellent speech made by the Prince of Wales at the opening of the above institution, His Royal Highness said :— *"That the New School of Modern Oriental Studies is a worthy object of material support by this country none can doubt, but the best aid and support it can receive will be derived from the extension of an active encouragement by public bodies and by the Government departments."* The nation will owe His Royal Highness a great debt of gratitude if his sensible remarks convince the Government of the importance of their attending to this matter; for the existence and success of such an Academy for Oriental languages must, to a great extent, unavoidably depend on support and encouragement from the State, and the public would now be disappointed if it did not flourish, as they have, by the medium of the press, fully endorsed the opinion of the Prince of Wales as to it being required and deserving of support.

One great impediment to the acquisition of the Turkish language hitherto has been the difficulty students have experienced in finding anything to read, after they had learnt the grammar, especially in England. This, perhaps, contributed not a little to the idea so prevalent in Europe that the Turks have no literature. The Turks have a literature, and a varied and interesting literature, but it consists chiefly of somewhat rare and costly standard works, sometimes only to be found in manuscript; and a collection of these involves the expenditure of a large amount of money. A Chrestomathy was, therefore, peculiarly necessary for the acquisition of Turkish, but not one was to be found in all Europe. The only Turkish Reading-book for the use of European students ever published was a small collection of tales from the "Forty Vezirs," printed by the French Government for the use of the students of the *Ecole des langues Orientales vivantes,* at Paris. It consists of some tales in Turkish, without translations or notes, and the Turkish text having been printed from an antiquated MS. the spelling is so obsolete and defective that the perusal of it is greatly impeded, and a student would learn to spell from it most incorrectly. Moreover, there is no variety of style, all the tales being from one

author; and even this most incomplete Reading-book is scarcely to
be had for love or money, as it was published nearly a hundred
years ago, in the reign of Napoleon I., who was fully alive to the
importance of a knowledge of Oriental languages, and copies of it
are now exceedingly rare. I am perfectly sure, therefore, that a
collection of extracts from standard Turkish authors will be welcome
to Turkish students, several of whom even have requested me to
prepare a book of this kind ; but I think, as I have given translations
in English of all the selections, the volume may have some interest
for the general public, as they will see from it that there are
Turkish historians, poets, novelists, dramatists, and journalists,
whose works possess decidedly some attraction for the student of
history, the literary man, and the politician.

# THE LITERATURE OF THE TURKS.

" Seek knowledge even in China."

*Words of Mahomet.*

It will be seen from the words of Mahomet I quote above that it is a great mistake to suppose that the religion of the Turks has prevented them from cultivating learning and literature. Mahomet also said, " It is permitted to the Moslems to possess all sciences ;" and again, in another place, he asserted that " Wisdom came from poetry " (*Inne min-esshiri hikmetun*), and that " There are treasure chambers 'neath the Throne of God, and the keys are the tongues of poets." (" *Lillahi Kunuz taht il arshi mefatihu elsinet es shuara.*") Most Europeans being unable to read Turkish books, and scarcely anything from their literature having been translated into European languages, it has been somewhat rashly presumed that they possess no literature, and some unscrupulous writers have not hesitated to represent the Turks as illiterate barbarians. This is very far from being the case. The Turks possessed a literature even before the conquest of Constantinople, and they have always had the greatest respect for learning and admiration for literature, and in no country, perhaps, in the world have literary men been so favoured by Royalty or so munificently rewarded. Numerous Sultans did not think it beneath their dignity to become authors themselves, and they delighted especially in the society of poets, historians, and other *literati*. Even the Conqueror of Constantinople, Mahomet II., was a poet himself, and he patronised literature not only in his own wide dominions but even in other lands. He is said to have pensioned thirty Turkish poets, and to have sent a thousand ducats a year to the Indian *Khoja'-i-Jihan* and the Persian Jami. Many of his vezirs were poets. Two universities were founded by him, that of Ayia Sofia and the Muhammedié. Over the public library, which he also built, was written this motto: "The study of all sciences is a divine precept for all True Believers." Mahomet II. did not destroy the library of the Greek Emperors. He was himself acquainted with the Greek and Arabic languages and literature, and delighted in reading the exploits of Alexander the Great, Scipio, Hannibal, and Julius Cæsar. He had several European works translated into Turkish. During the reign of the first Sultans many Greek and Latin works were translated into Turkish. A translation of Plutarch was made by order of Mahomet II., the Conqueror, and the commentaries of Cæsar were circulated amongst the Turks in the reign of Suleyman the Magnificent. Aristotle and Euclid are also to be found in Turkish, and it is natural to suppose that many other great classical productions were translated into Turkish, although copies of them are not now to be seen. Historical, astronomical and poetical works are still extant, although rare, which were produced by the Turks before they conquered Constantinople. There is a history of the Turks written by Ahmed-Ben-Yahya, which was produced in the reign of Orkhan. I venture, therefore, to slightly alter the words of Mahomet, and to say to the English public, and especially students of Turkish : "Seek knowledge even in Turkey !" Few people know that the idea of inoculation came from Turkey, from which country Lady Montague introduced it into England. It is possible, therefore, that we may learn something more from the Turks—fresh facts connected with European history, their customs, and their opinions of ourselves, if we take the trouble to peruse their literature ; and it must not be supposed that the love of literature and the production of it in Turkey are things of the past only. One of the greatest of modern Turkish writers, Kemal Bey, who only died last year, says : "A people without a literature are like a man without a tongue ;" and he has himself produced poems, novels and dramas, which are quite on a level with similar works in European countries. His description of London, from which I give an extract hereafter, is very clever and interesting, as showing us what impression our great capital makes on an intelligent Oriental.

The Turks possess numerous works on history, geography, astronomy, and scientific subjects, but they particularly excel in history. Sa'd-ud-Din, who lived more than three hundred years ago, wrote a history of the Turks called "*Taj-ut-Tevarikh*," "The Crown of Histories," which is considered one of the finest specimens of Turkish prose, and made him immortal. The book is remarkably well written, and the facts in it are related with a truthfulness and boldness which are very surprising when one considers the age and the country he lived in. He was the tutor of Murad III., and he had such influence over that monarch that it is reported that Queen Elizabeth of England sent him presents to induce him to prevail on his sovereign to send a fleet to help the English against Philip of Spain, when the latter was preparing the Armada. Sa'd-ud-Din was one of the few men who not only could write history but make history. He accompanied Sultan Mahomet III. in his campaign in Hungary, and the great victory the Turks gained at the battle of Keresztes was due in great part to the courage and firmness of Sa'd-ud-Din, who prevented the Sultan from flying when the battle at first seemed lost. He exhorted his master to remain, telling him in the words of the Koran that "Patience brings victory and joy succeeds to sorrow," and the sequel proved him to be right.

Another great historian whose writings are well worthy of perusal is Naïma. He was one of the Imperial historiographers who continued the history of Turkey after Sa'd-ud-Din. His works were printed at Constantinople as long ago as 1734 A.D., and consist of two folio volumes. His style is not so ornate as that of Sa'd-ud-Din, but it is clear and elegant. It throws great light on the history of Europe in connexion with Turkey, and it is amusing and instructive sometimes to hear events in European history related by a Turk from a Turkish point of view. His account of the conquest of Crete by the Osmanlis possesses a peculiar interest at the present moment, and I have consequently given rather copious extracts from that, from which it will be seen that the Turks took the island from the Venetians, and that the population were not very loth to receive the Turks as their masters, as the Turkish Generalissimo treated non-combatants with a certain amount of wise clemency and forbade wanton destruction of life and property. This, and other such facts in the history, may probably be depended on, as the author did not write for Europeans, and never imagined that his words would be translated into English or any other European language. The history of Turkey was continued by Rashid Effendi and Chelebi Zadé. This work also forms two large folio volumes. Amongst other curious and instructive things which it contains is a journal kept by a Turkish ambassador who was specially sent to the Court of France in 1720 A.D. It is very quaint and entertaining, as we see from it how European manners and customs really strike a Mahommedan. He was particularly struck with the respect the men in France had for ladies, and their politeness to them. "The French women," he says, "go where they please and do what they like. France is a real paradise for women, for there they live free from all care, and get everything which they can possibly desire."

Another great writer was the celebrated Haji Khalifé, the author of the "History of the Naval Wars of the Turks," in which he depicts in glowing colours the naval achievements of the Turks in the reign of Suleyman the Magnificent. The details he gives respecting the Turkish Lord High Admiral, Khaïr-ud-Din, or Barbarossa, and the Genoese Admiral, Andria Doria, are very valuable. He wrote many other important works on history and geography.

The Turks always were, and still are, very much addicted to writing poetry, for which they have an extraordinary love and admiration. High and low amongst them have cultivated poetry. The Sultans, themselves, were often poets. Indeed, from Murad II. to Murad IV., inclusive, there was an unbroken succession of Poet-Sultans. Verses by all these twelve monarchs are still extant, and they were not the only Sultans who indulged in verse. It may, therefore, justly be said that the Ottoman Sultans have been the most poetical royal family in the world. The learned von Hammer gives translated extracts in German from more than two thousand Turkish versifiers; but all of these can scarcely be called poets. The Turks have, however, produced some really good poets, amongst whom we may mention Baki, Mesihi, Nejati, Fouzouli, Misri, Kemal Pasha Zadé in ancient times, and Izzet Molla, the father of the celebrated Ali Pasha (Prime Minister of Turkey), Ziya Pasha, and Kemal Bey in recent times. Abd-ul-Hak Hamid Bey, at present First Secretary at the Ottoman Embassy in

London, is also a well-known modern poet of great promise. Turkish poetry is open to the objection that it is not very original, as it is almost always an imitation of Persian poetry; and most Turkish poets indulge in such extravagant metaphors and similes that their works, if translated into English at all closely, would be distasteful to most of us. They have, however, sometimes pretty and quaint ideas cleverly expressed, as in the case of Mesihi's Ode to the Spring, which I have translated. Probably our poetry appears to them rather tame and insipid, so different are oriental and western taste.

In the same way Turkish music is not agreeable to most European ears, and cultivated Turks have frankly confessed to me that they could not appreciate our operas, until they became accustomed to them by long residence in Europe. Although Turkish music is distasteful to the ears of most Europeans, it is sweet to the Turks, and that it is capable of exciting deep feeling is proved by the incident which led to the introduction of music amongst the Osmanlis. The Turks of Constantinople were without the art of music, it is asserted on good authority,* before 1047 *Anno Hegiræ*, when Murad IV. captured Bagdad. This cruel tyrant ordered that thirty thousand Persians should be slaughtered before his eyes. Before the massacre was over, Shah-Kouli, a famous Persian musician, managed to present himself before the Sultan, singing to the harp. His music so touched the hard heart of Murad that he burst into tears, and stopped the massacre. Murad took him and four other musicians back with him to Constantinople, where they introduced the science of music. There are even some few works on music written in Turkish, but they are rare. One, entitled "*Tarif-i-ilm-i-Musiki*," was written by Prince Cantimir, and dedicated to Sultan Ahmed III. It is said to have been once very much in use, but nowadays scarcely a copy can be found. The Turks are indebted to Cantimir for musical notes, which were first applied to Turkish airs by him. Afterwards, however, the Turks again returned to composing and executing everything by memory, according to their old custom.

With regard to fiction, the most famous book is a collection of

---

* Todorini, *Letteratura Turchesca*, Vol. I., page 222.

tales called the " Kirk Vezir " (The Forty Vezirs). It is a sort of Turkish " Arabian Nights," but neither so good nor so voluminous. Some of the stories are curious and quaint, and valuable as illustrations of Oriental manners and customs. The style is clear and simple, and therefore the book is very suitable for students of Turkish, and especially beginners. An abridgment of it, published by the French Government, has hitherto been the only Turkish Reading-book for the use of Europeans, but it is so full of errors in spelling that it is embarrassing and misleading for a learner. The " Kirk Vezir " is still popular in Turkey, and printed copies now are numerous in Constantinople, several editions of it having been printed. The orthography in these modern editions has been corrected, and in this form the book is very serviceable for students of Turkish, especially as it contains much colloquial Turkish. Hence I have given long extracts from it with these improvements.

During the present generation a number of novels on the European model, written by Turks acquainted with the French or English language and literature have appeared, some of which are very creditable. Amongst these I may mention "Jezmi," and the " Adventures of Ali Bey," by Kemal Bey, and *Ishtiyak*, by Mehemet Tevfik, published last year, which one might imagine had been written by Alexander Dumas. Numerous translations of French romances, such as the " Mysteries of Paris," have been published, and the "Merchant of Venice" and " Othello " have been turned into Turkish. Dramatic literature was quite unknown amongst the Turks until recently, but now there are several Turkish melodramas and comedies. The best drama we have seen is one called " Vatn " (The Fatherland), founded on the heroic defence of Silistria by the Turks, a very good subject for a dramatic author. *Iki Chaoush* ("The Two Sergeants "), by Mehemet Hilmi, is also good. These plays, although good reading, are intended for the stage, there having been now for some years a Turkish theatre at Stamboul. These modern books of fiction, and these entirely novel dramatic productions, are not only a sign that the Turks have not declined as regards their literary ability, but a decided proof of advancement.

CHARLES WELLS.

# CONTENTS.

## APPENDIX.

# CORRIGENDA.

| | | | | | | |
|---|---|---|---|---|---|---|
| PAGE | 3, line | 16, | *for* | اولهمر | *read* | اولهمز |
| ,, | 4, ,, | 14, | ,, | دوید | ,, | دووید |
| ,, | ,, ,, | 15, | ,, | صکر | ,, | صکره |
| ,, | 14, ,, | 18, | ,, | شنجی کمدر | ,, | سنجی کیمدر |
| ,, | 16, ,, | 6, | ,, | گوپریدر | ,, | کور پریدر |
| ,, | ,, ,, | 7, | ,, | adami | ,, | adamé |
| ,, | ,, ,, | 12, | ,, | bridge | ,, | blind fairy |
| ,, | ,, ,, | ,, | ,, | it | ,, | her |
| ,, | ,, ,, | 13, | ,, | it | ,, | her |
| ,, | 21, ,, | 10, | ,, | اکلمك | ,, | اکنمك |
| ,, | 22, ,, | 16, | ,, | المسه | ,, | اولمسه |
| ,, | 26, ,, | 9, | ,, | احن | ,, | احسن |
| ,, | ,, note | 15, | ,, | nedemter'am | ,, | nedemtev'am |
| ,, | ,, line | 10, | ,, | ایتدبکی | ,, | ایتدیکی |
| ,, | 29, ,, | 18, | ,, | کولدیلر | ,, | کلدیلر |
| ,, | 32, note | 2, | ,, | foreigners | ,, | foreigner |
| ,, | 44, line | 12, | ,, | کاورکن | ,, | کلورکن |
| ,, | 46, ,, | 16, | ,, | سکانندن | ,, | سکانندن |
| ,, | 49, ,, | 5, | ,, | اولنمغمیك | ,, | اولنمغین |
| ,, | ,, ,, | 9, | ,, | الصلانین | ,, | الصلاتین |
| ,, | 53, ,, | 17, | ,, | *Musselman* | ,, | *Mussulman* |
| ,, | 60, note | 5, | ,, | *Oakela* | ,, | *Oukela* |
| ,, | 61, ,, | 7, | ,, | obsolete or provincial | ,, | (obsolete or provincial) |
| ,, | 64, line | 4, | ,, | ارلوب | ,, | اولوب |
| ,, | ,, ,, | 11, | ,, | محاصرمنك | ,, | محاصرونك |
| ,, | 66, ,, | 1, | ,, | ادبر | ,, | ادبار |
| ,, | 67, ,, | 12, | ,, | height ; | ,, | height, |
| ,, | ,, ,, | 27, | ,, | gigantic walls | ,, | a gigantic wall |
| ,, | 72, ,, | 5, | ,, | نیسم | ,, | نسیم |
| ,, | ,, ,, | 7, | ,, | قورلمشر | ,, | دورلمش |
| ,, | 73, ,, | 1, | ,, | ولان | ,, | اولان |
| ,, | 74, ,, | 13, | ,, | محربه | ,, | محاربه |
| ,, | 75, ,, | 15, | ,, | رلحیره | ,, | زنحیره |

## Corrigenda.

| | | | | | | | |
|---|---|---|---|---|---|---|---|
| PAGE | 80, | last line, | *for* | his | *read* | his accession in |
| ,, | 82, | line 6, | ,, | chronicaling | ,, | chronicling |
| ,, | 88, | ,, 17, | ,, | ترتيبنى | ,, | ترتيبنى |
| ,, | 89, | ,, 6, | ,, | اردمجه | ,, | اردنجه |
| ,, | 90, | last line, | ,, | بولنه‌حق | ,, | بولنه‌جق |
| ,, | 99, | line 17, | ,, | مريمله ايله | ,, | مريمله |
| ,, | 100, | ,, 2, | ,, | تعطيما | ,, | تعظيما |
| ,, | 101, | ,, 5, | ,, | عجو | ,, | عجوز |
| ,, | ,, | ,, 13, | ,, | دبو | ,, | ديو |
| ,, | 108, | ,, 17, | ,, | صحابلري | ,, | اصحابلري |
| ,, | 110, | ,, 15, | ,, | word | ,, | world |
| ,, | 114, | ,, 5, | ,, | كسى | ,, | كس |
| ,, | 162, | ,, 2, | ,, | سير | ,, | شير |
| ,, | 165, | ,, 6, | ,, | كوجك | ,, | كوچك |
| ,, | 166, | ,, 2, | ,, | اولديفيچيون | ,, | اولديغيچيون |
| ,, | ,, | ,, 9, | ,, | اتمكه | ,, | ايتمكه |
| ,, | 169, | ,, 11, | ,, | قاعمقام | ,, | قائممقام |
| ,, | ,, | ,, ,, | ,, | انكنجى | ,, | ايكنجى |
| ,, | 172, | ,, 10, | ,, | بولرى | ,, | بورالرى |
| ,, | 176, | ,, 13, | ,, | بكله | ,, | بلكه |
| ,, | ,, | ,, 21, | ,, | قاشدر | ,, | قاشدر |
| ,, | 207, | ,, 13, | ,, | قاندها | ,, | قاندها |
| ,, | 211, | ,, 1, | ,, | فدر | ,, | قدر |
| ,, | 226, | ,, 21, | ,, | بورك | ,, | يورك |
| ,, | 228, | ,, 2, | | مغ ما فيه | ,, | مع ما قيه |

# PART I.

TURKISH PROVERBS, APHORISMS AND ANECDOTES,

*WITH INTERLINEAR AND FREE TRANSLATIONS*
*AND PRONUNCIATION.*

N.B.—In reading the transliteration of the Turkish text in European letters, the vowels must be pronounced as in French, and the consonants as in English.

Words marked " A " are Arabic, and those marked " P " are Persian, although used in Turkish.

# LITERATURE OF THE TURKS.

## TURKISH PROVERBS AND SAYINGS.

*اولمز انسان انسان ایله مال*

*olmaz — insan — insan — ilé — mal*

does not become — man — man — with — wealth

**One does not become a man by wealth.**

*عیبدر تنبللك دکل عیب فقیرلك*

*dir aïb — tenbellik — déil — aïb — fakirlik*

is shameful — laziness — not — shameful — poverty

**Poverty is no sin, but laziness is.**

*اولور عالم یاكیله یاكیله ادم*

*olour — alim — yanilé — yanilé — adam*

becomes — learned — by making — mistakes — a man

**By making mistakes one learns.\***

*اولهمز قیمتی نصیحتك اما در وار قیمتی جواهرك*

*olamaz — kimeti — nasihatin — ama — dir — var — kimeti — jevahirin*

cannot be — its price — of advice — but — is — existing — price — jewels

**Jewels** have a price, but there can be no price (high enough) for advice.

*كچمز یارﻩسی نﺎﻣﻮس اما كچر یارﻩسی بیچﺎق*

*gechmaz — yarési — namous — ama — gecher — yarési — bichak*

passes not — its wound — honour — but — passes — its wound — a knife

**A wound from a knife gets well, but a wound in one's honour does not.**

---

\* This exactly corresponds to the Italian proverb :—*Sbagliando s' impara.*

*[margin note: b. sweet — b. bitter]*

| حدت | طاتليدر | اما | ثمرهسى | اجيدر | نصيحت | اجيدر |
|---|---|---|---|---|---|---|
| hiddet | tatli dir | ama | semerési | aji dir | nasihat | dir aji |
| violence | sweet is | but | its fruit | bitter is | advice | is bitter |

| اما | ميوهسى | طاتليدر |
|---|---|---|
| ama | méïvési | dir tatli |
| but | its fruit | is sweet |

Impetuosity is sweet, but the fruit of it is bitter; advice is bitter, but its fruit is sweet.

*[margin note: lazim — ...]*

| يالكز | عبادتله | جنته | كيرلمز | سلامت | قلب | لازم |
|---|---|---|---|---|---|---|
| yaliniz | ibadetlé | jenneté | girlilmaz | selamet | kalb | lazim |
| only | by worship | in paradise | cannot be entered | of goodness | heart | necessary |

One cannot get to paradise by worship alone; goodness (soundness) of heart is necessary.

*[margin note: yoksa / or ...]*

| دوهيه | صورمشلر كه | انيشيمى | سور سين | يوقسه |
|---|---|---|---|---|
| devéyé | ki sormoushlar | enishi mi | seversin | yoksa |
| to a camel | that they asked | the descent (?) | dost thou like | or |

| يوقوشيمى | اوده | يوك | اولدقدن | صكر | ايكيسنىده |
|---|---|---|---|---|---|
| yokoushoumou | odé | yuk | oldakdan | sora | ikisinidé |
| the ascent | he | load | having become | after | both |

| شيطان | السون ! | ديمش |
|---|---|---|
| shéïtan | alsin† | démish |
| the devil | take | he said |

They asked the camel which he liked best, going up hill or down hill. He said:—"When I have got a load, the devil take them both!"

*[margin note: Menfrood of ...]*

| دوهجى | ايله | كوريشك | قاپوسونى | بيوك | اچملو |
|---|---|---|---|---|---|
| devéji | ilé | ghieurushun | kapousounou | buyuk | achmali |
| a camel-driver | with | who visits | his door | wide | must open |

He who is on visiting terms with a camel-driver must open his door wide.

---

* در ' is,' is often understood as in this sentence. † Or *Alsoun.*

| التون | اتشده | انسان | محنتده | تجربه | اولنور |
|---|---|---|---|---|---|
| altoun | ateshdé | insan | mihnetdé | tejribé | olounour |
| gold | in fire | man | in trouble | tried | is |

Gold is tested by fire, man by affliction.

| انسان | طاشدن | پك | كلدن | نازكدر |
|---|---|---|---|---|
| insan | tashden | pek | ghiulden | nazikdir |
| man | than stone | hard | than the rose | is delicate |

A man is harder than stone and more delicate than the rose.

| بشقهسنك | سوزندن | زياده | كندى | كوزيكه | اينان |
|---|---|---|---|---|---|
| bashkasinin | seuzinden | ziadé | kendi | ghieuziné | inan |
| of another | than his word | more | own | to his eye | believe |

Believe a man's eye more than his words.

| ديلنجينك | طوربهسى | طولمز |
|---|---|---|
| dilenjinin | torbasi | dolmaz |
| of the beggar | his bag | does not fill |

The beggar's bag does not get full (ever).

| كوپكسز | كوى | بولمش | دكنكسز | كزيور |
|---|---|---|---|---|
| kieupeksiz | kieui | boulmoush | deyneksiz | ghézéyor |
| without a dog | a village | having found | without a stick | promenades |

He who has discovered a village without dogs, goes walking without a stick.

| كوره | موم | بهايه | چيقدى | ديمشلر | بنم | ايچون | دكل ديمش |
|---|---|---|---|---|---|---|---|
| kieuré | moum | bahayé | chikdi | démishler | benim | ichun | déil démísh |
| to a blind man | candles | in price | have risen | they said | me | for | not he paid |

They said to the blind man: "Candles have risen in price!" "No," said he, "they have not—for me."

| مركبه | التون | سمر | اورسهك | ينه | مركب | ينه | مركب |
|---|---|---|---|---|---|---|---|
| merkebé | altoun | sémer | woursén | yiné | merkeb | yiné | merkeb |
| to a donkey* | gold | a saddle | if you put on | still | an ass | still | an ass |

If you put a gold saddle on a donkey, still he is a donkey, and remains a donkey.

---

\* *Merkeb* means any beast that is ridden, either a horse, donkey, mule or ass. We have something similar in the word 'mount.'

باغ دعا دكل چاپا ايستر

bagh    dua    déil    chapa    istér

a vineyard   prayers   not   a hoe   it wants

A vineyard does not require prayers, but it does require a hoe.

كوك يوزنده دوكون وار ديسلر قادينلر نردبان*

ghieuk   yuzindé   dughun   var   déséler   kadinler   nerdiban*

sky   in the face   a feast   existing   if they say   the ladies   ladder

قورمغه قالقارلر

kourmagha   kalkarlar

to erect   they get up

If any one said:—"There is a wedding feast in the sky," the ladies would begin putting up ladders.

بويه بوصه باقمه خويه ارصه باق

boïyé   bosé   bakma   khouïyé   ousé   bak

to stature   to appearance   don't look   to disposition   to good behaviour   Look!

Do not look at (a man's) stature and appearance; look at his disposition and behaviour.

وقتسز اوتن خروسك باشني كسرلر

vakitsiz   euten   khorosin   bashini   keserler

at the wrong time   crowing   cock   his head   They cut off

A cock who crows at the wrong time has his head cut off.

قوردك دعوتنه كيدن كوپكی برابر الملی

kourdoun   davetiné   ghiden   { kiupéyi / kiupéghi }   beraber   almali

of the wolf   to his invite   going   a dog   together   It is necessary to take

He who accepts an invitation from a wolf must take a dog with him.

كوزل سوز تیمور قپویی اچار

ghiuzel   seuz   démir   { kapouyou / kapiyi }   achar

pretty   words   iron   door   opens

Nice words open an iron door.

---

\* ' Nerdiban ' is a Persian word, which the Turks mispronounce and call ' mérdivén.'

باصمه    قویروغنه    ییلانك    اویویان

*basma*    *kouïroughina*    *yilanin*    *ouyouyan*

do not tread    to his tail    snake    sleeping

Do not tread on the tail of a sleeping snake.

یرده   یا   ارده   یا   قیز   یاشنده   بش   اون

*yérdé*   *ya*   *erdé*   *ya*   *kiz*   *yashindé*   *besh*   *on*

in the earth   or   married   either   girl   in her age   fifteen

A girl fifteen years of age ought either to be married or buried.

بسلر   فاره لری   بسلمین   کدی

*besler*   *faréleri*   *beslémeyen*   *kédi*

feeds   the mice   not feeding   a cat

He who does not feed a cat feeds the mice.

چیقاریر   دلیکندن   ییلانی   دیل   طاتلی

*chikarir*   *délikinden*   *yilani*   *dil*   *tatli*

brings out   from his hole   the snake   tongue   sweet

A sweet tongue brings out the snake from his hole.

پاتلر   باشنه   قباق   اکنك   قباق   ایله   شیطان

*patlar*   *bashina*   *kabak*   *ekenin*   *kabak*   *ilé*   *shéitan*

its bursts   to his head   who sows   gourd   with   the   devil

If you sow gourds along with the devil, they will burst against your head.

قازار   دیشیله   مزارینی   یین   یمك   ایکك   طوق

*kazar*   *dishilé*   *mezarini*   *yéyen*   *yémek*   *iken*   *tok*

digs   with his teeth   his grave   { eating who eats }   dinner   being   full

He who eats dinner when he has eaten his full digs his grave with his teeth.

اولور   یقین   بغداد   ایسه   ایی   رفیقك

*olour*   *yakin*   *Bagdad*   *isé*   *éï*   *refikin*

becomes   near   Bagdad   is   good   for thy friend

If your friend (companion) is a good one, Bagdad becomes quite near.

| اوركتمه | طوشنی | ارسلان | ایدرسین |
|---|---|---|---|
| eurketma | tawshani | arslan | edérsin |
| do not frighten | the hare | a lion | you make |

Do not cause a hare to take fright or you may make him a lion.

| چالشمق | عبادتك | نصفيدر |
|---|---|---|
| chalishmak | ibadetin | dir nisfi |
| { working to work | of religion | is the half |

Working is the half of religion.

| اولمش | ارسلانه | طاوشانلر | بیله | هجوم | ایدرلر |
|---|---|---|---|---|---|
| eulmush | arslana | tawshanlar | bilé | hujoum | edérler |
| dead | to a lion | the hares | even | attack | |

Even the hares attack a dead lion.

| اتش | كذارى | قیش | كوننك | لاله زاریدر |
|---|---|---|---|---|
| atesh | kenari | kish | ghiununun | lalézaridir |
| fire | its edge | of a winter-day | | its bed of tulips is |

The fire-side is the tulip-bed of a winter day.

| آلتون | انختار | قلعه | قپولرینی | اجار |
|---|---|---|---|---|
| altoun | anakhtar | kala | kapilerini | achar |
| gold | key | castle | gates | opens |

A gold key opens the gates of a castle.

| اق | كوپك | قاره | كوپك | ایكیسیده | كوپكدر |
|---|---|---|---|---|---|
| ak | kieupek | kara | kieupek | ikisidé | kieupekdir |
| white | dog | black | dog | both of them | a dog is |

A white dog and a black dog are both dogs.

| ار | اولان | اتمكنى | طاشدن | چیقارر |
|---|---|---|---|---|
| er | olan | etmeghini | tashdan | chikarir |
| a man | who is | his bread | from a stone | extracts |

He who is a man will extract his bread from a stone.

| اشك | آلتون | یولار | طاقسه | ینه | مركب | ینه | مركب |
|---|---|---|---|---|---|---|---|
| éshek | altoun | yoular | taksa | yiné | merkeb | yiné | merkeb |
| an ass | gold | headstall | if he fix | still | a beast | still | a beast |

If an ass has a gold headstall, he is still (only) an ass.

| كوسترمز | ديشنى | ايت | اصران |
|---|---|---|---|
| ghiustermaz | dishini | it | isiran |
| does not show | his tooth | a dog | who bites |

**A dog who bites does not show his teeth.**

| طوتيلور | يولارندن | حيوان | اقرارندن | انسان |
|---|---|---|---|---|
| tontoulour | yoularindan | haïwan | ikrarindan | insan |
| is held | by his headstall | a beast | by his admission (confession) | a man |

**A man is held fast by his words, and a beast by his headstall.**

| بيلمز | قدرينى | انسان | اولميان | انسان |
|---|---|---|---|---|
| bilmaz | kadrini | insan | olmayan | insan |
| does not know | his value | a man | who is not | a man |

**He who is not a man does not know the value of him who is a man.**

| دكلدر | سرو | اغاج | اوزون | هر |
|---|---|---|---|---|
| déildir | serv selvi | aghaj | ouzoun | her |
| is not | a cypress | tree | tall | every |

**Every tall tree is not a cypress.**

| دوشر | يره | ميوه | ايرن | كماله |
|---|---|---|---|---|
| dusher | yeré | méivé | eren | kemalé |
| falls | to the ground | fruit | attaining to | perfection |

**Fruit which has reached perfection falls to the ground.**

| اولمز | دولت | كبى | قناعت |
|---|---|---|---|
| olmaz | devlet | ghibi | kanaat |
| is not | grandeur | like | contentment |

**There is no grandeur like contentment.**

# TURKISH APHORISMS.

| بر | ملتك | نسوانى | درجه | ترقيسنك | ميزانيدر |
|---|---|---|---|---|---|
| bir | milletin | niswani | deréjé | terakkisinin | dir mizani |
| a | of nation | its women | the degree | of its progress | is its scales |

The women of a nation are the best measure of the degree of
progress it has reached.*—(*Abd-ul-Hak Hamid Bey.*)

| انسانلر | خلقت | عالمك | صباح | اولندن | زوال | ایامنه قدر |
|---|---|---|---|---|---|---|
| insanler | khilkat | alemin | sabah | evvelinden | zewal | eyyaminé |
| men | creation | of the world | morning | its first | disappearance | up to its days |

| اضطراب | چكمك | كوز | ياشى | دوكمك ایچون | خلق | اولنمشدر |
|---|---|---|---|---|---|---|
| iztirab | chekmek | ghieuz | yashi | deukmik ichin | khalk | olounmoushdour |
| tribulation | to suffer | the eye† | moisture | to shed for | created | were |

Men, from the first morning after the creation till the end of days
(time), were created to suffer tribulation and shed tears.—(*Seza'i
Bey.*)

| معرفتسز | انسان | میت | متحرکدن | فرقلى | دکلدر |
|---|---|---|---|---|---|
| marifetsiz | insan | méit | muteharrikden | farkli | déïldir |
| without knowledge | a man | corpse | from moving | different | not is |

A man without knowledge is like a moving corpse.—(*Ekrem.*)

| امیدسز | انسان | بخارسز | ماکنه | کبی | معطلدر |
|---|---|---|---|---|---|
| umidsiz | insan | boukharsiz | makina | ghibi | muattaldir |
| without hope | a man | without smoke | a machine | like | is useless (inactive) |

A man without hope, like a machine without smoke, is inactive
and useless.—(*Mehcmct Nadir.*)

---

* Many English people will be surprised at this being written by a Turk and a
Mussulman, a living Ottoman poet, who is at present First Secretary to the Turkish
Embassy in London.—C. W.
† Tears.

| مورخڭ | الڭ بيوك | خصيصهسى | بيطرفلقدر |
|---|---|---|---|
| muverrikhin | biyuk en | khasisési | bitaraflik dir |
| of the historian | the greatest | quality | impartiality is |

The greatest quality of a historian is impartiality.—(*Suleyman Pasha.*)

| تاريخ | انسانلری | ينه | كندى | مشابهلری ايله |
|---|---|---|---|---|
| tarikh | insanleri | yiné | kendi | ilé mushabihleri |
| history | men | again | own | with fellow creatures |

| تعليم | و | تربيهيه | خدمت | ايدر | بر | فن | جليلدر |
|---|---|---|---|---|---|---|---|
| talim | ve | terbiyéyé | khidmet | edér | bir | fen | jelildir |
| teaching | and | to educating | service | doing | an | art | glorious is |

History is a noble art, which aids the education and instruction of men by their own fellow-creatures.—(*Suleyman Pasha.*)

| زمان | او | قدر | صارپ | او | قدر | ديك | يولدركه | اوزرنده |
|---|---|---|---|---|---|---|---|---|
| zeman | o | kadar | sarp | o | kadar | dik | ki dour yol | uzerindé |
| time | a | such | steep | a | such | perpendicular | that is road | on it |

| توقف | ممكن | اولهماز | يووارلنوب | دوشمه مك | ايچون | دائما |
|---|---|---|---|---|---|---|
| tévakkuf | mumkin | olamaz | yivarlanip | dushmémek | ichin | daïma |
| stopping | possible | cannot be | rolling over | not to fall | for | always |

| سرعتله | چيقمق | اقتضا | ايدر |
|---|---|---|---|
| suratlé | chikmak | iktiza | edér |
| with rapidity | to ascend | requisite | it is |

Life (time) is such a steep and perpendicular road that standing still is impossible. In order not to roll over and fall, it is requisite constantly to ascend with rapidity.*—(*Sami Bey*).

---

* How many English people ever supposed the 'unspeakable' Turks uttered such sentiments as those above!—C. W.

حال   ایچون   قورتلمق   أضمحلالدن   و   تدنی   امت   بر

*hal*   *ichin*   *kourtoulmak*   *izmihlalden*   *vé*   *tédenni*   *ummet*   *bir*

state   for   to be saved   from disappearance   and   decline   people   a

قوتنی   ایتمکه   ترقی   دائما   ایتمیوب   قناعت   ایله   حاضر

*kuvvetini*   *etmeyé*   *terakki*   *daïma*   *etméyip*   *kanaat*   *ilé*   *hazir*

its power   to make   progress   always   not being   satisfied   with   its present

ایلریلتمکه   معارفنی   یالکز   معارفنی   خیر   خیر   ثروتنی

*ilériletmeyé*   *maarifini*   *yaliniz*   *maarifini*   *khaïr*   *khaïr*   *servetini*

to advance   its knowledge   only   its knowledge   No!   No!   its prosperity

چالیشلملیدر

*chalishilmali*

must be striven

A people, in order not to decline and decay, must not be content with its present condition. It must always strive to progress. It must strive to advance in power and prosperity—No! No! in knowledge, only in knowledge.—(*Sami Bey.*)

سرخوشلق   لکن   یوقدر   مشروب   بر   لذیذ   قدر   حریت

*serkhoshlik*   *lakin*   *dour yok*   *meshroub*   *bir*   *léziz*   *kadar*   *hurriyet*

intoxication   but   There is not   drink   a   delicious (nice)   as   liberty

در   وار   احتیاجی   بر *مزیه   دنیلن   اعتدال   ایچون   ویرمامك

*dir*   *var*   *ihtiyaji*   *mezéyé bir*   *dénilen*   *itidal*   *ichin*   *vérmémek*

there is   its necessity   appetizer an   called   moderation   for   not to give

There is no beverage so delicious as liberty, but in order that it may not intoxicate one, a little something must be taken with it called "moderation."—(*Sami Bey.*)

---

* The word *mezé* means a whet before dinner, which it is customary in Turkey to take. It consists of salt condiments, or fruit, and *Raki.*

تجارت    چیقارمقدر    الماس    قازوب    طوپراق    زراعت

*tijaret*    *chikarmakdir*    *elmas*    *kazip*    *toprak*    *ziraat*

commerce    to produce is    a diamond    digging    earth    agriculture

دمیر صاتوب التون قزانمقدر

*kazanmakdir*    *altoun*    *satip*    *démir*

to earn is    gold    selling    iron

Agriculture is digging the ground and (thereby) bringing forth diamonds; commerce is selling iron and (thereby) winning gold.— (*Abd-ul-Hak Hamid Bey.*)

پادشاهیدر    عالمنك    کندی    کیمسه    هر

*dir padishahi*    *aleminin*    *kendi*    *kimsé*    *her*

is the king    of his world    own    person    every

Every one is king of his own world.—(*Mahmoud Nedim Pasha.*)

حریت    اعطای    ملته    بر    ایدهمیان    تقدیر    حریتی    قیمت

*hurriyet*   *itaí*   *milleté*   *bir*   *edéméyan*   *takdir*   *hurriyeti*   *kimet*

freedom   of the giving   to a nation   not   being able to appreciate freedom   the value

عصیان   خنجر   بر   اغزینه   افرادینك   ملت   او   ایتمك

*isyan*   *khanjer*   *bir*   *aghzina*   *efradinin*   *millet*   *o*   *etmek*

rebellion   of dagger   a   in their mouth   of its individuals   nation   that   to do

ویرمك    کبیدر

*dir gibi*    *vermek*

is like    to give

To give freedom to a nation which does not appreciate the value of liberty is like putting the dagger of rebellion into their hands (mouths).—(*Saïd Bey.*)

سلاح   خیاله   بر   ایچنده   ظلمت   سرزنش   طالعه

*silah*   *khayala*   *bir*   *ichindé*   *zoulmet*   *serzenish*   *talié*

an arm   to chimera   a   in   darkness   rebuke   to fortune

قبیلندندر    چكمك

*dir kabilinder*    *chekmek*

is of the category    to draw

Complaining of fortune is like drawing one's sword against a chimera.—(*Abd-ul-Hak Hamid Bey.*)

| تحصّن | دائرهٴ | مهابتنده | بدن | و | برج | ایچون | قوم | بر |
|---|---|---|---|---|---|---|---|---|
| tahassun | daïréï | mahabetindé | béden | vé | burj | ichin | kavm | bir |
| fortification | circle | in its grandeur | walls | and | tower | for | people | a |

| ملیدر | اتحاد |
|---|---|
| dir mili | itihad |
| is national | unity |

National unity is the best thing to support the walls and towers
of a nation's grandeur.—(*Idem.*)

| هنغیسیدر؟ | خیرلوسی | مظفریتك |
|---|---|---|
| dir hangisi | khaïrlisi | muzafferiyetin |
| is which | the most advantageous | of victory |

| كلن | حصوله * | دوكولمكسزین | قان |
|---|---|---|---|
| ghelen | housoula | dukulmeksizin | kan |
| coming | to accomplishment | without spilling | blood |

Which is the most beneficial victory?
That which is achieved without shedding blood.—(*Abou'l Zia Tevfik.*)

| شنی كمدر؟ |
|---|
| dir kim sékhi |
| is who generous |

| مالندن | بشقهسنك | و | سخاوت | مالیله | كندی |
|---|---|---|---|---|---|
| malinden | bashkasinin | vé | sekhavet | malilé | kendi |
| from his wealth | of another | and | generosity | with wealth | own |

| ایدندر | صیانت | نفسنی |
|---|---|---|
| dir eden | siyanet | nefsini |
| is he who | restrains | his passions |

Who is liberal?
He who is generous with his own property and restrains his desire
for the wealth of others.—(*Abou'l Zia Tevfik.*)

---

* *Housoula ghelmek* means ' to be realized, accomplished.'

| حر | اولمق | ايستر ايسك | اولمه | جهانك | ذوقنده |
|---|---|---|---|---|---|
| hur | olmak | ister isén | olma | jihanin | zevkindé |
| free | to be | if thou wishest | do not be | of the world | in its amusement |

| صفاسنده | غمنده | كدرنده |
|---|---|---|
| safasindé | gheminé | kéderindé |
| in its pleasure | in its sorrow | in its care |

If you wish to be free do not enter into the amusements and pleasure of the world (nor) into its cares and sorrows.—(*Zia Pasha.**)

| اخلاق | مليهسى | اولميان | اقوامده | مدنيت | اولمز |
|---|---|---|---|---|---|
| akhlak | miliyési | olmayan | akwamdé | médeniyet | olmaz |
| moral qualities | national | not being | peoples in | civilization | does not become |

Amongst nations who have no national moral qualities, civilization is impossible (does not exist).—(*Zia Pasha.*)

| عطالت | موتك | كوچك | قرداشى | سفاهت | حياتك | بيوك |
|---|---|---|---|---|---|---|
| atalet | mevtin | kiuchuk | kardashi | sefahet | hayatin | buyuk |
| inertia | of death | little | brother | ostentation | of life | great |

| در | دشمنى |
|---|---|
| dir | dushmeni |
| is | enemy |

Idleness is the little brother of death (half death), and ostentation is the great enemy of life.—(*Kemal Bey.*)

| وار | سعادت | بر | حقيقى | ايچون | انسان | فانيده | جهان | بو |
|---|---|---|---|---|---|---|---|---|
| var | saadet | bir | hakiki | ichin | insan | fanidé | jihan | bou |
| be | happiness | a | real | for | man | fleeting in | world | this |

---

* Zia Pasha, a really good modern Turkish poet, a couplet of whose we give above, was a very remarkable man. Although Secretary to Sultan Abd-ul-Aziz, he took up with liberal ideas, and urged reforms on the government. For this he was obliged to leave Turkey, and lived for a long time in England in retirement, when the author of this volume had the pleasure of meeting him. He did not give up the world for ever, as he advises above, but returned again to the Turkish Court, got again into favour, and was promoted to the rank of Pasha, which he did not possess when I met him. He died only a few years ago.

ايسه اوده وقتنى مطالعات و تفكرات عاليه ايله كچيرمكدر

| isé | odé | vakitini | mutalaat | vé | téfekkiurat | aliyé | ilé | gechirmekdir |
|---|---|---|---|---|---|---|---|---|
| if there | that also | his time | studies | and | reflections | exalted | with | to pass is |

In this fleeting world, if there be real happiness, it is passing one's time in exalted studies and reflections.—(*Mustapha Reshid.*)

طالع بنی ادمه ترفیق اولنمش بر کوپریدر انسان انی ایستدیکی

| tali | beni adami | terfik | olounmoush | bir | kieuprudur | insan | ani | istédighi |
|---|---|---|---|---|---|---|---|---|
| luck | to mankind | accompanyings | is | a bridge | man | him | that he wished |

طرفه چکوب کتوره بیلیر

| tarafa | chekip | ghetiré | bilir |
|---|---|---|---|
| side to | drawing | to bring | it can |

Luck is a bridge sent to help men, and a man can pull it and bring it in the direction he wishes.—(*Abd-ul-Hak Hamid Bey.*)

تنبل ارباب حياتدن اولهمز بر میتدر که دفن اولهمز

| tenbel | erbab | hayatdan | olamaz | bir | méitdir | ki | defn | olamaz |
|---|---|---|---|---|---|---|---|---|
| a lazy (person) | of the living | cannot be | a corpse he is | which | buried | cannot be |

A lazy person is a dead body which does not belong to the living but cannot be buried.—(*Kemal Bey.*)

خسیس اولان غنی ایلقسز خزینه بکجیسي دیمکدر

| khasis | olan | ghani | aïliksiz | khaziné | bekjisi | démekdir |
|---|---|---|---|---|---|---|
| who is a miser | a rich man | without salary | a treasure | its watchman | may be called |

A rich man who is a miser may be called an unpaid watchman for a treasure.—(*Ekrem.*)

انسان بر غریب حیواندر که هر شیئه الشیر هر

| insan | bir | gharib | haïwandir | ki | her | shéiyé | alishir | her |
|---|---|---|---|---|---|---|---|---|
| man | one | strange | an animal is | who | to everything | gets accustomed to | every |

الشمدیغی شیدن قورقار

| alishmadighi | shéidan | korkar |
|---|---|---|
| to which he is not accustomed | thing | fears |

Man is a strange animal who gets accustomed to everything, but who is frightened of anything to which he is not accustomed.—(*Kemal Bey.*)

اممدر | انكار | خادم و | عالم | عبرتنمای | مرآت | غزته
--- | --- | --- | --- | --- | --- | ---
*umémdir* | *efkiar* | *khadim vé* | *alem* | *ibretnuma-i* | *mir'ét* | *ghazeta*
peoples is | thoughts | the servant and | the world | warning | mirror | a newspaper

A newspaper is a mirror of the world, containing warnings for us, and it is the servant of the thoughts of nations.—(*Ziver Bey.*)

يشار | ایله | سعی | كچنیر | سایهسنده | زمان | آدم
--- | --- | --- | --- | --- | --- | ---
*yashar* | *ilé* | *saï* | *gechenir* | *sayésindé* | *zeman* | *adam*
he lives | by | exertion | exists | by the help of | time | a man

A man exists by the help of time, but he only *lives* by exertion.—(*Kemal Bey.*)

غربادر | ادبا | اراسنده | بی ادبلر
--- | --- | --- | ---
*ghurebadir* | *édeba* | *arasindé* | *édebler bi*
foreigners are | literary men | amongst | the illiterate

Literary people are like foreigners amongst the illiterate.—(*Ekrem.*)

كلسه ایدی | لازم | اورلمق | كلید | دهاننه | ادبسزلرك
--- | --- | --- | --- | --- | ---
*ghelsé-idi* | *lazim* | *vouroulmak* | *kilid* | *dihaniné* | *édebsizlerin*
were it | necessary | to put | a lock | to their mouth | impudent people

اشتهار | كسب | ثروتلریله | چلینكیرلر | میاننده | اصحـٰب صنایع
--- | --- | --- | --- | --- | ---
*ishtihar* | *kesb* | *servetlerilé* | *chilinghirler* | *miyanindé* | *sanaï ashab*
celebrity | acquire | with their wealth | locksmiths | among | artisans

ایدرلر ایدی
*ederleridi*
they would

If it were necessary to put a lock on the mouth of impertinent people, locksmiths would become famous for their wealth amongst artisans.—(*Abou'l-Zia.*)

c

# ANECDOTES.

بر آدم تراش اولمق ايچون بر بربرهٔ مراجعت ايدر .

| edér | murajaat | bérbéré | bir | ichun | olmak | trash | adam | bir |
|---|---|---|---|---|---|---|---|---|
| has | recourse | to a barber | a | for | to be | shaved | man | it |

حريفك باشني تراش ايدرايكن بر قاچ يريني كسر . مرقوم

| merkoum | kesér | yerini | kach | bir | edériken | trash | bashini | herifin |
|---|---|---|---|---|---|---|---|---|
| the aforesaid | cuts | places | few | a | while | shaving | his head | the fellow |

تراش اولوب بيتنجه چيقاروب بربرهٔ ايكي قات اجرت ويرر .

| verir | ujret | kat | iki | bérbéré | chikaroup | béitinjé | oloup | trash |
|---|---|---|---|---|---|---|---|---|
| he gives | pay | gold | two | to the barber | taking out | to his house | being | shaved |

بربر يوزينه باقنجه . مرقوم بري تراش بری‌ده * حجامت

| hajamet | biridé | trash | biri | merkoum | bakinjé | yuziné | bérbér |
|---|---|---|---|---|---|---|---|
| cupping | one | shaving | one | the aforesaid | on looking | to his face | the barber |

پارہ سی دير .

| dér | parési |
|---|---|
| is | its money |

## Translation.

A man went to a barber to get shaved. While the fellow was shaving his head † he cut some places in it, the aforesaid person having been shaved, and being about to go home, took out double the price and gave to the barber. The barber having stared at him, he said: "One (the half) is for shaving and the other is for cupping me."

---

     * *Dé* means "also," and follows the word it applies to.
     † The Turks have the tops of their heads shaved.

بر خسيس بر جادّه اوزرنده بر او صاتون المش . پك
bir khasis bir jaddé uzerindé ev bir satoun* almish pek
a miser a highway road on house a bought having very

چوق ديلنجيلر كلوب صدقه ايسترمش خسيس هيچ برينه
chok dilenjiler gheloup† sadaka istérmish khasis hich biriné
many beggars coming alms wished the miser any to one

بر شى ويرميوب " عنايت " اوله ! ديرك صاودرمش .
bir shéi verméyoub inayet olé déyérek sawdirmish
a thing not giving grace be! saying dismissed (them)

زوجه‌سي بر كون ياهو بو اوى صاتالم ديلنجيسى پك
zevjési bir ghiun yahou bou evi satalim dilenjisi pek
one day Oh! (God) this house let us sell beggars very

چوق دينجه خسيس باس . يوق ديلنجيسى چوق ايسه
chok dénjé khasis bé's yok dilenjisi chok isé
many on saying the miser matter (harm) no its beggars many if they be

بنده‡ " عنايت " اوله " دها چوق " ! ديمش .
bendé inayet olé daha chok démish
in me grace be! more much He said

## Translation.

A miser having bought a house on a high road, very many beggars came and asked for alms. The miser did not give anything to any of them,§ and sent them away, saying: "May God show you favour." ‖ One day his wife said: "Oh, God! let us sell this house. There are so many beggars here." The miser replied: "No matter! If the beggars be many, I have more *Inayet olés* ["May God show you favour"s] than there are beggars."

---

\* Or satin. † Or ghelip.
‡ *Bendé,* 'in me,' is equivalent to 'I have.'
§ The singular is often used in a collective sense for the plural.
‖ This expression is always used when one wishes to get rid of a beggar.

مشهور  شيخ  سعدى  كوچكلكندن  هر  كيجه  صباح  اولمزدن

*meshour*  *sheikh*  *Sadi*  *kiuchiuklughinden*  *her*  *ghejé*  *sabah*  *olmazden*

celebrated  Sheikh  Sadi  from his childhood  every  night  morn  it became

اول  قالقوب  پدرينك  ياننده  طوريرو  پدريله  برابر

*ev-vel*  *kalkoup*  *pédérinin*  *yanindé*  *dourour*  *vé*  *pédérilé*  *bérabér*

Before  rising  of his father  at his side  stands  and  with his father  together

عبادت ايار ايدى  شيخ  ينه  بر  كيجه  معتادى وجه ايله  قالقدى

*éilér-idi-ibadet*  *sheikh*  *yiné*  *bir*  *gejé*  *mutadi vejé ilé*  *kalkdi*

they worshipped  the sheikh  again  one  night  as usual  rose

فقط  خانه  ايچنده  پدرندن  و  كنديسندن  بشقه  هر

*fakat*  *khané*  *ichinde*  *pédérinden*  *vé*  *kendisinden*  *bashka*  *her*

but  house  inside  his father  and  himself  except  every

كسك  اويومقده  اولادقلارينى  كوروب  ده  پدرينه  باقسهكز  بونارك

*kessin*  *ouyoumakda*  *oldouklarini*  *ghieuroup*  *dé*  *pédériné*  *bakséniz*  *boularin*

person  in sleeping  that they were  seeing  dé  to his father  look!  of these

هپسى  نصل  اوبويورلر  عبادت ايتمه ايچون*  هيچ  بريسى بيله

*hepsi*  *nasl*  *ouyouyorlar*  *ibadet etmé ichoun*  *hich*  *birisi bilé*

all  how  they sleep  for to worship  not one of them  even

باشنى  قالديرميور  دينجه  پدرى  كاشكى  سن  ده  انلر  كبى

*bashini*  *kaldirmayor*  *dénjé*  *pédéri*  *késhki*  *sen*  *dé*  *anlar*  *ghibi*

his head  does not raise  on saying  his father  would that  thou  also  them  like

اويومش  اولسهيدك  كيمسهنك  عيبنى  قصورينى  كوره يهيدك

*ouyoumoush*  *olsaïden*  *kimsénin*  *aïlini*  *kousourini*  *ghieurmayaïden*

slept  you had  of no one  his fault  his defect  you had not seen

ديمش .

*démish*

he said

## Translation.

The celebrated Sheikh Sadi in his childhood used to get up every night, just before daybreak, and stand by his father's side and say

---

* Or *ichin.*

his prayers with his father. One night he got up as usual, but seeing that everybody in the house but his father and himself were still sleeping, he said: "Look! see how they are all sleeping! Not one of them even raises his head for devotion." His father replied: "Would that you were asleep too, so that you could not see anybody's faults and failings."

---

ديوانەلرك زنجير بستەء كيدوب خانەيە تيمار بری حريفك

diwanélerin  beste-i-zinjir  ghidip  khanéyé  timar  biri  herifin

maniacs   chained   going  to a madhouse  one  fellow

اوزرە الكمك طوروب اوكندە پنجرەسی بر محلك اولديغی

uzeré  eghlenmek  douroup  eunindé  penjerési  bir  mahalin  oldoughou .

to amuse himself  standing  in front  window  a  place  where they were

كورنجە بونی دە بری ديوانەلردن چيقارمش طيشاری ديلنی

ghieurunjé  bounou  de biri  diwanélerden  chikarmish  tishari  dilini

seeing  this  one  from the maniacs  stretching  out  his tongue

نە زنجيرسز زنجيرلی اولنمز سوأل حكمتدن رب ا يا امان

né  zinjirsiz  zinjirli  olounmaz  sual  hikmetden  reb ya  aman

how many and not chained  chained  is not  asked  from wisdom  Lord oh  Dear me!

ديوانەلرك وار ا ديمش .

démish  var  diwanélerin

he said  there are  madmen

### Translation.

A fellow went to a madhouse, and, standing before the window where the chained lunatics were, amused himself by putting out his tongue at them. One of the maniacs seeing this, said: "Dear me, Oh Lord, thy ways are inscrutable. What a lot of lunatics there are, some chained, and some unchained!"

ديدكده "نه اغلايورسن؟" چوجغه بر بولنان اغلامقده بريسى

| dédikdé | aghlayorsin | né | chojougha | bir | boulounan | aghlamakdé | birisi |
|---|---|---|---|---|---|---|---|
| on his saying | are you crying | what | to child | a | who | was crying | someone |

ايچون انك ده ايتدم غائب غروشى بر ويرديكي انامك

| ichin | anin | dé | etdim | ghaïb* | ghroushi | bir | vérdighi | anamin |
|---|---|---|---|---|---|---|---|---|
| therefore | | | I have lost | | piastre | a | which she gave | of my mother |

ده آل ويروب غروش بر اكا ده ذات او . دير اغلايورم

| dé al | vérip | ghroush | bir | ana | dé | zat | o | dér | aghlayorim |
|---|---|---|---|---|---|---|---|---|---|
| take | givings | piastre | a | to him | also | person | that | he says | I cry |

دها اولكندن الوب پاره‌يى جوجق دينجه اغلامه ارتق

| daha | evvelkinden | alip | parayi | chojouk | dénjé | aghlama | artik |
|---|---|---|---|---|---|---|---|
| more | than before | taking | the money | the child | on his saying | do not cry | any more |

صورلدقده ديه اغلايورسين؟ نيچون شمدى باشلار اغلامغه زياده

| sorouldoukda | déyé | aghlayorsin | nichin | shindi | bashlar | aghlamagha | ziadé |
|---|---|---|---|---|---|---|---|
| having asked | saying | do you cry | why | now | he begins | to cry | more |

ايكى شمدى المسه‌ايدم ايتمش غائب ويرديكنى‌ده انامك اكر

| iki | shindi | olmasaïyidim | etmish | kaïb | vérdighini-dé | anamin | éyér |
|---|---|---|---|---|---|---|---|
| two | now | I had not | | lost | what she gave | of my mother | if |

دير . اغلايورم ايچون انك . اوله‌جقدى غروشم

| dér | aghlayorim | ichin | anin | olajaghidi | ghroushoum |
|---|---|---|---|---|---|
| he says | I cry | therefore | | would have been | my piastres |

### Translation.

Some one said to a child who was crying: "What are you crying for?" The child replied: "Because I have lost a piastre which my mother gave me." The gentlemen gave him another piastre, and said: "Take that, and cry no more." Whereupon the child took the money, and began to cry more than before. The gentleman asked: "What are you crying for now?" The child replied: "If I had not lost the piastre which my mother gave, I should now have had two!"

---

\* Generally pronounced *kaïb* in Turkish.

# PART II.

*EXTRACTS FROM STANDARD TURKISH AUTHORS, WITH FREE TRANSLATIONS AND EXPLANATORY NOTES.*

—◆—

## SAD-UD-DIN.

Sad-ud-Din is the most celebrated of Turkish historians. His great work, called تاج التواريخ (*Taj-ut-Tévarikh*), 'The Crown of Histories,' is remarkable for the elegance and grandeur of its style and the truthfulness of the author. This work gives the history of the Ottomans from the earliest times up to Sultan Selim I. Sad-ud-Din was the tutor and historiographer of Sultan Murad III., and also of Mahomet III. He was a great favourite with both, and his influence and advice to the latter, whom he accompanied to the war in Hungary, was the cause of the Turks achieving a grand victory, in 1596 A.D., over the Archduke Maximilian and the Imperialists, when the Sultan, despairing of success, had wished to retreat. Sad-ud-Din's courage and eloquence at the Battle of Ke-resztes, when, after two days fighting, all seemed lost for the Turks, induced the Sultan to remain, and led to a crushing defeat of the Christians in the East. Fifty thousand Germans and Transylvanians perished in the marshes or by the sword, and ninety cannon were taken by the Turks, who, at the beginning of the battle, had lost all their own. Sad-ud-Din died Mufti of Constantinople in the year of the *Hejira* 1006, that is to say about three hundred years ago. The extracts made in this volume are taken from a beautiful manuscript, once the property of the celebrated Orientalist Silvestre de Sacy.*

---

* Kindly lent to me by Mr. Quaritch, whom I have to thank for the loan of several other rare works in Turkish.

# THE TYRANNY OF TIMOUR.*

ذكر بعض مظالم تيمور

متتبع' اثار و مطّلع' اخبار تيموري اولان نكته شناس' بادئ' نظرده درك

و احساس' ايدر كه منتهای مرامي و قصاداى مهامى' تخريب' بلاد

و مجامع عباده القاى فتنه و فساد ايدی . و مقتضای خلق' و سيرتی'

و مطمع' نظر سرير'' تخريب عالم و تعذيب بنى آدم ايدی . مرحمت

و اشفاق نفوسى صحيفة قلبندن محكوك'' و مسلوب الانصف ايدوكى

غير مشكوك'' ايدي . بر فظّ'' غليظ القلب ايديكه قتل اطفالى

و غصب اموالى احسن اعمالى بيلوب و غارته و ايصال خسارته جسارتيته

تامهسى و قدم ندم توأمنى'' و ضع ايتديكى مواضعه نفرت'' عامه سى

وار ايدى . جبّار بدكردار'' و ستمكار'' مردم آزار'' ايدي . يوركى سنك

و سبعينده'' مانند پلنك'' و نام نيكو'' تحصيلنده پاى همتى لنك ايدى .

هر محله كه سپاه مردار غول كرداری'' هلول ايتسه كشت و زرعتى

و اصل و فرعنى نهب و يغما و سلب منافع و نعما'' ايدر لرايدى و هرقنده

قونسه امن اندن كوچر ايدی . و هر مقامده اوتورسه قيامت قالقار ايدی .

و هر ديارہ كه كذار ايتسه ديار قالمز ايدی .

(1) A. *Mutétebba*, ‘who follows.’ *Mutétebba-i-assar*, ‘one who reads works.’—
(2) A. *Mutétalli*, ‘one who studies.’—(3) P. *Shinass*, ‘one who knows, or is
acquainted with.’—(4) *Badi' Nazrdé*, ‘at the first glance.’—(5) *Ihsas*, ‘feeling.’—
(6) *Méham*, ‘important affairs.’—(7) A. *Takhrib*, ‘ruining.’ (8) A. *Khulk*, ‘nature,
disposition.’—(9) *Siret*, ‘course of life.’—(10) A. *Matmah*, ‘an object one has in
view.’—(11) *Serir*, ‘a throne, government.’—(12) A. *Mahkiuk*, ‘scratched out.’—
(13) *Meshkiuk*, ‘doubted.’— (14) A. *Fazz*, ‘a brutal fellow.’—(15) A. *Nedemter'am*,
‘the twin-brother of repentance,’ *i.e.* ‘which will be rued.’—(16) A. *Nefret*,
‘disgust.’—(17) P. *Bed-kirdar*, ‘whose deeds are evil.’—(18) P. *Sitem-kiar*, ‘oppressive.’—(19) P. *Merdum-azar*, ‘vexing men.’—(20) A. *Seba*, ‘a wild beast’ (a lion).—
(21) P. *Pelenk*, ‘a leopard, panther.’—(22) P. *Nam-niku*, ‘good name.’—(23) *Ghoul
kirdar*, ‘monstrous.’—(24) *Numa*, ‘a favour.’

* Timour the Tartar, better known in Europe as Tamerlane, was one of the most
formidable enemies the Ottomans ever had to encounter, and he nearly overthrew
their empire. His name ‘Timour’ means ‘Iron;’ but he was also called *Timour-
lenk*, which signifies ‘Timour the Lame,’ he having been lamed by a wound he once
received: the European word Tamerlane is a corruption of this. He was a greater
conqueror than even Alexander, Cæsar, or Napoleon, and shed more human blood,
and caused greater misery in the world, than any man who ever lived.

### *Translation.*

Those who study the history of Timour, see at the first glance that his object was to destroy countries, and to sow disorder and trouble amongst the worshippers (of God). The tendency of his disposition, and the aim of his rule, was the destruction of the world, and torturing mankind. Mercy and compassion were 'erased from the page of his heart,' and conscience he had none. He was a hard-hearted brutal man, who looked upon the slaughter of infants, and plunder, as good deeds. He had unlimited courage for rapine and destruction, and in the places where he set his cruel foot he was universally detested. He was an oppressive, tyrannical doer of evil. His heart was of stone, and he was like a wild beast. He limped * in his efforts to make a good name. Wherever his filthy soldiery—whose deeds were like those of *ghouls*†—appeared, they plundered and destroyed crops and agriculture, root and branch, and all the blessings of God. Wherever he halted, safety departed therefrom; and wherever he dwelt, it seemed as if the last day had arrived; and if he traversed a country, no country remained afterwards.

---

* This refers to Timour being lame, and means that he was lame in mind as well as body.

† *Ghoul* (غول) means 'a demon,' or 'goblin.'

## TIMOUR AND THE MOLLA.*

لطيفه

qıldekdeh

تيمور ديار رومه كلدكده مولانا * احمدي مصاحبتنه مائل اولدى بر كون

بيله حمامه كيروب مولانايه ديدى كه بو حمامده اولان امرانك هر

برينى تقويم ايله | مولانا دخى هر برينه بر قيمت تعيين ايلدى | تيمور

ايتدى بنى دخى تقويم ايله مولانا سكسن¹ اقچه تعيين ايلدى | تيمور

ايتدى عدالت ايتمدك ايتمدك | اول مبلغ تنها فوطهنك² بهاسى در مولانا بندخى

فوطهنك بهاسنى تعيين ايتدم | يوخسه سن بر پوله دكمزسن تيموره خوش

كلوب بى اختيار خندهء³ بسيار⁴ ايدوب حمامده اولان آلات نضه⁵

و ذهبى⁶ مولانايه هبه⁷ ايلدى .

(1) Usually spelt سكان, although pronounced *seksen*.—(2) *Fouté*, a kind of apron.
—(3) P. *Khandé*, 'laughter.'—(4) P. *Bisiar*, 'much.'—(5) *Fiddeh*, 'silver.'—(6) A.
*Zéheb*, 'gold.'—(7) A. *Hibé*, ' to present gratis.'

### Translation.

### A Joke.

Timour (Tamerlane) having come to the country of *Roum*†
(Turkey), liked to converse with Molla Ahmedi. One day he
entered a bath, and said to the Molla : " State what you think
the value of each of the commanders (gentlemen) in the bath."
The Molla set a price on each. Timour then said : " Value me
also." The Molla priced him at eighty *akché* ‡ (about 1½*d*). Timour
said : " You have not done me justice. That amount is only the
price of a *fouté* (an apron)." The Molla said : " I meant only the
price of an apron ; or rather, that you are not worth a farthing."
This pleased Timour. He involuntarily laughed, and made the
Molla a present of all the gold and silver vessels in the bath.

* مولا, A., when pronounced *Mevla*, means God, ' the Lord,' or ' Master.' *Na*
means in Arabic ' our.' Thus *Mevlana* signifies ' Our Lord ;' a title applied to God,
and to any high dignitary of the law. When pronounced *Molla*, it means ' a judge '
of a large town.
† The Eastern Empire, or Turkey.
‡ An *akché* was about ₁/₁₀ of a penny.

# THE CAPTURE OF CONSTANTINOPLE.

مار الذكر اولان مارپیكر¹ و اژدرسر² طوپلری مواضع لازمهده قوروب مترسلر
تعبیه³ ایتدیلر و یكیچری و عزب⁴ لشكرینی اول خدمته موكل⁵ ایدوب دیر
و دیوار و حصاری درون عشاق پر زاری كبی رخنه و سوراخ و تتابع
ضروب طوب طوپ قلعهكوب ایله پیدا اولان شكافی فراخ ایلدیلر اول
اهنین‌تن و آتشین دهن قزغانلر دهانندن نمایان اولان اتش چشم تیرهٔ
كفاری حیرة و مشوش ایدوب عیوقه صعود ایدن دود ممدود راه نفوذ
قوت باصرهٔیی مسدود اتمكله روز روشن نمودار شب تار و روی جهان
مانند بخت تیرة كفار سیاه روزگار اولور یدی سفیر تیر دهان كمان پیردن
"اینما⁶ تكونوا یدرككم الموت" پیامنی ارفع صوت ایله كوش بی سروش
دشمن مدهوشه ابلاغ ایلدیدی . . . . . . .

كفار ستمكار جانبندن نزول ایدن سنك طوپ و تفنك پنچه
مجاهدك قلعهٔ وجودینی بیم بنیادندن قلع ایدوب عرصهٔ پیكار نمودار⁷
لاله زار اولوب خون غزاتله روی زمین آل و خود و مغفر ایله معركهٔ⁸ قتال
مالامال اولمشیدی .

اول اثنادہ فرنك جانبندن امداد ایچون ایكی عظیم كوكه⁹ كه
سرنلرینك¹⁰ اوچی كوكه اتمشیدی دامن حصاره كلوب ایچنده اولان
جهنمی‌لر درون حصارده كوادیلر و نمایان اولان رخنه و سوراخلری سدہ
و عسكر اسلامی پیرامن حصاردن دفع و ردہ شروع ایدیجك بارو نشین
اولان دوزخیان¹¹ بی دین كشف وار¹² درون حصاردن باش چقاروب اطالهٔ¹³
لسانه اغرا ایتدیلر .

---

(1) P. *Mar-péïker*, ‘serpent-faced.’ — (2) P. *Azhder-sér*, ‘dragon-headed.’ —
(3) A. *Tabïh*, ‘to arrange, settle in battle array.’—(4) *Azb*, the name of a body
of troops under the old Turkish system.—(5) *Muvekkel*, ‘appointed.’—(6) An
Arabic sentence taken from the Koran, meaning: ‘Wherever you may be death
will reach you.’—(7) P. *Noumoudar*, ‘an example, likeness, like.’—(8) A. *Mareké*,
‘a battle-field.’—(9) *Kïouka*, ‘a kind of ship’ (obsolete).—(10) *Seren*, ‘spars.’—
(11) P. *Douzakhi*, ‘one who is doomed to hell.’—(12) *Keshef-var*, ‘like a tortoise.’—
(13) A. *Italé'-lissan*, ‘abuse.’

ارکان سلطنتده خليل پاشايه موافقت ايدوب صوب قتال و مكاوحه¹ دن
سمت مصالحهيه عطف عنان تصويبنه ذاهب اولدلر شاه كشوركير ضميرنده
امتناع تسخير دلايلني تصوير ايدوب صلحه ترغيب و لزوم مراجعت
مقدماتنى ترتيب ايتديلر كوش² هوشلرى³ استماع پيام خام و اصغاى
كلام ملام⁴ انجام⁵ دن اعراض و اجتناب اوزره مفطور⁶ اولمغين اول بد
اموزارك مقال مردود غرض اندودنه⁷ التفات اتميوب صوابديد علما و مشايخ
ايله عرصۀ داد و كيرده ثابت قدم و صدمۀ مهر و پيكانله پاس برج ايدن
پنچه ناسياسى افكندۀ خندق عدم ايلديلر علماى عظامدن شيخ احمد
كورانى و مشابخ كرامدن شيخ اق شمس الدين و وزرا عليمقامدن زغنوس
پاشا سلطان كشور كشا ايله يكدل و يكزبان اولوب تجويز مصالحه و مساهلهدن
امتناع ايدوب شاهد فتح دامنندن ال چكمك صدق عزيمت نشانهسى
دكلدر ديو سپاه ظفرپناهه نصيحتلر ايتديلر . و لطف ادايله " ثم يفتح لكم
الروم"⁸ مضمونندن مفهوم اولان وعد صداقت مقرونى اعلام ايدوب "الملحمة
العظمى فتح قسطنطنيه"⁹ فحواسندن مستفاد اولان لزوم سعى و اهتمامى
مجاهدينه افهام ايتديلر . و دلاوران عرصۀ جهاد دخى تن و جانلرينى
دين يولنده بذله اعداد¹⁰ ايدوب شب و روز مشاعل سيوفله معركه افروز
اولديلر . جمال دلاراى ظفر مجلاى ظهورده جلوهكر¹¹ اولمايجق شهريار
خجسته¹² تدبير جمع امراى روشن ضمير ايدوب بيوردنلر كه بو جانبك
مداخلى خندق عميق ايله مسدود و اسباب حفظ و حراستى نا معدود
در . نه بى تكلف¹³ خندقدن مرور ايتمك اولور و نه بريد¹⁴ افكار سور

---

(1) Fighting.—(2) P. *Ghioush*, 'the ear.'—(3) P. *Housh*, 'intelligence, mind, sense.'
—(4) *Melam*, 'reproach, rebuke.'—(5) P. *Enjam*, 'the end, upshot.' Thus *melam-enjam* means 'productive of rebuke, reproach.'—(6) A. *Meftour*, 'inclined by nature.'—(7) *Gharazendoud*, 'interested.'—(8) Arabic words from the Koran which mean : 'Then *Roum* (Greece) will be opened to you.' (9) Other Arabic words meaning : 'The greatest fight will be the conquest of Constantinople.'—(10) A. *Idad*, 'preparing.'—(11) P. *Jilvégher*, 'coquettish.'—(12) P. *Khujesté*, 'auspicious.'—(13) A. *Tekelluf*, 'labour and bother.'—(14) A. *Berid*, 'a courier ; ' 'a running foot-man.'

استوارندن جای کذار بولور · دیوارلری اوچ قاتدر · تنها بو طرفدن چالشمق تضییع اوقتدر · محل واحددن محاربه ایله دشمنه ظفر عسیر و مستتبع اهلاك جمع کثیردر · جانب بحردن دخی حصاری دکمك چاره بولمق کرکدر ·

استانبول ایله غلطه میاننی قطع ایدر خلیج اوزره زنجیر چکیلوب ممر سفنه مسدود اولمغین اول جانبه کمی کچرمك غیر مقدور و امكان عادی حیزندن دور اولدیغی جهتدن ارکان دولت بو ملاحظه صحراسنده هرچند که باد پای[2] افکارلرینی تکاپوی[3] ایتدردیلر نهایتنه ایرمدیلر · عاقبت ضمیر الهام[4] پذیر شاه کشورکیره[5] بو لایح اولدیکه · یکی حصار جانبندن کمیلر سوروب غلطه اردندن دریابه اشوریه لر · و اشوب علوپله حصاریلری جانب بحردن دخی شاشوره لر · اکرچه بو ملاحظه قوتدن فعله خروجی ممتنعات عادیدن ایدی · لکن دستیاری[6] امداد بخت خداداد[7] سلطان عدل استاد ایله اهون طرق اوزره میسر اولوب علم جرالاثقال ماهرلرینك حیرت افزا تدبیرلری ایله بحردن بره کشتی چکوب ادهان ایله تربیه اولنمش اشجار تعبیه ایدوب زمین خشك اوزره نشیب[8] و فرازده[9] نیچه کره شکوه[10] کشتیلر چکوب دریابه صالدیلر · و اول کمیلر اوزره کوپری بغلیوب متزسلر وضع ایدوب دلیران[11] جنك و استانبول کبی حصار وسیعی چشم کفاره تنك ایتدیلر ·

تکور[12] مردار[13] دریا جانبنك دخی رخنه دار اولدیغندن خبردار اولیجق کفار نابکارك[14] بر بلوکنی دخی بو جانب محافظه لرینه ضم ایلدی · مواضع عدیده ده اشکار اولان رخنه لر اوجندن متوزع[15] النحاطر اولمغین کاه اول جانبه کاه بو جانبه مقید اولمغله تدارکدن قالوب ادرنه قاپوسنك جانب

---

(1) Difficult.—(2) P. *Bad-pa*, 'a horse swift as the wind.'—(3) P. *Tekia-pouï*, 'running here and there, seeking.'—(4) *Ilham-pézir*, 'inspired.'—(5) P. *Kishvér-ghir*, 'conqueror of countries.'—(6) P. *Dest-yari*, 'assistance.'—(7) P. *Khoudadad*, 'the gift of God.'—(8) P. *Neshib*, 'a descent.'—(9) P. *Firaz*, 'an ascent.'—(10) P. *Kiouh-shukiouh*, 'majestic as a mountain.'—(11) P. *Diliran*, 'brave men.'—(12) *Tekir*, or تکفور *Tekfour*, 'the Greek Emperor.'—(13) *Mourdar* (*moundar*), 'filthy, unclean.' —(14) P. *Na-bekarin*, 'worthless.'—(15) Distracted.

جنوبی‌سنده پیدا اولان رخنه‌لر سدینی فرنك لشكرینه تفویض ایلدی .

خواص عسكری بو معنادن رنجیده' اولوب حفظنده جمله‌دن زیاده اهتمام

ایده‌جك محالك حفظنی انلره بیورمیوب اجانب عهده‌سنه تحویل

و بیكانه‌لره' اعتماد و تعویل ایتدیكندن بی‌حضور اولمغله میانلرنده انقلاب

صورتی نمایان اولدی . بو حال كروه' ضلال' امرینك انتظامنة باعث

اختلال و سلطان اقالیم كشانك مزید اقبالنه و طلوع كوكب امالنه دال

بر دلیل رافع الملال اولدی .

اول مخانیلك' كار و بارلرینه پریشانی و تفرق تطرق ایتدیكی اوضاعلرندن

ناشی اولان تلاشیلرندن تحقق بولیجق جان متاعنی ارزان' كورن دلاوران

بارو' افكن ادرنه' دروازه‌سنك' جانب جنوبندن اولان رخنه‌لر اوزره یوربش

ایدوب تار' اقدام و اوتار' اهتمام ایله بالای بروجه عروج صددنده' ایكن

طالع دیجور' افق غربی قله سندن ظهور ایدوب داور' دلاور عسكر ظفر

رهبرینه' بویله امر ایتدیكه نیزه' و رماح اوزره مشاعل و اشماع مهر' التماع

دیكوب اول قوم مذموم' قارشوسنده موملر یاقالر . و مشعل طارم' چارم'

عالمه پرتو صالیجه تیغ' بی دریغ' مشاعلنه فروغ' ویرلوب كافره امان و رخنه‌لر

سدنده زمان ویرمیه‌لر .

بر حسب فرموده شهریاری پیشكاه حصاری مشاعله مصابیح ایله روشن

و پرامن' سوری' افروخته' چراغلردن كویا كه سرخ' و زرد' كل و لاله مزین'

بر كلشن ایتدیلر . و بامدن' شامه و رواحدن' صباحه‌دك قتاله میل و جمع

---

(1) *Renjidé,* 'annoyed.'— (2) P. *Bighiané,* 'foreigners.'—(3) P. *Ghiurouh,* 'people.'
—(4) Error.—(5) A. *Makhazil,* 'rascals.'—(6) P. *Erzan,* 'cheap.'—(7) P. *Barou-efken,*
'overthrowing castle walls.'—(8) Adrianople.—(9) P. *Dervazé,* 'a gate.'—(10) P. *Tar,*
'a cord.'—(11) A. *Evtar,* pl. of وتر *vatr,* 'a cord, string.'—(12) Intention.—(13) A.
*Dcy-jour,* 'darkness.'—(14) P. *Daver,* 'a monarch.'—(15) Victorious.—(16) P. *Nizé,*
'a dart, javelin.'—(17) P. *Mihr,* 'the sun'; mihr iltima, 'shining like the sun, glittering.'—(18) A. *Mezmoum,* 'blamed, detestable.'—(19) P. *Tarim,* 'the sky, heaven,
a dome.'—(20) P. *Charum,* 'fourth.'—(21) P. *Tigh,* 'a sword.'—(22) P. *Bi-Dirigh,*
'never-failing' (which never refuses).—(23) P. *Furough,* 'light, splendour.'—(24)
P. *Piramen,* 'circuit, inclosure, environ.'—(25) P. *Efroukhté,* 'lighted, on fire, illuminated.'—(26) P. *Sourkh,* 'red.'—(27) P. *Zérd,* 'yellow.'—(28) A. *Muzeyyen,* 'ornamented.—(29) P. *Bam,* 'the dawn.'—(30) A. *Rewah,* 'the evening time.'

مثوبات[1] غزای احیای لیل ایتدیلر . و ماء شهادتله الایش[2] اثامدن[3] تطهیر ذیل ایتدیلر .

مجاهدین ایله اهنك[4] جنك ایدن فرنك مخاذیلنك سرداری حصار دیواری اوزره چیقوب قصد مدافعهء فریق جهاد ایتدكده بر جوان دلاور چالاك[5] سیف بی حیفنی[6] هلال آسا اویزهء افلاك ایدوب عنكبوت وار[7] حصار دیوارینه كمند همت ایله چیقوب نشیبدن فرازه تیغ بی دریغنی دراز و اول لهیب مهیبی دوزخیء مزبرك جوف[8] پر خوفنك نصیبی ایتمكله روی ادبارنه[9] عدم دریچهسنی[10] رخنهء حصار باز[11] ایدوب طعنه واحده ایله بوم[12] جانفی اشیان[13] شومندن[14] پران[15] ایتدی .

خیل فرنك سردارلرنیه یوبله رنك اولدیغنی كوریجك جنك چنكلرزندن[16] دامننی رها ایدوب هر بری سارع سلوك شارع فرار و متوجه وجهه ادبار اولوب كشتیلرینی جوبان[17] و جوی[18] سریع الجریان[19] كبی دریا جانبنه روان اولادیلر . . . همانندم[20] غازیبان شیر[21] نخجیركیر[22] كبی زنجیر تاخیردن بوشانوب[23] باران[24] تیر وسنكه و همواره[25] اتلان طوب و تفنكه باقمیوب مردانه میدانه كیردیكر . و اول رخنهلری دریچه فتح بیلوب خراب ایتدكلری مواضعة شتاب[26] ایتدیلر . . . . . شمشیرلر برهنه[27] اولوب چالشدی و نیزه و پیكان[28] اكباد[29] كروه عنادیله قان یلاشوب[30] الشدی . . . . . . . . . آن[31] واحدله بروجه عروج ایدوب لوای فتحی بالای سورهء قودیلر و زبان شمشیر طلیق اللسانله سورهء فتح اوقودیلر تكور كوردل مدافعهء محاصران حصاره

(1) A. Mesoubat, 'rewards promised for good actions.'—(2) Pollution.—(3) Sins.
—(4) P. Ahenk, 'intention.'—(5) Nimble.—(6) A. Haïf, ' injustice.'—(7) Like a
spider.—(8) The belly.— (9) A. Idbar, 'retrogression,' 'adversity.'—(10) A window.
—(11) Opening.— (12) An owl. — (13) P. Ashyan, ' a nest.'—(14) Unlucky.—
(15) Flying, adj.—(16) A hook.—(17) Seeking, desiring.—(18) A river, torrent.—
(19) Swiftly running.—(20) That very moment.—(21) P. Shir, 'a lion.'—
(22) P. Nakhjir-ghir, 'a hunter.'—(23) To be let loose.—(24) P. Baran, 'rain.'—
(25) P. Hemvaré, 'continually, constantly.'—(26) P. Shitab etmek, 'to hasten.'—
(27) P. Birehné, 'bare, naked.'—(28) P. Péïkan, 'an arrow.'—(29) Plural of كبد, kebd,
' the heart, the liver.'—(30) Yalashmak, ' to lick.'—(31) A moment, instant, time.

مشتغل اولوب ادرنه دروازه سنك جانب شماليسنده اولان سراينده وار

قوتنى بازويه كتوروب جوانب اطرافنى محافظه يه صرف[1] مقدور ايدرايكن

ناكاه رافعان[2] لواى كلمة الله درون حصاره راه بولديغندن اكاه اولوب ملحوظى[3]

معكوس وعلم دولتى منكوس[4] اولديغنى بيلوب بيرون سرايه شتاب و بخت

بر كشته سنه عتاب ايدوب اول سقر[5] مقر اين[6] المفر[7] كلامنى ازبر و راه

كريزه[8] كذر ايكن دلاورلردن بر جمع اندك[9] شمارى[10] غنايم جمعنه فراغ بال

ايله اشتغالده بولوب دائره[11] كينه[12] سينه[13] تيره سنه[14] اول خشك سالرى

اتشكيره ايدوب دامن شمشير ايله حاصل[15] عمرلرينى بچدى[16] و تيغ خون

فشانى[17] اول كروه بى اندوه قاننى ايچدى . بو ميانده عزب طايفه سندن بر

مجروح ناتوان جروحندن اقان قان مانند[18] جوى روان اولوب اول

جاى اشوبده دوشوب قالمش و زخم كنارىسندن جارى اولان خون ايچره

غرق اولوب اول افتاده رنجور[19] منظور تكور اوليجق تيغنى حواله[20] ايدوب

ديلديكه[21] بقيه رمقنى[22] ازاله ايده . اول ناتوان دخى بيم[23] جان ايله

چالشوب امداد واهب المراد ايله اول دشمن بى دينى زين[24] اوستندن

آيروب خاك[25] سياه ده دوشوردى . و شمشير جهاد مورچه[26] لرينى باشنه

اوشوردى . هماندم باشنى كسمكى زخمنه مرهم[27] وخدم[28] حشمنى[29] پريشان

و درهم[30] ايلدى . پيشكاه انظاردن كيتديلر . عرصه جنكده درنك[31] ايدوب

دست شكسته سنى شمشيره دراز ايتمكله اقدام ايدر بر احد قالما يجق

دروازهلرى باز و خارج حصارده اولان سپاه ظفرپناه شاه سرفراز اوكنچه درون

---

(1) Doing his utmost.—(2) Bearers.—(3) A. *Melhouz*, 'anticipated, expected.'—
(4) Inverted, turned upside down.—(5) *Sakar-makar*, 'whose abode will be in hell.'
—(6) Where?—(7) A. *Mefer*, 'a place of refuge.'—(8) *Ghiriz*, 'flight.'—(9) Small.
—(10) Number.—(11) Fire—(12) P. *Kiné*, 'rancour, malice.'—(13) The breast.—
(14) Dark, gloomy.—(15) The harvest, produce.—(16) To reap.—(17) Shedding,
scattering.—(18) Like.—(19) Suffering.—(20) Directing against.—(21) To desire.—
(22) The last spark of life.—(23) P. *Bim*, 'fear;' *Bim-i-jan-ilé*, 'in desperation.'—
(24) P. *Zin*, 'a saddle.'—(25) P. *Khak*, 'earth.'—(26) P. *Mourché*, 'a little ant; the
marks on Damascus steel.'—(27) A. *Merhém* (*melhém*), 'a plaster.'—(28) P. *Khadem*,
'servants.'—(29) A. *Hashem*, 'retinue.'—(30) P. *Dér-hem*, 'in confusion.'—(31) P.
*Direngh*, 'procrastination.'

حصنه كيرمكه اغاز ايتديلر . و تنفيل[1] علم سلطانى ايله اوچ شبانه روز[2] عسكر

فيروز اغتنام غنايمله دست[3] ارزولرينى كردن[4] مقاصدلرينه[5] حمايل[6]

ايدوب جوارى[7] حوارى[8] شمائل ذوايبنه[9] اويزه دللر ينى بند . و خوبان[10]

شكرخند[11] مشاهده سيله ديده اميدلرينى بهره[12]مند ايتد يلر . . . . .

يوم ثلثده چاوشان دركاه[13] عالى نهب و غارته مشغول اولان مجاهدلرى

بر موجب فرمان همايون منع و زجر[14] ايدوب دست درازلرينى بسته،

و چنكل طمعلرينى شكسته ايتديلر . و فرمان قضا[15] مضا جريان رسوم امن

و امان اقتضا ايتديكنى اعلام[16] ايدوب رضاى مسرت[17] افضاى سلطانى

غازيلر ارامده[18] و تيغلر نيامده[19] اولديغنه متعلق ايدوكنى اخبار ايتديلر. فرمان

شهريارى بو وجه اوزره جارى اوليجق شمشيرلر كوشه كير[20] اولدى . . . . .

بالجمله زلال[21] نوال[22] شهريار كامكار ايله غبار[23] كيرودار[24] باصلدى . و اوقلر

اتيلوب يايلر باصلدى . و اول كشور اشيان بوم ضلال ايكن استان مجد

و اقبال اولدى . مساعى[25] جميلهء سلطان محمدى ايله صداى بداداى

ناقوس[26] بى ناموس يربنه كلبانك[27] و زمزمه[28] پنج نوبت دبن اشرف

آيين احمدى بدل قيلنوب نواى[29] اداى[30] اذان ايله اذان اهل جهان

پر[31] اولدى و درون شهرده اولان كنيسه لر اصنام[32] خسيسه دن[33] تخليه[34] اولنوب

(1) *Tenfil,* 'giving the whole of the spoil to soldiers.'—(2) Day and night.—
(3) P. *Dest,* 'the hand.'—(4) *Gherden,* 'the neck.'—(5) Intentions.—(6) A sword-
belt.—(7) Female slaves, girls.—(8) Like the houris of paradise.—(9) A. *Zuabé,* 'a
tuft of hair, forelock.'—(10) P. *Khouban,* 'Belles.'—(11) Sweet smiles.—(12) P.
*Behrémend,* 'participating.'—(13) A court, gate.—(14) A. *Zejr,* 'restraining.'—
(15) A. *Kaza-maza,* 'which must be executed.'—(16) A. *Ilam,* 'making known.'—
(17) A. *Meserret,* 'joy.'—(18) P. *Aram,* 'repose.'—(19) P. *Niyyam,* 'scabbard.'—
(20) Sitting in a corner.—(21) A. *Zulal,* 'sweet-water.'—(22) A. *Newal,* 'grace,
favour.'—(23) A. *Ghoubar,* 'dust.'—(24) P. *Ghirudar,* 'conflict, fighting.'—
(25) Efforts.—(26) A. *Nakous,* 'a bell.'—(27) P. *Ghiul-bangh,* 'the Mussulman call
to prayer.'—(28) A. *Zemzemé,* 'a soft murmur of voices.'—(29) *Nuwa,* 'note,
tone.'—(30) A. *Eda,* 'grace of manner or tone.'—(31) P. *Pur,* 'full.'—(32) A.
*Esnam,* 'idols.'—(33) A. *Khasis,* 'ignoble.'—(34) A. *Takhliyyé,* 'emptying, or
evacuating.'

انجاس<sup>1</sup> ارجاس<sup>2</sup> و تبنيتدن<sup>3</sup> تطهير<sup>4</sup> و وضع پيشينلرى<sup>5</sup> تغيير قيلينوب
و ضع محاريب<sup>6</sup> و منابر<sup>7</sup> اسلامليه ايله نيچه دير<sup>8</sup> و كنشت رشك فراديس
بهشت<sup>9</sup> اولدى . معابد<sup>10</sup> كفره<sup>11</sup> مساجد<sup>12</sup> بررو<sup>13</sup> قيلينوب پرتو انوار اسلام اول
مقر ديرينۀ كفار لثامدن رفع افواج ظلام ايدوب تباشير صبح ايمان ايله
ظلمت ظلم ليثمان مضمحل و فرمان قضا جريان سلطان كامران<sup>14</sup> او ملك
جديد ضبطندۀ مستقل اولدى .

(1) The impure, or the dirty, pl. of نجس *nejis.*—(2) Crime, filth.—(3) Making any-one a son, adopting; probably referring to the Christians calling Christ the Son of God.—(4) Cleaning.—(5) Old, ancient.—(6) *Pl.* of *miḥrab,* a niche in the wall of a mosque indicating in which direction one ought to turn when praying.—(7) *Pl.* of *minber,* 'a pulpit.'—(8) A convent.—(9) Heaven.—(10) Places of worship, *pl.* of معبد *ma'bed.*—(11) *Kéferé,* 'infidels;' *pl.* of كافر *kafir,* 'an infidel, pagan.'— (12) *Pl.* of مسجد *mesjid,* 'a small parish mosque.'—(13) Pious people; *pl.* of بار *barr.*—(14) Successful.

### *Translation.*

(The Turks) planted the aforementioned serpent-faced * and dragon-headed * cannon in the requisite positions, and constructed intrenchments. The Janissaries and the *Azebs* were entrusted with the duty. They made the gate and walls and fortifications as full of rents and holes as the hearts of lovers are full of groans, and they widened the breach made by the repeated blows of the tre-mendous "castle-levelling" cannon. The fire from the mouths of these iron-bodied and fiery-muzzled engines (of destruction) spread confusion and dismay amongst the infidels. The smoke, which rose up to the sky, prevented any one seeing any thing, and the bright day became like dark night, and the face of the world became as dark as the fate (which awaits) unbelievers. The arrow from the bow, like an envoy, conveyed to the wretched † ear of the stupified enemy, in a loud voice, the following message (from the Koran) : " Wherever you may be death will overtake you." ......

However, the stone cannon-balls, and the musket bullets, which fell like rain, destroyed many a martyr, who were strewn like a bed of

---

* These compound Persian adjectives continually occur in Sad-ud-Din's work, and form one of the beauties of it, but when translated literally into English, as is necessary for the learner, they may sound peculiar, or even awkward; but we have similar expressions in English, as, for example, Richard the Lion-Hearted.

† *Bi-souroush* means, literally, ' without a guardian angel.'

tulips, and the ground was red with the blood of our champions of religion, and the battle-field covered with casques and helmets.

In the meantime two large vessels, whose masts reached the sky, came, bringing succour from the Franks. The devils who were in them entered the fortifications and began stopping the breaches and holes, and driving the Mussulman army from the fort. Then the infidel children of the devil put out their heads from the walls and abused us.

Those amongst the great men in the government (pillars of the State) who agreed with Khalil Pasha, and approved of relinquishing the combat and making peace, argued that it was impossible to conquer, and urged our victorious sovereign to retreat; but he, being by nature averse to giving ear to crude advice, or listening to talk " which leads to sorrow," took no notice of their perverse and interested counsels, and remained steadfast in battle, with the *oulema* and the *sheikhs,* and cast into the ditch of death the ungrateful creatures of God who defended the walls with arrows and other missiles.

Sheikh Ahmed Kourani, one of the *oulemas,* and Sheikh Ak Shems-ud-Din, one of the doctors of Law and Divinity, and the Vezir, Zagtous Pasha, opposed peace and conciliation, and exhorted the glorious troops, saying : " It is a sign of want of resolution to withdraw one's hand from the hem of victory;" and explained the promise implied by the words (of the Koran): " Then Roum (the Eastern Empire) shall be opened to you (conquered by you) ;" and gave them to understand that it was necessary to use every effort (as it was said in another place) " The *greatest* battle will be the conquest of Constantinople." (Hence) the valorous men in the Holy War prepared to sacrifice their lives for the sake of religion, and the battle-field was illuminated night and day by the flashing of their swords.

(However) as the goddess of victory was coquettish in making her appearance, the ingenious monarch assembled his brilliant-minded commanders, and said : " Entrance on this side is stopped by a deep ditch, and the means of guarding and defending it are numberless. We cannot cross the ditch without much trouble, nor can the courier of our thoughts find a place through which to pass

over the ramparts. There are three walls. It is waste of time to
work only on this side. By operating (warring) in one place only
victory will be difficult, and it will cause the death of a large number.
It is necessary to find a way to attack the fortifications on the side
of the sea."

(However) as a chain was drawn over the Strait (canal) dividing
Galata and Constantinople, closing it against the passage of ships,
(the above idea) was beyond the range of ordinary possibility; however much the great men of the State thought the matter over they
could come to no conclusion. Finally, it occurred to the mind of the
inspired monarch that they should drag ships from the direction of
the new Fort (Yeni Hissar), and bring them round the back of
Galata to the sea, and guns round to attack the fortifications
from the direction of the sea also. The execution of this idea
was one of those things which are ordinarily impossible, but by
the help of the divinely-inspired monarch it was easily carried out.
By the astounding arrangements of his skilful mechanicians they
dragged great ships along on greased rollers over the rough ground,
uphill and down dale. They erected a bridge on these ships, and
breast-works, and ranged valorous troops and intrenchments as
extensive as Constantinople, before the eyes of the unbelievers.

The unclean Emperor of the Greeks, hearing that there were
breaches in the direction of the sea, sent an additional division of
the infidels to that side. Distracted by the breaches made in
numerous places, he was forced to attend now to this side and now
to that, and entrusted the stopping of the breaches made on the
south side of the Adrianople gate to the Frank soldiers. His own
soldiers were annoyed by this, and uncomfortable because he had
not entrusted the defence of the place which required the greatest
zeal of all to them, and that he had confidence in strangers. Hence
disturbance arose amongst them; and this state of things caused
disorder amongst these misguided people, and increase of good
fortune to our glorious Sultan, and was a joyful sign that the star
of his hopes was in the ascendant.

As soon as the mighty Turkish heroes ascertained that the affairs
of those rascals were upset, and that they were in a state of alarm,
they stormed the breaches on the south side of the Adrianople gate;

but when they were about to climb up the ramparts " with the rope of perseverance," the scouts of the night appearing on the western horizon, our valourous monarch ordered his glorious troops to fix lanterns and lighted candles on their javelins and spears to throw light on the detestable people, and thus give splendour to the flashing of their own unfailing swords, "until the torch of the Fourth Heaven shone," in order that the infidels should have no repose, and no time to stop their breaches. In accordance with the royal command the front of the fortifications, and the circuit of the ramparts were lit up, and they made them, as it were like a rose-garden decorated with red and yellow roses and tulips. From dawn to evening, and from evening to morning, they fought steadily, like religious heroes, and they cleansed the stain of sins from their garments in the water of martyrdom . . . . . .

The leader of the Frank rascals who were fighting with our heroes, having mounted on the ramparts to repel the champions of religion, a valiant nimble youth climbed up the castle wall like a spider, and, drawing his "crescent-like" sword, with a single blow caused his owl-like soul to fly from the unclean nest of his body.

As soon as the Franks saw the plight their leader was in, they withdrew their garments from the clutches of war and all took to flight, and rushed down to the sea to join their ships like an impetuous torrent. Immediately our champions of religion, like lion-hunters, without delay, disregarding the shower of arrows and stones, and the cannon and musketry continually being fired, bravely entered the battle-field, and looking upon the breaches as the gates of victory, hastened to the places they had demolished. . . . . . They bared their swords and fought, and their javelins and arrows drank the heart's blood of the hardnecked people.* In a moment they mounted the walls and planted the flag of victory there, and with the tongue of the sword proclaimed the triumphal verses (in the Koran). . . . . .

The wretched Greek Emperor, busy repelling the besiegers of the fortifications, in his palace situated to the north of the Adrianople gate, did his utmost to defend the approaches to it. Suddenly he became aware that the " Flagbearers of the Word of God" (*i.e.* the

---

* This means the people who refuse to hear Mahomet's teaching.

Mussulmans) had found their way into the fortress, and knowing that his hopes were blighted, and the flag of his fate overthrown, he rushed out of the palace. Cursing his unfortunate lot, that infidel (whose abode will be in hell) fled, crying : " Where is there a place of safety." Meeting a small group of the heroes who were cheerfully engaged in gathering the spoil, the fire of malice in his gloomy breast was kindled ; with his sword he reaped the harvest of their lives, and his " blood-shedding" sword drank the blood of those inoffensive men.

Amongst them, one of the *Azeb* soldiers, who was helpless and wounded, his blood flowing in a stream, fell down and was bathed in his gore. The Greek Emperor noticing this suffering man raised his sword, wishing to extinguish the last spark of life in him. The poor wretch made a supreme effort, and, with the help of God, tore that enemy of religion down from his saddle, and, felling him to the ground, knocked him on the head with his Damascus blade. His decapitating the Emperor was a plaster to his own wounds, and put the Emperor's servants and retinue in confusion and disorder, and they vanished from sight. Losing all ardour for fighting, not one dared to handle his sword, and (the Mussulmans) opened the gates, and the glorious (Turkish) troops outside the walls began to enter in the presence of their proud sovereign.

By permission of the Sultan they were allowed to sack the town for three days and nights, and being attracted by the black-eyed (Greek) girls they feasted the eyes of their hopes with the sight of beauties whose smiles were like sugar.

On the third day the officers of the Court, in accordance with the royal orders, restrained the heroes who were engaged in plunder. They stopped their hands and controlled their avarice, and proclaimed that the royal command, which must be obeyed, required that mercy should be shown. The King's orders being obeyed, their swords were sheathed . . . . In a word, with the sweet water of the imperial grace, the dust of combat was layed. Arrows were thrown away and bows trodden under foot. (Thus) the land which had been the abode (nest) of infidelity became the threshold of glory and good fortune . . . . By the laudable efforts of the Sultan, instead of the evil sound of the disreputable Church-bells the Mussulman call to prayer, and the sweet murmer of voices repeating the confession of faith, five times a day, was substituted. The ears of the people of the world were filled with this sweet sound. The churches in the city were emptied of their vile idols, and cleansed from their impurities. The old rites were changed, and *Mihrabs* and (Mussulman) pulpits being erected in them, many chapels became like Paradises. The temples of the infidels were turned into the mosques of the faithful. The splendour of Islamism drove away the legions of darkness from the ancient abode of the infidels, and the darkness of wickedness disappeared on the announcement of the glad tidings of the Faith; and the orders of the august monarch, which all must obey, became supreme in the management of that new dominion.

## NAÏMA (Imperial Historiographer).

NAÏMA is, perhaps, the most celebrated historiographer, after Sad-ud-Din. He gives the annals of the Ottoman year by year from *Anno Hejirae* 1000 to 1050. His history was one of the first books ever printed in Turkey, and appeared in print in the year Anno Domini 1734. It consists of two thick volumes, in folio. His style is clear and good, and the facts he gives are sometimes remarkably interesting.

### The Conquest of the Island of Crete.

ابتدا غزوات      الف      و خمسين و      وقائع سنه خمس

كريد      جزيرهٴ

سنهٴ سابقهده ذكرى مرور ايدن مالته كميلرى استانهدن مصره كيدن دار السعاده اغاسى سفينهسنه مستولى اولوب الدقلرى سمع همايونه واصل اولدقده كفاردن اخذ انتقام و ثارهٴ همت شهر يارى اولوب اق دكزه سفر فرمان ايلديلر . . .

سابقا حرم همايونده مقرب پادشاه سلحدار يوسف پاشا كه طشره چيقرب قپوران ذيشان اولمشيدى دوننماى همابونه سردار اولمسى

---

(1) P. *Asitané*, 'a threshold,' 'a royal court,' 'Constantinople.'—(2) A. *Dar-us Seadet*, 'the house of felicity,' *i. e.* the Sultan's harem. *Dar-us-Seadet-aghasi* is the title of the Sultan's chief eunuch.—(3) A. *Sar*, 'vengeance.'—(4) *Ak-Deniz*, 'the Mediterranean.' — (5) One who comes close to the sovereign; hence 'a courtier.'—(6) P. *Silahdar* (*silihdar*), 'an esquire, or sword-bearer.'— (7) *Kapoudan*, 'a sea captain;' *Kapoudan Pasha*, 'Lord High Admiral.'— (8) *Serdar,* 'Commander.'

قرارداده¹ رأى پادشاه اولامغين قپودانلق منصبنه لشكر بحرو بر سپهسالارلغى²
دخى ضم و الحاق بيورلدى بو الطاف³ عظيمهدن ماعدا شرف⁴ مصاهرت⁵
ايله سائر اركان دولتدن سرافراز بيوريلوب ابكى بچوق ياشنده دختر پادشاه
جهان كندويه نامزد⁶ قلنوب عظيم نخللر⁷ ايشلنمكه شروع فرمان اولدى
ات ميدانه⁸ ناظر⁹ ابراهيم پاشا سرايى ترميم و بر ايكى قصر¹⁰ دلارا¹¹
و غرفهء¹² بيهمتا¹³ ضمى ايله تعمير اولندى و نخللر مرور ايدهجك يوللرده
مضايقه¹⁴ ويرر شهنشينلر¹⁵ ازاله¹⁶ توسيع¹⁷ طريق قلنوب لوازم ترويجه اهتمام تام
ايلديلر . . . . . . . چون يوسف پاشا حضرتلرى بو نوازش¹⁸ عظيم و عنايت
عميمه¹⁹ مظهر اولوب بويله بر مصالح عظيمه ايله مأمور اولدى همان روز
تدبير مهماته مباشرت ايدوب قضاة²⁰ مسلمينه كوزجى ايچون اوامر ايله
ادملر كوندردى و روم ايلى ايالتى دخى بغداددن معزول كوچك حسن
پاشايه توجيه اولنوب اول هفته سلانيكه ارسال اولنديكه روم ايلى عسكرينى
جمع ايدوب بنفشه ساحلنده قپودان پاشايه منتظر اوله بغداددن كلوب
رغرجى باشليقدن يكيچرى كتخداسى²¹ اولان مراد اغا يكيچرى اغاسى يرينه
سفره تعيين بيورلدى و صمصونجى باشى ابراهيم اغا و خاصكى على اغا
دخى سائر چورباجيلر²² ايله مأمور اولديلر و وزراددن بسنوى قوجه موسى

(1) *Karardadé*, 'settled, resolved.'—(2) P. *Sipahsalar*, 'Commander-in-Chief.'
—(3) A. *Eltaf*, pl. of *lutf*, 'favours.'—(4) *Sheref*, 'honour.'—(5) A. *Mousaheret*, 'relationship by marriage;' from صهر *sihr*, 'a son (or brother)-in-law.'—(6) P. *Nam-zed*,
'betrothed.'—(7) A. *Nahl*, 'an engagement present.'—(8) *At méidani*, 'Hippro-
drome,' (a place in Constantinople).—(9) A. *Nazir*, 'overlooking.'—(10) A castle;
a royal pavilion.—(11) P. *Dilara*, 'charming.'—(12) A. *Ghiurfé*, 'an upper chamber.'
—(13) P. *Bi-hemta*, 'unique.'—(14) A. *Muzayaka*, 'inconvenience, pressure, obstruc-
tion.'—(15) P. *Shahnishin*, 'a balcony, or bow-window.'—(16) A. *Izalé*, 'to remove.'
(17) A. *Tevsi i-tarik*, 'to widen a road.'—(18) P. *Nuwazish*, 'a caress, kindness,
attention.'—(19) A *Amim*, 'general.'—(20) A. *Kuzat* is the pl. of *Kazi*, or *Kadi*,
'a judge.' Two of these, called *Kazi-i-asker*, or 'judges of the army,' one for
Roumelia and one for Anatolia, exercised the office of supreme judges in Constantinople, although at first they were only the judges of the army.—(21) P. *Khet-
khuda*, 'a steward, manager, warden' (generally pronounced *Kiaya*).—(22) *Chor-
baji*, 'the master of a household, or a shop;' 'colonel of the Janissaries, in former
times.'

پاشا دخی سفر مرقومه تعیین بیورلدی که سردار ذیشانه رفیق و سمیر<sup>1</sup>
اولامغله تسخیر<sup>2</sup> بلاده حسن تدبیر ایده‌لر حسن پاشا سلانیکه واروب روم ایلی
امراسنی دعوت و جمع ایلدی و بو طرفدن اجرتلا ایله اللیدن متجاوز
بازرکان کمیلری استیجار اولنوب عساکر مذکورهنك زاد و زواده‌لرینی
تحمیل و دوننمادن اول ارسال قلندی طقسان پاره قالیون<sup>3</sup> و شیقه<sup>4</sup> سلانیکه
و التمش پاره سفینه دخی چشمه‌یه واروب لیماندرده لنکر<sup>5</sup> انداز اولدیلر
و بو کمیلره مهماتدن اون بش بیك قنطار باروت و اللی بیك آهنین
یوالاق<sup>6</sup> و اللی قطعه طوپلر و قازمه<sup>7</sup> و کورك<sup>8</sup> و سائر الت جبه‌خانه<sup>9</sup> و لوازم<sup>10</sup>
قلعه کیریکه بیحساب<sup>11</sup> ایدی تحمیل اولنوب کوندرلدی .

نمونه<sup>12</sup> نمای مقدمه‌ء<sup>13</sup> غزا<sup>14</sup> بو اثناده امرای بحر حضور سردار باوقاره<sup>15</sup> یوز
سورمکه اغاز ایتدیلر انلردن ممی پاشا اوغللری رودسدن<sup>16</sup> چیقوب عازم<sup>17</sup>
سدهء<sup>18</sup> سعادت اولوب کاورکن اق دکز اطه‌لرندن اسکری اطه‌سی لیماننه
واصل اولدقده لیمان مزبوردن اوتوز التی کافر ایله اون بندرمه طوپ چکر
بر مالته کمیسنه راست کلوب عون الهی ایله مسخر ایدوب ضرب
شمشیر ایله ملاعینی<sup>19</sup> در زنجیر و کمیلرینی تسخیر ایدوب یدکلیوب<sup>20</sup> حضور
سرداره کتوروب خلعتلر ایله انوع رعایتلریفه مظهر اولدی و بو قصه همان
فتحه‌دال و برفال فرخنده<sup>21</sup> مآلدر دیدیلر. . . . . . . . . .

---

(1) A. *Simmir*, 'a companion.'—(2) *Teskhir-etmek*, 'to conquer.'—(3) *Kalyon*, 'a man-of-war.'—(4) *Shaïka*, a *Saic*, 'a kind of ship.'—(5) P. *Lengher-endaz-olmak*, 'to anchor.'—(6) *Youwalak*, 'a ball, bullet.'—(7) *Kazmé*, 'a pickaxe.'—(8) *Kiurek*, 'an oar.'—(9) Or جبخانه *Jebkhané*, 'a powder magazine, or powder in store.' *Alat-i-jebkhané*, 'armoury implements.'—(10) *Lewazim kala-ghiri*, 'necessaries for a siege.' —(11) *Bi-hissab*, 'innumerable.'—(12) P. *Numouné-i-numa*, 'setting an example.' —(13) A. *Mukaddemé*, 'the advanced-guard.'—(14) *Ghaza*, 'a holy war, crusade.' —(15) P. *Ba-vékar*, 'dignified, majestic.'—(16) *Rodos*, 'the island of Rhodes.'— (17) A. *Azim*, 'departing.'—(18) A. *Suddé*, 'a threshold;' *Suddé-i-Saadet*, 'the threshold of felicity,' the seat of empire, the capital.—(19) A. *Melain*, 'accursed people.'—(20) *Yédeklémek*, 'to tow.'—(21) P. *Firkhende*, 'happy.'

تونس و طرابلس و جزائر<sup>1</sup> اوجاقلرینه<sup>2</sup> احکام مطاعه<sup>3</sup> و صدر اعظم مکتوبلری
کلوب اول بهارده اق دکزه سفر وار در کمیلریکز ایله عموماً غزایه حاضر
اولوب کلوب دوننمای همایونه ملحق<sup>4</sup> اولهسز دیو دعوت اولندیلر اوجاق
خلقی غزایه دعوت اولندقلرنده جوش و خروشلری زیاده اولوب جان و
باش ایله اوغور همایونده خدمته حاضر و قدوم سپهسالاره<sup>6</sup> منتظر اولدقلرینی
عرض ایتدیلر . . . . . . .

حضرت پادشاه دربادن<sup>7</sup> تدارك<sup>8</sup> و امور غزاده كمال اهتماملر<sup>9</sup> ینه بناء
هر كون ترسانهء<sup>10</sup> عامرهیه<sup>11</sup> بالذات<sup>12</sup> كندولر تشریف<sup>13</sup> ایتمکله سفائن<sup>14</sup> دوننما<sup>15</sup>
و سائر آلات قلعه كیری احضارینه<sup>16</sup> كندولر اقدام<sup>17</sup> و كمیلر و عسكر اموربنه
اهتمام تام بیوررلردی ماه صفرك یکرمی ایكنجی چهارشنبه كونی وقت
عصرده<sup>18</sup> مأمور اولان اوجاق اغالرینه و چورباجیلره خلعت سفر كید
یریلوب همان عزیمت<sup>19</sup> فرمان ایتدیلر قپودان یوسف پاشا دخی ماه ربیع
الاولك دردنجی روز یکشنبه ده عظیم دوننما و شنلكلر<sup>20</sup> ایله مالته سفری<sup>21</sup>
نامیله عزم غزا ایدوب جانب بحرسفیده<sup>22</sup> بادبانكشای<sup>23</sup> متوجه اولدی
دوننما ایله ساقز<sup>24</sup> جزیرهسنه واردقلرنده سلانیك<sup>25</sup> لیماننده<sup>26</sup> اولان كمیلر
ایچون ردوس<sup>27</sup> بكی ابراهیم بیك كه قره خواجه دیمكله معروفدر سكر مكمل
قدرغه<sup>28</sup> ایله كوندرپلوب قزلحصار لیمانننده جمع اولملری تنبیه<sup>29</sup> بیورلدی
و ساقزه داخل اولدقده اناطولی<sup>30</sup> سرعسکری احمد پاشا سیواس<sup>31</sup> و

---

(1) *Jezaïr,* 'Algiers.'—(2) *Ojak,* 'a colony, a corps,' and especially the corps of the Janissaries.—(3) P. *Muta,* 'obeyed.'—(4) A. *Mulhak olmak,* 'to be joined, attached.'—(5) *Joush-ou-Khouroush,* 'commotion, ebullition.'—(6) P. *Sipéhsalah,* 'a captain, or commander-in-chief, of an army.'—(7) *Derya,* 'the sea.'—(8) A. *Tédaruk,* 'preparation.'—(9) A. *Ihtimam,* 'effort.'—(10) *Tersané,* 'an arsenal.'—(11) A. *Amir,* 'busy,' 'public.'—(12) A. *Biz-zat,* 'in person.'—(13) *Teshrif etmek,* 'to honour.'—(14) A. *Sefaïn,* pl. of *Séfiné,* 'vessels.'—(15) *Donanma,* 'a fleet.'—(16) A. *Ihzar,* 'bringing into one's presence, producing.'—(17) Perseverance.—(18) A. *Asr,* 'the time for the afternoon prayer.'—(19) A. *Azimet,* 'departing.'—(20) *Shenlik,* 'rejoicings.'—(21) A. *Sefr,* 'a campaign, or expedition.'—(22) *Bahr-i-Séfid,* 'the Mediterranean.'—(23) P. *Baduban-kushaï,* 'unfurling sails.'—(24) *Sakiz* 'the island of Scio.'— (25) *Selanik,* 'Salonica.'— (26) *Liman,* 'a harbour.'—(27) *Rodos,* 'Rhodes.'—(28) *Kadirghé,* 'a galloy.'—(29) A. *Tenbih,* 'giving notice.'—(30) *Anatoli,* 'Anatolia.'—(31) *Sivas,* 'a town in Asia Minor.'

قرمان' و اناطولى بكلرى ايله دامنبوس' كاوب مظهر' التفات' اولديلر
ربيع الاولك يكرمى بشنجى كونى اناطولى عسكرى كميلره كيروب قرق
پاره شيقه ايله ساير ليماننده وضع لذكر اولديلر سكز كون استراحتد' نصكزه
كو چيلوب' قزلحصار ليماننه كلديلر يولده عظيم فورتنه' ظهور' ايدوب كميلر
پراكنده' و پريشان'' اولمشيدى مدللى'' بكى ولى بك كزوب جمله سنى
ترمش نام محله كلمسز ديو جمع ايلدى اوچ كونده قرق طقوز سفينه
جمله كلديلر روم ايلى سپهسالارى حسن پاشا دخى ايالتى عسكريله ربيع
الاولك يكرمى درندنده صالوب روم ايلى عسكرى قزل حصارى كچوب غرهء
ربيع الاخره ترمش سواحلنه كلوب طقسان سكز پاره سفينه ايله و بوقدر
جبه خانه و مهمات ايله دوننماى همايونه ملاقى'' اولديلر .

ايرتسى اوتراق'' فرمان اولنوب على الصباح يوسف پاشا باشترده
دن چيقوب اوتاقده'' جمله امراء كرام و سالاران لشكر اسلام مير'' ميران
حسن پاشا ايله كلوب دامنبوس سردار ايله مشرف'' اولوب تشريفات
شاهانه ايله سرافراز'' اولديار سردار كامكار'' هر برينى تطييب'' وغزا و
جهاده'' ترغيب'' ايلدى .

قرون سكانندن قره بتاق بك فرقتهسنه بنوب بر كريد فرقتهسنه اقتارمه''
ايدوب قپودان پاشايه كتوردكده خلعت ايله رعايت اولندى ايچنده بولنان
اون ايكى كافر كوركه'' قوديلر ايرتسى كوچيلوب بنفشه سواحلى مقابله سنده
كلدكلرنده بامر الله بر عظيم روزكار پيدا'' اولدى كرچه موافق'' ايدى لكن

(1) *Karman,* 'Caramania.'—(2) *Damen-bous,* 'kissing the hem of one's garment.'
(3) A. *Mezher,* 'a recipient.'—(4) *Iltifat,* 'favours, attentions.'—(5) A. *Istirahat,*
'rest.'—(6) *Ghieuchmek,* 'to migrate.'—(7) *Firtina,* 'a storm.'—(8) *Zuhour etmek,*
'to appear, arise.'—(9) *Prakendé,* 'scattered.'—(10) P. *Perishan,* 'in disorder.'—
(11) *Midilli,* 'Mytelene.'—(12) *Mulaki olmak,* 'to meet.'—(13) *Otourak,* 'a halt.'—
(14) *Otak,* or *otagh,* 'a large tent.'—(15) *Mir-i-Miran,* 'a governor of a district, with
the rank of lieutenant-general.'—(16) A. *Musherref,* 'honoured.'—(17) *Ser-efraz,*
'who holds up his head,' 'exalted.'—(18) P. *Kiamkiar,* 'successful.'—(19) A. *Tatyib*
*etmek,* 'to make pleased and happy.'— (20) A. *Jihad,* 'the good fight.'—(21) A.
*Terghib,* 'inciting.'—(22) *Aktarmak,* 'to turn over.'—(23) *Kiurek,* 'an oar,' 'the
galleys.'—(24) *Peida olmak,* 'to appear, arise.'—(25) A. *Muwafik,* 'favourable.'

شدتندن' دوننما ليمانه كيرديلر و بعض شيقه[2] و بورتنلرى[3] مانيه بوروننه
طوغرى چكدى دريادﮤ بولنان بعض امرا ليمانه كيرمك ممكن اولميوب
چوقه[4] اطهسنه دوشديلر .

سردادردن دور[5] اولدقلرينه تأسفده[6] ايكن مَكِر[7] ونديك[8] طرفندن كريد[9]
امدادينه[10] برصبا[11] رفتار[12] ايچى باورت[13] و دانه[14] و قورشون[15] وخمبرﮤ[16] وتفنك[17]
و فتيل[18] مالامال[19] كمى ارسال ايتمشلر لطف كردكار[20] ايله مزبور بكلر اوزرينه
دوشوب بى زحمت[21] جنك[22] اخذ و قبض ايدوب حقا بو خصوص دخى
بر فال[23] مبارك اولدى ايچندن خيلى كافر چيقوب كوركه قوديلر . . . .

اهل سفرﮤ مالته سفرى تدارك ايلك ديو فرمان اولندى و عسكر اسلام
خيام[24] ايله صحرايه چيقوب سفائن دوننمايى بغلمغه باشلاديلر واندﮤ ايكن
طرابلس[25] و تونس[26] پاشاسى عبد الرحمن پاشا و سكز پارﮤ چكدر قدرغهلرى
غظيم الاى ايله كلوب دوننمايه ملاقات[27] ايتديلر . امرا مغرب و سفينه
قپودانلرى و اوجاق ضابطلرى سراسر[28] ديبا خلعتلر[29] ايله سربلند[30]
اولنديلر . . . . .

اوارين ليمانندن چيقلوب هر كس انكينه[31] صالنور[32] قياسنده[33] ايكن امراى
دريا و قپودانلر دعوت[34] اولنوب كريد سفرينه مأمور اولدقلرينه خط[35] شريفى

(1) A. *Shiddet*, 'violence.'— (2) *Shaïka*, 'a kind of vessel called *Saïc*.'—
(3) *Bourtoun*, 'a lighter, flat-bottomed barge, store-ship.'— (4) *Choka*, ' the
island of Cerigo.'— (5) P. *Dour*, 'far off.'— (6) A. *Té-essuf*, 'regret.'— (7) P.
*Megher* (*méyer*), 'but.'—(8) *Vénédik*, 'Venice.'—(9) *Ghirid*, 'Crete.'—(10) A. *Imdad*, 'help, assistance.'—(11) A. *Seba*, 'a zephyr.'—(12) P. *Reftar*, 'walking.'—
(13) *Barout*, 'gunpowder.'—(14) *Dané*, ' A cannon, or musket-ball.'—(15) *Kourshoun*, 'lead.'—(16) *Khumbara*, 'a bomb.'—(17) *Tufenk* (*Tufék*), 'a market.'—
(18) *Fitil* 'a wick of a candle,' 'a quick-match.'—(19) P. *Malamal*, 'quite full.'—
(20) P. *Kirdighiar*, 'God.'—(21) A. *Kahmet*, 'trouble;' *Bi-zahmet*, 'without trouble.'
(22) P. *Jenk*, 'war, battle.'—(23) A. *Fal* (*Fé'l*), 'an omen.'—(24) *Khiyam* ( pl. of
خَيمَه *Khaïmé* ), 'tents.' — (25) *Tirabalous*, 'Tripoli.' — (26) *Tounous*, 'Tunis.' —
(27) *Mulakat etmek*, 'to meet.'—(28) P. *Seraser*, 'from end to end.'—(29) A. *Khilat*,
'a dress of honour.'—(30) P. *Ser-bulend*, 'their heads high.'—(31) *Enghin*, 'the
open sea.'—(32) *Salmak, v.n.*, 'to rush;' *v.a.*, 'to send, cast.'—(33) A. *Kiyas*, 'thinking, supposing, calculating.'—(34) *Davet olounmak*, 'to be summoned, called.'—
(35) *Khat-i-sherif*, 'an imperial decree.'

ابراز' و مضموننی' اعلام' و كشف' راز' ايدوب جزيره كريد فتحی' نيتنه
حانيه' بورننه' طوغری كتديلر اتفاقات حسنهدندر كه بعنایة الله' بر ايام'
لطيف'' و روزكار موافق و شريف اولديكه سفائن دونلما اصلا'' بری برزدن
متباعد'' اولميوب معيت ايله شوكت'' و مهابت'' كوسترهرك اولكون
كيدوب كيجه چوقه اطمسی قربنده لنكر انداز اولديلر ايرتسی ينه يورييوب
ايكندی'' زمانی كريد قربنده سكليه نام خرابه'' اطهيه واردقلرنده كوزجی'
كافرلر دخان'' ايله دونلما كلديكنی كريده اعلام ايلديلر ايرتسی روز جمعه
ايدی اخشام زمانی كريد طاغلری سچيلوب'' كميلرده فانوسلر'' ياندی''
روزكار قوی اولمغله فی الحال'' عسكر اسلام سواحل كريدده لنكر انداز اولديلر
همان اول ساعت مرقوم قره بتاق ديدكلری فرقته'' ريئسی'' تبديل شكل
ايله سكليه اطهسنه واروب كوزجی كافرلرك ايكيسی جنك ايتمكله
مقتول'' اولوب دردی زنده'' اخذ اولنوب'' ديل كتيردی .

اول كون عسكر اسلام سردار صاحب احتراملمه' كناره'' دوكياوب'' قری''
و بيوت'' كفاری'' فی الحال تارمار'' ايلديلر و بر قاچ كافرك سری''
پيشكاه'' سردارہ غلطان اولدی'' جمعه ايرتسی سحری'' كريدك قليچ بورنی

<hr/>

(1) *Ibraz*, 'displaying.'— (2) A. *Mazmoun*, 'sense.'— (3) A. *Ilam*, 'to make known.'—(4) A. *Keshf*, 'revealing.—(5) P. *Raz*, 'a secret.'—(6) A. *Feth*, 'conquest.' —(7) *Hania*, 'Canea.'—(8) *Bouroun*, 'a nose, cape, promontory.'—(9) A. *Bi*, 'by;' *inayet*, 'grace;' *Allah*, 'God;' *Bi-inayet-i-'llahi*, 'by the grace of God.'— (10) A. *Eyyam*, 'days.'— (11) A. *Latif*, 'pleasant.'— (12) *Asla*, 'not at all.'— (13) A. *Mutébaïd*, 'distant.'— (14) A. *Sherket*, 'majesty.'— (15) A. *Mahabet*, 'dreadness.'— (16) *Ikindi*, 'the prayer in the middle of the afternoon, or the time thereof.'— (17) A. *Kharabé*, 'deserted.'— (18) *Ghicuzju*, 'a scout.'— (19) A. *Dukhan*, 'smoke.'—(20) *Sechmek*, generally means 'to choose,' but here it means 'to discern.'—(21) Lights.— (22) *Yanmak*, 'to burn.'— (23) A. *Fil-hal*, 'immediately.'—(24) *Firkate*, or فرقتین *firkatéin*, 'a frigate.'—(25) A. *Réis*, 'a captain.'—(26) A. *Maktoul*, 'killed.'—(27) P. *Zindé*, 'alike.'—(28) *Akhz olounmak*, 'to be taken.'—(29) *Ihtiram*, 'respect, veneration;' *Sahib-i-ihtiram*, 'a possessor of respect,' *i. e.*, 'respected.'—(30) P. *Kénar*, 'the shore.'—(31) *Deukmek*, 'to pour, pour on.'—(32) A. *Koura*, pl. of قریه *Kariyyé*, 'a village.'—(33) *Buyout*, pl. of بیت *béit*, 'a house.'—(34) A. *Kufar*, pl. of كافر *Kiafir*, 'an infidel.'—(35) P. *Turmar*, or *Tar-ou-mar etmek*, 'to scatter, demolish.'—(36) P. *Ser*, 'a head.'—(37) P. *Pishghiah*, 'the front.'— (38) *Ghaltan olmak*, 'to roll,' *v.n.*— (39) A. *Sahri*, 'early in the morning.'

طولاشیلوب <sup>1</sup> كرید ایله تودوری اراسنده لیمان مثل بر موضعده لنكر

انداز اولوب طشره چیقلدی كفار باش كوسترمیوب روم ایلی بكار بكیسی

حسن پاشا روم ایلی عسكریله و یكیچری كتخداسی مراد اغا و صمصونجی

بشی ابراهیم اغا یكیچرینك اوكنه دوشوب كمیلردن مهمات<sup>2</sup> اخراج<sup>3</sup>

اولندقدن صكره خانیه حصاری<sup>4</sup> محاصرهسی<sup>5</sup> فرمان اولنمغهیك اخشام وقتی

حصار مزبور جانبنه توجه<sup>6</sup> اولدی اول كیجه كیدیلوب نصف<sup>7</sup> الليلده

صباح<sup>8</sup> اولنجه برنهر<sup>9</sup> خوشكوار<sup>10</sup> كنارنده ارام<sup>11</sup> ایتدیلر. اول اثنده دشمن<sup>12</sup>

ایرشدی<sup>13</sup> دیو برآوازه<sup>14</sup> ظهور ایدوب اصلی<sup>15</sup> یوتقدر دینلنجه خیلی<sup>16</sup> تفنك

اتلدی<sup>17</sup> ایرتسی بین<sup>18</sup> الصلاتین<sup>19</sup> خانیه قلعهسی<sup>20</sup> مقابلهسنده<sup>21</sup> اولان جسر<sup>22</sup>

سنكین<sup>23</sup> قربنده<sup>24</sup> دیولرده<sup>25</sup> نزول<sup>26</sup> اولنمغله بو طرفده<sup>27</sup> كفار فارغ البال<sup>28</sup> باغ<sup>29</sup>

و باغچهلرنده<sup>30</sup> اثواب<sup>31</sup> كرانبها<sup>32</sup> ایله مزین<sup>33</sup> و محتشم<sup>34</sup> ذوق<sup>35</sup> و صغارلرنده

ایكن عسكر منصور<sup>36</sup> اول مقهورلرك<sup>37</sup> سور<sup>38</sup> وقتنی باصوب غنایم<sup>39</sup> غنایم<sup>40</sup> بیشمار<sup>41</sup>

ایله مغتنم<sup>42</sup> اولوب وافر<sup>43</sup> مال<sup>44</sup> و اسیر<sup>45</sup> الدیلر لكن سردارك حسن تدبیرزندن<sup>46</sup>

بری بو اولدیكه كرفتار<sup>47</sup> غازیان اولان رعایا<sup>48</sup> و اهل قریةنك اطفال<sup>49</sup>

---

(1) *Dolashmak*, 'to go round.'—(2) *Muhimat*, 'military stores, ammunition.'—
(3) *Ikhraj olunmak*, ' to be got out.'— (4) *Hisar*, ' a fort.'— (5) A. *Muhaseré*,
' a siege.'— (6) *Tévejjuh olmak*, ' to turn one's face towards, proceed towards.'—
(7) A. *Nisf-u-'l-léil*, ' midnight.'—(8) A. *Sabah*, ' morning.'—(9) A. *Nehr*, ' a river.'—
(10) P. *Khoshghiuvar*, ' delicious.'—(11) *Aram etmek*, ' to rest.'—(12) P. *Dushmen*,
' an enemy.'—(13) *Erishmek*, ' to reach, to come up.'—(14) P. *Avazé*, ' a rumour, a
voice.'—(15) A. *Asl*, ' origin, foundation.'—(16) *Khalli*, ' much, many.'—(17) *Tufék
atmak*, ' to fire a gun.'—(18) A. *Béin*, ' between.'—(19) A. *Es-salatéin*, ' the two
prayers.'—(20) *Kala*, ' a castle.'—(21) A. *Mukabelé*, ' the front.'—(22) A. *Jisr*, ' a
bridge.'—(23) P. *Senghin*, ' of stone.'—(24) A. *Kurb*, ' vicinity.'—(25) *Tepé*, ' a hill.'—
(26) A. *Nuzoul*, ' descending.'—(27) A. *Taraf*, ' a side, direction.'—(28) *Farigh-u-l-
Bal*, ' free from care, light-hearted.'—(29) P. *Bagh* 'a vineyard.' (30) *Bagché*, ' a garden.'
—(31) A. *Eswab*, ' clothes.'—(32) P, *Ghiran*, ' heavy, dear;' *baha*, ' price;' *Ghiran-
taha*, ' high-priced.'— (33) A. *Muzeyyen*, ' adorned.'—(34) A. *Mutahshem*, ' respectable.'—(35) A. *Zevk*, ' enjoyment.'— (36) A. *Mansour*, ' victorious.'—(37) A. *Makhour*,
' subjected.'— (38) P. *Sour*. ' merry-making.'— (39) *Basmak*, ' to put down, suppress.'—
(40) A. *Ghanaïm*, ' plunder.'—(41) P. *Bi-shumar*, ' innumerable '—(42) A. *Muqténim*,
' seizing' (booty).—(43) A. *Wafir*, ' abundant.'—(44) A. *Mal*, ' wealth.'—(45) A. *Esir*,
' a prisoner, slave.'—(46) A. *Tedbir*, ' arrangement.'—(47) P. *Ghiriftar*, ' seized.'—
(48) A. *Ra'aya*, ' subjects, peasants.'—(49) *Itfal*, ' children.'

و نسواني ۱ كتورادكده كتورن غازيلره انعام ۲ و احسان ايدوب كرفــتارلرى ازان ۳
ايدوب احراق ۴ ممالك ۵ و قطع ۶ اشجار ۷ و قتل ۸ اسيردن عسكرى منع ۹
ايلدى ...

جناب ۱۰ سرداردن بو مرحمتى ۱۱ استماع ۱۲ ايدن اهالى مملكت ۱۳ هر طرفدن
اوردويه ۱۴ كلوب ذخيره ۱۵ ايله خدمت ۱۶ ايلديلر عسكر اسلامه مائل ۱۷
و جزيره ۱۸ اذارك اولمغه قائل ۱۹ اولديلر .

(1) A. *Niswan*, ' women.'—(2) *In'am*, ' to bestow favours on.'—(3) *Azad*, ' free.'
—(4) *Ihrak*, ' burning.'—(5) *Memalik*, ' territories.'—(6) *Kat*, ' cutting.'—(7) A.
*Eshjar*, ' trees.'—(8) A. *Katl*, ' killing.'—(9) *Men etmek*, ' to prohibit.'—(10) A.
*Jenab*, ' honour, excellency.'—(11) A. *Merhamet*, ' mercy.'—(12) *Istima etmek*, ' to
hear.'—(13) A. *Memléket*, ' a country.'—(14) *Ordou*, ' an army.'—(15) A. *Zakhiré*,
' provisions.'—(16). A. *Khidmet* (*hizmet*), ' service.'—(17) A. *Ma'il*, ' inclined.'—
(18) A. *Jéziré*, ' an island.'—(19) A. *Ka'il olmak*, ' to consent, be satisfied.'

### Translation.

*Events of the year* 1055 *(Anno Hejiræ) and the commencement of the Holy War
in Crete.*

It having come to the ears of the Sultan that some Maltese ships,
as mentioned in the preceding year, had seized on the vessel of
His Majesty's chief eunuch going from Constantinople to Egypt,\*
the Sultan exerted himself with a view to taking vengeance
on the infidels, and an expedition in the Mediterranean was
ordered . . . . . .

It was resolved that Yusuf Pasha, formerly Sword-bearer, and
one of the high officials in the Imperial Seraglio, who, leaving
there had become Lord High Admiral, should be the commander of
the Imperial fleet, and, by the wish of the Padishah, the title of

\* The Sultan Ibrahim at first wished to send armaments against the Knights of
Malta, but he was persuaded not to attempt the conquest of Malta, which even the
great Suleyman had failed to accomplish, but to wreak his vengeance on the Venetians who held Crete, a rich island conveniently situated for annexation to Turkey,
and who had permitted the Maltese to anchor with their Turkish prizes on the
south coast of that island. Venice was at peace with Turkey, and offered apologies,
which the Turks pretended to accept, but only the better to surprise the Venetians.

Generalissimo of the land and sea forces was added to that of Lord High Admiral. In addition to these favours he was honoured by being made a son-in-law of the Sultan, and thus raised above his fellow statesmen. He was affianced to a daughter of His Majesty, two years of age, and orders were given for the betrothal presents to be prepared. The palace of Ibrahim Pasha, overlooking the Hippodrome, was repaired, and one or two charming royal pavilions, and a peerless upper chamber, were added to it. The arrangements for the betrothal were set about energetically, the roads were widened through which the presents would pass, and balconies in them which blocked the way were demolished. . . . . .

When His Excellency Yusuf Pasha was honoured with these favours and attentions, and was entrusted with such important matters, he at once set about making arrangements, and sent messengers to the two *Kazi-Askers* (the Supreme Judges of the army) with commands. . . . . . The province of Roumelia was conferred on Kiuchuk Hasan Pasha, who had been removed from Bagdad, and he was sent that week to Salonica, to assemble the army of Roumelia, and to await the Lord High Admiral on the coast of Benefshé. Murad Agha, the *Kiaya* of the Janissaries from Zagherji-Bashlik, coming from Bagdad, was appointed to the expedition, in the stead of the Agha of the Janissaries; and Samsounji-Bashi Ibrahim Agha, Khaski Ali Agha, with other colonels of the Janissaries, were ordered to join it. One of the Vezirs also, Bosnavi Koja Mousa Pasha, was sent with the expedition, to be a companion and coadjutor to the Commander-in-Chief, so that they might manage the war well.

Hasan Pasha proceeded to Salonica and summoned and assembled the commanders of Roumelia. Upwards of fifty merchant vessels were hired from these parts, laden with provisions for the above troops, and sent before the Imperial ships. Ninety men-of-war and *Saics* * came to Salonica, and fifty vessels to Cheshmé, and anchored in the harbours; and these ships were loaded with ammunition—fifteen thousand quintals of gunpowder, fifty thousand

---

* A kind of vessel now out of fashion.

iron balls, and fifty pieces of cannon, pick-axes, oars, and other armoury implements, and innumerable siege requisites. . . . . .

The naval commanders, the advanced-guard of the Holy War, in the meanwhile, began to come and prostrate themselves in the Majestic presence of the Generalissimo. Amongst these, the sons of Mimi Pasha, leaving Rhodes for Constantinople, while on their way, having reached the port of the island of Eskeri, one of the Mediterranean islands, encountered a Maltese vessel from that port carrying thirty-six infidels, captured it, and put the accursed (wretches) in chains, after overcoming them with the sword. They then took the ship in tow, brought her to the Generalissimo, and received dresses of honour, and other favours. This episode was regarded as a happy omen of victory. . . . . . .

Orders were sent to the regencies of Tunis, Tripoli, and Algiers, and letters from the Grand Vezir, saying that there would be an expedition to the Mediterranean in the spring, and that they should all be ready with their ships and join the Imperial fleet. The people of the regencies, on being invited to the Holy War, were in a state of great ebullition, and answered that they were ready to serve the Sultan with body and soul, and were awaiting the arrival of the Generalissimo.

The Padishah, taking a great interest in the preparations for sea, and the affairs of the expedition, honoured the Imperial dock-yard every day with his presence, exerted himself about the ships of the fleet and the siege requisites being got ready, and carefully attended to naval and military matters. On Wednesday, the 22nd of the month of Safer, about the time of afternoon prayer, the officers and colonels of the Janissaries were invested with war dresses of honour, and then immediately orders were given to start. The Lord High Admiral, Yusuf Pasha, also sailed for the Mediterranean on Sunday, the 4th of Rabbi-ul-Evvel, with a large fleet and great rejoicings on the expedition, said to be, to Malta. On their arriving at the island at Scio, the Bey of Rhodes, Ibrahim Bey, known as Kara Khoja, was sent, with eight fine galleys, for the ships in the harbour of Salonica, and notice was given for them to assemble in the harbour of Kizil Hissar. On entering Scio, Ahmed Pasha, Commander-in-Chief of Anatolia, came, with the Beys of Sivas,

Karamania and Anatolia, to do homage, and had favours bestowed
on them. On the 25th of Rebbi-ul-Evvel the troops from Anatolia
embarked, and with forty *Saics* anchored in the harbour of Scio.
After eight days' rest they proceeded to Kizil Hissar harbour. On
their way a great storm arose, and the ships were scattered and
thrown in disorder. Veli Bey, the Bey of Mytelene, proceeded and
directed all to assemble at a place called Termish, and in three
days forty-nine vessels came together. The Commander-in-Chief
of Roumelia, Hassan Pasha, also, with the troops from his province,
on the 24th of Rebbi-ul-Evvel, began to move. The troops from
Roumelia passed Kizil Hissar, and on the first of the month
of Rebbi-ul-Akhir came to the shores of Termish, and, with
ninety-eight vessels and a large quantity of stores and ammunition,
joined the Imperial fleet.

The next day a halt was ordered, and early in the morning
Yusuf Pasha, disembarking from his galley, all the noble commanders of the Musselman army, together with the "Mirmiran"
(Lt.-General), Hassan Pasha, came into a large tent and had the
honour of kissing the hem of the Generalissimo's garment (paying
their respects) and receiving Imperial favours. The august Commander-in-Chief encouraged every one of them, and incited them to
the Holy War. . .

Kara Batak Bey, of Coron, embarking on board his frigate, captured a ship from Crete, and bringing it to the Lord High Admiral
had a dress of honour conferred on him. The twelve infidels who
were on board of her were put to the oars (condemned to the
galleys). The next day they moved on, and when opposite the
coast of Benefshé a mighty wind arose. Although it was favourable, it was so violent that the fleet put into harbour, and some
*Saics* and store-ships (barges) rowed for Cape Mania. Some
of the commanders who were at sea, finding it impossible to put
into harbour, fell off to the island of Cerigo.

While they were regretting that they were separated from the
Generalissmo, by the grace of God they fell in with a fine ship sent
from Venice to the assistance of Crete, which was full of gunpowder
and cannon-balls, bullets, bombs, muskets and matches, which
they captured without fighting; which was really a blessed omen.

There were several unbelievers in the ship who were put to the oars (condemned to the galleys). . . . . .

Orders had been given to the members of the expedition to prepare for a war with Malta. The troops landed and went into tents, and they fastened the vessels of the Imperial fleet. While there, Abdur-Rahman Pasha, the governor of Tripoli and Tunis, came with eight galleys and a great lot of men, and joined the fleet. The commanders of Morocco, and their sea-captains, and the officers of the Janissaries, had dresses of honour bestowed on them. . . . . . While everybody was under the impression that they would start from the port of Navarino for the open sea, the admirals and captains were summoned, and an Imperial Decree produced and explained to them ordering them to proceed on an expedition to Crete. The secret was thus divulged, and they then started straight to Cape Canea, for the conquest of Crete.

It happened fortunately that, by the favour of God, the weather being fine and the wind favourable, the vessels of the fleet were not at all separated from one another; they sailed majestically and imposingly that day, and at night anchored near the island of Cerigo. The next day they sailed again about the time of the afternoon prayer, and on their reaching the desert island, called Siklaya, in the vicinity of Crete, some infidel scouts made it known to Crete by smoke that the fleet was coming. In the evening the mountains of Crete were discernible, and lanterns were lit on board the ships. The wind being strong the army of the Moslems immediately anchored on the shore of Crete. Then at once the aforementioned captain of a frigate, Kara Batak Bey, turned about and went to the island of Sekliya to gain intelligence of the enemy's movements, and two of the infidel scouts were killed in fight and four taken alive.

That day the Moslem army, with the Generalissimo, landed on the shore, and immediately demolished the villages and houses of the unbelievers, and a few infidel heads rolled before the Commander-in-Chief. On Saturday, early in the morning, they rounded Cape Kilij, and anchored in a place like a harbour, between Todori and Crete, and disembarked. The infidels did not show their heads. The Governor-general of Roumelia, Hasan Pasha, with the troops from Roumelia, and the *Kiaya* of the Janissaries, Mourad Agha, and Samsounji Bashi Ibrahim Agha, at the head of the Janissaries, after having taken out ammunition from the ships, proceeded, in the evening, in the direction of the Fort of Canea, for the siege of which orders had been given. They went on that night, but rested from midnight until morning. During that time a report was spread that the enemy had come up, and until it was announced that it was without foundation, several shots were fired. The next day, between the two prayer times, the Moslems descended on the hills near the stone bridge opposite the castle of Canea, and while the unbelievers in this part were enjoying themselves, decked out in their finest clothes, quite free from anxiety, in the vineyards and gardens, our victorious troops suddenly put a stop to their joy, took enormous lots of booty, much wealth and many prisoners. But, by one of the merciful arrangements of the Commander-in-Chief, when the peasants captured by the Turkish troops, and the women and children of the villages were brought in, he rewarded the brave soldiers, but set their prisoners free, and forbade the troops to set the country on fire, or to cut down trees or to kill captives. . . . . . The inhabitants of the country who heard of this clemency on the part of the Commander-in-Chief, came from all parts to the camp and served it with provisions, and were well disposed to the Moslem army, and agreeable to the island becoming theirs.*

---

* It appears that the native population hated the rule of the Venetians, and were not unwilling to change masters. See Creasy's "History of the Ottoman Turks," vol. ii., p. 25.

## THE TAKING OF AYA-TODORI.

كريد جزيرهسنه قريب اوچ درت ميل مدور[1] بر جزيره صغيره[2] كه ايكى

طرفنده[3] يالك[4] قيه[5] اوزرينده بنا اولنمش ارالري بر ميل ايكى حصار[6] متين[7]

كه ايا تودورى قلعهلرى ديمكله معروفدر ممالك حانيهنك نكهبانلرى[8] شكلنده[9]

واقعدر[10] ديوارينك[11] عرضى[12] اللى ذراع[13] وارتفاعى[14] اون ايكي ذراع هربري

خسروانه[15] باليمز[16] طوپلر ايله و جبهخانه و ذخائر ايله[17] مالامال[18] ايدى اول

ايكى قلعه كه برىبالاتر[19] محافظ[20] بيرون[20] وبرى زيرتر[22] كه خارس[23] درباى

اندروند[24] درت ساعتنده قبضهء[25] تسخيره[26] كلدى .

دونانماى همايون ليمانه واصل[27] اولديغنى كفار خاكسار[28] مشاهده[29] ايتدى

بونلر محاصره[30] ايدهجكلريني بلوب قلعهء زير متانتنه[31] اعتمادلرى[32] اولمغله

جملهسى[33] اشاغى قلعهيه اينوب[34] جمع[35] اولديلر لشكر[36] اسلامك قدومنه[37]

منتظر[38] طورديلر بو طرفده سردار كامكار[39] كيجه عسكرى حانيه جانبنه ارسالدنصكره

اماسيه ميرلواسى[40] احمد پاشا وترجالله بكى احمد بك و يكيچيرى[41] و تونس

(1) A. *Mudevver*, 'round.'—(2) A. *Saghir*, 'small;' put in the feminine by the addition of ة to agree with جزیره *jezire*, an island, which is feminine.—(3) A. *Tarof*, 'side, direction.'—(4) *Yalin*, 'bare, naked.'—(5) Or كايا *kaya*, 'rock.'—(6) A. *Hisar*, 'a fort, castle.'—(7) A. *Metin*, 'strong, firm.'—(8) P. *Nighéban*, or نكاهبان *nigiah-ban*, 'a guardian, protector.'—(9) A. *Shékl*, 'form.'—(10) A. *Vaki*, 'situated.'—(11) P. *Diwar* or *douwar*, 'a wall;' T. ديوارجى *diwarji*, 'a bricklayer.'—(12) A. *Arz*, 'breadth.'—(13) A. *Dira*, the Turkish yard (30 inches).—(14) A. *Irtifa*, 'height.' —(15) P. *Khusrevané*, 'princely, royal,' from خسرو, *khusrev*, 'a prince.'—(16) *Bal-yeméz* (بال يمز), 'of large calibre,' 'culverine.'—(17) A. *Zakhaïr*, 'provisions.'— (18) P. *Malamal*, 'full.'—(19) P. *Balater*, 'higher.'—(20) A. *Muhafiz*, 'a protector, guardian, governor.'— (21) P. Outside.— (22) P. *Zirter*. 'lower.'—(23) A. *Kharis*, 'drinking,' 'who drinks.'—(24) P. *Enderoun*, 'interior.'—(25) A. *Kabzé*, 'the grip of the hand;' 'handle (of a sword).'—(26) A. *Teskhir*, 'conquest.'— (27) A. *Vasil*, 'arriving.'—(28) P. *Khaksar*, 'vile, contemptible.'—(29) A. *Musha-hedé etmek*, 'to see, observe.'—(30) A. *Muhaseré*, 'to besiege.'—(31) A. *Métanet*, 'strength, firmness.'— (32) A. *Itimad*, 'confidence.'—(33) A. *Jumlé*, 'all.'— (34) *Inmek*, 'to descend.'—(35) *Jem olmak*, 'to assemble.'—(36) P. *Leshker*, 'troops.'—(37) A. *Kudoum*, 'approach.'—(38) A. *Muntézir*, 'expecting, awaiting.'— (39) P. *Kamkiar*, 'successful, fortunate.'—(40) A. *Mira-liwa*, 'a major-general,' or a governor of corresponding rank.—(41) *Yenichéri*, 'Janissary.'

و طرابلوس¹ عسكرندن برر مقدار عسكر كميلاردن چقاروب صندالله² و پلاشكرمه

ايله ساحل³ جبل جزيرهء مزبورهيه ارسال اولندى لشكر مرقوم كيچه ايله

حصار ميانه⁴ واردقلرنده⁵ حصار⁶ بالايى كورديلر قپوارى اچلمش فى الحال

بى جنك⁷ و جدال⁷ كيروب قبض⁸ ايتديلر على الصباح⁹ كه روز شنبه¹⁰

و ربيع¹¹ الاخرك يكرمى سكزى ايدى غازيلر اشاغى قلغهيى محاصره ايدوب

ايكى طرفدن طوب و تفنك جنكنى ايتديلر سردار دخى جمله دونما

كميلر ايله عزم رزم¹² ايدوب باشترده‌دن¹³ قلعهيه طوپلر اتدى سائر امرا

دخى اقتدا¹⁴ ايدوب قدرغهلردن¹⁵ و ماونهلردن¹⁶ اول قدر طوپ اوردىلركه

صداسى¹⁷ آسمانه¹⁸ پيوسته¹⁹ اولدى همان اول ساعت²⁰ قدرغهلردن ايكى

طوپ اخراج²¹ اولنوب قلعهيه حواله²² ايتدكلرنده غازيلر غيرته²³ كلوب بر

اوغوردن²⁵ حصاره هجوم²⁶ ايدوب اعلام²⁷ نصرت انجام²⁸ نصب²⁹

ايدكلريفى كفار كوردكده خلاصدن مأيوس³⁰ اولوب بر بى‌دين³¹ و حيلهكار³²

پيشكاه كنكرهء³³ حصاره كاوب يد نامبارکنده³⁴ بر بياض³⁵ مقرمه³⁶ الوب

كلك قلعه سزكدر الك ديدكده غازيلر هجوم ايدوب اول محله ازدحام³⁷

(1) *Tirabolous*, ‘Tripoli.’—(2) *Sandal*, ‘a ship’s boat.’—(3) A. *Sahil*, ‘shore.’—
(4) P. *Miyan*, ‘middle.’— (5) *Varmak*, ‘to arrive,’ ‘to go on furlough,’ ‘to go
close to ;’ قوجهيه وارمق *Kojayé varmak*, ‘to get married.’— (6) P. *Bala*, ‘high.’—
—(7) A. *Jidal*, ‘fighting, quarreling.’—(8) A. *Kabz etmek*, ‘to seize.’—(9) *Al es-
sabah*, ‘in the morning.’—(10) P. *Shenbé*, ‘Saturday.’—(11) A. *Rebi‘*, ‘the spring
season ;’ the name of two Muhammedan lunar months, the first called *Rebi‘ u’l-Evvel*,
and the other *Rebi‘ u’l-akhir*.— (12) P. *Rezm*, ‘combat.’— (13) *Bashtarda*, or باشطرده,
‘a galley.’— (14) A. *Iktida*, ‘following, imitating.’— (15) *Kadirgha*, ‘a galley.’—
(16) *Maghouna*, ‘a barge.’—(17) A. *Sada*, ‘sound.’—(18) P. *Asiman*, ‘the heavens, the
sky, a ceiling.’— (19) *Peïvesté*, P. adj.; ‘reaching, attaining ;’ T. adv. ‘uninterruptedly.’—(20) *Heman ol-saat*, ‘immediately, at once.’— (21) *Ikhraj olumak*, ‘to be
taken out, extracted.’— (22) *Hawalé etmek*, ‘to direct against.’— (23) *Ghazi*, ‘a
champion of the faith.’—(24) A. *Ghairet*, ‘zeal.’—(25) *Bir oghourdan*, ‘all at once,
all together.’—(26) A. *Hujoum*, ‘attack.’—(27) *Alam* (pl. of علم *alem*), ‘flags, standards.’—(28) P. *Nusret enjam*, ‘victorious.’—(29) *Nasb*, ‘setting up.’—(30) A. *Mé-
yous*, ‘despairing.’—(31) P. *Bi*, ‘without ;’ *din*, A. ‘religion ;’ *bi-din*, ‘an atheist,
irreligious person.’—(32) P. *Hilékiar*, ‘crafty,’ ‘a knave.’—(33) P. *Kiunghéré*,
‘crenelated battlements of a castle,’ ‘a small tower,’ ‘a hill-top, peak,’ ‘the
summit.’—(34) A. *Mubarek*, ‘blessed ;’ but with the Persian privative particle
نا *na* before it, it means just the reverse, i. e., ‘accursed.’—(35) A. *Béyaz*, ‘white.’
— (36) A. *Makrama* (*mahrama*), ‘a pocket-handkerchief.’— (37) A. *Izdiham*, ‘a
crowd, multitude.’

ايله واردقلرنده سائر ارباب$^1$ ضلال اجرو فرار$^2$ ايدوب انجق بر كافر قالدى
مگر مقدما قپو يانده بو محل ايچون آماده$^3$ ايلد كلرى باروت لغمنه$^4$
آتش$^5$ و يرمشلر زير$^6$ زميندن الوب اوستنده و يانده بولدلرك كمى
انلاكه$^7$ پرتاب$^8$ و كمينى مثال كباب$^9$ بريان$^{10}$ ايلدى غازيان كرام$^{11}$ و
كفار لئامدن$^{12}$ خيلى اجسام$^{13}$ طعمه$^{14}$ اتش اولدى ديوار حصار رخنه دار$^{15}$
اولدقده غازيان ظفرقرين$^{16}$ هجوم دليرانه$^{17}$ ايله قلعه يى فتح ايدوب ايچنده
بولنان كفار يكسر$^{18}$ طعمه تيغ$^{19}$ ابدار$^{20}$ اولوب كلهلرى$^{21}$ حضور سرداره كلدكده
انعام فراوان$^{22}$ ايله بهادرلرى$^{23}$ شادمان$^{24}$ ايلدى بعده$^{25}$ دوننماى همايون
صفاى$^{26}$ خاطر ايله ليمان$^{27}$ راحت$^{28}$ رسان$^{29}$ اياتودوريده آسوده$^{30}$ اولديلر.

(1) A. *Erbab-zelal,* 'people in error.'—(2) *Firar etmek,* 'to flee.'—(3) P. *Amadé,* 'prepared.'—(4) *Laghem,* 'a mine.'—(5) *Atesh,* 'fire.'—(6) *Zir-zémin,* 'a subterranean place.'— (7) A. *Eflak,* 'the heavens.'— (8) P. *Pertab,* 'a jump.'— (9) *Kébab,* 'roast meat.'— (10) P. *Birian,* 'roasted.'— (11) A. *Kiram* (pl. of كريم *kerim*), 'noble.'—(12) A. *Liam* (pl. of لئيم *léim*), 'blameable, vile, base, worthless.' — (13) A. *Ejsam* (pl. of جسم *jism*), 'bodies.'— (14) A. *Toumé,* 'prey-food.'— (15) P. *Rachnédar,* 'pierced, rent, breached.'—(16) A. *Zafr-karin,* 'whose companion is victory,' *i. e.* 'victorious.'—(17) P. *Delirané,* 'valiant.'—(18) P. *Yekser,* 'all at once, all together.—(19) P. *Tigh,* 'a sword, dagger,' 'the prow of a caïque,' 'a sun-beam.'—(20) P. *Abdar,* 'watered,' 'tempered,' 'lustrous.'—(21) P. *Kellé,* 'the head, pate ;' T. *Ghiullé,* 'a cannon-ball, a shot;' P. *Kiulé,* 'a cap, spire.' —(22) P. *Feravan,* 'abundant.'—(23) P. *Bahadir,* 'a hero.'—(24) P. *Shadman* (or شاد *shad (shaz),* or شادان *shadan*), 'delighted, merry, happy.'—(25) A. *Badu,* 'afterwards.'—(26) A. *Safa,* 'purity,' 'freedom from care,' 'enjoyment ;' صفاى خاطر *safayi-khatir,* 'peace of mind, without anxiety or scruple.'—(27) *Leman,* 'a harbour.'— (28) A. *Rahat,* 'repose, comfort.'—(29) P. *Resan,* 'which brings.'—(30) P. *Asoudé,* 'at rest, tranquil.'

### Translation.

A little island, three or four miles round, near to the island of Crete, which has two strong forts, built on the solid rock, a mile apart, one on each side of it, which are called the Castles of Aya Todori, stands like a sentinel near the district of Canea. The breadth of the walls was fifty yards and the height twelve, and each of them was full of enormous heavy cannon and ammunition, and provisions. These two ports, of which one, the higher, defended the outside, and the other was near the interior sea, were captured in four hours.

The vile unbelievers perceived that the Imperial fleet had reached the harbour, and they knew that it would besiege them. Believing in the strength of the lower fort, they all descended and collected there, and awaited the approach of the Moslem troops.

The Commander-in-Chief, after having despatched troops in the night in the direction of Canea, disembarked the Governor of Amasia, Ahmed Pasha, and the Bey of Terhalé, Ahmed Bey, and a portion of the Janissaries and of the Tunisian and Tripoli troops, and sent them in boats to the shore of the mountain of the aforesaid island. They came in the night to the upper fort, and seeing the gates open captured it immediately, without firing a shot. The next morning, which was Saturday, the 28th of Rebi-ul-akhir, the champions of the Faith besieged the lower fort and fired cannon and muskets at it from two sides. The Commander-in-Chief also, joining in the combat, fired guns from his galley at the fort. The other commanders followed his example and fired such a number of shots from the galleys and barges, that the report reached up to the heavens. Immediately two guns were taken out of the galleys and turned against the fort, and thereupon our champions coming all at once, stormed the castle. On the infidels seeing them raise our victorious standards, despairing of safety, one crafty villain, coming to the front of the battlements, waving a white handkerchief in his accursed hand, cried : "Come on ! the castle is yours : take it ! Our champions attacked, and on their arriving at the place in crowds all the misguided unbelievers but one fled inside ; a mine was sprung, which they had previously prepared for this place near the gate, which sent those who were above it, or near it, some flying into the air, and burnt some like roast meat. Many bodies of our noble warriors, and of the vile unbelievers, became the prey of fire.

A breach having been made in the wall of the castle, our victorious troops took it bravely by storm, and the infidels in it were put to the sword. Their heads were brought into the presence of the Commander-in-Chief, who munificently rewarded the brave soldiers. After that the Imperial fleet comfortably moored in the Bay of Aya Todori without anxiety.

## THE SIEGE OF CANEA.

وصف' قلعهٔ حانیه

قلعه مزبوره<sup>2</sup> بناسنده<sup>3</sup> عقل<sup>4</sup> عقلا<sup>5</sup> قاصر<sup>6</sup> بر حصار در که روی زمینده<sup>7</sup>

مانندی<sup>8</sup> یوقدر و ممالک محروسهده<sup>9</sup> بو طرز<sup>10</sup> اوزره قلعه کورلمامشدر امرا

وندیک درت یوز سنهدن برو بو حصارك عمارت<sup>11</sup> و بنیاننه<sup>12</sup> و سایر

جبهخانه و مهماننه بذل مقدور<sup>13</sup> ایلوب کمال مرتبه<sup>14</sup> استحکام<sup>15</sup> و متانت

ویرمشلرابدی کرچه<sup>16</sup> ارتفاع<sup>17</sup> و وسعت<sup>18</sup> و متانتده ممالک محروسه قلاعی<sup>19</sup>

چوقدر لکن بو حصار معتبرك<sup>20</sup> طرزی غیری<sup>21</sup> مکرر در اولا بر دوزیرده

غلطه قدر طولانی واقع<sup>22</sup> اولوب یدی برج<sup>23</sup> رفیعی<sup>24</sup> که هر بری وسعت<sup>25</sup>

و ارتفاعده<sup>26</sup> برر حصاره بکزر<sup>27</sup> وهر برنده یکرمیشر بالیمز<sup>28</sup> طوپ قونوب بیك

نفر جنك اری آدم الور دیوارینك عرضی<sup>29</sup> بش اتلو<sup>30</sup> همرکاب<sup>31</sup> رفتار<sup>32</sup>

ایده جلك قدر در و پس دیوارده اولان طولمه<sup>33</sup> طوپرقده خود یکرمی اتلو

مراد اوزره یورر دیوار مرقومك کنکرهٔ والاسندن<sup>34</sup> یوقارو<sup>35</sup> اون ذراع قدر طوپراق

مرتفعدر که جای رزمی انده اولمق اوزره نه طوپ کار ایدر و نه غیری شی

---

(1) A. *Vasf,* 'description.'—(2) A. *Mezbour,* 'aforementioned.'—(3) A. *Bina,* 'building.'—(4) A. *Akl,* 'intellect.'—(5) A. *Oakela,* 'people of intellect.'—(6) A. *Kasir,* 'deficient.'—(7) P. *Rou-i-zemin,* 'the face of the earth.'—(8) P. *Manend,* 'like.'—(9) A. *Memalik-i-mahrousé,* 'the well-defended dominions,' *i. e.* Turkey,'—(10) A. *Tarz,* 'a fashion, way.'—(11) A. *Imaret,* 'being in a state of cultivation or good repair,' 'any public building,' 'a kind of soup-kitchen for the poor.'—(12) A. *Bunyan,* 'building.'—(13) A. *Bezl-i-makdoor,* 'doing one's utmost.'—(14) A. *Mertébé,* 'a degree.'—(15) *Istihkiam,* 'solidity;' استحکامات *istihkiamat,* 'fortifications.'—(16) P. *Gherchi* or *gherché,* 'although,' 'it is true.'—(17) A. *Irtifa,* 'heights.'—(18) A. *Vusat,* 'extend.'—(19) A. *Kila,* pl. of کاله *kala,* 'a fort, castle.' —(20) A. *Mutéber,* 'respectable.'—(21) A. *Ghaïri mukerrer,* 'not repeated, unique.' —(22) A. *Vaki,* 'situated (is).'—(23) A. *Burj,* 'a tower.'—(24) A. *Refi,* 'high.'—(25) A. *Vusat,* 'extent.'—(26) *Irtifa,* 'heights.'—(27) *Benzémek,* 'to resemble.'—(28) *Balyémez,* 'large (cannon).'—(29) A. *Arz,* 'breadth.'—(30) *Atli,* 'a horseman.'—(31) P. *Hemrikiab,* 'abreast.'—(32) *Reftar,* 'going'—(33) *Dolma,* 'anything filled in.'—(34) P. *Vala,* 'high.'—(35) *Youkari,* 'up, upwards, the upper part.'

تأثیر¹ ایدر و بناسی محکم مرتب² سنك³ تراشیده‌دن⁴ دیوارلو طقوز عدد

طابیه‌لر⁵ که سائر بروجدن⁶ یوجه⁷ آسمانه عروج⁸ ایلمشدر اون بشر بالیمز

و صاچمه⁹ طوپلر ایله شهری محافظه¹⁰ ایدر بعده ایکی ایکی کوشه‌لرنده¹¹ ایکی

خاکی¹² طاغ¹³ چیقارلمشدر که جمیعا¹⁴ بروج و تابیه‌لره و بر¹⁵ و بحره¹⁶ ناظرلر¹⁷

در و هر برنده یکرمیشر خسروانه طوپ کرانبها وضع¹⁹ اولنمشدر که

جوانب¹⁹ اربعه‌یی²⁰ محافظه ایدر و بو کهسارك²¹ التی²² یکسر مجوف²³

و قبه²⁴ اندر²⁵ قبه در که طوپ دانه‌لری و جبه‌خانه ایچون محزنلر²⁶ در اما

جانب²⁷ بحریسی دیوار عظیم البنیان ایله چکلمش بر لیمان لطیفدر²⁸ که

قپوسندن انجق قدرغه کیروب²⁹ و ینه³⁰ قپرسنده دریابه ناظر³¹ عظیم طوپلر

قونمشدر و کارکیر³² قبه‌لو قورشوك³³ اورتیلور³⁴ یکره‌ی اوچ دانه ترسانه‌سی³⁵ که

روی³⁶ زمینده بردخی نظیری³⁷ یوقدر هر برینه نیجه خزینه³⁸ صرف³⁹

اولنمشدر .

خصوصا⁴⁰ بیوت⁴¹ و سرایلر⁴² که شهر ایچنده در صافی⁴³ مرمردن⁴⁴ کسلمش

شدادی⁴⁵ بنالر⁴⁶ و خسروانه کاشانه‌لر⁴⁷ که قصر⁴⁸ خورنق⁴⁸ یانلرنده بر شی دکلدر

---

(1) *Té'ssir etmek,* 'to have effect.'— (2) *Muretteb,* 'arranged.'— (3) P. *Sengin,* 'stone.'—(4) P. *Trashidé,* 'hewn, cut.'—(5) *Tabia,* 'a redoubt.'—(6) A. *Burouj,* 'towers.'— (7) *Youjé,* 'tall;' obsolete or provincial.— (8) A. *Urouj,* 'ascent.'— (9) *Sachma,* 'small shot.'—(10) A. *Muhafezé,* 'defence.'—(11) P. *Kiushé,* 'a corner.' —(12) *Khaki,* 'earthen, earthly.'—(13) *Dagh,* 'a mountain, hill, mound.'— (14) A. *Jemia* (or جمعا *jemian*), 'all together.'—(15) A. *Ber,* 'the land.'—(16) A. *Bahr,* 'the sea.'—(17) A. *Nazir,* 'looking to, or one who looks at or over; a director or overseer.'— (18) *Vaz olounmak,* 'to be placed.'—(19) A. *Jewanib,* 'sides.'— (20) A. *Erbaa,* 'four.'—(21) P. *Kiuhsar,* 'a hill district.'— (22) *Alt,* 'the space underneath.'—(23) A. *Mujevvef* (*mujevf*), 'hollow.'— (24) A. *Koubbé,* 'a dome, vault, arch.'—(25) P. *Ender,* 'in, inside.'—(26) A. *Makhzen,* 'a magazine, storehouse, cellar.'—(27) A. *Janib,* 'a side.'—(28) A. *Latif,* 'pleasant.'—(29) *Ghirmek,* 'to enter.'—(30) *Yiné,* 'yet, still.'—(31) A. *Nazir,* 'looking to, or over.'—(32) P. *Kiarghir* (*kiavghir*), 'built of brick or stone.'—(33) *Kourshoun,* 'lead, a bullet.'— (34) *Eurtmek,* 'to cover.'—(35) *Tersané,* 'dockyard, arsenal.'—(36) P. *Rou-i-zemin,* 'the face of the earth.'—(37) A. *Nazir,* 'a peer, equal.'—(38) A. *Khaziné,* 'treasure.'— (39) *Sarf olounmak,* 'to be spent.'—(40) A. *Khusousa,* 'especially.'—(41) A. *Buyout* (pl. of بیت *béit*), 'a house.'—(42) A. *Serai,* 'a palace.'— (43) A. *Safi,* 'pure.'— (44) *Mermer,* 'marble.'—(45) *Shidad,* 'strong' (pl. of شدید *Shedid*).—(46) A. *Bina,* 'a building.'—(47) P. *Kiashané,* 'a hall, large apartment.'—(48) A. *Kasr,* 'a castle.'— (49) A. *Khawarnak* is the name of a castle often alluded to as the type of a magnificent edifice. It was built, in Babylonia, for King Bebram, by Numan-ben-Muzir.

. صنع¹ چشمەلر² و اسواق³ و دكاكين⁴ كه كوزلر كورممشدر خلقى⁵ اصحاب⁶

اموال⁷ و اهلى⁸ جمال⁹ اولەمغله معروفلردر¹⁰ فتحى میسر¹¹ اولدقدە قبضەء

تصرفه كلن جبه خانەلرى حددن¹² بیرون¹³ ایدى یالكز او چیوز طقسان بش

پارە طوپ كرانبها¹⁴ دفتر¹⁵ اولندى و بیرون حصار خندقك¹⁶ عمقى¹⁷

اون بش ذراع و عرضى یتمش ایكى ذراع معماریدر و اكثر¹⁸ لب¹⁹

خندقسنك²⁰ تراشیدەدر . . . . .

رزم حصار ماه مرقومك دردنجى كونى كه روز سەشنبه²¹ و جزیرانك²² اون

یدیسى ایدى على الصباح طوپلر ایله قلعه دوكلمكه²³ باشلایوب كفار خاكسار

دخى پاى²⁴ ثبات²⁵ و وقارى²⁶ محكم²⁷ باصوب²⁸ جنك و محاصرەدە اصلا

قصور²⁹ ایتمدیار محاصرەنك اون ایكنجى كونى سردار طوپخانەیه³⁰ كلوب غزاتى

جنكه تحریص³¹ ایدر كن كافر بدكار بر طوب صاعقه³² بارە اتش و بیروب وزیر

طوردیغى یرە كلدى روم ایلى سپاهیلرندن³³ بش ادمى شهید³⁴ ایدوب وزرا

و اركان³⁵ حرز³⁶ الهیدە³⁷ مصون³⁸ و محفوط³⁹ اولدیار اما لحوم⁴⁰ و دماء⁴¹ شهداء⁴²

الباس⁴³ سردار عالى مقدارى آلودە⁴⁴ ایلدى طوپ مزبور دانەسى اولقدر

(1) A. *Musanna*, 'made with art.'—(2) P. *Cheshmé*, 'a fountain, a spring.'—
(3) A. *Eswak* (pl. of سوق *souk*), 'a street of shops.'—(4) A. *Dekakin* (pl. of
دكان *dukian*), 'a shop,'—(5) A. *Khalk*, 'people.'—(6) A. *Ashab*, 'possessors.'—
(7) A. *Emwal* (pl. of مال *mal*), 'wealth, riches.'—(8) A. *Ehl*, 'a person connected
with anything.'—(9) A. *Jemal*, 'beauty.'—(10) A. *Marouf*, 'known.'—(11) A. *Muyesser*, 'facilitated' (by God).—(12) A. *Had*, 'a limit.'—(13) P. *Biroun*, 'out of,
beyond.'—(14) P. *Ghiranbaha*, 'heavy in price.'—(15) P. *Daftar*, 'a register, list.'
—(16) A. *Hendek*, 'a ditch, moat.'—(17) A. *Umk*, 'depth.'—(18) A. *Ekser*, 'most.'
—(19) P. *Leb*, 'the lip, edge, brink.'—(20) P. *Sengh trashidé*, 'hewn stone.'—
(21) P. *Seh*, 'three ;' *seh-shenbeh*, 'Tuesday.'—(22) A. *Haziran*, the Syro-Roman
month of June.'—(23) *Dughmek*, 'to beat, cannonade, bombard.'—(24) P. *Paï*, 'the
foot.'—(25) *Sebat*, 'firmness.'—(26) *Vekar*, 'gravity.'—(27) A. *Muhkem*, 'strong, firm.'
—(28) *Basmak*, 'to press, to tread.'—(29) A. *Kusour*, 'deficiency,' 'a fault, defect.'
—(30) *Tophané*, 'an artillery arsenal.'—(31) A. *Tahris*, 'inciting.'—(32) *Saïka*, 'a
thunderbolt.' The Persian termination بار *bar* means 'which pours forth, or rains.'
Thus the compound word *saika-bar* signifies 'thunderbolt casting.'—(33) P. *Sipahi*,
'a soldier, a *spahi*.' This word is that from which our word 'sepoy' has been corrupted.—(34) A. *Shéhid*, 'a martyr.'—(35) A. *Erkian*, 'pillars' (of the State).—
(36) A. *Hirz*, 'an amulet or charm.'—(37) A. *Ilahi*, 'divine.'—(38) A. *Masoun*,
'protected.'—(39) *Mahfouz*, 'preserved.'—(40) A. *Luhoum* (pl. لحم *lahm*, 'flesh.'—
(41) A. *Dema*, 'blood.'—(42) A. *Shuheda*, 'witnesses, martyrs.'—(43) A. *Elbas*,
'clothes.'—(44) P. *Aloudé*, 'stained.'

ضرب¹ شديد² ايله كلدى كه اوچ عظيم طبراق طلو سپتدن³ كچوب كندى

محل مرقوم قلعه به بر مقدار بعيد⁴ اولمغله محاصره‌نك اون اوچنجى كونى

جمعه كيجه‌سنده مترسلر دكيشلوب اناطولى عسكرى دخى سردارلرى اولان

احمد پاشا ايله ايكى طوپ كتورب روم ايلى مترسلرينه ملحق⁵ اولدى و قرمان

عسكرى ايكى طوپ ايله صهصوبجى قولنه تعيين⁶ بيورلدى و بوزاق بكى

دخى سنجاغى⁷ عسكرى ايله قبه‌لو كليسه‌ده⁸ قراوله⁹ امر¹⁰ اولندى على الصباح

محل¹¹ مزبوردن¹² قلعه‌يى سنكسار¹³ ايتديلر كرچه حصاره و شهره بو محلدن

خيلى خسارت¹⁴ اولندى اما كفار طوپلرينك آتش شراره¹⁵ پاش¹⁶ خيلى

كزنى پروانه¹⁷ مثل سوخته¹⁸ ايلدى مراد اغا مترسفى ايلرو¹⁹ سوروب²⁰

اقدام²¹ ايلدى سردار كامكار دخى كفارك طوپلرينه و تفنكلرينه²² باتميوب

اوردى همايونى قالديروب مقابله حصارده مقدما²³ طوپخانه اولان²⁴ تل رفيعه‌ده²⁵

قوردوردى سپاه و لشكر ظفرپناه جمله مترسلرده ثابت²⁶ قدم²⁷ اولوب

جنكه اهتمام²⁸ تام ايلديلر . . . .

كفار لئام غازيان ظفر انجامك هجومنى²⁹ كوروب درد³⁰ بى درمانلرينه³¹

چاره³² جوى اولوب ممالك³³ كريدده اولان بعضى³⁴ سوارى و پياده كفاره

---

(1) A. *Darb*, 'a blow.'—(2) A. *Shedíd*, 'violent.'—(3) *Séped*, 'a small open-mouthed basket.'—(4) *Baïd*, 'distant.'—(5) A. *Mulhak*, 'joined,' 'an arm,' 'a branch of anything' (not trees or plants), 'a patrol.'—(6) *Tayin etmek*, 'to appoint.'—(7) *Sanjak*, 'a flag, ensign, banner,' 'a minor province.'—(8) *Kélissa*, 'a church.'—(9) *Karaol* (sometimes spelt قراغول *karaghol*), 'a picket, outpost, guard;' قراغول خانه *karaghol khané*, 'a guard-house.'—(10) *Emr olounmak*, 'to be ordered.'—(11) A. *Mahal*, 'a place.'—(12) A. *Mezbour*, 'aforementioned.'—(13) *Senghsar etmek*, 'to stone.'—(14) A. *Khasaret*, 'damage.'—(15) *Shiraré*, 'a spark.'—(16) P. *Pash*, 'scattering.' Thus *Shiraré-pash* means 'which scatters sparks' (flaming).—(17) P. *Pervané*, 'a moth.'—(18) P. *Soukhté*, 'burnt.'—(19) *Ileri*, 'forward,'—(20) *Surmek* 'to push, drive.'—(21) *Ikdam etmek*, 'to persevere, strive.'—(22) *Tufenk* (*tufék*), 'a musket.'—(23) *Mukademma*, 'formerly, before.'—(24) A. *Tel*, 'a hill.'—(25) A. *Refi*, 'high.'—(26) A. *Sabit*, 'firm.'—(27) A. *Kadm*, 'a foot.'—(28) *Ihtimam*, 'exertion.'—(29) A. *Hujoum*, 'attack.'—(30) P. *Derd*, 'ailment, pain, grief.'—(31) P. *Derman*, 'a remedy;' *bi-derman*, 'incurable.'—(32) P. *Charé*, 'a resource;' *jouï*, 'seeking.'—(33) A. *Mémalik*, 'dominions.'—(34) *Bazí*, 'some.'

ناءءلر' كوندروب صحرادن اغاز جنگه تحريك' ايتديلر اوله‌كه عسكر انلره

مشغول' ايكن محصوره‌يه' برمقدار' راحت كله لاحرم' اهالى كريد و سوده

ليمانينده ياتان' اون يدى پاره قدرغه و اون درت قليونك لشكرى جمع

ارابوب زعملرنجه هجوم' ايتمكله عسكرى حصاردن قالديروق تدبيرينى كورديلر

بو طريقله" دوقه كين بكى على بك و سردنكچدى عسكرى اوزرينه كاوب عرض

شوكت' ايلدكلرينده بيكدن زياده پياده و سوار كفار الات' حرب"

و جبه' و جوشنله' ماننده ديوار استوار' ايكن اوچيوز قدر غازى بى پروا'

بونلره قويلوب' رزم بيشماردنصكره عنايت بارى' ايله غالب' كلوب

كروه' مكروه' مغلوب' و مقهور اولديلر ايات ـزيمت اثرلريله اوتوز قدر

باش حضور سرداره عرض و اعلام اولندقده عنايت عليه‌لرى مقارن' حال

غازيان اولدى . . . . . محاصرينك اون النجى كونى يوزدن زياده كافر

مترسلره' چيقوب هجوم ايتدكارنده مراد اغا و نجه بهادر حاضر' بولنوب

اول كافرلرى تفنكه' طوتوب دونديرديلر' روم ايلى' و سائر عسكر تيغ

خونريز' ايله ايريشوب' اكثرينى قتل' ايدوب باشلرينى سرداره كتوريلر

قورتيلان ملاعينى مجروح' و مقهور خندقه دوكلديلر' روزكار فرسوده كفار

<hr />

(1) P. *Namé,* 'a letter.'— (2) A. *Tahrik,* 'to urge.'— (3) A. *Meshghoul,* 'busy.'—
(4) A. *Mahsour,* 'besieged.'—(5) A. *Mikdar,* 'a portion, a bit.'—(6) A. *La-jérem,* ' without fail, in any case.'— (7) *Yatmak,* 'to lie.'— (8) *Jem olmak,* 'to be collected,
assembled.'—(9) *Zum,* 'illusion.'— (10) A. *Tedbir,* 'arrangement, management.'—
(11) A. *Tarik,* 'a road, a way.'— (12) A. *Shevket,* 'pomp.'—(13) A. *Alat,* 'implements.'—(14) A. *Harb,* 'war.'—(15) P. *Jebé,* 'armour, arms.'— (16) P. *Joushen,* ' a
cuirass.'—(17) P. *Ustuvar,* 'firm, strong.'—(18) P. *Perva,* 'fear;' *Bi-perva,* 'fearless.'— (19) *Komak* or *koïmak,* 'to put, let.'—(20) A. *Bari,* 'the Creator;' a Turkish
adverb meaning 'at least,' 'just only.'—(21) A. *Ghalib,* 'conquering, a conquerer.'—
(22) P. *Ghiuruh,* 'people.'—(23) A. *Mekrouh,* 'disgusting.'—(24) A. *Maghloub,* 'conquered.'—(25) A. *Mukarin,* 'close to, nigh to.'—(26) A. *Meteris,* 'an intrench-
ment.'—(27) A. *Hazir,* 'ready.'—(28) *Tufek,* 'a musket;' *tufeké toutmak,* 'to
fusillade.'—(29) *Doundourmek,* 'to turn, cause to turn.'—(30) *Roum élli,* 'Roumelia.'— (31) P. *Khounriz,* 'running with blood.'—(32) *Erishmek,* 'to reach, come
up.'—(33) *Katl etmek,* 'to kill.'—(34) *Mejrouh,* 'wounded.'—(35) *Doukmek,* ' to
pour;' or *dughmek,* 'to beat.'

خاكسار عسكر اسلامك دست برد۱ رستمانه۲ سنی مشاهده۳ ایدوب بر دخی۴
حصاردن چیقمغه جرأت۵ ایده مدیلر

بو محلده طرابلوسدن اوچ سفینه و بر قاچ شیقه کلوب مصر۶ عسکرندن
دخی خیلی دلاوران باروت فراوان ایله کلوب دوننمای همایونه ملاقاتا یتدیلر
و مصر عسکری دخی سوده لیمانی بوغازنده۷ پوصوده۸ طوروب قراول بكلمك
فرمان اولندی

روز مزبورده درون حصارده حالا سردار كامكار جامع۹ ایلدیکی کلیسهده که
صان فرانچسقو دیمکله معروف معبد۱۰ قدیمدر۱۱ چاكلغی۱۲ که اعجوبهء۱۳
دهر۱۴ ایدی جمله۱۵ انبیهء۱۶ حانیهءنك سر افرازی۱۷ بر بلند میل۱۸ اولوب
ذروهء۱۹ اعلا سنده بر صلیب۲۰ آهنین۲۱ وار ایدیکه بر قاچ فرسنخ۲۲ یردن
کور ینوردی طوپ ایله اور یلوب خاكله۲۳ یكسان۲۴ قلندی

آمدن۲۵ كفار بامداد۲۶ حصار و غلبهء۲۷ اسلامیان

· چون بو دیارك۲۸ فتحی مراد پروردگار۲۹ او لمشیدی لا جرم۳۰ هر امورده۳۱

---

(1) A. *Berd*, 'coldness, cold.'—(2) P. *Rustemané*, 'Rustem-like;' Rustem was a celebrated hero of romance.— (3) *Mushahedé etmek*, 'to behold, see.'— (4) *Bir-daha* (generally spelt بر دها), 'again.'—(5) *Jeraet etmek*, 'to have courage, be bold.'—(6) A. *Misr*, 'Egypt.'—(7) *Boghaz*, 'the throat, windpipe,' 'a defile, strait, channel, the mouth of a river,' the Bosphorus *par excellence.*—(8) *Pousou*, 'an ambush.'—(9) A. *Jami*, 'a mosque.'—(10) A. *Mabed*, 'a place of worship.'— (11) A. *Kadim*, 'ancient.'—(12) *Changlik*, 'a peal of bells' (from *chang*, 'a big bell').— (13) *Ujubé*, 'a wonder, miracle, prodigy.'—(14) A. *Dehr*, 'an age.'— (15) A. *Jumlé*, 'all.'—(16) A. *Enbiyé*, 'buildings.'—(17) P. *Ser-efraz*, 'eminent illustrious.'— (18) P. *Mil*, 'a landmark.'— (19) *Zirwé*, 'summit.'—(20) A. *Salib* 'a cross.'—(21) P. *Ahenin*, 'of iron.'—(22) A. *Fersekh*, 'a parasang,' 'an hour's journey on horseback at a walk.'—(23) P. *Khak*, 'the earth, ground.'— (24) *Yeksar*, 'level.'—(25) P. *Améden*, 'to come, the coming.'—(26) A. *Bi-imdad ; bi*, 'with;' *imdad*, 'help, succour.'—(27) A. *Ghalebé*, 'victory.'—(28) A. *Diyar*, 'a country, a district.'—(29) P. *Perverdighiar*, 'God.'—(30) A. *La jerem*, 'without fail, in any case.'—(31) A. *Oumour*, 'affairs.'

تدبیر¹ اهل اسلام² بالجمله² موافق³ تقدیر⁴ اولوب⁴ كار⁵ كفار صورت ادبره⁶ يوز⁷
طوتدی امیر الامراء⁸ كریدكه انلر اصطلاحنده⁹ جنرال ديررل دار¹⁰ الملك
كريد اولن قندیهده اوتروب حانیهنك محاصره اولندیغی تحقیق¹¹ ايتدكده
كتخداسفی بش يوز تفنك انداز¹² فدایی¹³ كافرلر ايله سوده ليماننه كوندروب
اندن دخی درت يوز قدر كمسنه الوب جمله سی محاصره نك طقوزنجی كونی
محصورينه استمالت¹⁴ نامه لر ايله كلوب قلعه قارشوسنده ايرشدكده قراول تعیین
اولنان دوقه كبن تونس و مصر عسكرينه كه بالجمله يش يوز قدر بهادر اولوردی
صبح¹⁵ كاذيب و قتنده راست¹⁶ كلوب كفارك كثرتندن¹⁷ اصلا پروا ايلمیوب
تفنك و تبر¹⁸ خدنك¹⁹ و شمشیر²⁰ ايله محكم جنك ايدوب بر ساعتده
كره مكروه بوزيلوب²¹ پريشان اولديلر اثنا جنكده سردن كچدی اغاسی
يحیالی زاده ارناود حسن اغا شهید اولوب كتخدای جنرال الليدن زياده
كافر ايله قلیجدن كچوب²² باشلر و ديلر و طبللر²³ ايله علی الصباح حضور
سردار عرض²⁴ ايلدكلرنده جمله سنه عنایتلر ايتدی . . . . . . بعون²⁵ الله تعالی
بونجه كافر واصل دار البوار²⁶ اولوب سائر دخی تلال²⁷ و جباله²⁸ فرار²⁹ ايليوب
بريسی قلعه يه كیرمكه مجال³⁰ او لمدی انجق³¹ عسكر اسلامدن درت كمسنه
شهید اولدی . . . . . .

---

(1) A. *Tedbir*, 'arrangement.'— (2) A. *Bil jumlé*, 'altogether.'— (3) *Muwafik*, 'agreeable to.'— (4) A. *Takdir*, 'fate.'— (5) P. *Kiar*, 'work, business.'— (6) *Idbar*, 'retrogression.'— (7) *Yuz toutmak*, 'to threaten.'—(8) A. *Emir-ul-umera*, 'commander of commanders, commander-in-chief.'—(9) A. *Istilah*, 'a technical way of speaking, a technical term.'—(10) A. *Dar*, 'a house;' *Milk*, 'sovereignty, dominion;' *Dar-ul-Milk*, 'the seat of government, capital.'—(11) *Tahkik etmek*, 'to ascertain, verify.'— (12) P. *Endaz*, 'throwing;' *tufenk-endaz*, 'a musketeer.'—(13) A. *Fedaï*, 'one who goes on a forlorn hope.'— (14) A. *Istimalet*, 'encouragement.'—(15) *Subh el-Kiazib*, 'the false dawn;' also called فجر كاذيب *Fejr-i-Kiazib*, after which darkness is said to fall again, in contradistinction to the true dawn or break of day, called فجر صادق *fejr-i-Sadik*.—(16) *Rast ghelmek*, 'to meet, encounter.'—(17) A. *Kesret*, 'quantity, abundance.'—(18) P. *Tebr*, 'battle-axe.'—(19) P. *Khadengh*, 'an arrow.'—(20) P. *Shemshir*, 'a sword.'—(21) *Bozmak*, 'to spoil, defeat.'—(22) *Kilijden gechmek*, 'to put to the sword.'—(23) A. *Tabl (dawoul)*, 'a drum.'—(24) *Arz etmek*, 'to present, offer, submit.'— (25) *Bi-avn*, 'by the help.'—(26) A. *Dar ul-Bevar*, 'The House of Destruction' (hell).—(27) A. *Tilal*, 'hills.'—(28) *Jibal*, 'mountains.'—(29) *Firar*, 'to flee, run away.'—(30) A. *Méjal*, 'power, ability.'—(31) *Anjak*, 'only, but.'

*Description of the Castle of Canea.*—The construction of this castle is such that the cleverest man cannot describe it, for there is nothing like it on the face of the earth; and in the Ottoman dominions a castle of this kind does not exist. The Lords of Venice for four hundred years had done their utmost in building and improving this fortress, and thus fortified and strengthened it most perfectly. Although there are many fortresses in the Imperial dominions equal to it in height, extent and strength, the fashion of this noble fortress is unique. It is situated in a level place, its circuit being as large as Galata, and has seven lofty towers, each of which resembles a fortress in extent and height; and is provided with twenty heavy cannons apiece. The breadth of the walls, which take a thousand fighting men, is such that seven horsemen can ride abreast on them, and then in the filled-in ground in the wall twenty horsemen can ride side by side. From the high battlements of the said wall, upwards, there are ten yards of raised ground, which, in case of fighting there, neither cannon nor anything else can have any effect upon. And there are nine redoubts with strongly built walls of hewn stone, bigger than the other towers, which reach up to the sky, and defend the city with fifteen heavy cannon apiece. Then, at their two corners two mounds of earth have been raised, which look on the towers and the redoubts, and land and sea. In each of them twenty enormous, valuable cannons have been placed, which defend the four sides. The space underneath these mounds is all hollow, and vaults within vaults, which are magazines for powder and cannon balls. As regards the sea-side of the fortress, it is a pleasant harbour surrounded by gigantic walls, which only a galley can enter, and then again at its entrance there are big cannon commanding the sea. And there are twenty shot-proof arsenals, arched over with stone or brick, which have not their like on the face of the earth, on each of which much treasure has been expended!

In particular there are houses and palaces inside the city which are of pure marble, fine buildings and princely halls, compared to which the famed palace of Khawarnak is nothing, artistic fountains and streets and shops, the like of which men's eyes have never beheld. The inhabitants are renowned for their wealth and beauty. After the conquest of the town, the magazines which fell into our hands were innumerable. Three hundred and ninety-five valuable cannon alone were registered. Outside the fortress the depth of the moat is fifteen yards and its width seventy-five, and most of the edge of the moat is of hewn stone.

The attack of the fortress began on the morning of the fourth of the above-mentioned (Muhammedan) month, which was Tuesday, (corresponding to) the seventeenth of June, by a cannonade of the castle. The vile unbelievers displayed great firmness and steadiness, and fought well. On the twelfth day of the siege the Commander-in-Chief came to the place where the guns were, and while he was animating our warriors an infamous infidel fired a tremendous ("thunder-bolt casting") gun, which struck the place where the Vezir stood. Five spahis from Roumelia were "martyred" (killed), and the Vezir and staff escaped by the divine protection; but the flesh and blood of the martyrs somewhat soiled the dress of the Commander-in-Chief. The ball of the above-mentioned cannon came with such tremendous force that it passed through three baskets filled with earth and went further. As the afore-mentioned place was somewhat distant from the fortress, on the thirteenth day of the siege the trenches were changed, and the troops from Anatolia, with their commander, Ahmed Pasha, brought two guns and joined the trenches of the Roumelians. The troops of Caramania, with two guns, were appointed to the patrol of Samsoungi; and the Bey of Bouzak also, with the soldiers from his province, were stationed as an out-post (guard) in a vaulted church.

In the morning early they cannonaded the fortress from the above-mentioned position; but although great injury was done from there to the fort and the city, the terrific fire of the enemy's guns burnt many Moslem warriors like moths (in a candle). Murad Agha persevered and pushed his trench closer. The glorious Commander-in-Chief also, disregarding the cannon and muskets of the infidels, broke up the Imperial camp and stationed it opposite the Fort, on the high hill, where previously the artillery had been planted. Our

" ever-victorious " troops stood firmly in all the trenches and executed themselves bravely. . . . . . . .

The abominable infidels, seeing the assault of our " ever-success-ful " warriors, tried to find a remedy for the incurable evil, and wrote letters to some infidel cavalry and infantry in the Cretan dominions, and urged them to come forth and fight, that the Moslem troops, being occupied by them, the besieged might have some rest. The inhabitants of Crete, and the troops from seventeen galleys and seven men-of-war which were lying in Souda Bay, collected together, and attempted to raise the siege by attacking our troops. Accord-ingly, they came on the Bey of Douka-Kin, Ali Bey, and the troops of Serdenkechdi in grand array, looking like a strong wall. More than a thousand infidel cavalry and infantry, with armour and cui-rasses and weapons of war, were opposed by about three hundred of our fearless braves. After a long struggle, by the grace of God, the latter were the victors and worsted the disgusting wretches. As trophies they brought thirty heads into the presence of the Commander-in-Chief, and were rewarded by his favour.

On the sixteenth day of the siege above a hundred of the infidels made a sortie and attacked the trenches ; but Murad Agha, and several valiant men, were ready for them, received them with musketry fire and turned them back ; and some Roumelian and other troops coming up, with their doughty swords killed most of them ; and they brought their heads to the Commander-in-Chief. Those who escaped, wounded, and beaten, were driven (cast) into the moat. Discomfited, the vile unbelievers, having felt the weight of the " Rustem-like " hand of the Moslem troops, did not venture to come out of the fortress again.

At this time three vessels from Tripoli, and a few " Saïcs," and also many heroes from the Egyptian army, arrived and met the Imperial fleets. The Egyptian soldiers also remained in ambush at the mouth of Souda Bay, and were ordered to remain as a guard.

On the same day an iron cross at the top of a church called San-fransisco, inside the town (since converted into a Mosque by the Generalissimo), an ancient place of worship, whose peal of bells was the wonder of the age, and which towered, like a lofty landmark over the other buildings of Canea, and was visible leagues away, was struck by a cannon ball, and levelled with the ground.

### Arrival of Infidels with reinforcements to relieve the fortress, and victory of the Mussulmans.

As it was the intention of the Almighty that this country should be conquered, every arrangement of the Moslems was entirely successful, and the affairs of the infidels threatened to get worse. Whereupon the Chief Ruler of Crete, who, in their phraseology, was called a "General," and resided in the capital of Crete, Candia, having ascertained that Canea was being besieged, sent his agent with a forlorn-hope of five hundred musketeers to Souda Bay, who took four hundred men from there and then arrived before the fortress, bringing letters of encouragement. On the ninth day of the siege they encountered the troops from Douka-Kin, Egypt and Tunis, who altogether were about five hundred, at the time of the "False Dawn." The Moslems, not at all frightened at the superior numbers of the unbelievers, fought stoutly with the musket, the battle-axe, the arrow and sword, and in an hour the disgusting wretches were defeated and scattered. During the combat, the Agha, of Serden-Kechdi Yahyali-zadé Hassan Agha, the Arnaoud, was killed; the agent of the General and more than fifty of the infidels were put to the sword, and their heads and their drums in the morning early were presented to the Generalissimo, who rewarded every one of our soldiers. By the help of God (may He be exalted!) so many infidels having been sent to perdition, the others fled to the hills and mountains, and not one was able to enter the fortress; but only four of the true-believers were killed. . . . . . . .

# SAD-UD-DIN, THE HISTORIAN, AND MAHOMET III.
## AT THE BATTLE OF KERESZTES.*

كفار دخى ظفريابِ¹ اوادق ملاحظه سياهِ² اوردو چادرلرينه كيروب يغمايه

ال اورديلر ايكى بيكدن زياده ملاعين³ ايلرو سوروب پادشاهك سجاده⁴

سنه بر اوق⁵ منزلى قدر محلده جنك⁶ ايدوب اوردو⁷ ايچنده تفنكدن

فراغت اولنوب مسلمان و كافر بربرينه سيف ايله كيريشوب يقه يه

يقه يه جنك ايدر اولديار . وزرا و اركانِ⁸ دولت پادشاهى احاطه ايدوب

طورديلر ملاعين اوتاغِ⁹ همايون طنابلرينه¹⁰ ال اوردقده اندرون¹¹ اغالرى قليم

اوشوروب قتل ايلديلر . اول روز رستخيزدن¹² بر ساعت ايديكه عامهء

عساكر بلغت¹³ القلوب الحناجر معذاسنى مشاهده ايلديلر . مولانا سعد

الدين افندى پادشاه حضرتلرينه ان النصر مع الصبر¹⁴ و ان مع العسر يسرا¹⁴

---

(1) *Zafryab*, 'victorious.'— (2) A. *Mulahaza*, 'observation, consideration.'—
(3) *Melain*, 'accursed ones.'—(4) A. *Sejjadé*, 'a prayer-carpet.'—(5) *Bir ok men-
zeli*, 'the range of an arrow.'—(6) P. *Jenk*, 'war, battle.'—(7) *Ordou*, 'a camp, an
army.'—(8) A. *Erkian-i-devlet*, 'the pillars of the state.'—(9) *Otagh*, 'a large
tent.'—(10) A. *Tinab*, pl. of طناب *tunub*, 'tent ropes.'—(11) P. *Enderoun*, 'the
harem;' *enderoun aghaleri*, 'the higher attendants attached to the Sultan's private
apartments.'— (12) P. *Restakhiz*, 'the last judgment.'—(13) A. *Balagat el-kuloub
el-hanajir*, an Arabic saying which means 'their hearts were in their mouths, they
despaired.'—(14) *En en-nasr ma es-sabr, wé en ma el-usr yusra*, two other Arabic
sayings to the effect that 'victory comes from patience, and happiness comes from
difficulty.'

---

* Sad-ud-Din accompanied the Sultan Mahomed III. in his campaign in Hungary. The battle of Keresztes lasted three days. The Turks had to contend with
the Imperialists under the Archduke Maximilian, and the Transylvanians under
Prince Sigismund, with whom they had effected a junction. On the first day, one
body of the Turks, after fighting bravely, were obliged to retreat, with a loss of
a thousand Janissaries, a hundred Spahis, and forty-three cannon. The Sultan
wished to retire himself, and that a general retreat of the Turkish army should
be ordered. A Council of War was held, and the author, Sad-ud-din, although not
a soldier, had the courage to tell his master that he ought not to turn his back
on the enemy. Owing to this advice it was resolved to fight, and the Sultan was
persuaded to remain. On the second day the Turks had some partial successes.
On the third day the Christians appeared completely victorious. They drove back
the Turks and Tartars, attacked the Ottoman batteries in flank, and routed the
Asiatic feudal cavalry. The Sultan wished to fly, and again it was only by the
exhortations of Sad-ud-Din that he was prevented. The Imperialists scattered
in order to plunder the Turkish camp, and while they were in disorder, Cicala
Pasha, who was in command of a large body of irregular cavalry, and who had
hitherto not been in action, rushed on them, and turned defeat into a victory,
which was in great part due to the firmness of a literary man.

مضمونلرينى¹ بيان و تفسير ايدوب اول پادشاه دين پناه حضرت پيغمبر

عليه الصلوة و السلامك خرقه² شريفلرينى كيوب بنايانى³ مرصوص⁴

جداروار⁵ ثابت⁶ و بر قرار اولوب حضرت عالم الاسرار و الخفياته⁷ مناجات⁸

و كريه⁹ و خضوع¹⁰ و نياز برله دركاه بينيازه رفع يد حاجات ايديجك

نسيم¹¹ فتح و ظفر پرچم¹¹ توغ¹³ محمديى¹ى تسريح¹⁴ ايلدى . كفار اتش نثار

عساكر اسلام چادرلرينى قاپليوب مال غنايمه پريشان اوليجق بعنايت

الله الرحمن صف مرتبلرى بوزيلوب قورلمشر چادرلره برر ايكشر كافر غالبانه

دخول ايدوب بى پروا غارته مشغول اولدقلرنده عسكر اسلامك ات

اوغلنلرى و اشجى¹⁵ و خربنده¹⁶ و دوه‌جى¹⁷ و سايس¹⁸ و اوردوجى

خدمتكار طائفه‌سى چادراره كيرن كفاره كيريشوب باطه و بچاق و بوندقلرى

الت ايله قيرمغه¹⁹ باشلاديلر . بو سبب ايله ملاعينه ضعف حال طارى²⁰

اولوب قرار مجاللرى²¹ قالميوب طابورلرينى²² اوزلديوب فرار²³ ايتدكلرنده كفار

بوزلدى ديو اوازه اولوب ايشيدن اهل اسلام دونوب ملاعينك اكسه‌سنه²⁴

دوشوب بر وجهله قيرديلركه روايت صحيحه اوزره زمان قليلده يوز بيك²⁵

قدر كفار زمين قهرزاده دوشوب وقت غروبده اول ميدان وسيعده كشته²⁵

لردن پشته‌لر يغيلوب پياده‌لرندن²⁶ خودجان قورتلميوب بقية²⁷ السيوف

---

(1) A. *Mazmoun,* ' a bon-mot, pun.'—(2) A. *Khirka,* ' a quilted jacket, a garment made of shreds and patches.'—(3) A. *Bunyan,* ' construction, physical constitution.'—(4) A. *Mérsus,* ' held firmly together with irons.'—(5) A. *Jidar,* ' a wall ;' *var,* P. ' like ;' *Jidar-var,* ' like a wall.'—(6) A. *Sabit,* ' firm.'—(7) *Alim-ul-israr wé el-khefiyat,* ' He who knows secrets and hidden things ' (*i.e.* God.)—(8) A. *Munajat,* ' prayers.' — (9) A. *Ghiryé,* ' weeping, tears.' — (10) A. *Khouzou,* ' humility.'— (11) A. *Nesim,* ' a zephyr, breeze.'—(12) P. *Pérchem,* the tuft of hair left on the head of a Muhammedan, the rest of the head being shaved. — (13) *Tough,* the special kind of banner or insignia of a Pasha in the olden times (a tail). A Pasha, received one, two or three of them according to his rank.—(14) *Tesrih etmek,* ' to set free, let go.'—(15) *Ashji,* ' a cook,'—(16) P. *Kherbendé,* ' a donkey-man.'— (17) *Devéji,* ' a camel-driver.'—(18) *Saïs,* ' a groom.'—(19) *Kirmak,* ' to break, to massacre, slaughter.'—(20) *Tari olmak,* ' to happen, overtake one.' — (21) *Mejal,* ' power, ability.'—(22) *Tabour,* ' a battalion, column.' — (23) *Firar etmek,* ' to run away, fly.'—(24) *Ensé,* ' the back part of the head, the back or hind part of anything.'—(25) P. *Kiushté,* ' killed.'—(26) P. *Piyadé,* ' infantry.'—(27) A. *Bakiyyet-es-suyuf,* or بقيا السيف , ' the leavings of the sword,' *i.e.* those who escape the swords of the enemy.

ولان سواريلر[1] ظالم ليلده بر يرده قرار ايده، يوب هرطرفه پريشان[2] و صبح
اولنجه دشت[3] و دره ديميوب كريزان[4] اولديلر . لله الحمد و المنه اول
پادشاه عالي جاه عون حق ايله منصور[5] و مظفر اولوب عزيمت صادقه و
ثبات قدم بركاتيله برنيك نام[6] تحصيل و عرض و ناموس دين و دولتى
تكميل ايلديكه اسلافندن[7] بو مرتبه يه بر پادشاه واصل اولمدى . . . . . . 

### Another account of the battle.

وقت اول عصرده[8] كفار حركته كلوب كروه كروه كورنديلر اولا پياده نمچه
الايلرى جملهسى آهن پوش[9] الزنده برر حربه و بر قاچ الاى دخى كوك[10]
تيموره مستغرق الزنده مشقتور ديدكار تفنك[11] كه اون بشر يكرميشر درهم
اتار . و بر قاچ الاى تفنك انداز[12] مجار[13] هايدورلرى[14] كه يوز الابدن زياده
پياده هر الاى بشر يوز قدر كافر ايديلر بعده مجارك اتلى الاىى صافى
صرقلى[15] و بيراقلى[16] كهسار پر اشجار[17] كبى كورينوردى و نيچه نمچه[18] چه[19]
و له[20] و سائر اجناسك[21] سوارى الايلرى كه هر بر كافر اوچر بشر مجار تفنكلرى
كتورر . بونلر دخى اللى الابدن زياده ايدى . . . . 

سنان پاشايه مراد پاشا و بوستانجى باشي على پاشا امداده كوندريلوب
ملحق[22] اولدى لكن كفار بالجمله تفنك اندار اولمغله مقاومت[23] ممكن اولميوب
اسلام الايلرى پراكنده[24] بتاغى[25] كچوب صحرايه[26] پايلديلر . كفار عسكرى طوب و

---

(1) *Suwariler,* 'cavalry.'—(2)—P. *Perishan,* 'scattered.'—(3) P. *Desht,* 'the open
country.'— (4) P. *Gherizan,* 'a fugitive,' 'who takes flight.'—(5) A. *Mansour,*
'helped' (by God), 'victorious.'—(6) P. *Nik nam,* 'a good name.'—(7) A. *Eslaf*
(pl. of سلف *sélef*), 'predecessors.'—(8) *Evvel asr,* or *asr-i-evvel,* 'the time of afternoon prayer.'—(9) P. *Ahen-posh,* 'dressed in iron,' *i. e.* in armour.—(10) *Ghieuk,*
'the sky;' *ghieuk, adj.,* 'sky-blue.'—(11) A. *Dirhem,* 'a drachm.'—(12) P. *Tufenk-
endaz,* 'who fire muskets, musketeers.'—(13) *Majar,* 'Hungarian.'—(14) *Haïdoud,*
'robber;' 'a Hungarian soldier.'—(15) *Sirik,* 'a small pole, a long, thick stick.'—
(16) *Baïrak,* 'flag, banner.'—(17) A. *Eshjar,* 'trees.'— (18) *Nemché,* 'German,
Austrian.'—(19) *Cheh,* 'Bohemia.'—(20) *Léh,* 'Poland.'—(21) A. *Ejnas* (pl. of جنس
*jins*), 'kinds, sorts.'—(22) A. *Mulhak,* 'annexed, joined to.'—(23) A. *Mukavémet*
'resistance.'—(24) P. *Perakendé,* 'scattered.'—(25) *Batak,* 'a morass.'—(26) *Sahra*
a desert, plain.'

تفنك اتارق و كوس ۱ و ترومپتهلريني ۲ چالارق ۳ بتّقدن ٤ كچوب اوردويه ظوغرى
يوريديلر . حسن پاشا روم ايلى عسكريله كچد ٥ باشنه واروب طورمق و كفارى
منع ايلمك فرمان اولنمشيدى كلوب او محلده طوردى لكن كفار هجومندن
بر آن قرار ايده ميوب تفنك زورندن ٦ سائر الايلره ملحق اولدى . كفارى
باك ۷ وبى پروا اوردويه و اصل اولوب هنوز ۸ عسكر اسلام منهزم اولمزدن
مقدم غارت ۹ و يغمايه قويلديلر . حتى بر ايكى بيراق ايله بر نيچه كافر خزينهء
عامرهيه ۱۰ هجوم ايدوب محافظهسنده اولان سپاه و يكيچرى طاغلديلر . كفار
خزينه صندوقلر اوزرينه چيقوب حاچلى ۱۱ بيراقلريني ديكديلر . و رقصه ۱۲
باشلديلر . چون بو حال منظور پادشاه دريا نوال اولدقده خواجه افندى
حضور همايونلرنده حاضر و بو امر عجيبه ناظر ۱۳ اولمغين افندى شمدنصكره
چاره و تدبير نه در ديو بيورمشلر انلر دخى پادشاهه لازم اولان يريكزده ثابت
و بر قرار طورمقدر جنك حالى بو در . اجداد ۱٤ عظامكز ۱٥ زمانلرنده اولان طابور
محربهلرى اكثر بويله اوله كلمشدر . معجزات محمديه ايله ان شاءالله تعالى فرصت
و نصرت ۱٦ اهل اسلامكدر خاطر شريفكزى خوش طوتك ديو تسليت ۱۷ ايتديلر .
منقولدر ۱۸ كه امراى كفاردن پادشاه عاليجاهى اول حالده ات اوزررينهء تمام
حيرت و انفعالده ۱۹ و خواجه افندى ركابى برابرنده طپروب اللرى دعايه
مرفوع ۲۰ تضرع ۲۱ و ابتهالده ۲۲ تصوير ايتديروب كويا كه اوقور اوزور ديو تصوير
ذيلنده نمچه لساننده خواجه افندينك دعاسى قبول اولدى ديو ياز مشلر .

---

(1) A. *Kious*, 'a kettle-drum, a drum.'—(2) *Tranpeta*, 'a drum.'—(3) *Chalmak*,
'to play' (an instrument).—(4) *Batak*, 'a morass.'—(5) *Gechid*, 'a pass, defile,'
'a ford, ferry.'—(6) P. *Zor (subst.)*, 'violence, strength, force;' Turkish, *adj.*, 'difficult, hard.'—(7) P. *Bak*, 'fear;' *bi-bak-ou-bi-perva*, 'without fear or dread.'—
(8) P. *Henouz (heniz)*, 'yet.'— (9) A. *Gharet*, 'plunder.'— (10) A. *Amir*, 'public.'—
(11) *Hachli*, 'having a cross on it.'—(12) A. *Raks*, 'dancing.'—(13) A. *Manzour*,
'seen.'—(14) A. *Ejdad*, 'ancestors.'—(15) A. *Izam* (pl. of عظيم *azim*), 'great.'—
(16) A. *Nusret*, 'victory.'—(17) *Tesliyyet etmek*, 'to console.'—(18) *Menkoul*, 'handed
down,' 'reported.' — (19) A. *Infial*, 'affliction, grief.'—(20) A. *Merfou*, 'raised.'—
(21) A. *Tézerru*, 'a humbling oneself.'—(22) A. *Ibtihal*, 'supplication, groaning in
prayer.'

اول و قندده ابچ ۱ اوغلانلرندن سراسر ۲ کسره و لباس ایله توز قدر غلام ۳
اکرلی ۴ و اکرسز ربر بارکیره سوار اولوب فرار ایتمکاه سائر عسکردن بر کوره
فرایلرك فرارلرینه باعث اولدیلر. سؤال ایدنلره بر قوچییه ۵ بنوب وقت
عصرده میر اخور ۶ اغا اوكنه دوشوب كتدیلر دیمكله عظیم پریشانلق ویردیلر.

چون لشکر کفار اوردویه کیروب عمرنده کورهدیكی غنایمی کوروب چادرلره
مستولی ۷ اولدی. و ایچنده اولان اشیایی قبضه تصرفه كتورمکه مشغول اولوب
حرب و قتالدن قالدیلر. عسکر اسلامك درت بلوکده بری كتمشدی و فرار
ایتمشدی و وقت غروب دخی قریب اولوب عسکر اسلام اسباب عادیه
دن تطع امید ایدوب مجرد عنایت الهیه یه مترقبلر ایکن ذاكاه رجال الله
ظهور ایدوب چادرلرده اولان ات اوغلانی ۸ و اشجی و قره قوللقچی ۹ نامنه
غازیلر یریر کفاره قوپلروب بالطه و کورك ۱۰ مقولهسی الات ایله هجوم
ایدوب وافر ملعون دپهلدیلر در حال اول قوم ضالده آثار هزیمت ۱۱ ظاهر
اولدی و کافر قاچدی صداسی قوپاردیلر اوردو اطرافنده سرسری ۱۲ کزن اورکمش ۱۳
الیارد ونوب هجوم ایدوب دشمنی قلچدن کچوردیلر. صف صف
رنجیره چكلمش حربی ۱۴ پیادهلر جسته ۱۵ جسته دوشوب اكثری خوفندن هلاك
نیچه بیك کفار طعمهء تیغ تابناك اولوب آن ۱۶ واحدده ۱۷ بی منت ۱۸ اللی
بیکدن متجاوز ۱۹ کافر قلچدن کچوب نیچهسی دخی بتاقلره باتوب ۲۰ انده
باشلری کسلدی. وزیر سنان پاشا یاندنده اولانلر ایله اوردوی همایونك صاغ

<hr>

(1) *Ich oghlanleri*, youths in the Sultan's palace brought up to be officers in the imperial palace in olden times.—(2) P. *Sérasér*. From end to end.—(3) A. *Ghoulam*, 'a lad, a slave;' in Persia, 'a courier.'—(4) *Eyerli éyersiz*, 'saddled or unsaddled.'—(5) *Kochou*, 'a large coach.'— (6) P. *Mir-i-akhor (emrakhor)*, 'Master-of-the-Horse.'—(7) A. *Mustevli*, 'overrunning, occupying, taking.'—(8) *At oghlani*, 'a stable-boy.'—(9) *Kara-koulloukjou*, 'a common soldier among the Janissaries placed at a guard-house.'—(10) *Kiurek*, 'a wooden shovel, an oar;' *kieuruk*, 'a pair of bellows.'—(11) A. *Hezimet*, 'defeat, a total rout.'—(12) *Sérseri*, 'wandering, a vagabond.'—(13) *Eurkmek*, 'to take fright, shy.'—(14) A. *Harbi*, 'an enemy, an alien.'—(15) P. *Jesté jesté*, 'little by little.'— (16) A. *An*, 'a moment.'—(17) A. *Wahid*, 'one.'—(18) A. *Minnet*, 'grace, favour.'— (19) A. *Mutéjariz (muté-jawuz)*, 'exceeding, more.'— (20) *Batmak*, 'to sink' (*v.n.*).

جانبنه كلن يكرمى بيك قدر كافر اتلوسنى بچق ساعتده غداى¹ شير²
شمشير ايليوب نيچهسنى دخى صوبه دوكدى جان حقيرلر ينى خلاص ايدنلر
قرار فرارہ تبديل ايلدكلرنده فتح كراى عسكر تاتار ايله هر طرفدن يورييوب
قيرہ قيرہ طابورلرينه دوكوب كفرہ چادرلرنده تحصن اتمكى مراد، ايتدكلرنده
اندہ دخى قرارہ محال بولميوب چادرلرينى جمله اشيا و مهماتى براغوب
يكتا³ باشلريله طاغلرہ دوشديلر . اونر بيك فلوريلك⁴ طقسان يدى بك اعلا
طوپلرى و خمبرہ و مكمل جبه خانهلرى ضبط اولندى

(1) *Ghida,* 'food.'—(2) P. *Shir,* 'a lion.'—(3) P. *Yekta,* 'only.'—(4) *Filouri,* 'a ducat, sequin.'

### Translation.

The infidels, thinking they were victorious, entered the tents of our army and began plundering. More than two thousand of the accursed wretches pushed forward and were fighting in a place only a bow shot from the Sultan's prayer-carpet. In the camp muskets were given up and Moslems and Christians fought with the sword hand to hand. The Vezirs and the Grandees of the State stood surrounding the Sultan. The accursed infidels having laid hands on the tent ropes of the Imperial pavilion, the attendants of the harem took swords and killed them. There was one hour that terrible day when our whole army felt the force of the (Arabic) expression *Balaghat el-Kulout el-hanajir* (their hearts were in their mouths). His Honour Sad-ud-Din Efendi reminded the Sultan of the (Arabic) saying: "Victory comes from patience, and happiness comes after difficulty;" and His Majesty, the "Asylum of the Faith," put on the *hirka** of the Prophet (prayers and peace be on him!), and then his body became as firm as a wall, and he put up prayers to Him "who knows all secrets and all hidden things," and wept, and humiliated himself, and raised his hands in supplication to Heaven, whereupon the breeze of victory unfurled

* *Hirka* is a kind of quilted jacket. The jacket of Mahomet is supposed to be a precious relic, having miraculous virtues.

the Muhammedan standard. On the Infidels who "scatter fire" *
falling on the tents of the Moslem army, and dispersing in order
to collect booty, by the grace of God, the Merciful, their regular
ranks were broken. The victorious unbelievers entered the tents
in twos and threes and set about plundering without fear or anxiety.
Then, the stable-boys, and cooks and donkeymen, and camel-drivers
and grooms, and servants of the Moslem army in the tents, en-
countering the infidels, began to slaughter them with hatchets and
knives, and whatever instruments they found. By reason of this the
accursed wretches begun to grow weak, and had not the power to
resist, and fled. On the cry being raised that the 'Ghiaours' were
beaten, the Muhammedans who heard it turned back, followed the
Christians and massacred them, so that, according to one truthful
account, in a short time, as many as a hundred thousand infidels fell
on our field of victory. In the evening that extensive plain was
heaped up with dead bodies. The infantry could not save their lives ;
and the cavalry, the only ones who escaped our swords, not being
able to make a stand anywhere, were scattered in every direction
and fled until day-break over hill and dale.

Thanks be to God, that great Sultan, by the Divine help, was
victorious, and thanks to his firmness and steadfastness he acquired
a great name and raised the honour and glory of his religion and
country more than any of his predecessors.

### Another account of the battle.

In the afternoon the infidels began to move, and appeared in
masses. First, the German infantry regiments, all in armour, with
lances in their hands, and some regiments with guns, which they call
"Muskets," which cast fifteen or twenty drachms (of lead), and the
Hungarian "brigands," some regiments with fire-arms,—who were
more than a hundred regiments of infantry,—each regiment containing five hundred infidels. Then came the Hungarian cavalry
regiment, who, with their flags and spears looked like a "hilly
country full of trees," and several cavalry regiments composed
of Germans, Bohemians, Poles and other races, every unbeliever

---

* This refers to the fire-arms the Christians used.

carrying three or five Hungarian guns apiece, of these there were more than fifty regiments . . . . . .

Murad Pasha, and the head of the " Bostanjis, " Ali Pasha, were sent to reinforce Sinan Pasha, and joined him; but, all the Christians having fire-arms, resistance was impossible, the Moslem regiments scattered and passed the morass and spread out in the plain. The infidel army fired cannon and small arms, beat their drums and passed the morass and marched straight on our army. Hassan Pasha had received orders to go to the head of the pass with the Roumelian troops, and stand there and hold back the enemy. He stood there, but owing to the violence of the fire-arms he could not make a stand for a moment, and joined the other regiments. The infidels, without any fear or dread, reached our army, and before the Moslem army had been defeated, set about plundering and pillaging. Some of the infidels even, with one or two flags, attacked our public treasury, and the Spahis and Janissaries, who had to guard it, were scattered. The Christians fell on the treasury chests, hoisted their flags with the cross on them, and began to dance. When this state of things was seen by the Sultan, he asked the professor, who was in the Imperial presence, and saw what had happened, what was to be done, who consoled him, saying : " Sire, what is necessary is that you remain firm and steady in your place. Thus were your great ancestors wont to do in most great battles. By a Muhammedan miracle, please God, the Moslems will have an opportunity to be victorious. Do not be cast down." It is stated in the German accounts that the Sultan sat on horseback, bewildered and afflicted, the professor by his side, and that they raised their hands in prayer and supplication, and that the professor's prayer was answered.

At that time a large number of the Sultan's pages mounted horses, saddled or unsaddled, and fled, and their flight caused another body of the troops to run. Great confusion was caused by it being said that they had fled in the afternoon with the Master-of-the-Horse in a coach.

When the enemy's troops entered our camp and beheld more booty than they had ever seen in their lives, they overran the tents, busied themselves with taking possession of the things there, and left off fighting and killing. One out of every four companies of the

Ottoman troops had gone and fled. The evening was drawing nigh; the Moslems despaired of success by ordinary means, and trusted only to the favour of God. Suddenly, men of God appeared, and the champions, in the form of stable-boys, cooks, and privates of the Janissaries, who were in the tents, fell on the infidels and attacked them with hatchets and wooden shovels and such things, and knocked lots of infidels on the head; and signs of defeat began to be visible amongst those misguided people. The cry arose that the "Ghiaours" had fled. The Ottoman regiments who had taken flight and were wandering round about, turned back and put the enemy to the sword. Strings of the enemy's infantry, dragged along in chains, fell little by little; many died from fear, and many thousands were put to the sword. In a very short time more than fifty thousand infidels were sabred without mercy, some of them also sank in the morass and there their heads were cut off. The Vezir, Sinan Pasha, and those by him, put twenty thousand Christian cavalry, who came to the right of the Imperial army, to the sword in half an hour, and drove many into the water. Those who saved their vile lives, instead of standing took to flight; and then Feth Gheraï, with the Tartar troops, pursuing them in every direction, slaughtered them, and broke their batallions. They attempted to fortify themselves in their tents, but they could not hold their ground, and abandoned all their effects and ammunition, and fled to the mountains with nothing but their heads. Ninety-seven splendid cannon, worth ten thousand ducats apiece, and bombshells and whole magazines of warlike muniments were captured.

## ARRIVAL OF AN AMBASSADOR FROM ENGLAND IN THE TIME OF CHARLES I.

امدن الچی انكليز

انكليز قرالنك¹ الچيسی² كلوب نامهسنده عرض مودت³ و باباسی يرينه
قرال اولديغنی بلدروب تونسليلر و جزائرلر ايله تجارت¹ ايچون عقد مصالحه
ايدوب در دولتدن دخی اذن⁴ همايون رجا ايتمكين جزاير و تونس بكلر
بكارينه قپوجی⁵ باشی كوندرلدی . و ممالك محروسه⁶ اسكلهلرنده⁷ دخی عهد⁸
نامهيه مخالف⁹ تكليفلر¹⁰ مثلاً¹¹ مصدريه نامهله و غيری بهانه¹² ايله بی
وجه اقچه النميوب انجق كمرك¹³ الله جزائر بكلربكيسی ايكن وفات ايدن
خسرو پاشا جزائرده اولان و تونسلی ياننده اولان انكليزلری حبس¹⁴ ايدوب
بر قاچ بيك غروش المغله مبلغ¹⁵ مزبور مقاطعات¹⁶ مالندن و يرلمك فرمان
اولندی و هند طرفندن يمن اسكله لرنده تجارته¹⁷ كلورکن يكرمی درت پاره
تجار¹⁸ كميلرينی انكليز جانبدن بورتونلر الوب ايچنده اولان تجار ايله اول
كميلری اطلاق¹⁹ ايدوب تلف²⁰ اولان ماللری²¹ اصحابنه²² رد²³ ايليه سزر ديو
نامه تحرير²⁴ و ارسال اولندی

(1) *Kral,* ' a king.'—(2) P. *Elchi,* ' an ambassador.'—(3) A. *Mévédet,* 'friendship, amity.'— (4) A. *Izn,* ' permission.'— (5) *Kapiji-bushi,* ' a chamberlain.'— (6) A. *Mahrousé,* ' well-protected ;' *Memalik-i-Mahrousé,* ' the well-protected dominions,' *i. e.* Turkey.—(7) *Eskelé,* ' a wharf, landing-place,' ' a port.'—(8) *Ahd-namé,* ' a written treaty.'—(9) A. *Mukhalif,* ' contrary.'—(10) *Teklif,* ' a tax.'—(11) A. *Messela,* ' for example, for instance.'—(12) P. *Bahané,* ' a pretext.'— (13) *Ghiumruk,* ' a custom-house,' ' a custom's duty.'—(14) *Habs etmek,* ' to imprison.'—(15) A. *Meblagh,* ' a sum, amount.'—(16) A. *Moukataat,* a fief attached to an office, the tithes from which went to the holder of the office (now abolished).—(17) A. *Tijaret,* ' commerce.'—(18) A. *Tujar,* ' merchants.'—(19) *Itlak etmek,* ' to set free, let go.'— (20) *Télef olmak,* ' to be destroyed.'—(21) A. *Mal,* ' property, wealth.'—(22) A. *Ashab,* ' owners' (pl. of صاحب, *sahib*).—(23) *Red éïlémek,* ' to restore.'—(24) *Tahrir olounmak,* ' to be written.'

### Translation.

An ambassador having arrived from the King of the English (Charles I.) with a letter proposing friendship, and announcing his

his father's stead, and asking for a Treaty, and the Imperial permission, in order to trade with Algiers and Tunis, a Chamberlain was sent to the Governors of Algiers and Tunis, and orders were sent that no taxes contrary to the Treaty should be exacted at any of the ports in Turkey, like the *Masderiyé*, and a letter saying that the late Khosrev Pasha, while Governor of Algiers, having imprisoned some English people in Algiers and in Tunis, and taken a few thousand piastres from them, the said sum should be taken from his receipts ; and that twenty-four merchant vessels, which had been taken from the English coming from India to Yemen to trade, be restored to the owners, with the property destroyed, and the merchants in them set free.

### RASHID EFFENDI (Imperial Historiographer).

RASHID EFFENDI, Imperial historiographer, a lawyer, continued the annals of the Turkish Empire after Naïma's death.  His work was printed at the Imperial press of Constantinople in 1734 A.D., and, with its continuation by Chelebi Zadé, relates the history of Turkey up to 1141 *Anno Πejiræ.*  Rashid, in chronicaling the events of the year 1133 A.H., gives nearly the whole of a journal written by Mehemet Effendi, describing his voyage from Constantinople to Paris, when sent as Turkish Ambassador to that city, which is very quaint and original.  The Turkish Ambassador was greatly pleased by the gardens and fountains at Versailles, and by Paris, which city, in his opinion, had no equal in the world, excepting Constantinople.  When surprised by some of the beautiful places he saw he consoles himself by the verse of the Koran, which says that "this world is the prison of true believers, but the paradise of the infidels."  The Turkish grandee was greatly amazed at the liberty enjoyed by ladies in France, and the respect shown to them by the men.  "In this country," says he, "the women go where they please and do what they like, live free from all care, and get everything.  In short, France is heaven for women."

## THE EVENTS OF THE YEAR 1093 (Anno Hegiræ).*

*Arrival of a Russian ambassador with presents, and a French ambassador with a letter of apology from the King of France.*

و قایع سنه ثلث و تسعین و الف .

چول¹ عربانی مفسدلریندن² اولوب حوالیء³ حلبده⁴ چوق خباثت⁵
ارتكاب⁶ ایدوب نچه مدت قطع⁷ طریق و. قتل⁸ نفوس⁹ ایله شهرتیاب¹⁰
اولان ملهم نام عرب حالا والیء ایالت¹¹ حلبڭ اولان قره محمد پاشا تدبیریله
كرفتار¹² چنكال¹³ نكال¹⁴ اولوب ركاب¹⁵ همايونه ارسال اولنمغله صفرڭ¹⁶
یكرمی بشنجی كونی باب همايون اوكنده جزاسی¹⁷ ترتیب¹⁸ و مزبورڭ
قتلیله سائر اشقیای¹⁹ عربان ترهیب²⁰ و تادیب²¹ اولندی .

ورود²² الچیء²³ چار²⁴ مسقو .

مسقو چاری طرفندن بیوك الچیسی استانهء²⁵ سعادته واصل²⁶ و رسم²⁷
قدیم²⁸ اوزره اعداد²⁹ اولنان قوناغنه³⁰ نازل³¹ اولوب بالجمله³² ذخائر لازمهسی

(1) *Cheul*, 'a desert;' عرب *arab*, pl. عربان *ourban*, 'Arabs.'—(2) A. *Mufsid*, 'one who causes strife,' 'malefactor.'—(3) A. *Hawali*, 'the environs.'—(4) A. *Haleb*, 'Aleppo.' —(5) A. *Khabaset*, 'villainy.'—(6) A. *Irtikiab etmek*, 'to commit.'—(7) A. *Kat'-i-tarik* means literally 'cutting the road,' *i.e.* stopping travellers and robbing them; hence 'highway robbery.'—(8) A. *Katl*, 'killing.'—(9) *Nufous*, 'persons, individuals, souls.' —(10) P. *Shevretyab*, 'celebrated.'—(11) A. *Eyalet*, 'a province.'—(12) P. *Ghiriftar*, 'scized.'—(13) P. *Chenghal*, or چنكل *chengel*, 'a hook, or fork.'—(14) A. *Nekial*, 'exemplary punishment.'—(15) A. *Rikiab*, 'a stirrup;' *Rikiab-i-humayoun*, 'the imperial stirrup,' *i.e.* 'the capital.'—(16) A. *Safer*, the 2nd month in the Muhammedan year. —(17) A. *Jeza*, 'punishment, retribution.'—(18) A. *Tertib*, 'arranging.'—(19) A. *Eshkiya*, 'rascals.'—(20) A. *Terhib*, 'frightening.'—(21) A. *Tédib*, 'punishing, correcting.'—(22) A. *Vuroud*, 'arrival.'—(23) P. *Elchi*, 'an ambassador.'—(24) *Char*, 'the Czar.'—(25) P. *Asitané*, 'a threshold;' *Asitané-i-saadet*, 'the threshold of felicity,' *i. e.* Constantinople.—(26) A. *Vasil*, 'arriving.'—(27) A. *Resm*, 'a custom, usage, ceremony.'—(28) A. *Kadim*, 'ancient.'—(29) A. *Idad olounmak*, 'to be prepared.'—(30) *Konak*, 'a mansion, a resting-place on a journey,' 'a day's journey,' 'a guest, a lodger, one billeted in a house;' *konak etmek*, 'to halt for the night or for a time.'—(31) A. *Nazil*, 'descending.'—(32) A. *Bil jumlé*, 'all, every one.'

---

* Anno Domini 1682, in the reign of Mahomet IV.

ترتیب اولندی بر قاچکون¹ مکث² و استراحتدن³ صکره شهر ربیع⁴ الاول

یدنجی کونی عاوفه⁵ اخراجیچون⁶ ترتیب دیوان همایون اولنوب یوم

مزبورده الچی مسفور⁷ دخی چهره⁸ سای⁹ در¹⁰ دولتمدار¹¹ اولمغه ماذون¹²

اولدی قانون قدیم اوزره چاوش¹³ باشی اغا دلالتیله¹⁴ رکاب مستطاب¹⁵

شهریاری یه¹⁶ یوز سوروب کندویه و مبعتبر آدملرینه خلعتلر¹⁷ الباس¹⁸ اولندقدن

صکره عرضه¹⁹ کیرن وزرای²⁰ عظام²¹ عقبنده²² پایهء²³ سریر²⁴ اعلیه²⁵ روبمال²⁶

ایدوب نامهسنی تسلیم²⁷ وهدایا²⁸ نامهنه کتوردیکی بیك یوز طقسان سکز

دانه سمور²⁹ و یکرمی دانه بالق دیشی و اون عدد جناح³⁰ سونقوری³¹ عرض³²

و تقدیم³³ ایلدی . . . . .

---

ورود اعتذارنامهء³⁴ قرال³⁵ فرانچه برای³⁶ فتنهء³⁷ ساقز³⁸ .

بالاده³⁹ تحریر⁴⁰ اولندیغی اوزره بوندن اقدم فرانچه قلیوزلریذك ساقز جزیره سنده

ایتدکلری فساد⁴¹ ایچون بو کیفیتدن⁴² اصلا خبریمز اولمیوب و اول مقوله⁴³

---

(1) بر قاچ کون *bir kach ghiun,* 'a few days.'—(2) A. *Meks,* 'staying.'—(3) A. *Isti-rahat,* 'repose, resting.'—(4) A. *Rebbi-ul-evvel,* the name of a Muhammedan month. —(5) A. *Uloufé,* 'pay, salary.'—(6) A. *Ikhraj,* 'causing to come out, drawing out. —(7) A. *Mesfour,* 'above-mentioned.' This word is only used when speaking of anyone for whom one wishes to show contempt.— (8) P. *Chehré,* 'the face.'— (9) *Saï,* 'who rubs.'— (10) P. *Der,* 'in.'—(11) P. *Devlet-médar,* 'the centre, focus, of sovereignty.'—(12) A. *Mé'zoun,* 'permitted.'—(13) *Chaoush,* 'a sergeant in the army, a herald or sergeant-at-arms in ancient times; *Chaoush-bashi* was in olden times even a sort of grand usher, and is now a kind of chief baron in the Court of Chancery.'—(14) A. *Delalet,* 'guidance.'—(15) A. *Mustétab,* 'good, approved.'— (16) P. *Shehriyari,* 'royal.'—(17) A. *Khilat,* 'a dress of honour.'—(18) *Ilbas olounmak,* 'to be dressed.'—(19) A. *Arz,* 'presenting;' *irz,* 'honour.'—(20) A. *Vuzera,* 'Vezirs.'— (21) A. *Izam,* 'great (in the plural.)— (22) *Akbindé,* 'after.'— (23) P. *Payé,* 'foot.'—(24) A. *Serir,* 'a throne.'—(25) *Ala,* 'very high.'—(26) P. *Rouï-mal,* 'who rubs his face.'—(27) A. *Teslim,* 'delivering.'—(28) A. *Hédaya,* 'presents.'— (29) A. *Semmour (Samour),* 'the sable.'— (30) A. *Jenah,* 'a wing.'— (31) *Sonkour,* 'a gerfalcon.'—(32) A. *Arz,* 'offering.'— (33) A. *Takdim,* 'presenting.'—(34) A. *Iti zar,* 'apologizing;' *Itizar-namé,* 'a letter of apology.'— (35) *Kral,* 'a king.'— (36) P. *Beraï,* 'for.'— (37) A. *Fitné,* 'disorder, riot, conspiracy, sedition.'— (38) *Sakiz,* the island of Scio.—(39) P. *Baladé,* 'above.'—(40) A. *Tahrir olounmak,* 'to be written.'— (41) A. *Fesad,* 'disorder,' 'wrong practice, villainy, sedition.'— (42) A. *Kéifiyet,* 'matter.'—(43) A. *Makoulé,* 'kind.'

خلاف<sup>1</sup> صلح<sup>2</sup> و صلاح<sup>3</sup> حرکت<sup>4</sup> شنیعه<sup>5</sup> لرینه طرفمزدن بر و جهله رضا<sup>6</sup>
و جواز<sup>7</sup> کوسترلدیکی یوغیکن جسارت<sup>8</sup> ایلدکلری ضرر<sup>9</sup> و خسارت<sup>10</sup>
مقابلهـسنده<sup>11</sup> سفائن<sup>12</sup> مزبوره قپودنلری کما ینبغی<sup>13</sup> تأدیب<sup>14</sup> و جزای
مایلیقاری<sup>15</sup> ترتیب<sup>16</sup> اولندی دیو اعتذاری مشعر<sup>17</sup> فرانچه قرالی طرفندن
نامه ایله طقسان کیسهلك قدر جوهر<sup>18</sup> و اوتوز کیسهلك مقداری سائر
تحف<sup>19</sup> و زواهرکه جمعا التمش بیك غروشلق هدیه<sup>20</sup> اتحاف<sup>21</sup> و کندو
جرم<sup>22</sup> و قصورلرینه<sup>23</sup> اعتراف<sup>24</sup> اولنهغله ماه جمادی الاولینك یکرمنجی کونی
فرانچه الچیسنك کتخداسی ترجمانیله<sup>25</sup> یالی<sup>26</sup> کوشکنده<sup>27</sup> رکاب همایونه حمره
سای مثول<sup>28</sup> و عرض هدایای مرقوم ایله نیازمند<sup>29</sup> قبول اولدقده صدر<sup>30</sup>
اعظم حضرتلری شفاعت<sup>31</sup> و رجاسیله<sup>32</sup> نوعا<sup>33</sup> مساعدهء<sup>34</sup> خسروانی ارزانی<sup>35</sup>
بیورلدی .

(1) A. *Khilaf*, 'contrary to.'— (2) *Sulh*, 'peace.'— (3) A. *Salah*, 'harmony.'—
(4) A. *Herekiat*, 'acts, behaviour.'—(5) A. *Shenié*, 'odious.'—(6) A. *Riza*, 'consent.'
—(7) A. *Jevaz*, 'permission.'—(8) A. *Jesaret*, 'boldness.'—(9) A. *Zarar*, 'damage.'
—(10) A. *Khasaret*, 'injury.'—(11) *Mukabelesindé*, 'in return for.'—(12) A. *Sefaîn*,
'vessels.'—(13) A. *Kema yambaghi*, 'as is fit.'—(14) A. *Té'dib*, 'correcting.'—(15) *Ma
yelik*, 'as is suitable.'—(16) *Tertib olounmak*, 'to be arranged.'—(17) A. *Mushiı*
'indicative of.'—(18) *Jevher*, 'a jewel, precious stone.'—(19) A. *Tuhéf*, 'elegant
things fit for presents.'—(20) A. *Hédiyé*, 'a present.'—(21) A. *Ithaf*, 'presenting.'
—(22) A. *Jurm*, 'a fault, culpability.'—(23) *Kousour*, 'defect, fault.'—(24) A. *Itiraf*,
'admitting.'—(25) A. *Terjuman*, 'an interpreter' (from which the word 'dragoman' has been corrupted).—(26) *Yali*, 'the sea-shore.'—(27) *Kieushk*, 'a pavilion,
or summer residence.'—(28) A. *Musoul*, 'standing respectfully waiting for orders.'
—(29) P. *Niyazmend*, 'a petitioner.'—(30) P. *Sadr-i-azam*, 'the prime minister.'—
(31) A. *Shifaet (shefaet)*, 'intercession.'—(32) A. *Rija*, 'request.'—(33) A. *Nevan*,
'in some manner; somewhat.'—(34) A. *Musaadé*, 'allowing.'—(35) *Erzani*, 'deeming fit.'

## Translation.

### The events of the year 1093 Anno Hejiræ.

An Arab, one of the malefactors of the Arabian desert, called
Melhem, who had committed many acts of villainy in the neighbourhood of Aleppo, and had been notorious for a long time for highway
robbery and murder, having fallen into the hands of the law, by

the management of Kara Mehemet Pasha, at present Governor-General of Aleppo, having been sent to the capital, was executed on the 25th of Safer, in front of the *Bab-i-Humayoun*,* as a warning and a lesson to other Arab rascals.

### *Arrival of the Ambassador of the Czar of Moscow.*

An Ambassador Extraordinary from the Czar of Moscow having arrived in Constantinople, according to an ancient custom, alighted at a mansion which had been got ready for him, and all the necessary provisions were provided for him. After he had rested himself for a few days, an Imperial Divan being held on the 7th of Rebi-ul-evvel, for drawing pay, the said ambassador was allowed to prostrate himself in the Imperial presence. According to an old law he was admitted to the Imperial levée under the guidance of the Grand Usher, and he and his principal followers having received dresses of honour, were admitted, coming after the great Vezirs, to the presence. He rubbed his face at the foot of the throne, delivered his letter and his presents, consisting of eleven hundred and ninety-eight sables, twenty *fishes' teeth* and ten gerfalcons.

### *Arrival of a Letter of Apology from the King of France respecting the disorders in Scio.*

On the 20th of the month Jumadi-ul-Evvel, the *Kiaya* of the French Ambassador, with his dragoman, presented a letter of apology from the King of France for what the French men-of-war had done, as we previously mentioned, in the island of Scio, saying that it was entirely without his knowledge, and that he had in no

---

* The principal entrance to the old imperial residence, near the mosque of St. Sophia. It would appear, from the above, that in old times, at any rate, the Turks took care to put down robbery and murder, whether committed by Mussulmans or Christians, by exemplary punishment.

way consented to or permitted such shameful acts, incompatible with peace and goodwill, and that, as compensation for the damage which they had been bold enough to commit, the captains of the said ships would be properly punished. He also brought ninety purses of jewels, and thirty purses of other presents and ornaments, which altogether amounted to sixty thousand piastres worth of gifts, acknowledging that the French had been in the wrong, and, coming to the Imperial levée at an Imperial sea-side kiosk, begged their acceptance, which, at the request of the Prime Vezir, and by his intercession, was graciously acceded to.

## EXTRACT FROM THE JOURNAL OF MEHEMET EFFENDI,
### TURKISH AMBASSADOR TO FRANCE IN 1720 ANNO DOMINI.

جمادى[1] الاولك طقوزنجى سبت[2] كونى پاريس شهرى كنارنده احضار[3]
اولنان سرايه[4] نزول ميسر[5] اولدى . سراى مزبورده بر هفته مكث اولندى
كيجهده و كوندوزده خلقك كثرتى و رجال و نسوانك وفرتى[6] بر وجهله
قابل تعبير دكل ايدى . دوكون اولرنده بو مرتبه زحام[7] اولديغى كورلمامشدر .
ايكنجى كونده بونلرده بر منصب واركه صاحبنه انتور دوقتور ديرلر ايلچيلره
مخصوص خوش كلديكز ديمكه و الايه بندرمكه و قراله كتورمكه متعيين[8]
ايمش اول كمسه كلوب قرال جانبندن تهنيه[9] قدوم[10] ايلدى و ايكى كوندن
صكره ينه كلوب قرالمز بازار كونى وقت ظهرده[11] سزى شهره دعوت ايدر
مخصوص خانه احضار اولنمشدر و مزين عسكر ايله الايكزه و سلامكزه دورمق
ابچون تر تيب ايتمشلردر سزى كتورمكه باش مرشال تعيين[12] اولنمشيدى
لكن قرال تربيه سيله مشغول و كندوسى اختيار و عليل[13] اولوب اته بنمكه
قدرتى اولمديغندن او چنجى مرشال دتره تعيين اولندى انشا الله تعالى
بازار كونى نصف نهاردن مقدم قرالك هنطويله سزى الايه بندر مكه كلور .
و كندو ايله رفاقات ايدر سزدر ديدى و ايرتسى مسفورك بر رفيقى كه بو خصوصه
ناظر ايمش كلوب الايكز تر تيبنى دفتر ايتمكه كلدم سوار اوله جق قاچ ادمكز
وار در قرال اخورندن[14] مكمل آتلر كتوره لم ديدكده وجه مناسبتله دفتر
اولنوب ويرلدى بعده قرال سر اخورندن[15] موسى قونيار كلوب هر كسه توزيع[16]

---

(1) *Jemaziyyul 'l-evvel,* the fifth Muhammedan month.—(2) A. *Sebt,* 'Saturday.'—
(3) *Ihzar oloumak,* ' to be prepared, to be produced.'—(4) P. *Sérai,* 'a palace, mansion.'—(5) A. *Muyesser,* 'facilitated,' 'permitted by God.'—(6) A. *Wefret,* 'abundance, a great number, or quantity.'—(7) A. *Ziham,* 'a crowd, crowding.'—(8) A.
*Muta'ayyen,* 'appointed, deputed, distinguished.'—(9) A. *Tehniyyé etmek,* ' to congratulate.'— (10) A. *Koudoum,* 'arrival, approach.'—(11) A. *Zouhr,* 'noon.'—
(12) *Tayin etmek,* ' to appoint, fix.'—(13) A. *Alil,* ' weak, sick.'—(14) P. *Akhir,* 'a
stable.'—(15) *Ser akhor,* ' head of the stable.'—(16) *Tevzi etmek,* ' to distribute.'

ایلدی بعده مرشال دترﮦ انتورﮦ دوقتور ایله قرال هنطورینه سوار اولمشلر کلدیلر .

بز-استقبال ¹ ایله رعایت ² ایلدك قرالمز کندو هنطونی سزك ایچون

کوندردیلر و جمله کبار ³ دولتمز کندو هنطورلرینی ⁴ سزﮦ اکراماً ⁵ ارسال

ایتمشلر دیو یوز قدر مزین ⁶ و رعنا ⁷ هنطور کلدیلر بعده وقتدر اذنکر ایله

الای یوریتمکه باشلادﮦلم دیوب قالقدیلر مقدماً ⁸ قرالك کندوبه مخصوص

عسکرندن بر رکمند یوریدوب اردمجه ⁹ بزم ادملری سوار ایدوب بر مقدارینه

کورکلر ¹⁰ کیدروب اللرینه تفنـکلر ویرمشیدك و بر مقدارینه کراکه ¹¹

کیدیروب اللرینه مزراقلر ¹² ویرمشیدك انلر یوریدوب اردلرنجه اغوات ¹³

مقولهسی ¹⁴ صقاللو ¹⁵ اولنلر یوریبیوب بعده امام ¹⁶ افندی و قپوجیلر ¹⁷ کتخداسی و

بعدهما اوغلنمز ایله کتخدامز همعنان ¹⁸ اولوب عقبلرنجه التی عدد یدك ¹⁹ اغر

کسمهلر ایله مزین و مسرج ²⁰ چکدیریلوب تمامنده قرالك سر اخوریله ترجماں

کیدوب کندیمز دیوان بساطی و عبا ایله مسرج اسبه سوار اولوب یمینمزده

مرشال و یساریمزده انتورﮦ دوقتور ایله عزیمت اولندی . و عقبمزده ²¹ دخی بر

رکمند اتلو دیزیلوب بعدهم هنطور علی مراتبهم ²² دیزلدیلر . ²³

پارس شهرینك زوقاقلری ²⁴ غایت و سعتلیدر یان یانه بش التی عربه

کتمك ممکن ایکن بعض محلرده زحام ²⁵ ناسدن اوچ سوار کوچﮦ مرور ایدرك

کویا شهرده اولان جمله خلق الای سیرینه ²⁶ کلمشلر ایدی و خانهلری دوردر

(1) A. *Istikbal*, 'going to meet anyone.'—(2) *Riayet etmek*, 'to show respect.'—
(3) A. *Kibar*, 'grandees' (used as a Turkish singular sometimes for a grandee).—
(4) *Hinto*, 'a carriage' (from the Hungarian).—(5) A. *Ikraman*, 'as an honour
to you, in your honour.'—(6) A. *Muzéyyen*, 'adorned, decorated.'—(7) P. *Rana*,
'beautiful.'—(8) *Mukaddeman*, 'in front,' 'formerly.'—(9) *Ardinjé*, 'behind.'—
(10) *Kiurk*, 'a fur.'—(11) *Keréké*, a silk mantle, part of a dress of honour, formerly
worn on grand occasions.—(12) *Mizrak*, 'a spear.'—(13) *Aghevat*, 'Aghas,' 'lords,
masters, chiefs.'—(14) A. *Makoulé*, 'a category, kind.'—(15) *Sakalli*, 'bearded.'—
(16) A. *Imam*, 'a leader, one who leads to prayers, a chief a priest.'—(17) *Kapou-
jilar kiayasi*, 'chief chamberlain.'—(18) *Inan* (A.), 'the reins of a horse; *heminan*,
(P.), 'abreast.'—(19) *Yédek*, 'a led horse.'—(20) A. *Muserrej*, 'saddled.'—(21) *Akbi-
mizde*, 'behind us.'—(22) A. *Ala meratibhim*, 'according to their rank;' *Meratib*
(pl. of مرتبه *mertebé*), 'degree, rank.'—(23) *Dizmek*, 'to range, draw up in a line.'—
(24) A. *Zokak*, 'a street.'—(25) A. *Ziham*, 'a multitude, a crowd.'—(26) A. *Seïr*,
'looking at, a spectacle, a sight.'

بشر قات<sup>1</sup> اولوب پنجرەلری زوقاقە ناظر در هر پنجرەسی كنجایش<sup>2</sup> پذیر اولەجق رتبەدن افزون<sup>3</sup> مرد<sup>4</sup> و زندن<sup>5</sup> متـزاحم<sup>6</sup> اولمشلر ایدی بو ترتیب ایلە احضار اولنان خانەیە نزول اولنوب سلامە دوران عسكرى دخی علی الترتیب خانەمز اوكندن كذار<sup>7</sup> ایدوب تمامندە مرشال دخي بزی وداع<sup>8</sup> ایدوب خانەسنە كتدى ٠

ينه رجال و نسا كيمى زيارت كيمى سير طريقيلە تزاحم اوزرە كلوب خصوصا طعام ايدو كمزى كورمكە زيادە طالب اولورلر ايدى فلان كمسنە نك قزى و فلان كمسنەنك قاريسى طعام ايدوكيكزە باقمغە اندنـكـز رجا ايدرلر ديو خبرلر كلوب كيمنى دفع ايدە ميوب ناچار رخصت ويررك پرهيزلرى<sup>9</sup> و قتنە مصادف اولمغين كندورلرى اكل ايتميوب سفرەيى احاطە ايدوب سير ايدرلر ايدى خاطر ایچون صبر ايدردك اذلر ايسە سير طعامە مألوف<sup>10</sup> اولمشلر فرضا قرالك طعام ايدوكنى سير اتمك استین واروب سير اتمكە رحصتياب اولور عادتلرى ایمش ٠ دخی غريب بوكە قرال فراشندن<sup>11</sup> نصل قالقار و نصل كينور سير اتمكە كيدرار ایمش بناء على ذالك بزە دخی بو كونە تكليفلر ایلە ثقلت<sup>12</sup> ایدرلر ایدى ٠

ایكی كوندنصكرە ينە انتورە دوقتور كلوب جمعە كونى قرال سزى دعوت ايدران شاءاللە كيدرسرز و سزە اكراما پرنجس لا نبسكی تعيين ایتمشلر معا كدرز و كالاول<sup>13</sup> همعنان كيدرز و بو انە دك كلن ايلچيلرە مرشال و پرنجس تعيين اولنديغى يوقدر ٠ و اولكيدن زيادە الای ترتيب اولمشدر ٠ و نامـﺌ همايونى تسليم ايتدكدە جوابكزى<sup>14</sup> لالا ویرە جکدر و قرالمز آياب<sup>15</sup> و ذهابكزدە قائم بولنەحقدر ٠ سز دخی دوستلغە لایق معاملە نە ایسه اوبلە ایدرسز دیدی

---

(1) *Kat*, 'a floor.'—(2) P. *Ghiunjayish-pézir*, 'measured.'—(3) P. *Efzoun*, 'more.'
—(4) P. *Merd*, 'a man.'—(5) P. *Zen*, 'a woman.'—(6) A. *Mutézahim*, 'crowding,
crowded, flocking.'—(7) *Ghiuzar etmek*, 'to pass.'—(8) *Veda etmek*, ' to say farewell, good-bye.'—(9) A. *Perhiz*, 'a Christian fast.'—(10) A. *Mé'louf*, 'habituated,
habitual.'— (11) A. *Firash*, 'a bed.'— (12) *Siklet vermek*, 'to worry, annoy.'—
(13) As before.—(14) *Lala*, 'a man who has charge of a child, a guardian.'—
(15) A. *Iyab*, ' coming back ;' *Zihab-ou-iyab*, 'a coming and going.'

و كتدى . جمعه كونى اولدقده مزبورلر كلديلر خلقمزى ترتيب ايدوب
انجق قليچلر قوشاتميوب و تفنك و مزراقلر ويرمدك و اوغلمز ديوان
افندیسی[1] مقامنده ايلمغله نامهٔ همايون شوكتمقرونى الله ويروب انك
ايچون بر مرصع لجاملو قصراق كتور مشلر ايدى اكا سوار و اوكمزه الوب كنديمز
دخى كاتبى دستار[2] و فراجه[3] و سمور كورك ايله ديوان رخت[4] و بساطيله
ايرلنمش كندى اسبمز سوار اولوب پرنجس لابنسك يمينمزده و انتوره دوقتو
يسارىمزده عزيمت ايلدك . قرال عسكرينى بزه سير ايتدرمك ايچون بعض
اطرافده قشلاقده اولان پياده و سوار ركمنداری كتوردوب و اكثرينه مجدد
لباسلر قطع ايتمشلر و جمعا اوتوز بيكدن متجاوز عسكر ترتيب ايدوب
اولديغمز خانهدن قرال سراينهدك ديزلمشلر ايدى .

قرال سراينه باغچه طرفندن واريلوب باغچه ايچنده ديزيلن ركمندك
بربنه اق اتلو و بربنه سياه اتلو ديرلر ايمش بو ايكى ركمند جمله عسكرك
زياده معتبرى ايمش و بونلرك نفراتى جمله كبار زاده و بكزادلردر سراى
قپوسنك نردبانى ديبنده يانشوب اتدن اينوب قپودن ايچرو كيردكده
تنفس ايتمك ايچون صاغ طرفده بر اوطهيه كتورديلر قرال كتخداسنك
اوطهسى ايمش برمقدار استراحتدن صكره قالوب يوقارى نردبانه عزم ايتدك
هر مقامه واردلردقده رجال دولتدن برر كمسنه استقبال ايدهرك ديوانخانه
قپوسنه واردق خلقك كثرتى بر مرتبهده ايديكه استقباله كلنلر اطرافمزى
احاطه ايدوب كوجله كذار ايدردك . ديوانخانه قپوسندن دخى اون ايكى
ادم ايله كذار ايلدك . قرالك تختى قربنه وارنجه ايكى طرفده دوكون اوزنده
وضع اولنان سريرلر كبى بر قاچ يوز سرير بربرندن يوكسك وضع و ترتيب
ايتمشلر . بونلرده نقدر كبار قارياری و قرالك خصملری[5] وار ايسه جمع اولوب
مجوهر[6] و مشعشع[7] لباسلر ايله اوتورمشلر . بز دخول ايتدكده جمله سى

---

(1) *Diwan-efendisi*, 'an official secretary.'—(2) P. *Déstar*, 'the cloth which
forms a turban, a turban.'—(3) A. *Ferajé*, 'a cloak worn by women, formerly a
cloak worn by the doctors of the law.'—(4) P. *Rakht*, 'dress, effects.'—(5) P. *Khism*,
'a relative.'—(6) A. *Mujevver*, 'jewelled.'—(7) A. *Mushashi*, 'glittering, flashing.'

قيام ايتديلر قريب اولديغمزده قرال دخى قيام ايلدى . نامهء همايون
شوكت مقرونى اوكمزه المشيدق اليمزى كوكسمزه قيوب كويا نامهء
همايونه سلام وبرر وضعنى<sup>1</sup> كوستردك . قرال يانه واردقده تمنا صورتده
اليمزى باشمزه قريوب بعده نامهء همايونى آلوب شوكتلو عظمتلو و قدرتلو
پادشاه اسلام ولى نعمتم افندم سلطان احمد خان ابن سلطان محمد خان
حضرتلرينك نامهء همايون شوكتمقرونلريدر ديدك . قرال طفل اولمغله
تعظيم ايله وزيرى اليمزدن الوب .قرال ياننده وضع اولنان صرمهلى<sup>2</sup> سفره
ايله پوشيده<sup>3</sup> اسكمله<sup>4</sup> اوزره وضع ايلدى . بعده صاحب دولت حضرتلرينك
نامهسنى آلوب بو دخى دولتلو سعادتلو وزير اعظم و داماد<sup>5</sup> محترم ابراهم
پاشا حضرتلرينك نامهء عاليسيدر ديدكده ينه وزير اليمزدن الوب نامه
همايون تختنه وضع ايلدى . بو ايكى دولت بيننده مرعى<sup>6</sup> اولان قوى
دوستلغى تأكيد ايچون و حشمتلو فراچه پادشاهى حضرتلرينه اولان محبت
و مودت واعتبار و رغبتلرينى عيان و بيان ايتمكيچون ايلچيلك ايله بنى
ارسال ايلديلر ديدم . قرال اون برياشنى تمام ايدوب اون ايكى ياشنه باصمش
غايت حسن و جمال صاحبى اولوب الماسرله مستغرق زربن لباسار ايله
مجلسه شعشعه انداز اولمشيدى . كندى جوابه تصدى<sup>7</sup> ايتميوب لالاسى
اولان مرشال شوكتلو بقدرتلو آل عثمان پادشاهى حضرتلرينك نامهلرندن و
ايلچييلكه جذابلرينك انتخاب اولندقلرندن قرال حضرتلرى زياده محظوظ
اولمشلردر ديو جواب ويردى و جمله يمين و يسارنده قائم دوررلر ايدى .
بعده اليمز باشمزه قريوب وبر قاچ خطوه<sup>8</sup> دنصكوه اليمز كوكسمزه قريوب وداع
ايلدك

---

(1) A. *Vaz*, 'attitude, pose, gesture.'— (2) *Sirma*, 'gold lace, gold embroidery.'—
(3) *Poushidé*, 'covered, hidden.'—(4) *Eskimlé*, 'a stool.'—(5) P. *Damad*, 'a son-in-law, or brother-in-law (of the Sultan).'—(6) A. *Meri*, 'observed, in force.'—
(7) A. *Tésaddi*, 'setting about.'—(8) A. *Khatvé*, 'a stop, a pace.'

On Saturday, the 9th of the month *Jemaziyyu'l-Evvel*, we alighted at a palace which had been prepared in the environs of the city of Paris, where we stayed a week. Day and night the multitudes of people, and the number of men and women, cannot be described. There was more crowding than at houses where there is even a marriage feast. On the second day a person came from the king to congratulate us on our arrival, called "Antoré Doctor," who holds an office here, which consists in welcoming Ambassadors and arranging processions, and bringing them to the king. After two days he came again, and said: "Our king invites you to come to the city next Sunday, at noon; and a mansion has been especially prepared for you. Troops in full dress have been prepared to attend you and salute you. The 'Chief Marshal' had been appointed to bring you; but as he is occupied with the education of the king, and is himself aged and infirm, and not able to mount a horse, the third Marshal (Detre), has been appointed. Please God, he will come next Tuesday before midday to take you in the king's carriage, and you will accompany him." The next day came a colleague of his, who had to look after this matter, and said: "I have come to arrange the programme of your procession; tell me how many people there are of yours to mount, and I will bring good horses from the king's stable;" whereupon a list was made and given to him. Afterwards, Monsieur Konyar, one of the king's equerries, distributed them to each person. Subsequently, Marshal "Detre," with "Antoré Doctor," came in the king's carriage; and we showed them respect by going to meet them. They stated that the king had sent his own carriage for me, and that all the grandees of the State had sent their own carriages in our honour, and as many as a hundred beautiful, ornamental carriages came. Then they rose and said: "It is time, with your permission, let us proceed." In front marched a regiment of the king's guards, behind them rode our men, part of whom I dressed in furs, and put muskets in their hands, and part of whom I dressed in silk mantles and put spears in their hands; behind them marched bearded "Aghas;" and then our priest (*Imam*) and the Steward of the Chamberlains.  Behind them rode our son and our steward, side by side.  Then followed six led horses, richly caparisoned and saddled.  After them came the king's equerry and the interpreter.  I mounted a horse saddled with court trappings, and, with the Marshal on my right, and Antoré Doctor on my left, we started.  Behind us came a regiment of cavalry followed by the carriages in the order of their rank.

The streets of Paris are extremely spacious.  Although it is possible for five or six carriages to drive abreast, in some places, owing to the throngs of people, three horsemen passed abreast with difficulty.  It seemed as if all the people in the city had come to see the procession.  The houses have four of five stories, and the windows look on to the streets.  Every window was crowded with an innumerable lot of men and women.  Thus arranged, we alighted at the mansion prepared for us.  The troops saluted, and passed before our house, and then the Marshal took leave and went home.

Again the men and women came in crowds, some to look at us, some to visit us.  They were especially desirous to see us eat.  One said : " My daughter, and another my wife, desires, with your permission, to look at you eating."  As we could not drive some of them away, we gave our permission *nolens volens*.  As this time happened to coincide with a Christian fast, they did not eat themselves, but surrounded the table and looked on.  Out of politeness to them, we had patience.  As for them, they were accustomed to look on while people ate, for anyone wishing to see the king eat was allowed to come and look on.  It is also a strange thing that they go and see how the king gets up out of bed, and how he dresses.  Hence it was that they bothered us with this kind of thing.

After a couple of days, " Antoré Doctor " came again, and said : " The king invites you on Friday.  Please God, you will go ; and he has appointed Prince " Lanheski " to do you honour.  We will come together ; and, as before, we will ride side by side.  Hitherto no Marshal or Prince has ever been appointed for Ambassadors who have come ; and a grander procession has been arranged than before.  When you have delivered the Sultan's letter, the Regent (guardian) will answer you ; and the king will rise on your coming and going.  You will behave as friendship requires."  So saying, he left.

When Friday came, the above persons arrived. I arranged my people as before, only I did not arm them with swords, or spears, or muskets. I put the Sultan's Imperial letter into my son's hand (as he was in the stead of an official secretary), for whom they had brought a mare, whose bridle and reins were ornamented with precious stones, which he mounted and went before me. I, in the sable furs and cloak, and turban of a *Kiatib*, mounted my own horse, saddled with court trappings, and had Prince Labinski on my right and Antoré Doctor on my left; and we started.

The king, in order to let us see his troops, caused some regiments of infantry and cavalry, from barracks in the neighbourhood, to be brought, and dressed most of them in new uniforms. Altogether there were upwards of thirty thousand troops, who were ranged from the mansion we were in as far as the king's palace.

We entered the king's palace from the side of the garden. Of the regiments ranged in the garden, one is called the White Horse-Guards, and the other the Black Horse-Guards. These two regiments are most esteemed of any in the whole army; and all the privates in them are the sons of great men and gentlemen. On coming to the bottom of the steps at the palace gate, we alighted and entered through the gate, and were conducted to a room on the right, to rest ourselves, which was the apartment of the king's steward. After a little rest we arose, and began to ascend the staircase. At every landing-place one of the grandees of the State met us, and on arriving at the door of the Court Room there were such a number of people that those who came to receive us surrounded us completely, and we could scarcely pass. We also passed through the door of the Court Room with twelve men. We arrived near the king's throne. On each side some hundred seats had been arranged one above another, like the seats at a marriage feast. On these sat the wives of the grandees, and the relatives of the king, in splendid apparel, covered with jewels. On our entering they all rose. On our coming near the king he also rose. I had taken the Sultan's Imperial letter in front of me. I put my hand on my breast,*

---

* One most respectful way of saluting in Turkey is to place one's hands on one's breast, and bow.

and assumed an attitude as if I were saluting the Imperial letter. On coming close to the king I raised my hand to my head to salute him. Then taking the Imperial epistle, I said : "This is the letter of His Majesty, the potent, great and mighty Emperor of the Moslems, my benefactor, Sultan Ahmed Khan, son of Sultan Mahomet Khan." The king being a minor, his Vezir took it out of my hand respectfully, and placed it on a stool concealed by a table covered with gold lace, at the king's side. Afterwards, I took the letter of our Prime Minister, and said : "This is the letter of His Excellency the most illustrious Grand Vezir, the respected brother-in-law of the Sultan." Whereupon the Minister again took it from my hand, and placed it on the stool with the Imperial letter; and I said : " I have been sent as an Ambassador, to cement the firm friendship which exists between these two countries, and to explain the love, friendship, and respect we have for His Majesty the King of France." The king, who was about twelve years of age, and very handsome, sat glittering amidst the company, in gold apparal covered with diamonds. He did not answer himself, but, the Marshal, his guardian, replied: " His Majesty the King is much pleased by the letter from His Majesty the potent, mighty Emperor of the Ottomans, and that he selected you as his Ambassador ;" and everybody right and left of him rose. Then I placed my hand to my head, and, after retiring a few steps, put my hand on my breast and took my leave.

## MIRÉ·T-I-KAÏNAT.*

### (A MUHAMMEDAN LIFE OF CHRIST.)

باب ثانى و ثلاثون در احوال عیسی نبى علیه السلام
ولادت عیسی .

تفاسیرده ¹ مذکور در که مریم ² حیض ³ کوردکجه دیزه ⁴ سی و زکریانك
خاتونی ایشاع یاننده کیدوب پاك اولدقده مسجده ⁵ کلوب دائما عبادته ⁶
چالشوردی پس بر کون دیزه‌سی اونده غسل ⁷ ایدرکن جبرائیل علیه
السلام تازه کوزل یکت صورتنده کورینوب مریم انی بیلمیوب سندن الله
صغنورم ⁸ دیوب جبرائیل کندوی بلدیروب قرانده حکایت اولندیغی
اوزره سویلشوب بعده مریمك قفتانی ⁹ یقاسنه ¹⁰ یا یكی ¹¹ ایچنه و یا
اغزینه یقیندن یا ایراقدن ¹² اوفوروب ¹³ قدرت حقله فی الحال حامل ¹⁴ اولوب
ابن عباس قولنجه ¹⁵ بر انده سائرلر قولنجه اوچ ساعتده یابدی ¹⁶ یا سکز
یا التی یا طقوز ایدنصکره مریم اون اوچ یا اون التی یا یکرمی یاشنده ایکن
عیسی علیه السلام وجوده کلدی .

(1) A. *Tefasir,* 'commentaries, especially of the Koran.'—(2) A. *Meryem,* 'Mary, the Virgin Mary.'—(3) A. *Haïz,* '*menstruus sanguis.*'—(4) *Teyzé,* also written زیزه, 'a maternal aunt, mother's sister.'—(5) A. *Mesjid,* 'a place of worship,' 'a small parish or private mosque. Our word mosque is derived from this word.—(6) A. *Ibadet,* 'worship, adoration.'—(7) A. *Ghousl etmek,* 'to wash the whole body.'—(8) *Siyhinmak,* 'to take refuge, to take shelter.'—(9) *Kaftan,* 'a kind of robe worn in former times.'—(10) *Yaka,* 'a collar.'—(11) *Yeng,* 'a cuff, lower part of a sleeve.' —(12) *Irak,* 'distant.'—(13) *Ufurmek,* 'to blow on, or in.'—(14) A. *Hamil olmak,* 'to become *enceinte.*'—(15) A. *Kavl,* 'an assertion, statement.'—(16) *Yaïmak,* 'to spread, extend.'

* The *Mirror of the Universe* is the title of a kind of universal history, in Turkish, printed at Constantinople in 1269 *Anno Hejiræ.* Most Europeans will be greatly astonished to see, from the above extract from this work, that Muhammedans not only admit that Christ was a great prophet, but believe that he was miraculously begotten, and performed miracles.

مرويدر' كه اثر² حملى³ طويدقده⁴ قدسدن⁵ چيقوب بر قاچ ميل
يرده قريهٴ⁶ بيت اللحمه واروب علايم⁷ ظهور⁸ ولد⁹ اشكار¹⁰ اولدقده
استناد¹¹ و استتار¹² ايچون بر قوريمش درخب خرمايه¹³ التجا¹⁴ و انكيا¹⁵
ايدوب عيسى طوغدقده جبرائيل عليه السلام اياغنى يره اوروب بر طلتلو
صو آقوب¹⁶ خرما اغاجى فى الحال بوداقلنوب¹⁷ خرما بتوروب حضرت
مريم خلقك طعن¹⁸ و تشنيع¹⁹ احتماليله پر²⁰ غم²¹ اولوب ("يا²² ليتنى
مت قبل هذا و كنت نسيا منسيا") ديدكـده جبرائيل ياخود
عيسى عليه السلام قرآنده بيورلديغى اوزره تسليت²³ ايدوب بعده مريم
عيسايى كوتوروب شهره كلدكده مريمك قومى باباسز اوغلانمى طوغر نه
عجب ايش ايلدك ديو لوم²⁴ و انكار²⁵ ايتدكلرنده زمان معينهدك²⁶ سوز
سوبلماهمّه نذر²⁷ ايتدم اوغلانجغه سويليك ديو اشارت ايدوب انلردخى
بشكدهكى اوغلانه نيچه سويليهلم ديو غضبه كلدكده عيسى عليه السلام
قرق كونلك اولوب ممه²⁸ امركن²⁹ براغوب ("انى³⁰ عبد الله آتانى الكتاب و
جعلنى نبيا و جعلنى مباركا اينما كنت و اوصانى بالصلاة و الزكوة ما
دمت حيا و برا بوالدتى") ديو سويليوب بعده³¹ عادتجه بيوينجه³² ارتق³³

<hr/>

(1) A. *Mervi*, 'narrated, handed down.'—(2) A. *Esr*, 'a trace, sign.'—(3) A. *Haml*,
pregnancy, or the fœtus.'—(4) Generally written دويمو *douïmak*, 'to feel' (*v.a.*); ' to
hear, learn;' pronounced *doïmak*, it means 'to be satisfied, satiated.'— (5) *Kouds*,
'Jerusalem.'—(6) A. *Kariyé*, 'a village.'—(7) A. *Alaïm*, 'signs.'—(8) A. *Zuhour*,
' appearance.'—(9) *Veled*, 'a child.'—(10) P. *Ashikiar*, 'evident.'—(11) A. *Istinad*,
'leaning on.'— (12) A. *Istitar*, ' seeking shelter.'— (13) A. *Khourma*, 'a date.'—
(14) *Iltija*, 'taking refuge, shelter.'—(15) *Ittikia etmek*, 'to recline, lean on, or
against.'—(16) *Akmak*, 'to flow.'— (17) *Boudaklamak*, 'to put forth branches.'—
(18) A. *Tan*, 'reproaching, speaking ill of.'—(19) A. *Teshni*, 'defaming, slandering,
reproaching.'—(20) P. *Pur*, 'full of.'—(21) A. *Gham*, 'grief, regret.'— (22) Arabic
words meaning : 'Would that I had died before this, and been forgotten !'—
(23) *Tesliyet etmek*, 'to console.'—(24) *Levm etmek*, 'to blame, reprimand.'—(25) *In-
kiar etmek*, 'to deny.'—(26) A. *Muayen*, 'appointed.'—(27) *Nezr etmek*, 'to make a
vow.'—(28) *Memé*, 'a nipple, a teat, udder.'—(29) *Emmek*, 'to suck.'—(30) Words in
Arabic, meaning : ' I am the servant of God. God gave me the Book, and made
me blessed wherever I may be, and commanded me to pray and be pious all my life,
and made my mother pure.'—(31) A. *Badéhou*, 'then,' 'afterwards.'—(32) *Buyumek*,
'to grow, get bigger, grow up.'—(33) *Artik*, *adv.* (with a negative) 'no more, never
again ;' (with an affirmative) 'now, at last ;' *adj.*, 'over and remaining.'

سویلمدی . بنی اسرائیل بو علامت پر كرامتی كوردكلرنده عیساننك
پیغمبر[1] اولهجغنی بیلوب مریمه سوء ظنلری دفع اولدی . . . . . . .

كشانده مذكور در كه یوسف مریمله عیسایی بر مغاره‌یه[2] ایلتوب[3]
یولده قتل ایتمك فكر ایتدكده جبرائیل كلوب عیسی زدن[4] دكل
روح[5] القدسدندر مریمی قتل ایتمه دیمكین فراغت ایدوب قرق كونه
دك مغاره‌ده طوروب مدت نفاس[6] كچدكده شهره كیدوب یولده عیسی
ای والده مژده[7] سكا كه بن الله تعالینك عبدی و مسیحی[8] یم دیو شهره
كیردكلرنده اقربا[9] و احبابری[10] جمله صلحا[11] اولمغین یا مریم بزی بدنام
و پر غم و الم[12] ایتدك دیو اغلاشوب[13] بعضلر قولنجه رجم[14] ایتمك
استیوب حضرت عیسی بونلره سویلدكده فراغت[15] ایتدیلر .


ارهاصات[16] .


هر پیغمبرك ولادتندن مقدم و ولادتی زه‌ٰننده و بعده پیغمبر اولحیه‌دك
اكا متعلق[17] ظهور ایدن علامات[18] و كرامانه[19] ارهاصات دینوب نبوتندن[20]
صكره اولنلره معجزات[21] دیرلر . پس حضرت عیسایه ارهاصات بی حد
و غایت اولوب بعضلری دخی بودر كه ذكر اولنور .

تفسیر لبابده و غیریده مرویدر كه حضرت یحیی[22] علیه السلامك
والده‌سی مریمله ایله بولشوب اویحیی‌یه بو عیسایه حامل ایكن دیمش

---

(1) P. *Péygamber*, or پيامبر *péyamber*, 'a messenger, a prophet.'—(2) A. *Meghare*,
'a cave, cavern.'—(3) *Iletmek*, 'to forward, send forward, send.'—(4) *Zina*,
'adultery.'—(5) A. *Rouh*, 'a spirit;' *Rouh-oul-Koudous*, 'the Holy Ghost,' according
to Christians, but 'Gabriel,' according to Muhammedans; *Rouh-ou'-llah*, 'the Spirit
of God (Jesus Christ).'—(6) A. *Nifas*, 'forty days after childbirth.'—(7) P. *Muzhdé*,
'glad tidings.'—(8) A. *Mesih*, 'the Messiah.'—(9) A. *Akréba*, 'relations.'—(10) A.
*Ahibba*, 'friends.'—(11) A. *Souléha*, 'righteous people.'—(12) A. *Elem*, 'pain,
anguish.'—(13) *Aghlashmak*, 'to weep together.'—(14) *Rejm etmek*, 'to stone.'—
(15) *Feraghat etmek*, 'to give up.'—(16) A. *Erhasat*, 'wonders proceding the birth
of a prophet.'—(17) A. *Mutaalik*, 'connected with, dependent.'—(18) A. *Elamet*,
'sign, wonder, phenomenon.'—(19) A. *Kéramet*, 'a marvel, wonder.'—(20) A.
*Nuburret*, 'being a prophet.'—(21) A. *Mujizé*, 'a miracle.'—(22) *Yahya*, 'John
the Baptist.'

كه يا مريم بذم حملم بلورميس اودخى بنمده حملم وار ديدكده يحيى
والدهسى ديمشكه قارنمده‌كى سنك قارنكده كى يه تعطيما سجده[1] ايدر
مشاهده ايدرم . . . . .

بری بو در كه حضرت مريم ديمشدر كه عيسى قارنمده ايكن تنها[2]
اولدقجه بر بريمزله عادتجه سويلشوب يانمه بر كمسنه كلسه ياخود تسبيحه[3]
مشغول[4] اولسم قارنمده تسبيح ايدوب بن انى بالتمام ايشيدر ايدرم .

بری بو در كه عيسى بر كونلك ايكن آيلق قدر كورينوب طقوز آيلق
اولدقده مريم انى خواجه‌یه ويرمك ايستدكده اى والده الله تعالى بنى
خواجه‌دن مستغنى[5] ايدوب دخى قارنكده ايكن بكا تورات[6] و انجيل[7]
اوكرتمشدر ديدى .

---

CHRIST'S MIRACLES.

خلق[8] طيور .

تاريخ مير خوانده مذكور در كه عيسى عليه السلام مرسل[9] اولدقده
قدسه كلوب يهود مردود[10] اهل جحودى[11] راه الهه[12] دعوت ايتدكده اول
قوم[13] مستحق[14] التعذيب[15] رسول مقبول حقيقى بالتصديقى تكذيب
ايدوب بعد انواع الشتم[16] عناده اصرارى[17] و قصد اضرارى[18] حسم و حتم
و دل[19] پر غل‌المزينى[20] مهر[21] كفره[22] ختم[23] ايتديلر .

تفسير لبابده مذكور در كه دعواى نبوّت و اظهار معجزات ايتدكده

(1) *Sejdé,* 'to bow the head, to worship.'—(2) P. *Tenha,* 'lonely, alone.'—(3) A. *Tesbih,* 'a rosary,' 'a kind of litany of masses for which the rosary is used in counting.'—(4) A. *Meshghoul,* 'occupied.'—(5) A. *Mustaghni,* 'independent of, not requiring.'—(6) A. *Tevrat,* 'the Pentateuch.'—(7) A. *Injil,* 'the Gospel.'—(8) A. *Khélk,* 'creating.'—(9) A. *Mursel,* 'an apostle.'—(10) A. *Merdoud,* 'rejected, disowned.'—(11) A. *Juhoud,* 'denying.'—(12) A. *Ilah,* 'a god, God.'—(13) *Kavm,* 'a people.'—(14) A. *Mustahik,* 'deserving.'—(15) A. *Tazib,* 'torment, punishment.'—(16) A. *Shetm,* 'abuse, abusing.'—(17) A. *Israr,* 'persisting.'—(18) *Izrar,* 'injuring.'—(19) T. *Dil,* 'the tongue, language,' 'information got by spies.' P. *Dil,* 'the heart.'—(20) A. *Ghil,* 'deceit.'—(21) A. *Muhur,* 'a seal.'—(22) A. *Kiufr,* 'unbelief, swearing.'—(23) A. *Khatm etmek,* 'to seal, to conclude (a speech).'

يهوديلر تركجه يراسه ` عربجه خفاش ديدكلرى قوش يراتمق ` تكليف `
ايتدكلرنده بالچقدن ` تصوير ` ايدوب اوئلدكده جللنوب هوايه اوچوب
كيدوب تنها يرده دوشوب ميت اولور ايدى تاكه الله تعالى بالذات
يراتديغيله مخلوق و اسطه سيله يراتديلانك فرقي ظاهر اوله .

احياء ` ابن العجوز ` .

ينه عيسى عليه السلام بر خاتونك وفات ايتمش 'اوغلنه تابوتله ` كوتور
يلور كن اوغرايوب دعا ايتمكين جانلنوب قفتانلرينى كيوب تابوتى اموزينه
اوروب اوينه كلدى .

معجزهٔ عجيبه .

تاريخ مير خوانده مذكور د، كه بر كون عيسى عليه السلام اصحابيله
سياحت ايدركن حصادى ` يقلاشمش ` بر ترلايه ` اوغرايوب ` يا روح ` الله
غايتده اجدق اشبو اكيندن ` قوپاروب ` يمكه اجازت ` ويرر ميسز ديد
كلرنده اجازتدر دبو وحى املنمغين اصحاب قوپاروب اكين صاحبى طوبوب
بوتارلا ابا ` عن جدّ ميراثله ملك ` صرىحمدر ` كيمك اذنيله ` تصرف
ـــز ديوب عيسى دور ` ادمدنبرو مالك اولنلرك حياتنه دعا ايتمكين
هر بغداى ` صاپى ` ديبندن ` كيمى ` ا، كيمى عوت برر آدم چيقوب

---

(1) *Yerasé,* 'a bat.'—(2) *Yeratmak,* 'to create.'—(3) *Teklif etmek,* 'to propose.'—
(4) *Balchik,* 'clay; the guard of a sword handle.'—(5) A. *Tasvir etmek,* 'drawing,
designing, modelling, shaping.'—(6) A. *Ihya,* 'to animate, bring to life.'—(7) A.
*Ajouz,* 'an old woman.'—(8) *Tabout,* 'a coffin.'—(9) *Hasad,* 'the harvest, reaping.'
—(10) *Yaklashmak,* 'to draw near, approach,' *v.n.*—(11) *Tarla,* 'a field.'—(12) *Oghramak,* 'to pass by or through, to meet with.'—(13) A. *Rouh,* 'a spirit,' *Rouh-
oullah,* 'the Spirit of God (Jesus Christ).'— (14) *Ekin,* 'a crop, seed-sowing.'—
(15) *Koparmak,* 'to pluck, gather.'—(16) A. *Ijazet,* 'permission.'—(17) A. *Eba-én-
jeddin,* 'hereditary.'—(18) A. *Mulk,* 'freehold property;' *Milk,* 'dominions, terri-
tory.'—(19) A. *Sarih,* 'clear.'—(20) A. *Tésérruf,* 'possessing, using, disposing of.'—
(21) A. *Devr,* 'a period, time.'—(22) *Boghdaï,* 'wheat;' مصر بغداى *Misr boghdayi,* 'Indian
corn.'— (23) *Sap,* 'a stalk, a straw, a handle.'—(24) A. *Dib,* 'the bottom.'—
(25) *Kimi,* 'some of them.'

هر بری صوت[1] اعلا[2] ایله بنم تارلامه کیمك اذنیله تصرف ایتدکز دیو
ندا ایتدکلرنده صاحب مزرعه[3] حیران[4] اولوب بو معجزهٴ عظیمه صاحبی
کیمدر دیو عیسی ابن مریم در دیدکلرنده یا روح الله سزی بلمدم
معذور[5] طوتك حالا جمله اكینمی اصحابكزه حلال[6] ایتدم دیوب عیسی
علیه السلام بهی کشی حقیقتده نه مزرعه نه مزروع سنك دكلدر زیرا
سندن اول جم[7] غفیر[8] و جمع کثیر بو مزرعهبی رجاء منفعت ایله مالکانه
تصرف ایتدیلر عاقبت حسرتله[9] قریوب کتدیلر سکا دخی اوبله اوله جقدر
دیو بیوردی . . . . . .

<br>

## رفع عیسی علیه السلام .

یهودیلر قتل عیسایه عزم ایتدکلرنده حواریون[10] بر چارطاقده[11] جمع اولوب
عیسی علیه السلام پنجرهدن ایچرو کیروب شیطان لعین[12] یهودی بی
دینه خبر ویرمکین درت نفر یهودیٴ خر[13] بداختر[14] قپویه کلوب عیسی
علیه السلام حواریونه کیمدر که چیقوب قتل اولنوب جنتده[15] بکا رفیق
اوله دیدکده بریسی اشته بن یا نبی دیمکین قفتان و دلبند[16] و عصاسنی[17]
اکا ویروب قدرت حقله عیسی صورتنه دونمکین طشره چیقدقده طوتنوب
قتل و صلب اولندی . بو طرفده عیسی حکمت خدا ایله قنادلنوب نور
مطلقه مستغرق ملائكه ایله کوکه اوچدی . . . . .

---

(1) A. *Savt*, 'a voice, a sound.'—(2) *Ala*, 'very high, excellent.'—(3) A. *Mezréa*, 'a sown field, an arable field.'—(4) A *Haïran*, 'bewildered, astounded.'—(5) A. *Mazour*, 'excused.'—(6) A. *Hélal*, 'permitted (by God), lawful;' *Helal etmek*, 'to give up.'—(7) A. *Jem*, 'a crowd, multitude.'—(8) A. *Ghafir*, 'great, immense.'—(9) A. Regretting, a sigh.—(10) A. *Héwari* (pl. *Hewariyyoun*), 'an apostle, companion of a prophet.'—(11) P. *Chartak*, 'an arbour.'—(12) A. *Laïn*, 'accursed.'—(13) P. *Khar*, 'an ass, donkey.'—(14) P. *Bed-akhter*, 'ill-starred, evil.'—(15) A. *Jennet*, 'paradise.' —(16) *Dulbend* (*Tulbent*), 'muslin.'—(17) A. *Asa*, 'a staff.'

TRANSLATION.

*Thirty-second Chapter, concerning the Prophet Jesus.*
(Peace be on Him!)

---

*The Birth of Jesus.*

It is recorded in the Commentaries that Mary (the Virgin Mary), on seeing the *menstruus sanguis* went to her maternal aunt, the wife of Zaccharia, *Ishaa* (Elizabeth), and, having become clean, repaired to the Temple and continued praying. Then, one day, while she was performing her complete ablution of her whole body, in the house of her maternal aunt, Gabriel (On him be peace!) appeared in the form of a handsome young man. Mary, not knowing who he was, said: "I will take refuge with God!" Gabriel made himself known, and, according as is related in the Koran, they conversed together, and then Gabriel blew, either on the collar of Mary's robe, or in her sleeve, or in her mouth, from a distance or close to her, and by the power of God she became immediately pregnant. According to the statement of Ibn Abas, she grew big in an instant, and, according to the account of others, in three months. After six, or eight, or nine months, when Mary was either in the thirteenth, or sixteenth, or twentieth year of her age, Jesus came into existence.

It is related that Mary, on feeling the symptoms of pregnancy, left Jerusalem, and went to a village a few miles off, called Bethlehem. On it becoming clear that a child would be born, she leaned against a dried-up date tree for support and shelter, and Christ was born. Gabriel (On him be peace!) striking the ground with his foot, sweet water flowed out, and the date tree immediately put forth branches and brought forth dates. Her Holiness Mary became full of grief, thinking that the people would probably reproach and slander her, and cried: "Would that I had died ere this, and been forgotten!" Whereupon, as is stated in the Koran, Gabriel, or Christ, consoled her. Then Mary took Jesus and came to the city; and when Mary's people reviled and denied her, saying: "Is a child born without a father? What a strange thing thou hast done;"

she said that she had taken a vow to be silent about this till a certain time, and suggested they should speak to the child. They waxed wroth, and added: "What can we say to the child in the cradle?" Jesus, who was forty days old, and sucking at the breast, left off, and said: "I am the servant of God, he brought me the 'Book' and made me a prophet, and made me blessed wherever I may be, and recommended me prayer and piety as long as I live, and made my mother pure."

After that he grew, as is usual, and said no more. The people of Israel, on seeing this wonderful miracle, knew that Jesus would be a prophet, and their evil thoughts about Mary were dispelled. . . . .

It is mentioned in the *Keshaf* that Joseph sent Jesus and Mary to a cave, and, on the way, thought about killing them. Whereupon Gabriel came and said: "Jesus is not (the fruit) of adultery, but of the Spirit of God. Do not kill Mary!" Wherefore he refrained.

Mary remained in the cave the forty days after child-birth (called 'Nifas'), and then came to the city. On the way, Jesus said: "Glad tidings for thee! for I am the servant of God the Most High, and His Messiah."

On their entering the city, their relations and friends, being all righteous people, wept, and said: "Oh Mary, thou hast given us a bad name, and filled us with grief and pain," and on their wishing to stone them (according to what some say), Jesus spoke to them, and they desisted.

### Wonders before Christ's Birth.

Before the birth of every prophet, and at the time of his birth, and afterwards, till he become a prophet, certain signs and wonders occur which are termed *Erhasat*. After his becoming a prophet, they are called miracles (*Mujizat*). Well, the wonders preceding His Holiness Jesus' birth are innumerable, but amongst those recorded are the following:—"It is related in the commentary of Libab, and others, that the mother of His Holiness John (the Baptist) (Peace be on him!), being in the company of Mary, while the former was pregnant with St. John, and the latter with Jesus, said: 'Dost thou know that I am with child?' Mary replied:

'And I am also.' Then the mother of John said : 'He who is in my womb bows his head to him in your womb to honour him.'"

Another narrative is this—Her Holiness Mary is reported to have said : "While Jesus was in my womb, when we were alone, we used to talk to one another. If any one came, or if I were engaged saying my rosary, I could plainly hear him in my womb saying his rosary."

Another is this—When Jesus was one day old he seemed a month old ; and when He was nine months old, and His mother wished to send Him to a master, Jesus said : "Oh, mother, God (May He be Exalted!) made me independent of masters, and while I was in thy womb taught me the Pentateuch and the Gospel."

### CHRIST'S MIRACLES.

#### *Creation of a Bat.*

It is related in the history of Mīr Khandā that Jesus (Peace be on Him!), having become a prophet, came to Jerusalem; and, on his urging the Jews, the disowned of God, and the people who denied Him, to enter the path of God, that nation, "worthy of punishment" contradicted the well-beloved apostle, whose truthfulness had been confirmed, reviled him in all kinds of ways, and persisted in their obstinacy, and sealed their deceitful hearts with the seal of unbelief.

It is stated in the commentary of Libab, that on his prophesying, and performing miracles, the Jews proposed to him to create a bird, called a Bat (in Turkish termed *Yerasé*, and in Arabic *Khuffash*), whereupon He shaped one out of clay, blew on it, and gave it life; and it flew into the air and went away, and on falling in a lonely place died, in order that the difference might be seen between a creature created by God Himself and one made by one of God's creatures.

#### *Raising a Woman's Son from the Dead.*

Again, on Jesus meeting the son of an old woman while they were carrying him in a coffin, Jesus prayed, and he, the young man, came to life, and, putting on his robe, took the coffin on his shoulder, and returned home.

### A Marvellous Miracle.

It is written in the chronicle of Mir Khandé that, one day, while Jesus (Peace be on Him!) was travelling with his companions (disciples) they came through a field where the harvest was at hand, and his disciples said: "We are extremely hungry. Dost thou permit us to pluck the crop and eat?" and Jesus said: "It is permitted." Whereupon, at his suggestion, his disciples plucked the crop. The owner of the field hearing this, cried: "This field is my undoubted property, by hereditary succession, by whose permission do you use it?" Jesus prayed that all those who had owned it from the time of Adam might come to life; and from the bottom of every straw of wheat rose human beings, some men, some women, and each one cried out, in a loud voice: "By whose permission did you use my field?" The proprietor of the field was bewildered, and said: "Who hath performed this great miracle?" On their telling him, "Jesus, the son of Mary," he exclaimed: "Oh! Spirit of God, I did not know you. Pardon me. I now give up all the harvest to your disciples." Jesus (On Him be Peace!) replied: "Oh man! in reality neither the field nor the produce is thine, because, before thee a great multitude of people have possessed it, in the hope of profit, and gave it up with regret, and thus will it be with thee."

### The Ascension of Jesus.

When the Jews had resolved on killing Jesus, the apostles were collected in a pavilion, and Jesus (On Him be peace!) entered through the window. The devil having given information to the unbelieving Jews, four ill-starred Jews came to the door. Jesus having said to his apostles: "Who will go forth and be killed, and become my companion in Paradise?" one replied: "I, Oh Prophet!" Whereupon he gave him his robe, and his staff, and, by the power of God, he was changed into the form of Jesus, and went out, and was taken and crucified. On the other hand, Jesus, by the will of God, obtained wings and ascended into heaven with angels, in a cloud of glory.

## SHEIKH-ZADÉ.

OF SHEIKH-ZADÉ, the author of the most celebrated collection of Turkish tales, called the "Forty Vezirs," nothing is known. It is supposed that he translated or adapted them from the Arabic, but no corresponding book of tales has ever been discovered in the Arabic language. The origin of the stories is probably Indian, and most likely they were carried from India to Persia and thence found their way westward. The tales in Turkish are at least between four and five hundred years old, as one edition, still extant, is dedicated to Murad II. (the father of Mahomet II. the conqueror of Constantinople), who reigned from 1421 to 1451 Anno Domini. It was from this ancient version that the selections from the Forty Vezirs were made by Belletête, which book was published at the expense of the government of Napoleon, in 1812, for the use of French students of Turkish. Apparently Napoleon was aware of the importance of Oriental languages, but this reading-book, in which the old spelling of the ancient MS. spoken of above was copied, was not by any means fit to teach students the current Turkish; but yet it has been the only Turkish reading-book in Europe until now! The tales are quaint and curious and have continued to be popular in Turkey up to the present time. Many editions have been issued at various times. In the more recent issues the spelling has been modernized and corrected, and in *this form* the book is still good Turkish, and the style being simple and clear, it is well adapted for students, and especially beginners. It is a sort of Turkish Decameron, but it is by no means so indecent as Boccacio's work. One tale, which I have called the "Wife with Two Husbands," reminds one of "Box and Cox," but I am sure that the author of that charming comedy did not plagiarise from this old Eastern tale, of which, probably, he never heard.

تاريخ قرق وزير *

*Tarikh Kirk Vezir.*

## THE HISTORY OF THE FORTY VEZIRS.*

بسم الله † الرحمن الرحيم

| و | كون | خالق | اول | بی پايان | شكر | و | فراوان | حمد |
|---|---|---|---|---|---|---|---|---|
| vé | kevn | khalik | ol | payan bi | shukr | vé | ferawan | hamd |
| and | existence | creator | that | endless | thanks | and | abundant | praise |

| قدرته | (جلت) | جان | و | انس | رازق | و | مكان |
|---|---|---|---|---|---|---|---|
| kudrethou | jellet' | jan | vé | ins | ruzik | vé | mékian |
| his omnipotence | magnified be | soul | and | mankind | maintainer | and | place |

| و | صلوات | و | اولسون | حضرتلرينه | عظمته ) | عظمتهٔ | و | عزت | و |
|---|---|---|---|---|---|---|---|---|---|
| vé | salawat | vé | olsoun | hazretleriné | azamethou | his magnificence | glorified be | azzet | vé |
| and | prayers | and | be ! | to his majesty | | | | | and |

| دخی | و | اولسون | اوزرينه | رسول | اول | يحصی | لا | تسليمات |
|---|---|---|---|---|---|---|---|---|
| dakhi | vé | olsoun | uzeriné | resoul | ol | yuhsa- | la | teslimat |
| also | and | be ! | on | prophet | that | innumerable | | salutations |

| الله | رضوان | اولوسون | اوزرينه | صحابلری | و | آل |
|---|---|---|---|---|---|---|
| Allah | rizwan | olsoun | uzeriné | ashabléri | vé | al |
| God | satisfaction | be ! | on | friends | and | family |

| اجمعين ٠ | عليهم | تعالی |
|---|---|---|
| ejmaïn | aléihim | ta'ala |
| all | on them | May He be exalted ! |

---

* This is the way in which this word ought to be spelt, and not *vizier*, as we often see it written in European books. It is an Arabic word, meaning one who bears a burden, and hence a minister of state. It is pronounced in Arabic *Wezir*, so that it may be spelt in English letters either with a *v* or a *w*.

† These Arabic words *Bism-i-'llah!* 'In the name of God!' are to be found at the beginning of every Turkish book, and are used as a sort of grace, not only before commencing a meal, but before beginning anything. Turks are very much astonished at our impiety in abruptly commencing a book without using any such words.

| كون | بر | سبكتكين* | محمود | سلطان | عدل آيين | پادشاه |
|---|---|---|---|---|---|---|
| ghiun | bir | Sabuktéghin | Mahmoud | sultan | ayin-adl | padishah |
| day | one | Sabuktéghin | Mahmoud | Sultan | just | the king |

| رائی | روشن | وزراى† | ايدر ايكن | صحبت | وزيرلرايله |
|---|---|---|---|---|---|
| ré'ï | roushen | vuzera-ï | eder iken | suhbat | vézirlerilé |
| opinion | brilliant | the Viziers | chatting | | with his Vezirs |

| پادشاهرى | كچمش | اولوب فوت و | غتمش | كلوب | دنيايه |
|---|---|---|---|---|---|
| padishahleri | gechmish | oloup fevt vé | ghitmish | gheloup | dunyayé |
| of kings | passed (away) | dying and | gone | coming to the world | |

| و | الخصال | محمود‡ | سلطان | ايتديلر | ذكر |
|---|---|---|---|---|---|
| vé | el-khisal | Mahmoud | sultan | etdiler | zikr |
| and | whose character was praiseworthy | Mahmoud | the Sultan | they made | mention |

| ندر | اسمى | پادشاهلرك | اول | بيورديكه | مسعود الفعال |
|---|---|---|---|---|---|
| nédir | ismi | padishahlerin | ol | buyourdiki | el-fïal messoud |
| what is? | the name | of those kings | those | asked | whose deeds were fortunate |

| ايتدى§ | وزير |
|---|---|
| ëïtdi | Vezir |
| said | the Vezir |

| اخرته | سراى | پادشاهلر | اول | زماندنبرو | بونچه |
|---|---|---|---|---|---|
| akhireté | seraï | padishahler | ol | zemandenberou | bounché |
| future life | the palace | kings | those | time ago | such a long |

---

\* Sabuktéghin is the name of the father of Sultan Mahmoud, the founder of the dynasty of the Gaznevids, who flourished at the beginning of the eleventh century.

† *Vuzera* is the Arabic plural of وزير *vezir*, 'a Vezir.' The sound of *i* inserted after it is given because it is followed by a Persian adjective. See *Wells' Grammar*, pp. 178, 179.

‡ The word *Mahmoud* means 'praised,' and خصال *khisal* means 'moral qualities.' The expression 'Mahmoud el-Khisal' thus signifies 'one who has praiseworthy qualities, and is a *jeu-de-mots* on Sultan Mahmoud's name.

§ The word ايتمك, when pronounced *etmek*, means 'to do,' but when pronounced *ëïtmek* means 'to say.' In this sense it is now somewhat obsolete. The same word, when pronounced *itmek*, means 'to push.'

| اسمی | برينك | بيكده | مرصو نده<br>بيورمشلار | انتقال |
|---|---|---|---|---|
| ismi | birinin | bindé | buyourmoushler | intikal |
| the name | of one | in a thousand | they condescended | transported to |

| وار | پادشاه | بر | زمانده | فلان | انجق* | بلنمز |
|---|---|---|---|---|---|---|
| var | padishah | bir | zemandé | filan | anjak | bilenmaz |
| existing | king | a | at a time | such and such | but | is not known |

| بيوردديكه | پادشاه | ديدكلرينده | سويلنور | ديو† | ايمش |
|---|---|---|---|---|---|
| buyourddiki | padishah | dédiklerindé | suïlenir | déyou | imish |
| { condescended to say } | the king | on they saying | it is said | saying | was |

| دكين | قيامته | تا | که | ايدەسز | تدبير | بر | بكا |
|---|---|---|---|---|---|---|---|
| déghin | kiyameté | ta | ki | edésiz | tedbir | bir | bana |
| until | the Resurrection | until | that (whereby) | make | contrivance | a | to me |

| مشهور | نامم | و | مذكور | جهانده | سرای | آدم |
|---|---|---|---|---|---|---|
| meshour | namim | vé | mezkiour | jihandé | serai | adim |
| celebrated | my name | and | mentioned | in the word | the palace | my name |

| اولسون . |
|---|
| olsoun |
| may be |

| بناسنه | عمارت | بر | که | بيان ايتديلر | وزيرلر |
|---|---|---|---|---|---|
| binasiné | imaret | bir | ki | etdiler béyan | vezirler |
| to its building | public building | a | that | explained | the Vezirs |

| اولور | خراب | ايله | ايام | مرور | بيورسەكز | شروع |
|---|---|---|---|---|---|---|
| olour | kharab | ilé | eyyam | murour | buyourséniz | shurou |
| it will become | a ruin | with | days | lapse | { if you condescend } | { to commence } |

---

\* *Anjak*, when an adverb, means 'only just, hardly,' but when a conjunction it means 'but, however, still.'

† In conversation pronounced *déyé*.

| نامکز | باقی قالمز | آخر | مملكتده | ...ویلنوب | مشهور |
|---|---|---|---|---|---|
| *naminiz* | *kalmaz-baki* | *akhar* | *memleketdé* | *suïlenip* | *meshoor* |
| your name | will not remain | another | in a country | being talked of | celebrated |

| اولمز | ديو | هر | بری | بر | درلو | سوز | سویلديلر . |
|---|---|---|---|---|---|---|---|
| *olmaz* | *deyou* | *hér* | *biri* | *bir* | *durlu* | *seuz* | *suïlédiler* |
| it will not be | saying | every | one of them | a | kind 4 | word | they said |

| عاقبت | سلطان | محمودك | خاص ایاس | نامنده | بر |
|---|---|---|---|---|---|
| *akibet* | *sultan* | *Mahmoudoun* | *éyas khas* / Khas-eyas | *naminé* | *bir* |
| at last | Sultan | of Mahmoud | | called | a |

| سوكلو | خدمتكاری * | وار | ایدی | غایت | تدبیر | صاحبی † |
|---|---|---|---|---|---|---|
| *sevghili* | *khidmetkiari* | *var* | *idi* | *ghayet* | *tedbir* | *sahibi* |
| favourite | his servant | existing | was | extremely | | ingenious |

| اولوب | مكر ‡ | پادشاهمك | آدینه | بر | كتاب | تصنیف |
|---|---|---|---|---|---|---|
| *oloup* | *mégher* | *padishahimin* | *adiné* | *bir* | *kitab* | *tasnif* |
| being | may be | of my king | to his name | a | book | composed |

| اولنه | كه | تا § | قیامته | دكین | قالوب | مملكتدن |
|---|---|---|---|---|---|---|
| *oluna* | *ki* | *ta* | *kiyameté* | *déjhin* | *kaloup* | *memléketden* |
| may be | that | until | to the Resurrection | until | remaining | from country |

| مملكته | شایع اولوب | اوقنه | و | اول | كتابك | سببیله |
|---|---|---|---|---|---|---|
| *memleketé* | *oloup-shayi* | *okouna* | *vé* | *ol* | *kitabin* | *sébebilé* |
| to country | being spread | it may be read | and | that | of book | by reason |

| پادشاهمك | اسم | شریفلری | یاد | اولنوب | الی | اخر |
|---|---|---|---|---|---|---|
| *padishahimin* | *ism* | *sherifleri* | *yad* | *olounoup* | *ila* | *akhir* |
| of my king | name | his noble | being remembered | | to | the end |

* Generally pronounced *hizmetkiar.*
† *Tedbir-sahibi* literally means 'a possessor of management, or contrivance.'
‡ *Mégher* generally means 'unless, and yet;' but here it means 'may be, it might be.'
§ *Ta* is a Persian word meaning 'as far,' and *déjhin* a Turkish word meaning 'until.' Sometimes both are used, the former before, and the latter after the word to express 'until.'

ديد،كده — dédikdé — on his saying
اوله — ola — may it be
مذكور — mezkiour — mentioned
ايله — ilé — with
دعا خير — dua- khaïr — blessings
الزمان — ezzeman — time

تدبيرى — tedbiri — arrangement (plan)
بو — bou — this
و — vé — and
لايق — laïk — fit
رأيى — réÿyi — opinion
بو — bou — this
دخى — dakhi — also
وزيرلر — vezirler — the Vezirs

ايتديلر — etdiler- — approved
تحسين — tahsin — approved
كوروب — ghieurub — seeing (considering)
موافق — mufavik — favourable propositions

نامنده — naminidé — called
طوسى † — tousi
فردوسى * — Ferdousi — Ferdonsi
محمودك — Mahmoudoun — of Mahmoud
سلطان — sultan — Sultan
محلده — mahaldé — place in
اول — ol — that
مثال

پادشاه — padishah — the king
ايدى — idi — was
وار — var — exerting
استادى — ustadi — master
آكاه — aghiah — intelligent
عارف — arif — learned
و — vé — and
كامل — kiamil — perfect
بر — bir — a

التمش — altmish — sixty
كه — ki — which
كتابنى — kitabini — the book of
شاهنامه — Shahnamé — Shahnamé
و — vé — and
ايلدى امر — éïlédi emr — ordered
كامله — kiamilé — to perfect
اول — ol — that

كندى — kendi — own
ويروب — véroup — giving
التون — altoun — a gold piece
برر — birér — apiece
بيتنه — béïtiné — verse
هر — hér — every
بيتدر — béïtdir — verses is
بيك — bin — thousand

ادينه — adiné — to his name
تأليف — té'lif
ايتديردى — etdirdi- — caused to be written

---

\* *Ferdousi*, the most celebrated of the poets of Persia, and of the whole East, author of the *Shah-Namé*, or 'King's Book.' He lived in the reign of Sultan Mahmoud the Ghaznevid, and died in the 421st year of the Hejira (or Anno Domini 1030), at Tous, where he was born. He flourished, therefore, before the Norman conquest of England, when this country was in a very illiterate condition.
† *Tousi* means 'one who was born in Tous.'

In the name of God the Merciful, the Clement! Abundant praise and endless thanks be to the Creator of all things, the maintainer of mankind and life (May His omnipotence and glory be magnified!) ; and may prayers and salutes innumerable be offered for His Apostle (Mahomet), and for his family and friends (May God be well pleased with them all !).

One day, while Sultan Mahmoud Sabuktéghin the Just* was chatting with the Vezirs, the latter brilliant-minded men made mention of past kings who had come into the world and gone, and died. Sultan Mahmoud (The Praised), whose qualities were praiseworthy and whose deeds were fortunate, condescended to say : "What is the name of those kings ?" A Vezir said : "It is such a long time since those kings have passed into (the palace of) eternity that the name of one in a thousand is not known. People, speaking of them, say :—'At a certain time there was a king.'" Thereupon, the king said : "Find out for me a contrivance whereby my name may be mentioned in the world, and celebrated until the Resurrection." The Vezirs replied : "If you erect a public building, by the lapse of time it will fall into ruins, and your name will not be perpetuated, and it will not be spoken of in other lands and become celebrated." They were all unanimous in speaking thus.

At last, a very ingenious favourite servant of Sultan Mahmoud, called Khas-Eyyas, said : " Suppose a book were written in the king's name, which may last till the Resurrection, be spread from country to country and read, and thus the king's noble name, by means of this book, be remembered to the end of time, and mentioned with blessings." The Vezirs approved, thinking this opinion good and the contrivance suitable.

Sultan Mahmoud had a clever, learned and intelligent tutor in that place, called Ferdousi ; the Sultan ordered him to write, in his name, the *Shahnamé* (The King's Book), which has sixty thousand verses, and for every verse he gave him a gold piece.

---

* The celebrated conqueror of India, who ruled at Ghazni from A.D. 998 to 1030.

# DR. AVICENNA AND THE MICE.

حلب[1] شهرنده[2] بر پادشاه[3] وار ایدی و اول شهرده سچانلر[4] چوق
اولمغین اهالیلر[5] هر کون سچانلردن شکایت[6] ایدرلردی بر کون شاه ابو علی
سینا[7] ایله کلام[8] ایدر کن سوز سچانلره کلدی شاه ایدر یا ابو علی شو
سچانلردن هر کسی شکایت ایدر نه اولیدی شونلره بر چاره بولسك
هر کس راحت[9] ایتسون ابو علی ایدر بن انلره بر ایش ایدهیم تاکه[10] بو
شهرده بر دانهسی قالمسون اما[11] شول[12] شرطله[13] سن بو شهرك قپوسنده
طوروب چوق عجائب کوره سن لکن زنهار[14] کولمیه سن[15] دیدی شاه راضی[16]
اولوب شاد[17] اولدی در حال[18] امر[19] ایلدی آت حاضر[20] ایلدیلر سوار[21]
اولوب قپیه کلدی ابو علی سینا دخی بو طرفده[22] بر سوقاقده[23] طوروب[24]
افسون[25] اوقویوب سچانلری[26] دعوت[27] ایلدی سچانلرك بریسی[28] کلدی ا
انی طوتوب[29] هلاك[30] ایلدی بر تابوت[31] ایچنه قویوب اول تابوتی درت
دانه سچانه یوکلتدی[32] کندی افسون اوقویوب اللرینی بری برینه اورمغه
باشلادی اول درت سچان اهسته اهسته[33] اهسته یوروومکه[34] باشلادیلر شهرده نقدر

<hr>

(1) *Haleb*, Aleppo.—(2) *Shehir*, 'city.'—(3) P. *Padishah*, 'a king.'—(4) *Sichan*,
'a mouse, or rat.' To distinguish them a mouse is called فندق سچانی *findik sichani*,
and a rat کمر سچانی *ghemér-sichani*.—(5) *Ehali*, 'people, inhabitants.'—(6) *Shikiayet*
*etmek*, 'to complain.'—(7) *Abou-ali-Sina*, the celebrated physician Avicenna, as
Europeans call him. He was born in Bokhara, A.D. 983, and died at Hamadan,
A.D. 1036.—(8) *Kelam etmek*, 'to talk.'—(9) *Rahat etmek*, 'to be comfortable.'—
(10) *Taki*, 'in order that.'—(11) *Ama*, 'but.'—(12) *Shol*, or شو *shou*, 'that.'—
(13) A. *Shart*, 'a condition, stipulation;' *shartilé*, 'on condition.'—(14) *Zinhar*,
'Beware! take care!'—(15) *Ghiulmek*, 'to laugh.'—(16) *Razi olmak*, 'to consent,
agree.'—(17) A. *Shad (shaz)*, 'delighted.'—(18) P. *Der hal*, 'at once, immediately.'
—(19) *Emr etmek*, 'to order.'—(20) A. *Hazir*, 'ready.'—(21) *Suwar olmak*, 'to
mount.'—(22) A. *Taraf*, 'side, direction.'—(23) *Sokak*, 'a street.'—(24) *Dourmak*,
'to stand.'—(25) *Efsoun okoumak*, 'to read an incantation.'—(26) *Sichan*, 'mouse.'
(27) *Davet eilemek*, 'to invite.'—(28) *Birisi*, 'one of them.'—(29) *Toutmak*, 'To catch.'
—(30) *Helak etmek*, 'to destroy.'—(31) *Tabout*, 'a coffin.'—(32) *Yukletmek*, 'to place
as a load (on anything).'—(33) *Ahesté ahesté*, 'slowly.'—(34) *Youroumek*, 'to walk.'

سچان وار ایسه اول جنازه‌یه¹ حاضر² اولدیلر بونلری سوره³ سوره شاهك⁴
طوردیغی قپویه كلدیلر كیمسی⁵ تابوت اوكنده⁶ كیمیسی اردنده⁷ شاه
دخی سیر⁸ ایدر كن اول تابوت⁹ اوموزلرنده اولان سچانلری كوردكده¹⁰
طیانه‌میوب¹¹ گولدی¹² همان گولنجك قپودن طشره¹³ نقدر سچان
چیقدیسه¹⁴ جمله‌سی¹⁵ هلاك¹⁶ اولدیلر و قپودن ایچرو¹⁷ نقدر قالدی ایسه
جمله‌سی ایچرویه طاغیلوب¹⁸ قاچدیلر¹⁹ ابو علی سینا ایتدی ای شاه اكر
نصیحتم²⁰ طوتوب بر دم²¹ دخی كولمامش اولیدك بو شهرده بر دانه سچان
قالمیوب جمله‌سی طشره چیقوب هلاك اولوردی و هر كس راحت
اولوردی دیدی شاه گولدیككنه پشمان²² اولدی اما نیلسون²³ صوڭ پشمانلق
فائده ایتمز.

(آرسلان) ٢٠

(1) *Jenazé*, 'a funeral.'—(2) *Hazir* here means 'present.'—(3) *Surmek*, 'to drive;' *suré suré*, 'driving and driving.'—(4) P. *Shah*, 'a king.'—(5) *Kimisi*, 'some of them.'—(6) *Euninde*, 'in front of.'—(7) *Ardinde*, 'behind.'—(8) *Séir etmek*, 'to look on.'—(9) *Omouz*, 'the shoulder.'—(10) *Ghieurmek*, 'to see.'—(11) *Dayanmak*, 'to bear support.'—(12) *Ghiulmek*, 'to laugh.'—(13) *Tashra*, or طشری *dishari* (adv.), 'out, beyond;' subst., 'the exterior,' 'a provincial place.'—(14) *Chikmak*, 'to go out.'—(15) *Jumlé*, 'all.'—(16) *Helak olmak*, 'to perish.'—(17) *Icheri*, 'inside.'—(18) *Daghilmak*, 'to be dispersed.'—(19) *Kachmak*, 'to run away.'—(20) A. *Nashihat*, 'advice.'—(21) *Dem*, 'a moment.'—(22) P. *Peshiman* (or *pishman*), 'to be sorry, to repent.'—(23) *Né éilésin*, 'what could he do?'

## Translation.

There was a king in the city of Aleppo, and as there were a great many mice in that city, the inhabitants were every day complaining of the mice. One day, while the king was talking with Abou-Ali-Sina (Avicenna), the conversation turned on the mice. The king said: "Abou-Ali-Sina, everybody is complaining of the mice. How would it be if you found a remedy for them, and everybody were made comfortable." Abou Ali Sina said: "I will do something for them, so that not one will remain in this town, but on condition that you stand at the gate of the city, and whatever strange things you see you must not laugh, or beware!" The king consented, and was delighted. He immediately ordered them to get a horse ready. He mounted and came to the gate.

Abou Ali Sina also stood in a street in that direction, and read an incantation and called the mice. One of them came, and he caught hold of it and killed it, put it into a coffin, and made four mice bear it. He again read an incantation, and they began to strike their hands together, and the four mice commenced slowly marching. All the mice in the city attended the funeral; and they came rushing along to the gate where the king stood, some in front of the coffin, and some behind it. The king looked on, but on seeing the mice carrying the coffin on their shoulders, he could not stand it, and laughed. At once, on his laughing, all the mice who had passed out of the town perished, and all the mice who were inside the gate were scattered inside the town and fled. Abou Ali Sina said: " Oh, king, if you had taken my advice and not laughed for one moment more, not one mouse would have remained in the city, all would have gone out and perished, and everybody would have been comfortable. The king repented of his laughing; but what could he do ? Repentance too late is of no avail.

## CHRIST AND THE DEAD WOMAN.

شويله روايت ايدرلر كه حضرت عيسى زماننده بر ترزى يكت وار ايدى
بر محبوبه عورتى وار ايدى بر بريله غايت سوشيلر ايدى بر كون شويله
اتفّاق ايدوب عهد ايتديلر كه عورت اول اولورسه ارى عورت المية
و عورتك مزارينى قوجقليوب¹ اخشامه دكين اغليه اكر يكت اولورسه
عورت دخى اويله ايده حكمت خدا عورت فوت² اولدى ترزى اغليوب
فرياد ايتدكدنصكره دفن ايلدى و اول ايتدكلرى عهدى يرينه كتوروب
اول عورتك مزارينى توجقليوب اغليوب و دائم قبرى اوزرنده بكلردى
بر كون عيسى اول محلدن كچركن كورديكه بر يكت بر قبر توجقليوب
اغلر ياننه واروب نيچون اغلاديغنى صوردى يكت دخى برر نقل ايلدى
همان عيسى دعا ايدوب عورت ديرلدى³ و كفن ايله مزاردن چيقدى
عيسى ينه يولنه كتدى يكت ايتدى بويله كفن ايله كتمك اولامز بر
دم⁴ سن بونده طور واردم اودن اسباب كتورديم سندخى اسبابكى كى صكره
برابر كيدهلم ديوب تيزجه اوينه كتدى خاتونى انده براقدى ناكاه اول
اقليم⁵ پادشاهنك اوغلو اول محلدن كچركن كورديكه بر محبوبه عورت
بر كفنه صارلمش⁶ اوتوررو شهزاده بو عورتى كورديكى كبى جان و كوكلدن
عاشق اولوب عورته ايتدى سن كيمسين عورت ايتدى بن غريبم⁷ حرامى⁸
بنى صويدى ديدى اول ساعت سهزاده خدادملرينه امر ايلدى بو عورتى
آلوب سرايه كتورديلر و پاك لباسلر كيدىرديلر چون يكت اسبابلرى كتوردى

---

(1) *Koujaklamak*, 'to take into one's arms, to encircle with one's arms.'—
(2) *Fevt olmak*, 'to die.'—(3) *Dirilmek*, 'to come to life.'—(4) P. *Dem*, 'a moment.'
—(5) A. *Iklim*, 'a clime, country.'—(6) *Sarilmak* (v.n.), 'to embrace, to twine;'
(v.p.) 'to be bound up, or bound round.'—(7) *Gharib*, 'stranger.'—(8) *Harami*, 'a
robber.'

عورتی انده بولمدی فریاد ایدرك كلوب كچنلردن سؤال ایلدی كمسه

كورن اولمیوب بیچاره صوره شهزاره خداملرینه راست كلدی انلر

بو ترزییه سؤال ایدوب ایتدیلر نه اغلارسین ترزی ایتدی نیچه زماندر

حرم فوت اولوب الحمد لله شمدی عیسی پیغمبرك دعاسیله حی

اولوب بن كتدم اسباب كتورهیم اول عورت غائب اولدی انكیچون اغلرم

دیدی بونلر ایتدیلر اول خاتونی بو كون سهزاده سرایه كوندردی دیدیار

همان ترزی شهزادهنك حضورینه كیدوب ایتدی كتوردیكك [1] عورت بنم

حلالم [2] دیو دعوا ایلدی شهزاده اول خاتونه سؤال ایلدی خاتون انكار

ایدوب ایتدی بو حرامیدر بنی صوبوب اسبابمی آلوب كتدی الحمد لله

شمدی كلدی اكر سن بونی اولدرورسن عظیم ثواب ایتمش اولورسن

دیدی شهزاده امر ایلدی ترزبنك ایكی الینی اردینه باغلادیلر بیچاره

ترزی نقدر فغان ایلدی اولمدی بوغازینه ایپ [3] طاقوب بر دار [4] ایتمكه

كتوردیلر یولده حضرت عیسی یی كوردیلر طوروب منتظر اولدیلر چونكه

یقین كلدی بونلردن احوالی سؤال ایلدی بونلر دخی خبر ویردیلر عیسی

بونلری توقیف ایدوب كندی شهزاده قاتنه [5] كلدی عورتی چاغروب سؤال

ایلدی ترزی بو عورت اول یكیدك عور تیدر بن دعا ایتدم دیری اولدی

عورت چونكه پیغمبری كوردی انكاره مجالی قالمیوب طوغریسنی سویلدی

تكرار عیسی دعا ایلدی اول عورت مرد [6] اولوب ترزی دخی دوشدیكی

ورطهدن خلاص اولدی و بونچه وقت اغلادیغنه پشمان اولدی .

---

(1) *Ghetirmek* means 'to bring,' but *gheuturmek* (generally spelt كوتورمك) means 'to carry off, to carry.' Evidently it is in the latter sense that the word is here used, and it would have been better spelt كوتورمك.—(2) *Halal*, 'lawful property.'—(3) *Ip* is 'a rope;' *ip takmak*, 'to adjust a rope round.'—(4) *Ber-dar* means 'on the gibbet, gibbeted;' and *Ber-dar etmek*, 'to hang.'—(5) *Kat* generally means 'a fold,' but here it signifies 'presence.'—(6) P. *Murd*, 'dead.'

### *Translation.*

It is related that in the time of His Holiness* Jesus, there was a young man, a tailor; he had a beloved wife and they loved one another extremely. One day they agreed to make a covenant that, if the wife died first the husband would not take another wife, but that he would embrace his (deceased) wife's tomb, and mourn (every day) till evening. If the young man died, the wife also would do thus. By the will of God, the wife died. The tailor, after lamentations, buried her, and, carrying out the covenant they had made, he embraced her tomb and wept, and always remained on her tomb. One day, while Jesus was passing through that place he saw a young man embracing a tomb and weeping. He approached him, and asked why he wept. The youth narrated all that had passed. Jesus at once put up a prayer, and the woman came to life; and she arose from the grave in her winding-sheet. Jesus went on his way again. The youth said: "It won't do for you to walk about thus in your winding-sheet. Stop a minute here, and I will go and bring some clothes from home. Put them on, and then we will go together." Whereupon, he went quickly to his home, and left the woman there. By chance the son of the king of that country happened to pass that way, and saw a lovely woman sitting with a winding-sheet wound round her. As soon as the prince saw her he fell madly in love with her, and exclaimed: "Who art thou?" The woman said: "I am a stranger; and a robber has stripped me." The prince immediately ordered his servants to take the woman and bring her to the palace, and put clean clothes on her.

When the young tailor brought the clothes, he did not find the woman. He began to weep, and made enquiries of the passers by. There was no one who had seen her, and the poor fellow, asking

---

* The Muhammedans, far from speaking of Christ disrespectfully, as we do of Muhammed, always prefix this title of respect to his name, as they consider he was a prophet, and even divinely inspired, but not God Himself. It would appear also from this tale that they even believe in his power of performing miracles.

and asking, at last met the prince's servants. They asked the tailor why he was weeping, and he said : "Some time ago my wife died, but (praise be to God) by the prayers of the Prophet Jesus she was brought to life. I went to get her clothes, and in the meanwhile the woman has been lost ; that's why I weep." They answered : "The prince sent that lady to day to the palace." The tailor went at once into the presence of the prince, and said : "The woman whom you carried off is my lawful wife ;" and claimed her. The prince asked the woman about this, and she denied it, and said : "This thief stripped me, and took my things and ran away. Thanks be to God he has now come. If you kill him you will do a meritorious action." The prince gave orders for them to bind the tailor's hands behind his back. His cries were of no avail. They put a rope round his neck and took him off to hang him. On the road they saw His Holiness Jesus. They stood and waited. When he came near, he enquired about the matter, and they informed him. Jesus stopped them, and went himself to the prince. He called the woman and asked her, and said : "This woman is the wife of that youth. I put up prayers and she was brought to life." The woman, as she saw there was no possibility of denying it, admitted the truth. Jesus again put up prayers, and the woman died. The tailor was saved from the precipice into which he had fallen, and he regretted that he had wept over the woman so long.

## THE WOOD-CUTTER'S WIFE.

زمان¹ سابقده² بر شهرده³ بر اودنجی یكت⁴ وار ایدی و اﻧك بر یاوز⁵
سلیطه⁶ عورتی⁷ وار ایدی دائم⁸ بو اودنجی هر نه كه قزانسه⁹ عورت الدن¹⁰
آلوردی¹¹ شویله¹² كه بر اقچه سنی¹³ یدنده¹⁴ براقمازدی¹⁵ و كاه¹⁶ كیجه¹⁷ یمكی
طوزلو¹⁸ اولوب اودنجی بو كیجه پشیردیﻚك¹⁹ یمك طوزلو كلدی
دیدكده²⁰ ایرتسی²¹ كیجه یمكه هیچ طوز قاتمیوب²² طوزسز پشیریردی
كذلك²³ طوزی یوق دیدكده وافر²⁴ طوز قاتوب اكلدن²⁵ عاری²⁶ ایدردی
بر كون اودنجی ایپ²⁷ المق²⁸ ایچون عورتدن برقاچ پاره²⁹ كیزلیوب³⁰
كیجه اولدقده عورت پاریی اودنجینك قوینده³¹ بولوب³² ایتدی سﻚك
بندن غیری³³ بر كیزلوجه³⁴ اویناشﻚ³⁵ وار در آتچه الوب سن اكا كتورور
سن دیدی یكت اند³⁶ ایچدی عورت اینانمدی³⁷ اودنجی ایتدی بهی³⁸
جانم³⁹ ایپ المق ایچون براقدم⁴⁰ عورت ایتدی سنی اول ایپ ایله
بردار⁴¹ ایتسونلر .

---

(1) A. *Zeman*, 'time.'—(2) A. *Sabik*, 'former.'—(3) *Odoun* (sometimes spelt اوطون)
means 'firewood,' and *odounji*, or *odounjou*, 'a wood-cutter.'—(4) *Yighit*, 'a young
man.'—(5) *Yawuz*, 'cruel, ferocious.'—(6) A. *Sélité*, 'a sharp-tongued, loquacious,
woman.'—(7) *Avret*, 'a woman, a wife.'—(8) A. *Daïm*, 'always.'—(9) *Kazanmak*, 'to
earn.'—(10) *El*, 'the hand.'—(11) *Almak*, 'to take.'—(12) *Sheuilé ki*, 'so that.'—
(13) *Akché*, 'money, cash, a small coin worth about $\frac{1}{15}$ of a penny.'—(14) A. *Yéd*,
'the hand.' — (15) *Brakmak*, 'to leave.' — (16) P. *Ghiah* (adv.), 'sometimes.' —
(17) *Gejé yéméyi*, 'supper.'— (18) *Touzlon*, 'salt.'— (19) *Pishirmek*, 'to cook.'—
(20) *Dédikdé*, 'on his saying.'—(21) *Irtési gejé*, 'the next night.'—(22) *Katmak*, 'to
add.'—(23) A. *Kezalik*, 'likewise, also.'—(24) A. *Wafir*, 'abundant.'—(25) A. *Ekl*,
'eating.'— (26) *Aari*, 'free from ;' *ekl-den aʻri etmek*, 'to make it uneatable.'—
(27) *Ip*, 'rope.'—(28) *Almak*, 'to buy.'—(29) *Para*, a small coin, $\frac{1}{15}$ of a penny.'—
(30) *Ghizlémék*, 'to hide.'—(31) *Koïn*, 'breast pocket.'—(32) *Boulmak*, 'to find.'—
(33) *Ghaïri*, 'another.'— (34) *Ghizli*, 'secret.'— (35) *Oïnash*, 'a prostitute.'—
(36) *And ichmek*, 'to swear.'—(37) *Inanmak*, 'to believe.'—(38) *Behé*, 'Oh !'—
(39) *Janim!* literally means 'My soul!' but it is often equivalent to 'My dear!
My good fellow! My dear madam!'—(40) *Brakmak*, 'to leave.'—(41) *Ber-dar etmek*,
'to hang.'

اونجی ایتدی نیچون بکا بویله بد[1] دعا ایدرسن عورت ایتدی دخی

بو ایلدیکم بد دعا سکا از در الحاصل[2] بونلر بر عظیم[3] غوغا[4] ایلدیلر

اونجی خ'تونی[5] ضرب ایدوب اول کیجه نه حال ایسه صباح[6] اولدی

اونجی قالقوب مرکبك[7] بریسنی آلوب طاغه[8] کیدرکن عورته ایتدی

ص'قین[9] اول بر مرکبی سندخی الوب کلمیه‌سن دیدی همان عورت

قالقوب او بر مرکبه بنوب[10] اردینك[11] اردنجه طاغه کتدی و ایتدی سن

بنسز اولیجق کیم بیلور نلر[12] ایدرسن دیدی اونجی باقدی[13] عورت کلیور

سس[14] ایتمیوب طاغه کتدی عورت دخی برابر کتدی اونجی اودون

کسمکه[15] باشلادی[16] عورتدخی اول طاغی طولانورکن[17] بر قیونك[18] باشنه[19]

کلدی[20] اونجی باقدی عورت باشنه قیویه نظر[21] ایدر حایقروب[22] عورته

ایدر صاقین قیو باشندن چکل[23] عورت بر مقدار[24] دخی ایلرو[25] کتدی[26]

تکرار[27] اونجی حایقروب ایتدی سکا کیرو چکل دیرم سن ایلرو کیدرسن

چکل کیرو دیدی عورت بر مقدار دخی ایلرو کیده‌یم دیو بر آدیم[28]

دخی ایلرو باصدی[29] ایاغی[30] التنده‌کی[31] طاش پایدار[32] اولمیوب قایوب[33]

عورت قیویه دوشدی[34] اونجی دخی چونکه الندن[35] عاجز[36] قالمش ایدی

مقید[37] اولمیوب مرکبلری یوکلدوب اوینه کلدی اول کیجه کچدی

فرداسی[38] کون ینه[39] مرکبلری آلوب طاغه کتدی شو عورته واره‌یم بقایم

---

(1) P. *Bed-dua*, 'bad prayers,' *i. e.* 'malediction.'—(2) A. *El-hasil*, 'in short.'—
(3) A. *Azim*, 'great, big.'—(4) *Ghavgha* (generally pronounced *khavga*), 'a quarrel,
or a fight.'—(5) *Khatoun*, 'a woman, lady, wife.'—(6) A. *Sabah*, 'morning.'—
(7) A. *Merkeb*, 'a beast.'—(8) *Dagh*, 'a mountain.'—(9) *Sakin!* 'Take care!'—
(10) *Binmek*, 'to mount.'—(11) *Ardinin-ardinjé*, 'behind him.'—(12) For نه‌لر *néler*,
'what things.'—(13) *Bakmak*, 'to look.'—(14) *Sess*, 'a sound, voice.'—(15) *Odoun*,
'firewood.'—(16) *Kesmek*, 'to cut.'—(17) *Bashlamak*, 'to begin.'—(18) *Dolanmak*,
'to wander about.'—(19) *Kouyou*, 'a well, pit.'—(20) *Bash*, 'head.'—(21) *Ghelmek*,
'to come.'—(22) *Nazr etmek*, 'to look.'—(23) *Haïkirmak* (often spelt حيقرق), 'to cry
out, call out.'—(24) *Chekilmek*, 'to withdraw, go back, retire.'—(25) A. *Mikdar*, 'a
quantity, bit.'—(26) *Ileri*, 'forward.'—(27) *Ghitmek*, 'to go.'—(28) *Tikrar*, 'again.'
—(29) *Adim*, 'a step, pace.'—(30) *Basmak*, 'to tread, step.'—(31) *Ayak*, 'foot.'—
(32) P. *Païdar*, 'firm.'— (33) *Kaïmak*, 'to slip.'— (34) *Dushmek*, 'to fall.'—
(35 & 36) *Ajiz kalmak*, 'to be unable, not powerful enough;' *elinden ajiz kalmish*,
'he could not help it.'—(37) A. *Mukayyed*, 'attentive.'—(38) *Ferdasi ghiun*, 'the
next day.'—(39) *Yiné*, 'again.'

ديوب اول قيوزڭ اغزينه[1] كلدى باقدى عورت كورنمز[2] يوركى[3] اجيوب[4]

بر ايپ صارقيدوب[5] ايتدى بره عورت طوت[6] بو ايپى سنى چكهيم[7]

ديدى باقدى ايپ اغر[8] اولدى غيرت[9] ايدوب چكدى بر عفريت[10]

ايه صارلمش چقار اوندجى خوف[11] ايلدى عفريت ايتدى اى يكت

بندن خوف ايتمه حق[12] تعالى[13] سندن راضى[14] اولسون بنى بر عذابدن[15]

خلاص[16] ايلدنكه قيامته[17] قدر خاطرمدن[18] كيتمك محالدر[19] اوندجى

ايتدى نصل عذابده ايدك عفريت ايدر بو قيو نيجه زماندر بنم مسكنمدر[20]

دونكى[21] كون برسليطه نحس[22] عورت اوزريمه دوشوب اموزى باشمه بنوب

بنى قولاقلرمدن[23] محكم[24] طوتوب شمديه قدر بنى براقمدى[25] شمدى

سن كلدك صارقدك طوت ايپى ديو چاغردك[26] بنى براقدى ايپى دخى

طوتمدى الحمد الله بن قورتولوب[27] خلاص[28] اولدم شمدى بن دخى

استرم[29] بو بكا ايلديك ايلك ايچون سكا مكافات[30] ايدهيم ديوب اوچ

يپراق[31] چقاردى يكته ويردى و ايتدى شمدى بن واروب بو اقليم

پادشاهنك قيزينى طوتارم نكه علاج[32] ايتسهلر براقمم تاكه سن كلوب بو

يپراقلرك برينى صويه قريوب صويلى اول قيزك يوزينه[33] سور[34] بن قريوب

كيدرم شاه سكا حوق نعمتلر[35] احسان[36] ايدر ديدى يكت دخى اول

يپراقلرى عفريتك الندن الدى عورته مقيد اولميوب اوه كلدى بزم

(1) *Aghz*, 'the month.'—(2) *Ghieurunmek*, 'to appear.'—(3) *Yurek*, 'the heart.'—
(4) *Ajimak*, 'to ache, to pity.'—(5) *Sarkitmak* (صارقتمق), 'to let down danglingly;'
from صرقمق *sarkmak*, 'to hang down' (*v.n.*).—(6) *Toutmak*, 'to hold, catch.'—
(7) *Chekmek*, 'to pull, draw.'—(8) *Aghir*, 'heavy.'—(9) *Ghaïret*, 'zeal.'—(10) *Ifrit*,
'a hideous genie.'—(11) *Khavf etmek*, 'to be frightened.'—(12) A. *Hak*, 'truth,'
'God.'—(13) A. *Taala*, 'May His name be exalted!' (Arabic).—(14) *Razi*, 'con-
tented.'—(15) A. *Azab*, 'pain, punishment, torture.'—(16) A. *Khalas etmek*, 'to
save.'—(17) A. *Kiyamet*, 'the resurrection.'—(18) *Khatir*, 'mind, memory.'—
(19) A. *Muhal*, 'impossible.'—(20) A. *Mesken*, 'place of abode.'—(21) *Dounki ghiun*,
'yesterday.'—(22) A. *Nahis*, 'unlucky, of evil omen.'—(23) *Koulak*, 'the ear.'—
(24) A. *Muhkem*, 'fast.'—(25) *Brakmak*, 'to let, let go, leave.'—(26) *Chaghirmak*,
'to call.'—(27) *Kourtoulmak*, 'to be delivered.'—(28) *Khalas olmak*, 'to be saved.'—
(29) *Istémek*, 'to wish.'—(30) *Mukiafat etmek*, 'to reward.'—(31) *Yaprak*, 'a leaf.'—
(32) A. *Ilaj*, 'medicine.'—(33) *Yuz*, 'the face.'—(34) *Surmek*, 'to rub.'—(35) A.
*Nimet*, 'a favour.'—(36) *Ihsan etmek*, 'to confer.'

قصه‌مز <sup>1</sup> عفریته كلدی عفریت اوراجقدن <sup>2</sup> چقوب طوغری <sup>3</sup> پادشاهك

سراینه <sup>4</sup> كلوب قیزینی طوتدی قیز در مست <sup>5</sup> لا یعقل یاتوب و ای باشم

دیو آه <sup>6</sup> و نغان <sup>7</sup> ایدر پادشاهه خبر <sup>8</sup> كوندردیلر پادشاه كلوب قیزی

باش اغریسی <sup>9</sup> طوتمش آه و نغان ایدر چابك <sup>10</sup> حكیم <sup>11</sup> تعیین <sup>12</sup> ایلدی

حكیم كار ایتمدی <sup>13</sup> بر حكیم دخی تعیین ایلدی ینه كار ایتمز بر دخی ینه

كار ایتمز القصه <sup>14</sup> اون قدر حكیم اولدی كار ایتمیوب قیز باباسنی كوردكده

امان بابا باشم دیو فریاد ایدر باباسی دخی ایدر اولادم <sup>15</sup> سن باشم فریاد <sup>16</sup>

ایتدكچه بنم باشم و یوركم سندن زیاده اجیر لكن نه یاپه‌یم واره‌یم سكا

منجم بولیم دیوب علم <sup>17</sup> نجومده ماهرلری <sup>18</sup> دخی دعوت ایتمكه باشلادی

انلردن دخی وافرلر كلوب درلو خواص <sup>19</sup> درلو <sup>20</sup> علاج ایتمكده اولوب بزم

قصه‌مز اوننجی یكته كلدی چونكه عفریت اول بیراقلری ویروب وما جرایی <sup>21</sup>

یكته تعلیم <sup>22</sup> ایتمشدی انجق <sup>23</sup> یكت ایذانمیوب <sup>24</sup> مقید اولمدی بر كون

اول پادشاهك شهرندن بر آدم كلوب بر فرمان <sup>25</sup> كتوردی مضمونی <sup>26</sup> بو

ایمش كه قیزم خسته <sup>27</sup> اولدی بو قدر <sup>28</sup> حكیملر و بو قدر منجملر <sup>29</sup> تعیین

ایلدم اصلا <sup>30</sup> فائده <sup>31</sup> اولمدی هركیم <sup>32</sup> ماهر ایسه كلسون علاج ایلسون اكر

مسلمان <sup>33</sup> ایسه قیزیمی اكا ویررم تك <sup>34</sup> شفا بولسون كافر <sup>35</sup> ایسه دنیا <sup>36</sup> قدر

---

(1) A. *Kisa*, 'a tale.'— (2) *Orajikdan*, 'thence.'— (3) *Doughrou*, 'straight.'—
(4) *Seraï*, 'a palace.'—(5) P. *Der mest la yakil*, 'in a state of insensibility.'—
(6) *Ah!* 'Oh!'—(7) P. *Fighan*, 'cry, lamentation.'—(8) A. *Khabr*, 'news;' *khaïr
ghiundermek*, 'to send word.'—(9) *Bash aghrisi*, 'a head-ache.'—(10) *Chabuk*,
'quick.'—(11) A. *Hékim*, 'a doctor.'—(12) *Tayin etmek*, 'to appoint.'—(13) *Kiar
etmédi*, 'he did nothing.'—(14) A. *El Kisa*, 'in short.'—(15) *Evlad*, 'children,'—an
Arabic plural used, strange to say, for the singular 'child.'—(16) *Feryad etmek*,
'to cry out.'—(17) A. *Ilm-i-Nujoum*, 'astrology.'—(18) A. *Maher*, 'skilful.'—
(19) A. *Khawas*, 'special things.'—(20) *Turlu*, 'kind, sort;' *turlu-turlu*, 'all kinds.'
—(21) A. *Ma-jera*, 'what had happened' (Arabic).—(22) *Talim etmek*, 'to inform.'—(23) *Anjak*, 'only, but.'—(24) *Inanmak*, 'to believe.'—(25) P. *Ferman*,
'order.'—(26) A. *Mazmoun*, 'purport.'—(27) *Khasta*, 'ill.'—(28) *Bou kadar*, 'so
many.'— (29) A. *Munajjim*, 'astrologer.'— (30) *Asla*, 'not ... at all, never.'—
(31) A. *Faïdé*, 'use, advantage.'—(32) *Her kim*, 'whoever.'—(33) A. *Mussliman*,
'Muhammedans,' but pronounced *Mousoulman*, and used as a Turkish singular, it
signifies 'a Muhammedan.'—(34) *Tek*, when an adverb, as in this case, means
merely, 'only, but once;' but used as an adjective it signifies 'odd' (not even), or
'quiet, alone.'—(35) A. *Kiafir*, 'an infidel.'—(36) A. *Dunya*, 'the world.'

انعام¹ و احسان ايتنسم كركدر² ديوب امضا³ ايلمش همان اونجى كلوب
ايدر بن وارهيم اللهك اذنيله⁴ علاج ايدهيم شفا⁵ بولسون ديدى فى الحال⁶
اونجى يكتى كلن آدمه تسليم⁷ ايلديلر طوغرى عزيمت⁸ ايتدى بر كون
پادشاهك ولايتنه⁹ داخل¹⁰ اولديلر شاهه خبر ويرديلر چابك¹¹ كلسون
ديو امر ايلدى حضورينه¹² چقارديلر¹³ پادشاه امر ايدوب قيز كتورديلر
اونجى يكت عفريتك تعريفيله¹⁴ عمل¹⁵ ايلدى قيز شفا بولدى شاه
دخى قيزى ويروب دامادا¹⁶ ايلدى مكر¹⁷ اول شاهك بر شاه دخى
دوستى¹⁸ وار ايدى اول عفريت انك قيزينى سوردى¹⁹ و دائم اول قيزى
انجيديردى²⁰ و بو شاهك قيزى خوش²¹ اولديغنى ايشد نجه²² آدم
كوندروب²³ شاهك دامادينى طلب²⁴ ايلدى تاكه²⁵ قيزينه بر چاره²⁶
اوله پس²⁷ شاه دخى كوندردى چون يكت شاهك قيزى يانه²⁸ كيردى²⁹
كورديكه اول ديو³⁰ انده در ديو يكتى كورنجه ايتدى باق بن سكا بر
ايولك ايلدم بن خود³¹ بو قيزى سورم بونى دخى المدن المغمى كلدك
اشته وارهيم اول قيزى دخى النذن الايم ديوب غايت³² طارلدى³³ يكت
قورقو³⁴ سندن حيران³⁵ قالوب³⁶ ايتدى بن بورايه قيز ايچون كلمدم لكن
قيزوهكى عورت بنم عورتم ايدى النذن قورتولهيم ديو قيويه براقمش ايدم
عورت شمدى قيودن چقوب³⁷ كلدى هرنه محله كيدرسم يانمدن ايرلمز³⁸

---

(1) A. *Enam* (pl. of *nimet*), 'favours, benefits.'— (2) *Gherek*, 'fitting, proper,'
corresponding to 'ought' in English.—(3) *Imza etmek*, 'to sign.'—(4) A. *Izn*, 'permission.'—(5) *Shefa boulmak*, 'to be cured, recover.'—(6) A. *Filhal*, 'immediately.'
—(7) *Teslim-etmek*, 'to deliver.'—(8) *Azimet etmek*, 'to depart.'—(9) A. *Vilayet*,
'country, province.'—(10) *Dakhil olmak*, 'to enter.'—(11) *Chabuk*, 'quick.'—
(12) A. *Huzour*, 'presence.'—(13) *Chikarmak*, 'to bring out, cause to go out.'—
(14) A. *Tarif*, 'explanation.'—(15) *Aml etmek*, 'to act.'—(16) P. *Damad*, 'son-in-
law.'—(17) P. *Mégher* (*méyer*), 'but, unless.'—(18) *Dost*, 'a friend.'—(19) *Sevmek*,
'to love.'—(20) *Injitmek*, 'to pain, hurt.'—(21) P. *Khosh*, 'agreeable.'—(22) *Ishit-
mek*, 'to hear.'—(23) *Ghiundermek*, 'to send.'—(24) *Taleb etmek*, 'to demand,
summon.'—(25) *Taki*, 'in order that.'—(26) P. *Charé*, 'a resource. cure.'—(27) *Pess*,
'then.'—(28) *Yan*, 'side.'—(29) *Ghirmek*, 'to enter.'—(30) *Div* (*dev*), 'a demon.'—
(31) P. *Khod*, 'self.'—(32) A. *Ghayet*, 'extremely.'—(33) *Darilmak*, 'to grow
angry.'—(34) *Korkou*, 'fear.'—(35) A. *Haïran*, 'stupefied.'—(36) *Kalmak*, 'to remain.'—(37) *Chikmak*, 'to go out.'—(38) *Aïrilmak*, 'to be separated.'

اندن قاچوب¹ بورايه سنك يانـنه كلدم شمدى اول دخى ايچرو كيرر
ديدى چـون شمدى ايچرو كيرر ديديكنى سوزى ايشيدنجـه امان
بورايه دخى كلديمى بو ير بكا حرام² اولدى ديوب شاهك قيزينى
قيووريروب³ كتدى و شاهك قيزى دخى شفا بولدى .

---

(1) *Kachmak,* ' to run away, flee.'—(2) A. *Haram,* unlawful.'—(3) *Koyouvermek,*
' to let loose, let go.'

### Translation.

In former times, in a certain town, there was a young man, a
wood-cutter. He had a cruel, sharp-tongued wife. Continually,
whatever the wood-cutter earned, his wife took it from him, so that
she did not leave him a farthing. Sometimes, if the supper were
too salt, and the wood-cutter said : " To-night the supper is too
salt," the next night she put no salt in and cooked it without salt.
In the same way, if he remarked : " There is no salt in it," then she
would put in too much, and make it uneatable.

One day the wood-cutter hid a few pence from his wife, to buy
rope with. When it was night, finding them in his pocket, she said :
" You have got another bad *girl* besides me, and you take the money
and bring it to her." The wood-cutter swore that he had not, but she
did not believe him. " Oh my dear, I left it to get rope with." The
woman replied : " I hope they may hang you with that rope!" He
said : " Why do you abuse me thus ?" She answered : " The curses
I uttered are too few for you." In a word, they had a big quarrel,
and the wood-cutter struck the woman ; and they passed the night
somehow, till day broke. The man arose and took one of his asses,
and when going to the mountains said to the woman : " Take care
you do not come with the other ass." The woman at once arose,
got on the other ass, and followed him to the mountains. She said :
" As soon as you are by yourself who knows what things you will do."
The wood-cutter looked, and saw the woman was coming. He went
to the mountains without uttering a sound. The wife went too.
He began to cut wood. The wife, wandering about the mountains,
came to the brink of a well. The wood-cutter looked at the well, near

which the woman was, and cried out to her, "Go back!" She went a little more forward. Again the wood-cutter called out, saying : "I tell you to go back, and you go forward. Go back—back!" The woman said: " I shall go forward," and went a step more forward. The stone under her was not firm, and slipped, and she fell into the well. The wood-cutter, as he could not help it, paid no attention, loaded his asses and went home. That night passed ; the next day, he again took his asses and went to the mountain. He said to himself I will go and look at that woman, and came to the well. He looked, the woman was not visible. He took pity on her, and, letting down a rope, said : "Hulloa! wife, catch hold of this rope, and I will pull you up." He looked, the rope felt heavy. He exerted himself and pulled, and an Ifrit who had wound himself in the rope, came forth. The wood-cutter was frightened. The Ifrit said: "Oh! youth, fear me not! May God be pleased with you. You have saved me from great torture, and I can never forget it till the Day of·Judgment." The wood-cutter answered : "What tortures were you in?" The Ifrit said: "This well has been my abode for a long time; yesterday an ill-omened virago fell on top of me; her shoulders came on my head, and she caught tight hold of my ears and has never let me go. You came, and, throwing me a rope, cried out : "Catch hold of this rope!" She let me go, and did not catch the rope, and, thanks be to God, I was freed and saved. Now, I want to reward you for the service you have done me ;" saying which, he drew forth three leaves, and gave them to the young man, adding: "Now I shall go and possess the daughter of the king of this country. However much they doctor her, I shall not leave her until you come, and putting one of these leaves in water you rub the juice on her face. Then I will leave her and go. The king will bestow great favours upon you." The young man took the leaves from the Ifrit's hand, and not caring about the woman, went home. But to return to the Ifrit. The Ifrit went from there direct to the king's palace, and possessed his daughter. The girl lay stupefied, crying: "Oh, my head!" They sent word to the king. He came, and looked, and cried : "She has got a headache," and ordered a doctor. The doctor was no use; he appointed another doctor, and he did no good ; and another, and he did no good; in short, there were as many as ten doctors, but they were all no use.

The girl, on seeing her father, cried : " Oh! father, my head ! " He answered : " My child, my head and heart ache when you cry so, and more than your head, but what shall I do ? I will go and find an astrologer." So saying, he went and called the most skilful astrologers. ·Several of them came, and applied all kinds of remedies. But to return to the wood-cutter. When the Ifrit gave him the leaves and told him what we have related, the youth did not believe him, and paid no attention. One day a man came from the city of that king and brought a firman, which was to this effect: " My daughter has fallen ill. I ordered many docters and astrologers, but they have been no use at all. Whoever is skilful, let him come and treat her. If he be a Mussulman, I will give him my daughter. Only let her get well. If he be an unbeliever, I must confer a world of favours upon him. ·The wood-cutter came, and said : " I will go and cure her, with God's permission." They immediately brought him to the man who came from the king. They started at once. One day they entered the king's country. They informed the king. He gave orders for him to come directly, and they brought him into his presence. The king ordered the girl to be fetched. The wood-cutter acted according to the Ifrit's directions, and the girl was cured. The king gave him his daughter, and made him a son-in-law. Now, that king had a friend, a king also, and the Ifrit loved his daughter, and was always plaguing that girl. Hearing that the other king's daughter had recovered, he (her father) sent a man and asked for his son-in-law to cure his daughter. The king sent him. When the youth came to the girl he saw that the Div was in her. When the Div saw the youth, he cried: " Look here! I did you a kindness ; and I like this girl. Have you come to take her from me ? " Thus he got into a great rage and said : " I will go and take that other girl from you." The wood-cutter, terror-stricken, said : " I have not come for the girl, but the woman in the well was my wife. I left her in the well to get rid of her; but now she has got out of the well, and has come here. Wherever I go, she will not leave me. I have fled and come to you. She will come in here too, directly." As soon as the Div heard the words, " She will come in here directly," he cried: " Oh, dear! she has come here too, has she ? This place is not for me then, and he let the girl go," and went off ; and the king's daughter also was cured.

# THE WOMAN WITH TWO HUSBANDS.

## (THE TALE OF THE TWENTY-FOURTH VEZIR.)

زمان سابقده مصر شهرنده دلۀ الـمحتال نامنده بر مكارۀ‎[1] عورت وار ایدی
ایكی‎[2] اری وار ایدی همان هر بری عورتی كندونك‎[3] بیلوردی و عورت
چوق زمان ایكیسنه دخی عورتلك ایلدی اما اول ادملر بری برینك بو
حالزندن هیچ آكاه اولمدیلر و بو ارلرك كارلری بری‎[4] عیار و اول بری اوغری‎[5]
ایدی و ایكیسی دخی عورتك شاكردلری ایدی . كونلرده بر كون اوغری
بازارۀ بر مال كتوروب بیع ایدر و آقچهسنی الور و اول مالی تسلیم ایلدیكی
آدم ایله بر غیری آدم راست كاوب ایدر الحمد للّٰه نشان بلیندی سائر
مالم دخی سنده در تیز بكا سویله دیدی اول ادم ایتدی سوزك ییبلده
سویله بن بومالی صاتون بها ایله آلدم سن ایسه بكا شویله دیهرك بندن
بریله مال استرسن اوغری بونلری كوررب همان طبان‎[6] قالدیروب اوبنه
كلدی خاتونه ایتدی خاتون اوغریلغم طویولدی بكا بر مقدار اتمك كتور بر
غیری یره كیدهیم بو غوغا بر طرف اولنجیه دكین دیدی خاتون بر چورك‎[7]
و بر قیون قویروغی حاضر ایدوب اول چوركك یاروسیله قویروغك یاروسنی
كسوب اوغرییه ویردی اوغری الوب یوله كتدی و بر زماندنصكره عیار
چیقه كلدی ایتدی خاتون بو كون عیارلغم طویولدی بكا بر مقدار اتمك
ویر بر قاچ كونه قدر كورنمیهیم بشقه محله كیدهیم دیدی خاتون دخی
اوغریدن باقی قالان یارم قویروغی عیارۀ ویردی الوب یوله كتدی مكر مقدم
كیدن اوغری واروب بر لطیف پیكارۀ‎[8] و لطیف كولكهیه ایرشوب اول لطیف

---

(1) The feminine of the Arabic word مكار mekkiar, 'a knave, or cheat.'—(2) Er,
an old Turkish word for 'a husband,' or 'a man.'—(3) Generally spelt كندی
kendi.—(4) A. Ayyar, 'a rogue, impostor, cheat.'—(5) Oghrou (obsolete), 'a
thief, robber.'—(6) Taban, 'the sole of the foot;' taban kaldirmak, 'to take to
one's heels.'—(7) Cheurek, 'a kind of cake, or bun.'—(8) Pounar, 'a spring, fountain;' often spelt پیكار pingar.

صويك باشنه اوتوروب چورك ايله قوبروغى چيقاروب يمك مراد ايلدى
همان عيار دخى اول محله چيقه كادى اول دخى بوكار كذارينه
اوتوروب اتمكى و قوبروغى چقارديكه بيه اوغرى قرنداش كل برابر طعام
ايدهلم ديدى عيار كلدى عيار كندينك چوركنه باقدى و اوغرينك چوركنه
باقدى كورديكه برى برينه بكزر ايكيسى بر يره كتورديلر كه بر چوركدر و
قوبروق پارچهلرينى دخى بريره كتوروب انى دخى كورديلر كه بر قوبروقدر
عيار تعجب ايدوب قرنداش صورمق عيب اولماسون نه محلدن كلورسن
ديدى خرسز ايتدى مصردن كلورم عيار ايتدى خانهكزنه يرده اولور اوغرى
مصرده بنم خانم دله المحتالك خانه سيدر و اول قارى بنم عورتمدر عيار
ايدر اول خانه بنمدر و اول قارى بنم عورتمدر و نيچه سنهدر بن انده ساكن
اولورم شمدى نيچون يلان سويلرسين اوغرى ايدر بره[1] آدم سن دلى ميسن
يوخسه لطيفهمى ايدرسن بونجه يلدر اول بنم نكاحلى عورتمدر ديروب
ارايرده غوغا چوغالدى پس عيار ايتدى بونده غوغا ايتمنك فائدهسى
يوقدر كل سنكله عورتك ياننه كيدهلم و اكا صورهلم قنغيمزك ايدوكى اول
وقت معلوم و عيان[2] اولور ديدى پس ايكيسى دخى قالقوب عورتك
ياننه كلديلر.

خاتون انلرى كورنجه حال نيدوكنى[3] بلدى ايكيسنه دخى ير كوستردى
كچوب ايكيسنك قرشولرنده اوتوردى عيار ايتدى بره عورت سن كيمك
عورتى سن عورت ايتدى و الله شمديه قدر ايكيكزك دخى عورتى ايدم
اما شمديدن صكره قنغيكزك هنرى زياده اولور ايسه بنم ارم اولدر ايكيكزه
دخى برر هنر اوكرتدم قنغيكزك هنرى زياده اولور ايسه انك عورتى
اولورم صحيح ديدى ايكيسى دخى بو قوله راضى اولديلر عيار ايتدى بو
كون بن عيارلق ايدهيم صكره سندخى هنريكى كوستر ديدى پس عيار
ايله اوغرى قالقوب بازاره وارديلر عيار كورديكه بر فرنك بر كيسهيه

---

(1) *Bré!* 'Sirrah! follow!'—(2) *Ayan,* 'manifest.'—(3) Or نه ايدوكنى

بيك التون قربدي و قوينينه قوريوب بازاره كتدى فى الحال عيار فرنكك

آردينه درشوب بازار اراسنده ايريشوب بر ظرافتله فرنكك قوينندن

التونفى چالدى بر مخفى يره واروب التونك طقوزينى الوب و كندزك

اسمى يازلمش بر كومش يوزوكنى پارمغندن چيقاروب كيسهنك ايچنه

قويوب و كلوب فرنكك قوينينه قويدى بو جمله ايشلرى اوغرى كوردى پس

عيار طولاشوب فرنكك اوكنه چيقوب يقاسنه ياپشوب بر قاچ كره

اوروب ايتدى بره لعين بنم كيسم ايله بنم التونلريمى نيچون الدك

فرنك ايتدى وار ايشكه كيت بنى قوى سن كيم سن هنوز بن بلمم

ديدى عيار ايتدى سن بنى بلمك لازم دكلدر كل سنكله محكمهيه كيدهلم

فرنك راضى اولدى معا كتديلر عيار دعوى ايلدى قاضى فرنكه صوردى

سنك التونلرك قاچ دانه در فرنك ايتدى بيك التوندر عياردن صوردى

سنك قاچ دانه ايدى طقوز يوز طقسان بر دانه در و هم بنم اسم يازلمش

كومش يوزوكم كيسهنك ايچنده بيلهدر ديدى قاضى كيسهيى چيقاروب

مايديلر تمام طقوز يوز طقسان بر و يوزك دخى ايچنده چيقدى پس

فرنك بر قاچ سله ايله اورديلر التونلرى عياره ويرديلر عيار الوب اوغرى

ايله برابر عورتك يانينه كلديلر عورت ايدر ايشته عيار بر هنر كوستردى بو

آنه قدر كمسه مثلنى ايشتمامش ديدى چون كيچه اولدى اوغرى دخى

كمندينى الوب عيار ايله شاهك سرايينه وارديلر اوغرى كمند الوب

يوقارو چيقدى اندن عيارى دخى چكوب يوقارى چيقاردى اندن اشاغه

اينديلر خزينهسنه واروب درلو درلو مفتاحلر چيقاروب قپويى آچدى و

شاهك خزينه سنه كيروب عياره ايتدى قالدر بلديكك قدرالتون يوكلن عيار

---

(1) *Koïn*, 'the bosom or breast pocket, a fob.'—(2) A. *Zarafet*, 'tact, elegance
or wit.'—(3) *Makhfi*, 'secret, hidden.'—(4) A. *Laïn*, 'accursed one, the devil.'—
(5) *Komak*, or *koïmak*, generally means 'to place, put,' but here it means
'to leave, or let alone.'—(6) A. *Mahkemé*, or *mehkemé*, 'a court of justice.'—
(7) A. *Sillé*, 'a smack on the face, or box on the ear.'—(8) Pronounced *messel*
this word means 'a proverb, or parable,' but pronounced *misl* it signifies 'a like
thing, the like.'—(9) P. *Choun* means 'when,' or 'as.'—(10) *Kemend*, 'a halter,
noose.'

دخی یوكلندی طشره چقدیلر اندن قاز خانیه كیدوب بر قاز دخی طوتدی
بوغازلیوب اتش یاقدی شیسه¹ طاقوب عیاره چوبردیدی كندوسی پادشاهك
یتاق اوطهسنه طوغرلدی عیار ایتدی نیلرسن² اوغری ایتدی واروب پادشاهه
سنك و بنم هنرلریمی عرض ایدهیم بقالم قنغیمزك هنری زیاده در عورت
سكاهی لایقدر یوخسه بكامی لایقدر دیدی عیار ایتدی كل الله عشقنه كیدهلم
بن عورتدن كچدم سنك اولسون دیدی اوغری ایتدی سن شمدی اویله
دیرسن اما یارین پشمان³ اولورسن لكن پادشاه حكم ایلدكده اول وقت
راضی اولورسن دیوب كندی قپودن كیزلنوب باقدی بركوله⁴ شاهك ایاقلرینی
اوغار⁵ و هم اغزینده ساقز⁶ چینار⁷ كاه اویور كاه اویانور اوغری آهسته⁸ اهسته
تخته التنده كیزلندی و آت قلینك⁹ اوچنی اوغلانك اغزینه صوقدی و
اوغلان قیلی ساقرایله چیذادی اوغلان اسنرابكن¹⁰ اغزی اچلدی اوغری
قیلی چكوب ساقزی اغزیندن چالدی اوغلان كوزینی آچوب ساقزی اول
یكا بویكا ارادی بولمدی چون اراسی بر از كچوب اوغلان اویودی اوغری بر
دارو¹¹ بوررنه طوتدی اوغلان تمام كندودن كچوب دوشدی اوغری بر زنبله¹²
قیوب دیواره اصدی و كندو پادشاهك ایاغنی اوغماغه باشلادی عیار قپودن
بر ایشلری كورورردی پادشاه قملداندی¹³ اوغری آهسته آهسته ایتدی شاهم
اكر دكلرسن بر حكایه نقل ایدهیم پادشاه ایدر سویله دكلیهلم اوغری باشلدی
عیارایله بینلرینده واقع اولان احوالی بیان ایتمكه و ارالق ارالق طشرهده اوتوروب
قازی كباب ایدن عیاره چوبرده قاز یاندی دیو خطاب ایدردی حتی عیارایله
خزینهسنه كیروب و عیار طشره اوتوروب قازی كباب ایتدیكنی و كندوسی

---

(1) *Shish*, 'a skewer, a spit,' 'a swelling.'—(2) نه ایلرسن 'What art thou doing?'
(3) *Pishman*, properly the Persian word پشیمان *peshiman*, 'to repent, be sorry.'—
(4) *Kieulé*, 'a male slave.'—(5) *Oghmak*, 'to rub with the palm of the hand,
shampoo.'—(6) *Sakiz*, a kind of gum which is chewed like tobacco in the East.—
(7) *Chinémek*, 'to chew, masticate,' 'trample on.'—(8) P. *Aheste*, 'softly, slowly.'
—(9) *Kil*, 'a hair, or bristle.'—(10) *Esnemek*, 'to yawn, gape,' 'to be elastic.'—
(11) P. *Darou*, or *dari*, 'a drug.'—(12) Generally spelt زنبل *zenbil*, 'a rush basket,
tool-basket.'—(13) *Kimildanmak*, 'to move,' (v.n.).

حيله ايله اوغلان اغزندن ساقزى چالديغنى الحاصل جمله واقع نه ايسه
بيان ايلدى اول سوپلر عيار دترر وهم كل كيدهلم ديو اشارت ايدر اوغرى
دخى چوپرقاز ينار ديوب خطاب ايدر و دونرب شاهه ايدر اى شاه
عياركمى هنرى زيادهيوخسه خرسزكمى زياده در عورت بونلرك قنغيسنه
لايقدر ديدى شاه ايتدى اوغرينك هنرى زياده در و عورت دخى انكدر
ديدى پس اوغرى برازدخى شاهك اياغنى اوغوب شاه اوبودقده اهسته
اهسته قالقوب عيارك يانه كلوب ايتدى شاه عورت اوغرينكدر ديديكنى
ايشتدنمى عيار ايشتدم ديدى اوغرى عورت كيمكدر ديدى عيار سنكدر
ديدى اوغرى ايدر يلان سويلرسن بن ينه واروب شاهدن سوال ايدهجكم
عيار ايدر الله ايچون اولسون كل كيدهلم قارى دكل استرسن بندخى سنك
اولديم اندن قالقوب اول مالى قارينك يانه كتورديلر اكا دخى بو احوالى
بيان ايلديلر عورت تحسين ايدرك اوغربى كندوبه ار ايدندى

(1) *Edinmek,* 'to provide for one's self,' 'procure for one's self,' 'gain for one's self.'

### *Translation.*

In former times there was a crafty woman, in the city of Cairo, called Dallat-ul-Muhtal. She had two husbands, and each one thought she was his own wife, and for a long time she was wife to both. The men were completely unaware of this state of affairs. As regards their calling: one of these men was a sharper, and the other a thief; and both were pupils of the woman. One day the thief went to the bazaar and sold an article, and took the money. Another person meeting the man to whom he had delivered the article, cried out, "Thanks be to God! I have found a clue, you have got my other property; come, speak quickly!" The man replied, "Don't talk nonsense! I bought this and paid for it. You talk thus because you want this property." The thief saw them, and at once took to his heels, and came home. He said to the woman: "Wife! my robberies have been found out; bring me a piece of bread and I will go elsewhere, until this row has blown over." The woman prepared a cake and a lamb's tail, and cutting them in two, gave the thief a half of the cake and a half of the lamb's tail. The thief took them, and went on his way. After a time the sharper came too, and said : "Wife ! my swindling has been detected, give me a piece of bread. I will not appear for a few days, and go somewhere else." The woman gave the sharper the remaining half of the lamb's tail, and he departed. However, the thief, who went first, coming to an agreeable shady place, and a nice spring of water, sat down by that agreeable water, and took out the bread and the lamb's tail, and was about to eat, when, lo ! the sharper also came to that place, and sat down at the edge of the spring. On his sitting down, and taking out the lamb's tail, the thief said : "Come mate, let us dine together." The sharper approached, and looked at his own cake and the thief's. He saw they resembled each other. They put them together, and it was one cake. They then put the pieces of the lamb's tail together, and found they were one tail. The sharper was astonished, and said : "There's no offence in asking. Where do you come from ? " The thief said : " I come from Cairo." The sharper replied : " Where is your house." The thief said : " My house is Dallat-ul-Muhtal's house, in Cairo ; and she is my wife." The sharper said : " That house is mine, and that woman is my wife, and I have lived there for how many years. Now why do you tell lies ? " The thief said : " Fellow ! are you mad, or are you joking ? She has been my married wife for many years." Thus talking the dispute waxed greater and greater. At last the sharper said : " There is no use in our quarelling here ; come, let us go to the woman, and ask her. Then we shall see whose wife she is." Then the two arose, and came to the woman. As soon as the woman saw them she knew what was the matter. She showed them both a seat, and sat down before the two. The sharper said : " Holloa, wife ! whose wife are you ?" She said : " Wallah,* hitherto I have been the wife of both of you, but henceforth he will be my husband who is the cleverer. I taught you both to be skilful, but whoever's skill is greater, I will be his wife." They both consented to this agreement. The

---

* ' By God ! '

sharper said : "To-day I will do some swindling, then you can show your skill." Then they both arose, and went to the bazaar. The sharper noticed that a Frank put a thousand pieces of gold into a purse and the purse into his bosom, and went to the market. The sharper at once followed the Frank, reached him in the middle of the bazaar, and, by a skilful trick, stole it out of his pocket. He then went into a secret place, took nine gold pieces out of the purse, and taking off his finger a ring engraved with his own name, put it into the purse, and came back and put it into the Frank's pocket. The thief saw all this. Then the sharper made a circuit, came in front of the Frank, seized him by the collar and beat him several times, saying : "Halloa, you devil ! why did you take my purse and my gold pieces." The Frank said : "Go about your business. Go, and let me alone. Who are you ? I have never seen you until now." "There is no necessity for you to know me. Come ! we will go together to a Court of Justice." The Frank agreed, and they went together. The sharper prosecuted, and the Cadi asked the Frank : "How many are your pieces of gold?" The Frank said : "A thousand pieces of gold." He (then) asked the sharper: "How many are yours?" "Nine hundred and ninety-one pieces, and even there is a silver ring of mine, on which my name is written, inside the purse." The Cadi took out the purse and counted. Exactly nine hundred and ninety-one came out, and a ring. They gave the Frank a few smacks on the face, and the money to the sharper, who took them and returned with the thief to the woman. The woman said : "Behold ! he has shown skill the like of which has hitherto not been heard of." When night came the thief took a slip-knot and went with the sharper to the king's palace. The thief took his slip-knot and climbed up, and then, pulling, got the sharper up. They descended (inside). They went to the treasury, and, taking out various kinds of keys, opened the door, and entered the king's treasury. The thief said to the sharper : "Pick up and carry as much gold as you can." The sharper loaded himself and they went out. They then proceeded to the poultry house, took a goose and killed it, lit a fire and put it on a skewer, which the sharper turned. The latter then went in the direction of the king's bedroom. The sharper said : "What are you doing ?" The thief said : "I am going to the king to submit our skill to him. We shall see which of us has the greater skill, and whether you or I deserve the woman." The sharper said: " Come! for God's sake let us go away, I have given up the woman. Let her be yours." The thief replied : "You say so now ; but to-morrow, you will be sorry for it, but when the king has arbitrated then you will be satisfied." So saying, he, hiding himself behind the door, peeped in. A male slave was shampooing the king's feet, and chewing mastic, sometimes awake, sometimes asleep. The thief softly hid himself under the throne ; and stuck the end of a piece of horse-hair into the boy's mouth. The boy chewed up the the hair with the mastic, but he yawned and opened his mouth. The thief pulled the hair, and drew the mastic out of his mouth. The boy opened his eyes and looked for the mastic on this side and on that side, but after a short interval fell asleep. The thief held a drug to his nose, the boy became quite unconscious and dropped down. The thief put him into a rush-basket and hung him up on the wall, and began to shampoo the king's foot himself. The sharper saw all things from the door. The king moved, the thief softly said : " Sire, if you desire it, I will tell you a tale." The king said : "Tell it me, and I will listen." The thief commenced to relate everything that had happened between him and the sharper, and from time to time looking out, addressed the sharper, who sat outside turning the goose, saying : "Turn, turn, the goose is burning." He even explained that he had entered the king's treasury with the sharper, that the sharper was sitting outside turning the goose, and that he by a trick had stolen the mastic out of the slave's mouth, in short all that had occurred. The sharper trembled and beckoned to him for them to go. The thief replied : " Go on turning, the goose is burning ;" and turning to the King said : " Oh, King! is the skill of the sharper greater or that of the thief? and which deserves the woman." The king said : " The skill of the thief is greater, and the wife is his." Then the thief sham-pooed the king's leg a little, and when he fell asleep, he softly arose, and coming to the sharper's side, said : " Have you heard that the king says that the woman is the thief's." The sharper said : " I have heard it." The thief said : " The woman is whose?" The sharper replied : " Yours." The thief said : " You are telling lies,

I will go again, and ask the king." The sharper said : " For God's sake, let it be. Come ! let us go. Not only the woman, but I will be yours, if you wish." Then they arose, and brought those riches to the woman, and explained how things were. The woman approved, and took the thief as her husband.

———————

# TOOTI-NAMÉ.

The *Tooti-Namé*, or "Parrot's Book," is a Turkish version of the Fables of Bidpaï.
The tales are amusing, and well adapted for practice in reading for students.

## THE STORY OF SAÏD.

حكايه سعيد

ديار¹ حلبده² بر بازركان³ وار ايدى اسمنه خواجه⁴ بهرام ديرلردى بونك
اون بش ياشنده بر محبوب⁵ اوغلى وار ايدى اسمنه سعيد ديرلر ايدى بر
كون سعيد اتنه سوار⁶ اولوب حلبك طشره⁷ باغلرينه كيدوب واقر كزينوب⁸
كيرويه رجعت⁹ و خانه‌سنه كلوركن يولى بر حمامه¹⁰ اوغرايوب¹¹ اننك
اياقلرى¹² سورچوب¹³ يقلدى¹⁴ سعيدك دخى عقلى باشندن كيدوب
بيهوش¹⁵ اولدى حمامدن عورتلر چقوب كيدركن سعيدى اول حالده كوردىلر
و اه يازق¹⁶ شول محبوب هلاك¹⁷ اوله‌جق ديو سعيدى برقاچى¹⁸ صقوب¹⁹ بو
حالى سويلديلر تيز طشره كلوب سعيد الوب حمامك بر تنها²⁰ يرنده
ياتوردى يبزينه صو سريوب²¹ معالجه²² تيدنده²³ ايكن مكر²⁴ شهر حلبده
خوجه يوسف نامنده بر بازركان وار ايدى بونك كلفوش نامنده بر محبوبه
قزى اولوب دنياده مثلى²⁵ ناياب²⁶ و سنى²⁷ اون بش ايدى اتفاق²⁸ اول
كون اولدخى حمامده بولندى سعيد بران²⁹ خوش³⁰ اولوب عقلى باشنه

---

(1) *Diyar*, 'a country.'—(2) *Haleb*, 'Aleppo.'—(3) P. *Bazirghian* (*bazirghan*), 'a merchant.'—(4) P. *Khajé* (*khoja*), 'a gentleman, schoolmaster, teacher, professor, a civil servant.'—(5) A. *Mahboub*, 'beloved, lovely.'—(6) *Suwar olmak*, 'to mount.'—(7) P. *Bagh*, 'a vineyard' (in poetry, 'a garden').—(8) *Ghezmek*, 'to promenade;' *ghezinmek*, 'to walk about without any object.'—(9) A. *Rijaat*, 'returning.'—(10) A. *Hammam*, 'a bath.'—(11) *Oghramak* (*v. n.*), 'to pass by, or through, to touch at.'—(12) *Ayak*, 'a foot.'—(13) *Surchmek*, 'to slip.'—(14) *Yikilmak*, 'to fall, or be pulled down.'—(15) P. *Bi-housh*, 'insensible.'—(16) *Ah! yazik*, 'What a pity!'—(17) *Helak olmak*, 'to perish.'—(18) *Bir katch*, 'a few.'—(19) *Sokmak*, 'to push in.'—(20) P. *Tenha*, 'lonely.'—(21) *Serpmek*, 'to sprinkle.'—(22) *Mualejé*, 'curing, medical treatment.'—(23) A. *Kaïd*, 'fixing one's attention on any thing.'—(24) P. *Méjher* (*méyer*), 'but, however.'—(25) A. *Misl*, 'a like thing, or quantity.'—(26) P. *Nayab*, 'not existing,' 'not to be found.'—(27) A. *Sin*, 'age.'—(28) A. *Itifak*, 'chance, by chance.'—(29) P. *Ber-an*, 'thereupon.'—(30) P. *K'hosh*, 'agreeable, well.'

سكاسا كلدی خالصهسی ¹ و جاریهلری ² سوندی ³ كلنوش بو احوالی ⁴ اشتدی كندی
كندیه ایتدی بو سعید كوزللكده و محبوبلقده مدح ⁵ ایدرلر بوندن ایو فرصت ⁶
اولمز باری ⁷ بر نظر ایدهیم دیو كلوب عورتلر ⁸ اراسندن جمال ⁹ سعیدهد نظر ¹⁰
ایلمكده بر كلهلم سعیده صو استدی ویردیلر ایچرن كلنوشك جمالی سعیدك
دیده ¹¹ مستانهسنه ¹² راست ¹³ كلوب یا بو ملك ¹⁴ صورت ¹⁵ تر كیمكدر دیوب
عشقنه ¹⁶ كرفتار ¹⁷ اولدی قر دخی تماشا ¹⁸ ایدر كن سعیده تعشق ¹⁹ ایدوب
ایكی طرفدن بازار عشق كرم ²⁰ اولدی حاصل مرام سعیدك بر یرنده علتی ²¹
قلمیوب خاله سنك النی بوس ²² ایدوب حمامدن طشره اتنه سوار اولوب
خانهسنه كلدی طایهسنی ²³ چاغروب ²³ تنها بویننه ²⁵ صارلدی ²⁶ احوالنی سویلهدی
و خاله قادین انده ایدی جاریهلر اول قزی بلیرلر كیمك قزیدر سندن خبر
استرم دیو نیاز ایلدی طایه ایتدی شهر حلبده خوجه یوسفك قزندن كوزل
قز یوقدر هله بر سؤال ایدهیم دیوب خالهسنك جاریهلرندن خبر الدی
خوجه یوسفك قزیدر دیو كلدی سعیده خبر ویردی سعید طایهنك الینه
و ایاغینه دوشوب او قزه بندن سلام كتوروب حالمی اعلان ²⁷ ایله دیدی
خلاصه طایه مشفقه ²⁸ او لمغله تیز ²⁹ واروب قز ایله بولشوب ابتدا ³⁰ ای نادره ³¹
دوران ³² سعید سنی حمامده كوروب سزه تعشق ایلمش دیو سلامنی تبلیغ
ایلدی كلنوش مسرور ³³ اولوب ابتدا ای طایه قدین اولكون بندخی انك

(1) *Xale*, ‘an aunt.’— (2) A. *Jariyé*, ‘a female slave, girl.’— (3) *Sevinmek*, ‘to
be glad.’— (4) A. *Ahwal* (pl. of حال *hạl*), ‘state.’— (5) *Medh etmek*, ‘to praise.’—
(6) A. *Fursat*, ‘an opportunity.’—(7) *Bari*, ‘at least, at any rate.’—(8) A. *Avret*,
‘a woman.’—(9) A. *Jemal*, ‘beauty.’—(10) *Nazr etmek*, ‘to look.’—(11) P. *Didé*,
‘an eye.’— (12) P. *Mestané*, ‘intoxicated.’— (13) *Rast ghelmek*, ‘to meet.’—
(14) A. *Mélek*, ‘an angel.’—(15) A. *Souret*, ‘form, figure;’ *mélek souret*, ‘who has
an angel’s form.’—(16) A. *Ashk*, ‘love.’—(17) P. *Ghiriftar*, ‘seized.’—(18) *Tamasha
etmek*, ‘to view, survey.’—(19) *Taashuk etmek*, ‘to fall in love.’—(20) P. *Gherm*,
‘warm,’ ‘swift.’—(21) A. *Illet*, ‘a disease.’—(22) P. *Bous*, ‘a kissing;’ *bous etmek*,
‘to kiss.’—(23) *Dayé*, ‘a foster-mother.’—(24) *Chaghirmak*, ‘to call.’—(25) *Boyoun*,
‘the neck.’—(26) *Sarilmak*, ‘to entwine one’s self, embrace.’—(27) *Ilan éilémek*,
‘to make known, inform.’—(28) A. *Mushfik*, ‘compassionate, kind.’—(29) P. *Tiz* (*téz*),
‘quick, quickly.’— (30) A. *Ibtida*, ‘a commencement, beginning;’ (adv.) Turkish,
‘first of all.’— (31) A. *Nadir*, ‘rare.’—(32) P. *Deveran*, ‘the world, time;’ thus
*Nadiré-i-deveran*, ‘Oh, rare one of the age!’—(33) A. *Mesrour*, ‘delighted.’

عشقنه كرفتار او لمشم او كوندنبرو سلام كوندره جك بر واسطه ٔ بولهمدم دليو
سعيده سلام و وافر هدايا ٔ كوندردى طايه كاوب سعيده هداياٯرى و سلمى
تبليغ ٔ ايلدى بونك اوزرينه بر قاچ كون مرور ٔ ايدوب كلنوش والدهسيله
خوجه بهرامك خانهسنه زيارتهده ٔ كلدى طايهيى مخفيجه بولوب ابتدا اى
طايه قدين بنى بو كون ديدار ٔ سعيده ملاقى ايله زيرا صبره قرارم قالمدى
ديدى طايه ايتدى بن واروب سعيد ايله مشاوره ايدهيم . . . . . . . .

(1) A. *Vasité,* 'a means.'— (2) A. *Hedaya,* 'presents.'— (3) *Tebligh etmek,* 'to
forward.'—(4) *Murour etmek,* 'to pass.'—(5) A. *Ziaret,* 'a visit.'—(6) P. *Didar,* 'the
sight of any one, after absence;' 'the face.'

## Translation.

There was a merchant in the country of Aleppo, called Khoja
Behram, who had a handsome son, fifteen years of age, whose name
was Saïd.

One day Saïd mounted his horse and went to the vineyards
outside Aleppo. After riding about for a long time he returned.
While on his road back he passed by a bath, and, his horse's foot
slipping, he was thrown off, and became senseless. The women
coming from the bath saw Saïd in that condition, and some of them
reported it, and they came and took Saïd and laid him down in a
quiet place in the bath, sprinkled water in his face and tried to
restore him.

Now there was (another) merchant in Aleppo who had a lovely
daughter called Gulnush, fifteen years of age, the like of whom was
not to be found in the world, who happened to be in the bath that
day. Saïd, in the meanwhile, had got better, and his senses returned;
and his aunt and her women rejoiced. Gulnush, hearing of this affair,
said to herself: "They extol this young man and say he is handsome
and nice. There could not be a better opportunity. I will just
have one look at least." So saying she came and looked at him, and
called for water for Saïd. They gave it to her, and while he was
drinking it, the beauty of Gulnush met his intoxicated gaze, and he
said: "Who is this maiden with the form of an angel?" and

fell in love with her. The maiden also, on beholding Saïd, fell in love with him, too; in short, the love was mutually ardent. Saïd being completely recovered, kissed his aunt's hand, left the bath, mounted his horse and went home. He then sent for his foster-mother, and, when they were alone, threw himself on her neck, and told her how matters stood, and that his aunt and her women had been there and knew whose daughter the maiden was, and that he wanted her to find out. The foster-mother said: "There is no girl in Aleppo prettier than Khoja Yousouf's daughter." She went and inquired of the aunt's women, and came and told Saïd that the girl was Khoja Yousouf's daughter. Saïd fell at the feet of his foster-mother and said: "Take my compliments to that maiden, and tell her my condition." Finally his foster-mother had compassion on him, and went directly to the girl, and bringing his compliments, addressed her thus: "Oh, rare one of the age! Saïd has seen you in the bath, and fallen in love with you." Gulnush was delighted, and said: "Oh, Madam! I also fell in love with him that day, and since then I have not been able to find a means of sending my greeting to him." So saying, she sent her salutation to Saïd, and numerous presents, and the foster-mother brought them to him. A few days having elapsed after this, Gulnush went with her mother on a visit to Khoja Behram's house. She saw the foster-mother privately, and said: "Oh, Madam, my patience is exhausted, let me see Saïd to day." The foster-mother replied: "I will go and speak to Saïd." . . . . . .

## SULTAN SULEYMAN THE MAGNIFICENT.*

### GRANDEUR.

خاق ايچنده ،عتبر<sup>1</sup> بر نسنه<sup>2</sup> يوق دولت<sup>3</sup> كبى

اولامىه دولت جهانده بر نفس<sup>4</sup> صحت كبى .

سلطان سليمان قانونى .

(1) A. *Mutéber,* 'esteemed.'—(2) *Nesné,* 'a thing.'—(3) A. *Devlet,* 'empire, prosperity.'—(4) A. *Néfes,* 'the breath;' *nefs,* 'the soul, the flesh, the passion.'

### *Translation.*

" There is nothing so esteemed by the people as grandeur (empire);
whereas there is nothing so good in worldly grandeur as one breath
of health."—(*Sultan Suleyman, the Law-giver*).

---

* This great monarch, who was distinguished both for his victories and his
literary talent, is called by Europeans 'Suleyman the Magnificent,' but by the
Turks 'Suleyman the Law-giver.'

## MESHIHI.

MESHIHI is a Turkish poet who excelled in describing the beauties of nature, and may be called the Longfellow of the Turks. He was born near Uskub. His productions were highly esteemed by his contemporaries; indeed so much so that the Grand Vezir, Ali Pasha, the Eunuch, gave him a fief on the revenues of which he existed, and also appointed him Secretary of the Divan, in consequence of a poetical petition Meshihi had addressed to the Prime Minister. This poem is still extant. It appears, however, that Meshihi was not so good an official as a poet, and neglected the duties of his office to indulge in dissipation. The Sultan, on learning this, considerably reduced his salary. After his patron Ali Pasha's death, Meshihi again solicited government employment, but unsuccessfully. He died in the year of Hejira 918 (1512 Anno Domini).

## THE MERRY SPRING.

دكله <sup>1</sup> بلبل <sup>2</sup> قصه <sup>3</sup> سن كم <sup>4</sup> كلدى ايام <sup>5</sup> بهار <sup>6</sup>

قوردى <sup>7</sup> هر باغده هنكامهء <sup>8</sup> هنكام <sup>9</sup> بهار

اولدى سيم <sup>10</sup> افشان <sup>11</sup> اكا ازهار <sup>12</sup> بادام <sup>13</sup> بهار

عيش و نوش ايت كم كچر بو ايام بهار

ينه انواع شكوفهله <sup>14</sup> بزندى <sup>15</sup> باغ <sup>16</sup> و راغ

عيش <sup>17</sup> ايچون قوردى چيچكلرى صحن كلشنده اوتاغ

كم بلور اول بهارهدك كه و كيم اوله صاغ

عيش و نوش <sup>18</sup> ايت كم كچر قالمز بو ايام بهار

طرف كلش نور احمد برله مالا مالدر

سبزهلرنده صحابه <sup>19</sup> لالهء <sup>20</sup> خير الالدر

هى محمد امتى وقت حضور <sup>21</sup> حالدر <sup>22</sup>

عيش و نوش ايت كم كچر قالمز بو ايام بهار

رخلرى <sup>23</sup> رنكين <sup>24</sup> كوزللر در كايله لالهلار

كم قولاقلرينه دراو جوهر اصمش ژالهلار <sup>25</sup>

الدانوب صنمه كه بونلر بويله باقى قالهلار

عيش و نوش ايت كم كچر قالمز بو ايام بهار

---

(1) *Dinlémek,* 'to listen.'—(2) P. *Bulbul,* ' the nightingale.'—(3) A. *Kisa,* 'a tale.'
—(4) *Kim* (in old books used for كه *ki*), 'for, because.'—(5) A. *Eyyam,* 'days.'—
(6) A. *Bahar,* 'spring.'—(7) *Kourmak,* 'to set going, to place in working order, to
pitch, to plan.'—(8) P. *Henghiamé,* 'a tumult.'—(9) P. *Henghiam,* 'time.'—(10) P. *Sim,*
'silver.'— (11) P. *Efshan,* 'scattering, who scatters.'—(12) A. *Ezhar* (pl. of زهر),
'flowers.'—(13) P. *Badam* (or بادم *badem*), 'an almond.'—(14) P. *Shughioufé,* 'a blossom,
flower.'—(15) *Bézenmek,* 'to adorn one's self, put on one's best clothes.'—(16) P.
*Bagh,* 'a garden.'—(17) A. *Ish,* 'pleasure, jollity, gaiety.'—(18) P. *Noush,* 'drinking.'—(19) A. *Sahabé* (pl. of صاحب), 'companions' (especially of Mohammad).—
(20) P. *Lalé,* 'a tulip.'—(21) *Husour,* 'tranquillity, pleasure.'—(22) A. *Hal,* 'the
present.'—(23) P. *Roukh,* 'the cheek.'—(24) P. *Renghin,* 'coloured, capital, funny,
varied in colour.'—(25) P. *Zhalé,* 'a dewdrop, dew.'

كتدى اول دیملر كه اولوب سبزلر صاحب فراش [1]

غنچه [2] فكرى كلشنك، اولمشیدى بغرنده [3] باش

كلدى بر دم كم قراردى لالهلله طاغ و تاش

عیش و نوش ایت کم کچر قالمز بو ایام بهار

ابر كلزار اوستنه هر صبح [4] كوهر [5] بارٔ یكن

نفحهٔ [7] باد [8] سحرٔ [9] پر نافهٔ [10] تاتار یكن

غافل اولمه عالمك محبوبلیغى وار ایكن

عیش و نوش ایت کم کچر قالمز بو ایام بهار

بوی [11] كلزار [12] اتدى شولدكلو [13] هوای مشكناب [14]

كم یره اینجه اولور قطرهٔ [15] شبنم [16] كلاب [17]

چرخ [18] اوتاق [19] قوردى كلستان اوستنه كونلك [20] سحاب [21]

عیش و نوش ایت کم کچر قالمز بو ایام بهار

(1) A. *Firash*, 'a bed ;' *sahib-firash*, ' ill in bed.'—(2) P. *Ghonché*, 'a rosebud.'—
(3) *Baghir*, ' the bowels ' (' the breast '), obsolete.—(4) A. *Soubh*, ' the morning.'—
(5) P. *Ghevher*, or *ghiuher*, 'a pearl, or precious stone.'—(6) P. *Bar*, 'pouring;'
*ghevher-bar*, ' which pours out pearls or precious stones.'—(7) A. *Nefhé*, 'a breath.'
—(8) P. *Bád*, ' the wind.'—(9) A. *Sahr*, 'the early morn.'—(10) P. *Nafé*, 'a
bag of musk;' ' the navel.'— (11) P. *Bouï*, 'scent.'— (12) P. *Ghiulzar*, 'a bed of
roses.'—(13) *Dinlou*, 'manner, kind;' *shol*, 'that;' *shol-dinlou*, ' in such a manner.'
—(14) P. *Mushk*, ' musk;' *nab*, ' pure.'—(15) A. *Katré*, 'a drop.'—(16) P. *Shebnem*,
' dew.'—(17) P. *Ghiulab*, 'rose-water.'—(18) P. *Charkh*, ' the universe, firmament.'
— (19) *Otak*, ' a large tent.'— (20) *Ghiunluk*, 'frankincense.'—(21) A. *Séhab*, 'a
cloud.'

## THE MERRY SPRING.

[The following free translation of the above appeared some years ago in a collection of Oriental tales, &c., in English, published by the Author of this volume.]

Hark ! 'tis the nightingale !
Come, let us spring-time hail ;
For joy's own bower,
'Neath the almond-flower
In the spring-time 's to be found.

L.

Oh ! hear the spring's voice,
And laugh and rejoice ;
  For the merry spring,
  On Time's swift wing,
Doth quickly, quickly pass.

Flowers cover hill and dale,
Arid heath and smiling vale ;
  But a fleeting thing
  Is the merry spring,
And ne'er may you see her more ;
So hear the spring's voice,
And laugh and rejoice ;
  For the merry spring,
  On Time's swift wing,
Doth quickly, quickly pass.

  The groves are all bright
  With " Ahmed's light." *
Oh, people of Mahomet, come,
For pleasure's season 's now begun.
  And hear the spring's voice,
  And laugh and rejoice ;
    For the merry spring,
    On Time's swift wing,
  Doth quickly, quickly pass.

The rose and the tulip, in the fresh, crisp air,
Look as blooming and charming as damsels fair ;
And the dew on the leaves, the dew-drops of morn,
With fairy-like diamonds these sisters adorn.
  Then hear the spring's voice,
  And laugh and rejoice ;
    For the merry spring,
    On Time's swift wing,
  Doth quickly, quickly pass.

* A kind of flower.

The season of darkness and sickness is o'er,
And the plants and the flowers recover once more,
And, passive and sorrowful, down on its breast,
Doth the rosebud no longer its sickly head rest.

> Then hear the spring's voice,
> And laugh and rejoice;
> For the merry spring,
> On Time's swift wing,
> Doth quickly, quickly pass.

The clouds in their passage, at early morn,
The rosebuds with fresh sparkling gems adorn,
And the gentle zephyrs, as on they sweep,
The earth in the musk of Tartary steep.

> Then hear the spring's voice,
> And laugh and rejoice;
> For the merry spring,
> On Time's swift wing,
> Doth quickly, quickly pass.

The scent of the roses, as it upward flies,
Meets the dew of the morn as it comes from the skies,
And together they mingle, and downward fall,
Every drop of the dew rosewater all.

> Then hear the spring's voice
> And laugh and rejoice;
> For the merry spring,
> On Time's swift wing,
> Doth quickly, quickly pass.

# MODERN WRITERS.

◆

## KEMAL BEY.

KEMAL BEY was one of the greatest of modern Turkish authors, if not the greatest. He was a poet, novelist, dramatist and journalist, and excelled in all branches of literature. His novels are nearly as good as those of Sir Walter Scott or Alexander Dumas, and his political articles in the *Ibret*, and other Turkish newspapers, are very ably written. His political ideas, which had been cultivated by the study of European history and literature, were in advance of his age in Turkey, and during the reign of Sultan Abd-ul-Aziz, he was exiled, and came to London, where he appears to have enjoyed himself and profited by what he saw, if we judge by the interesting description of London which he has bequeathed to his countrymen. He was acquainted with the languages and literatures of Persia, Arabia, England and France. While in London he published a Turkish journal called the *Hurriyet* ("Liberty"), which contained some remarkable articles suggesting reforms in the government of Turkey. He seems certainly to have been a good patriot, although some of his ideas were not approved of by his government. After a long stay in England he was allowed to return to his native land, and became eventually governor of the island of Scio. Notwithstanding his official duties his devotion to literature still continued. Unfortunately, last year, death put a stop to his literary activity at the early age of forty-eight.

I may, I think, appropriately conclude these few remarks about this great author, whom I had the privilege of being personally acquainted with, by a quotation from his own works, which shows that he deeply felt what a fleeting thing life is :—

"لايقيله دوشونلسون . انسانك حياتى يالكز استقبالدن عبارت دكلميدر ؟

ماضى نه در ؟ بر موت ابدى ... حال نه در؟ بر نفس واپسين"

" If we rightly reflect, the life of man consists only of the Future. What is the Past ? A perpetual death. What is the Present ? One's last breath."

## LONDON.

بتون ممالك متمدنهيى ¹ طولاشمغه ² نه حاجت ³ . انسان يالكز لوندرهيى
امعان ⁴ نظرله تماشا ⁵ ايلسه كورهجكى بدايع ⁶ عقله وله ⁷ كتورر . لوندرهيه
انموزج ⁸ عالم دينلسه مبالغه ⁹ دكلدر . روى ارضده موجود اولان اثار ترقينك ¹⁰
فوطوغراف ايله رسمى النمش اولسه مدنيت ¹¹ حاضرهيى انجق لوندره قدر
كوسترَه بيلور . بناء عليه بزده مثال ¹² اولهرق انى اختيار ايتدك .

بو مملكت ريب ¹³ و كمان ¹⁴ بلوطلرى ايچنده مستور اولان اقبال ¹⁵ بشر ¹⁶
كبى اكثريت اوزره بر قره دومان ايله محاط ¹⁷ و حتى كوبا كه عادات
مدنيت احجار ¹⁸ واشجارينه وارنجه يه قدر سرايت ¹⁹ ايتمش كبى خانهلرى
بيله سياهلرَه ²⁰ مستغرق كورينور . فقط او نقاب ²¹ ظلمانينك ²² ماوراسنه
تعلق نظر اولنورسه نازنين ²³ دلرباى ²⁴ تمدن ²⁵ نظره قريب افكار اولهجق بر
زينت وسلطنت ايله عرض ديدار ايتمكه باشلار كه بدايع پسند اولان
كوكللر ايچون حسن اندامه ²⁶ مفتون اولمامق احتمالك خارجنده در .

لوندرهده بولنان بر آدم احكام ²⁷ عدالتك ²⁸ جرياننى ²⁹ كورمك ايسترسه
اوكنه هر شيدن اول مركز تشريع اولان و دنياه كورديكمز قواعد سياستدن
همان بر چوغنك مهد ³⁰ ظهورى بولنان او توجه پارلمنتو چقار كه ـ يالكز

---

(1) A. *Mutémeden*, ' civilized.'—(2) *Dolashmak*, ' to go round, walk round, travel
round.'—(3) *Né hajet*, ' what necessity ?'—(4) A. *Iman*, ' regarding attentively.'—
(5) *Temasha*, ' viewing, seeing' (any sight).—(6) A. *Bedaï*, ' wonders.'—(7) A. *Velé*,
' astonishment, amazement.'—(8) *Unmuzaj*, ' type, pattern, model.'—(9) A. *Mubalagha*, ' exaggeration.'—(10) A. *Terakki*, ' progress.'— (11) A. *Médeniyyet*, ' civilization.'—(12) A. *Misal*, ' an illustration, an example, a counterpart.'—(13) A. *Réïb*,
' doubt.'— (14) A. *Ghiouman*, ' doubt, suspicion.'—(15) A. *Ikbal*, ' good luck.'—
(16) A. *Besher*, ' mankind, a human being, a man.'—(17) A. *Mouhat*, ' surrounded.'
—(18) A. *Ahjar*, ' stones' (pl. of حجر *hajar*). — (19) *Sirayet etmek*, ' to be com-
municated,' ' to be contagious.'— (20) P. *Siyah*, ' black, blackness, a black spot.'—
(21) A. *Nikab*, ' a veil.'— (22) A. *Zoulmani*, ' dark.'— (23) P. *Nazénin*, ' a beautiful
girl.'—(24) P. *Dilruba*, ' charming.'—(25) A. *Témeddun*, ' civilization.'—(26) P. *En-
dam*, ' figure, stature, symmetry.'—(27) A. *Ahkiam*, ' influences,' ' principles,' ' commands.'—(28) A. *Adalet*, ' justice.'—(29) A. *Jéréyan*, ' a being current, happening
taking place.'—(30) A. *Mehd*, ' a cradle.'

بناسنه باقلسه افكار¹ عمومیهنك دهشت و مقاومتی نظر اداریه قارشو بر
جسمانیت² كسب ایتمش و كوبا كه اوجسم هائل دكمه³ بر صدمه ایله
زوالدن مصون اولدیغنی كوسترمك ایچون تحجر⁴ ایلمش قیاس اولنور .

ایچنه كیربابورسه یوز سكسان ملیون اعضادن مركب اولان و كمالات
مدنیهده برنجی دكلسه برنجیلردن صایلان بر ملتك الك ممتازلرندن اوچ
درتیوز مبعوث⁵ كورپلور كه – هربری آمال⁶ قومه و مطالب استقباله بر
فصاحت فوق العاده ایله ترجمه اولمش زور بازوی عرفان ایله احكام
عدالت و اسباب ترقی یی سرائر⁷ خانه طبیعتدن استخراجه چالشمقده حد
امكانه تقرب ایدهجك قدر مهارت كوستررلر .

بو هیئت ممتازهنك قوه استذادی⁸ ایسه هر بری وسعتده بر بشقه
مملكت دنیلمكه شایان اولان عمومی بر مقصد اوزرینه افكارجه اتفاق
ایتمش قرق اللی و بعض كره یوزیوزاللی بیك كشیدن مركب انجمن⁹
سیاسیلر در كه – اجتماعلرنده تجاوز¹⁰ ویا دغدغه¹¹ ظهور ایتمك دكل
ارهلرنده جریان ایدن مباحثات¹² ادیبانهدن¹³ بشقه صیقیجه¹⁴ بر اوكسورك¹⁵
سسی¹⁶ بیله ایشیدیلمز . اوقدر ادم بر یره طوپلانور . ایچلرندن بر قاچی سوز
سویدر . قصوری سكوتله استماع ایلر . جملهسی بردن¹⁷ خلوص¹⁸ نیت و
اداب¹⁹ مطاوغتله²⁰ حكومتلرینه كیدرلر . عرض حاجت ایدرلر . استدعالرینك
یوزده طقسانی حقه موافق و برقوه غالبه ایله مؤید اولدیغی ایچون مقبول
اولور هله پارلمنتونك ویردیكی احكامی تطبیقه مأمور اولان محكمهلرده حاكملر²¹

(1) A. *Efkiar-i-umoumiyyé*, 'public opinion.'—(2) A. *Jismaniyyet*, 'incarnation, embodiment.'— (3) *Deghmé*, 'not every one.'— (4) A. *Tehajjur*, 'to turn to stone' (*v. n.*).—(5) A. *Mebus*, 'a deputy, representative.'—(6) A. *Amal*, 'hopes.'—(7) A. *Seraïr*, 'secrets.'—(8) A. *Istinad*, 'relying on for support,' 'taking as a basis.'—(9) P. *Enjumen*, 'an assembly, society.'—(10) A. *Téjavuz*, 'an offensive act, infringement.'—(11) A. *Daghdaghé*, 'turmoil.'—(12) A. *Mubahasat*, 'discussions.'— (13) P. *Edibané*, 'well-behaved, polite, refined,'— (14) *Sikjé*, 'often.'—(15) *Euksuruk*, 'a cough.'—(16) *Séss*, 'a sound.'—(17) *Birden*, 'at once.'—(18) A. *Khulous*, 'candour, sincerity, friendship, purity.'—(19) A. *Adab*, 'gentlemanly behaviour.'—(20) A. *Mutave'et*, 'conformity, obedience.'—(21) A. *Hakim*, 'a judge, a ruler.'

كوريلور كه طرفين صورلسه انصاف[1] و عدالـتـلرينه پدرلرينك شفقت[2]
ابوتقدن[3] زياده استناد ايدرلر . اوحاكملره تعيين[4] حقيقتده حكم و جدانيسنى
كتم ايتمامكه يمين (زورى)[5] ايتمش هيئتى مشاهده و معاونت ايدركه
جملهسى ايكى خصمك دخى جان جكرى قومشوسى اقرباسيدر . بونلرك
حضورنده طرفين مدعاسنى تربيح ايچون ـ فقيرلره بادهوا[6] خدمت ايدر .
وكيل و معينلر بولنورکه حقلى دعوايى قزانمق اتك[7] طولوسى التون قزانمغه
ترجيح اولنه كلمشدر .

ايشنته عدالت بوحالده وهله معرفت اندن زياده كمالده در . هانكى
مكتبه كيديلورسه كيدلسون ايچنده بولنان اون اون ايكى ياشنده اطفالى[8]
عادتا يكرمى اوتوزياشنه كيرمش ادملر قدر هر درلو انتظام و تربيهيه مألوف[9]
بولنور . رشديهلر وار در كه شاكردان اوچ درت لسان اوقور و علـوم الـيـه
وعاليهدن التى يدى اساسلى فن بيلور .

اون اون ايكيشر ياشنده يكرمى يكرمى بـش چوجق بـر باغچهيه كيدرلر .
كاه اللرنده بر غزته بولنور . او واسطه ايله دنياتك حالندن خبردار اولمغه
چالشورلر وكاه بر كوشه ده اوتورهرق هواتك لطافتنى و اشجارك طراوتنى
مدركانه بر نظرله تماشا ايدرك طبيعتدن وجدانى تلذذلر ايدرار .

كميلرده طائفه كوريلور كه بوش وقت اولدقچه رياضياتك[10] قوّ جاذبه[11]
قانونلرى كبى اك عميق[12] مسائلنى[13] مطالعهيه اوغراشور . دكانلرده يازيجى
كوريلور كه فرضا المانيا حكماسنك[14] حكمت حقوق حقنده اولان فكرلرينى
محاكمهيه[15] قالقيشور . . . . .

بر حيوانات باغچه سى وار . قفسلرنده بولنان حيوانات برر برر نظردن

---

(1) A. *Insaf*, 'conscience.'—(2) A. *Shefket*, 'compassion, clemency, indulgence.'—
(3) A. *Ubuvvet*, 'paternity.'—(4) A. *Tayin*, 'pointing out.'—(5) *Yemin etmek*, 'to
swear.'—(6) P. *Badi-héva (bedawa)*, 'gratis.'—(7) *Etek*, 'a skirt.'— (8) A. *Etfal*,
'children.'—(9) A. *Mé'louf*, 'accustomed.'—(10) A. *Riyazat*, 'mathematics.'—(11) A.
*Kuvvé-i-jazibé*, 'the attracting power' (power of gravity).—(12) A. *Amik*, 'deep,
profound.'—(13) A. *Mesail*, 'questions.'—(14) A. *Hukema*, 'wise men.'—(15) *Mu-
hakeme etmek*, 'to judge of.'

كچوراسه سفينهء[1] نوح هنوز طوفاندن[2] قورتيلهرق اوراجه قارهيه واصل اولمش
ده دروننده نه موجود ايسه كناره اوغرامش تصورنده بولنيليور .

كتبخانهلرينه[3] كيريلسه هر لساندن ايكى اوچ مليون كتاب و انلرى بولمق
ايچون همان علامهء[4] هر فن وصفنه لايق يوزلرجه حافظ[5] كتب موجود در .
اصحاب مطالعه ايسه اك خالى وقتنده سكز يوز كشيدن نقصان اولمز .
و ايچلرنده طقسان ياشنده خواجهلر و اون سكز ياشنده قزلر بولنور .

هله نمونه خانه[6] دروننده اولان دارالكتب[7] هر كيم كيدرسه نه قدر
نامعروف[8] بر لساندن اولورسه اولوسون مطبوع[9] بر كتاب استرسه و يرمهيه
و موجود دكلسه سرعت ممكنه ايله كتورتمكه مجبوردر[10] .

پارلمنتوده[11] بر خزانة الكتب وار . يالكز بر لورد اكا اوتوز بو قدر بيك
جلد كتاب وقف[12] ايتمش ! ! !

بر تربيهلى اكانجه محلنه كيدلديكى حالده كيميا[13] و حكمت[14]
طبيعيهيه دائر بر طاقم مسائل عميقهنك براهين[15] علنيهسنى كورر كه
چينده[16] مشهود[17] اولسه معجزهيه حمل[18] ايدرلر . . . .

بازارلرنده اولان جواهر[19] و نفايسه[20] باقلسه دنياىنك دفاىن[21] طبيعت و
خزائن[22] ثروتى[23] سراپا[24] يغما ايدلمشده اورايه كتورلمش ظن اولنور . . . . .
دور حركتك كثرتى او در كه سوقاقلرك هر برى دورى دائمى و حريانى
سريع بر كردباب[25] عظيمه دونمش . لاينقطع[26] بر طرفدن بر طرفه انسان اقار

(1) A. *Sefiné-i-Nouh,* 'Noah's Ark.'— (2) A. *Toufan,* 'the Flood.'— (3) *Kitab-khané,* 'a library.'—(4) A. *Allamé,* 'a very learned man.'—(5) *Hafiz-i-Kiutub,* 'a librarian.'— (6) *Numouné-khané,* 'a museum.'— (7) A. *Dar-ul-kiutub,* 'a library.'—(8) *Na marouf,* 'unknown, outlandish'—(9) A. *Matbou,* 'printed.'—(10) A. *Mejbour,* 'obliged.'— (11) *Parlamento,* 'parliament.'— (12) *Vakf etmek,* 'to bequeath.'— (13) A. *Kimiya,* 'chemistry.'—(14) A. *Hikmet-i-tabiiyyé,* 'natural philosophy.'—(15) A. *Berahin,* 'proofs ;' *aleni,* 'public, open ;' *Berahin-i-aleniyyé,* 'experiments, illustrations.'— (16) *Chin,* 'China.'— (17) A. *Meshhoud,* 'seen, witnessed.'— (18) *Haml etmek,* 'to attribute.'—(19) A. *Jevahir,* 'jewels.'—(20) A. *Nefaïs,* 'precious, beautiful things.'—(21) A. *Defaïn* (pl. of ذفينه *definé*), 'buried treasures.'—(22) *Khazaïn,* 'treasures, treasuries.'—(23) A. *Servet,* 'wealth, opulence.'—(24) P. *Serapa,* 'entirely, totally.'—(25) P. *Ghirdab,* 'a whirlpool.'—(26) A. *La-yenkati,* 'continually, uninterruptedly.'

طورر . شهر ايچنده قرق بيكى متجاوز اولان او عربه لرندن بشقه اوتوز بش
بيكدن زياده كيرا عربه سى و اون بش بيكدن زياده اومنيبوس وار در .
بونكله برابر شهرده اولان تيمور يوللرينك مركزنده[1] يومى اون درت ساعت
هر ايكى دقيقه ده التمش . عربه لى بر واپور حركت ايدر . بوحال ايله دخى
ينه شمندوفره ويا اومنيسوسه بنمك ايچون نوبت[2] بكلمك و شهرك پك
غلبه لك يرنده عربه بوله مامق اراصيره[3] هر كسك باشنه كلور حاللردندر .

شهرك ايچنده ير وار در كه اوج قره واپورى كوپريلره بربرينك اوزرندن
كچر . بغچه وار در كه سير[4] زه انلرى اللى التمش بيك عربه دور[5] ايدر .
تايمس نهرينك كنارنده اولان مخزنلره[6] كيدلسه ده هر كون وقوعبولان
ادخالات[7] و اخراجاته[8] باقلسه آدم دير كه نهرك كونده بر كره يو كسلوب بر
كره الچالمسنى موجب[9] اولان جزر[10] و مد ايله دنيانك نه قدر محصولاتى[11]
وار ايسه بورايه دوكليوب كليور . انسانك نه قدر معمولاتى[12] وارسه بورادن
طاغيلوب كيدييور . فابريقه لرينه[13] كيدلسه دهشتدن[14] وجودده تويلر
اورپرير . ايشليانلر ماكنه دكل كويا طاغ پارچه سى قدر بر ديو[15] اهنين[16]
بدندر[17] كه اغزندن اتشلر پوسكوره رك[18] و هر عضوى[19] حركت ايتدكچه بشقه
بر صداى مدهش[20] پيدا[21] ايدرك كندينى زنجير[22] حكمنه[23] اسير[24] ايدن
ملك[25] العقلك[26] كبجه كوندز بلا[27] ارام[28] انفان[29] فرماننه چاليشور . ايچارزنده

----

(1) A. *Merkez*, 'a centre.'—(2) *Noubet beklemek*, 'to wait one's turn.'—(3) *Arasira*, 'sometimes.'—(4) *Séir*, 'a promenading.'—(5) *Devr etmek*, 'to circulate' (v.n.).—
(6) A. *Mahzen*, 'a warehouse.'—(7) *Idkhalat*, 'imports.'—(8) *Ikhrajat*, 'exports.'—
(9) *Mujib olmak*, 'to cause.'—(10) A. *Jezr-vé-med*, 'the tide' (the ebb and flow).—
(11) A. *Mahsoulat*, 'productions, produce.'—(12) *Mamoulat*, 'manufactures, manufactured articles.'—(13) *Fabrika*, 'a manufactory.'— (14) A. *Dehshet*, 'terror.'—
(15) *Div*, 'a monster.'—(16) P. *Ahenin*, 'of iron.'—(17) P. *Bedn*, 'a body.'—
(18) *Puskiurmek*, 'to spout out of the mouth in a fine shower.'—(19) *Ouzr*, 'a member of the body.'—(20) A. *Mudhish*, 'terrible.'—(21) *Péïda etmek*, 'to get, to find, to get into one's possession;' *Péïda olmak*, 'to spring up, appear.'—
(22) P. *Zenjir*, 'a chain.'— (23) A. *Hukm*, 'authority, power, influence;' 'a decree.'
—(24) A. *Esir*, 'a captive, slave'—(25) A. *Melik*, 'a king's.'—(26) A. *Akl*, 'intellect.'— (27) A. *Bila*, 'without.'— (28) P. *Aram*, 'rest, repose.'— (29) A. *Infaz*, 'causing an order to be put in force.'

الات¹ طبعيه كوريلور كه عبرتنك² سكزى بيوكلكنده بر غزتهدن بر ساعتده
ايكى يوز بيك نسخه³ باصار : بر مطبعه⁴ ده اللى بيك عمله⁵ استخدام⁶
اولنديغى بر بيره فابريقهسنك اون بش بيك عربه باركيرى بولنديغى
كورلمشدر .

سرايا يالديزلره⁷ مستغرق⁸ و سرايلره غبطه⁹ رسا اولهجق صورتده مزين
اوتللرى واردر كه ايچنده اوچ بيك آدم يتار سفرهلرنده درت بيك كشى
يمك ييه بيلور . دكانلرى موجود در كه مثلا ترزى الذنه اولان بر مغازهده
بزم اسكدار¹⁰ خلقنك يدى ياشندن يتمش ياشنه قدر كافه افرادينى
كيديروب قوشاتمغه كافى¹¹ البسه كوريلور . و ايچنده مشترى يه¹² اشيا كوسترمك
ايچون يدى سكز يوز اركك¹³ و بش التيوز قادين خدمتكار بولنور . . . .

نهر التنده منتظم¹⁴ چارشرلر¹⁵ هوا ييزنده مكمل كپريلرى وار ! ! !

آيينه¹⁶ سراى نامنده بر مسيرهلرى¹⁷ موجوددر اوزاقدن باقيلورسه انعطاف¹⁸
شعلهدن¹⁹ حاصل اولان هوايى²⁰ ماﺋى²¹ بر زمين²² اوزرنده جولان اولان علايم²³
سما پارچهلرى نظر خيال اوكنه بر مجف كوه²⁴ الماس²⁵ كتورر .

كوندزلرى فسقيهلرندن²⁶ فوران²⁷ ايدن صولر نوردن ياپيلمش بر مناره
شكلنى باغلار . كيجهلرى غازلره مهتابلره مستغرق اولان ستونلرى عمود صبحنى

---

(1) A. *Alat* (pl. of الت, *alet*), 'an instrument, tool;' *Alat-i-Tabiyyé,* 'printing machines.'—(2) *Ibret,* the name of a Turkish newspaper.—(3) A. *Nuskhé,* 'a copy.' —(4) A. *Matba,* 'a printing-office.'—(5) A. *Amélé,* 'workmen, labourers.'—(6) *Istikhdam olounmak,* 'to be employed.'—(7) *Yaldiz,* 'gilding;' يالدز التونى *yaldiz altini,* 'a Venetian ducat,' 'a gold sequin.'—(8) A. *Mustaghrak,* 'immersed, drowned,' 'covered.'—(9) P. *Ghibta-resa,* 'causing longing.'—(10) *Uskiudar,* the village of Scutari, near Constantinople.—(11) A. *Kiafi,* 'sufficient.'—(12) A. *Mushteri,* 'a customer.'—(13) *Erkek,* 'male.'—(14) A. *Muntazem,* 'regular.'—(15) *Charshi,* 'a bazaar, market.'—(16) P. *Ayiné,* 'a mirror, reflector;' *ayiné seraï,* 'the Crystal Palace.'—(17) A. *Mesiré,* 'a promenade.'—(18) A. *Initaf,* 'reflection.'—(19) A. *Shulé,* 'flame.'—(20) A. *Hawaï,* 'belonging to the air.'—(21) A. *Ma'ï,* 'blue' (generally, in *Turkish,* pronounced—written even—ماوى *mavi*).—(22) P. *Zémin,* '.the surface of the ground,' 'the ground' (of colours).—(23) A. *Alaïm-us-sema,* 'a rainbow' (commonly pronounced *Eléïm-sama*).—(24) P. *Kiouh,* 'a mountain.'—(25) A. *Elmas,* 'a diamond.'—(26) *Fiskiyyé,* 'a fountain, jet d'eau.'—(27) *Fevéran etmek,* 'to spirt up, bubble.'

اندیرر نور نظر باغچهنك بر باشندن بر باشنه یتیشور . اویله بر باغچه که

ریاض¹ خلدی² تماشایه مقتدر اولان بر آدم بو دار محنت ایچنده اندن

مكمل بر تقلیدی³ یاپمغه مقتدر⁴ اوله بیلمش مشكوكدر .⁵

حكومتلرینك سطوتنی⁶ كورمك ایچون بر كره نهر كنارینه اینلمك

یاخود شهرك اسكی قلعهسنه كیرلمك كافیدر . زرهلی⁷ سفینهلر كوریلور

كه تیموردن دوكلمش بر بیوك مملكت حكمنده‌در . . .

خلقك مكنتی⁸ اكلاشلمق استنیلورسه یالكز غزه‌هلرك اعلان ایتدیكی اعانه

دفترلرینی كورمكله بوكا بر علم اجمالی حامل ایتمك قابلدر .

بر طول قادین⁹ ایتام¹⁰ مكتبنه اوچیوز بیك التون اهدا¹¹ ایدیور .

قوندره بویاسی یپار بر آدم وصیتنامه¹² سنده فقرایه یكرمی بیك لیرا

براقور . غریب¹³ شوراسیدر كه او قدر سطوتلی بر حكومتك یالكز اسایش¹⁴

خلقی محافظهیه¹⁵ مأمور اولان ضبطیهلرندن¹⁶ بشقه اورته‌ده بر اثری كورلمز .

ضبطیهلرك كاری ایسه كوندزلری عربهلرك چارپمامسنه¹⁷ نظارت ایدرك

مثلا احاد¹⁸ ناسدن برینك بندیكی كرا عربهسنی نوبتندن كیدرو براقمامق

ایچون اك بیوك اصحاب حیثیتك¹⁹ بر اشارتله²⁰ فیتونلرینی طوردیرمق

و كیجهلری بر قاچ سر خوش مجادلهسی باصدیرد قدن صكره صباحلره

قدر خانهلرك دكانلرك قپوسی قپالی و پنجرهلری محفوظ اولوب اولمدیغنی

كوزتمك كبی عدالت و اسایش خدمتلرندن عبارتدر .

خلقك ایسه او قدر مكنتله برابر خزینهلره مالك اولان اك بیوك اصحاب

---

(1) A. *Riyaz* (pl. of روضه *ravza*), ‘gardens.’—(2) A. *Khouldi*, ‘eternal.’—(3) A. *Tak-lid*, ‘imitation.’—(4) A. *Muktédir*, ‘able.’—(5) A. *Meshkiouk*, ‘doubted, doubtful.’—(6) A. *Satvet*, ‘military strength, might.’—(7) *Zirhli*, ‘iron-clad.’—(8) A. *Muknet*, ‘what one is able to do.’—(9) *Doul-kadin*, ‘widow lady.’—(10) A. *Eytam*, ‘orphans.’—(11) *Ihda etmek*, ‘to give a present.’—(12) *Vasiyyet-Namé*, ‘a will.’—(13) A. *Gha-rib*, ‘strange.’—(14) P. *Asayish*, ‘order, tranquillity.’—(15) A. *Muhafezé*, ‘protection, preservation.’—(16) *Zabtiyyélér*, ‘policeman.’—(17) *Charpmak*, ‘to knock or dash anything against another’ (*v. a.*).—(18) A. *Ahad*, ‘individuals.’—(19) A. *Haï-siyyet*, ‘status, dignity, consideration;’ *Ashab-i-Haïsiyyet*, ‘people of quality or position.’—(20) A. *Isharet*, ‘a sign.’

ثروتی ¹ سكسان ياشنده اولديغی حالدهينه مغازهسنه كيدر اقشاملره قدر
ايلقلی خدمتكار كبی ايشيله اشتغال ايدر .

دائما سعی و علم جهتلرينه مصروف اولان فكر حقيقت قوتيله اوبله بر
جهان رفاهيت ² پيدا ايتمشلردر كه بيك درلو مبالغات ³ ايله محاط اولان
ايران ⁴ خيالات شاعرانهسنك ⁵ هند ⁶ و چينده تصوير ايتديكی جوهرين ⁷ قلعهلر
زرين ⁸ سرايلر رنكين ⁹ كلستانلر ¹⁰ ياننده هيچ حكمنده قالور . . . .

اوت شويله بر قاچ سنه ايچنده استانبولی لوندره و يا روم ايلییی فرنسه
حالنه كتورمك ممكن اولمديغنی بزده بيليورز . فقط مادامكه اوروپا بو حاله
طوبی ¹¹ ايكی عصر ¹² ايچنده كلمش و مادامكه اسباب ¹³ ترقيجه ¹⁴ انلر
موجد ¹⁵ اولمش بز او وسائط ¹⁶ حاضر بولهجغز ايش اطرافلی ¹⁷ طوتيلورسه هيچ ¹⁹
اولمازسه ايكی عصر ايچنده اولسون بزده اك متمدن مملكتلردن صاييلهجق
بر حاله كله بيله جكز هيچ اشتباه ¹⁹ وار ميدر؟ ايكی عصر ايسه حيات ²⁰
جمعيتة ²¹ نسبتاً ²² لمحهء ²³ بصر حكمنده قالمزمی ؟

(1) A. *Servet*, 'opulence;' *Ashab-i-servet*, 'opulent people.'—(2) A. *Refahiyyet*, 'prosperity, comforts, good circumstances.'—(3) A. *Mubalaghat*, 'exaggerations.' —(4) *Iran*, 'Persia.'—(5) *Shaïrane*, 'poetical.'—(6) *Hind*, 'India.'—(7) P. *Jevherin*, 'of jewels, jewelled.'—(8) P. *Zerin*, 'of gold, golden.'—(9) *Renghin*, 'coloured,' 'gorgeous.'—(10) P. *Ghiulistan*, 'a rose garden, a flower garden.'—(11) *Top*, 'the whole of anything, all.'— (12) A. *Asr*, 'an age, century.'—(13) A. *Esbab*, 'causes.'— (14) A. *Terakki*, 'progress.'—(15) A. *Movjid*, 'an inventor.'—(16) A. *Vesaït*, 'means.' —(17) *Etrafli*, 'thoroughly.'— (18) *Hich olmazsa*, 'at least, at any rate.'—(19) A. *Ishtilah*, 'doubt.' — (20) A. *Hayat*, 'life.' — (21) A. *Jemiyyet*, 'a community.'— (22) A. *Nisbeten*, 'in relation to.'—(23) A. *Lemhé*, 'a glance;' *i-basr*, 'the twinkling of an eye, a moment.'

### Translation.

What necessity is there to travel through all civilized countries? If one only visits London with observant eyes, the wonders one will see will amaze one. If all the improvements in the world were photographed in a picture, the whole civilized world could only show as much as London. It is no exaggeration to say that London is a type of the world. Therefore we have chosen it as a sample (of the civilized world).

This city is generally enveloped in a black mist, like the happiness of mankind is involved in clouds of doubt and uncertainty, and its houses are as deeply covered with blacks as its very stones and trees are affected by the habits of civilization. But if we look behind that dark veil, the beauty of civilization is revealed to us in such splendour and majesty that an intelligent man must be smitten by it.

If any one who is in London wish to see the principles of justice in full play, before all things, there is that gigantic House of Parliament, which was the cradle of many of the constitutions (rules of politics) which we see in the world. If one looks at its construction, it seems as if the power and resistance of public opinion with regard to the administration had been embodied, and that that tremendous body had been turned to stone, to show as it were, that it is protected from destruction by any shock. If one enters it, he sees three or four hundred representatives, the most distinguished men of a nation (composed of one hundred and eighty millions of members) which, if not the first of all civilized nations, is one of the first, every one of whom explains, with extraordinary eloquence, the wishes of the people and the wants of the future, and displays all possible skill in expounding the principles of justice and the secrets of progress.

This distinguished body has, as its basis and support, political assemblies, each one as extensive as a town, which consists of forty or fifty, and, sometimes, a hundred, or a hundred and fifty thousand people, who have all agreed about a common object. When they meet, not only is there no disorder or turmoil, but very often, except the polite discussions which are going on, not even a cough is to be heard. So many men meet together in one place; some of them speak, and their defects are listened to in silence, and then, at once, they go candidly and politely to their government, and explain what they need. Ninety out of a hundred of their demands are granted, as they are consistent with right and supported by overwhelming force.

Judges in the Court of Justice, appointed in accordance with the principles laid down by the Parliament, are to be seen, whom all parties trust even more than the indulgence of their own fathers.

These judges are helped and controlled by a body called the "Jury," who swear to do their utmost to investigate the truth, and who are themselves the friends and neighbours of the two litigants. There are lawyers to state clearly both sides of the question in the presence of the Jury, who (some of whom) would prefer gaining a deserving case to a lap full of gold.

Behold, this is the state justice is in, but education is still more perfect. If you go into any school, children ten or twelve years of age are accustomed to order and education only to be found amongst men of twenty or thirty (elsewhere). There are higher schools where the pupils study three or four languages, and know six or seven sciences.

Twenty, or five-and-twenty children, ten or twelve years of age, will go to a garden (park). Either they have a newspaper in their hand and try to make themselves acquainted with what is going on in the world, or they sit in a corner and enjoy the pleasantness of the air, and freshness of the trees, which they survey with an intelligent glance. In their ships, crews are to be found who study the most abstruse mathematical questions, like the laws of gravitation. In the shops clerks are to be found who will discuss the ideas of the *savans* of Germany about the philosophy of rights.

There is a Zoological Garden. When all the animals in the cages pass before one's eyes, one by one, one fancies that Noah's Ark has just arrived there saved from the Flood, and all in it just landed.

If you enter their libraries, there are two or three millions of books, in all languages, and hundreds of librarians, who deserve to be called "Universal Geniuses," to help you find them. There are never less than eight hundred readers, and, amongst them, there are professors ninety years of age, and girls of eighteen.

Well! in the Museum Library, if any one wants a printed book, in no matter how outlandish a language, they must give it him, or if they have not got it, they must send for it as quickly as possible.

There is a library in the House of Parliament to which one lord alone bequeathed thirty thousand volumes!

If one goes to a " refined place of amusement," * he can see experiments in difficult matters connected with chemistry and natural philosophy which, if they were made in China, would be considered miracles.

If one sees the jewels and precious things in the shops, one thinks that the hidden treasure of nature, and the wealth of the world, have been plundered and brought there.

The traffic is such, that in every street the rapid and continual circulation is like a whirlpool of men, which flows from one end to another without cessation.

In the town, besides more than forty thousand private carriages, there are more than thirty-five thousand hired vehicles, and more than fifteen thousand omnibuses. At the centre of the railways of the town, for fourteen hours every day there is a train with sixty carriages every two minutes. Nevertheless, it often happens to any one that he has to wait his turn to get into a train or an omnibus, and sometimes, in a crowded part of the town, he can find no vehicle.

There is one place in the town where three trains run one above the other by the means of bridges ; and there is a park, in which, at promenade times, fifty or sixty thousand carriages circulate.

When one goes to the warehouses on the banks of the River Thames, and looks at the exports and imports every day, he thinks that the tide,† which causes the river to rise and fall every day, casts all the productions of the world here, and that all the manufactures made by man go from here to be distributed.

If one goes to the factories here, his hair stands on end ! He thinks the thing at work is not a machine, but an iron monster as big as a piece of a mountain, who spouts forth fire from his mouth, and every member of whom, when it moves, gives out a terrible cry, and that he is continually working without repose, day and night, to carry out the orders of " King Intellect," who has made him his prisoner.

There are printing-machines, which print in one hour two

---

* I suppose this refers to the Polytechnic.
† The Turks have no tide in their own country, as the Mediterranean is a tide-less sea, and they only know of such a thing from books or hearsay.

hundred and fifty thousand copies of a newspaper eight times as large as the *Ibret*.\*   In one printing-office fifty thousand workmen are employed, and in one beer brewery they have fifteen thousand cart horses.

There are hotels one mass of gilding, ornamented in a way to make palaces envious, where three thousand people can sleep, and four thousand persons can dine at their tables.   There is a tailoring establishment where sufficient clothes are to be seen to dress all the people in our town of Scutari, from seven to seventy years of age; and there are seven or eight hundred shopmen, and five or six hundred shopwomen, to show the goods to customers.

There are regular markets under the river ;† and splendid bridges up in the air ! ! !

There is a place of amusement called the " Mirror Palace " (Crystal Palace), which, owing to all the colours of the rainbow sparkling on it from the reflection of the light, on a sky-blue ground, looks, from a distance, like a mountain of diamonds.

In the daytime the water from the fountains forms steeples of light !  In the evening, when the gardens are flooded with gas and moonlight one thinks it is day, and one can see from one end of them to the other.   These gardens are such that it is doubtful whether any one who was capable of visiting Paradise could produce any better imitation of it in this world of affliction.

To see the military strength of their government, it is sufficient to go down to the banks of the river, or to the old castle of the town (the Tower).   There are iron-clad vessels to be seen which are like a big city made of iron.

If you wish to know what the people can do, you need only look at the lists of subscriptions in the newspapers.

One widow lady presents three hundred thousand pounds to an orphan asylum !

A blacking manufacturer, in his will, leaves twenty thousand pounds to the poor !

It is very wonderful that one sees no other signs of such a

---

\* The name of a Turkish newspaper.
† We suppose this refers to the Thames tunnel.

powerful government in public but the police, who are employed only in preserving public order.

As regards the police, their work consists in the daytime of such things as seeing that carriages do not collide, and stopping the greatest people of quality with a sign, if they wish to go out of their turn before some ordinary individual : and at night, in quelling a few drunken squabbles, examining the doors of shops and houses to see if they are closed, and windows to see if they are fastened, and such like things connected with order and justice.

Although the people are so opulent, the greatest millionaire will go to his shop when he is eighty, and work till evening, like a shopman.

By continual effort and knowledge they have produced a world of opulence, compared to which, all the golden palaces and jewelled castles, and splendid flower-gardens which the imagination of the Persian poets described in the most exaggerated way in India and China, are as nothing.

Well, we know it is impossible in a few years to make Constantinople like London, or Roumelia like France. But, as Europe has got into this condition in two centuries, and they had to discover the means of progress, whereas we find those means ready to our hands, if the work be properly taken in hand, there is no doubt that in two centuries, at any rate, we shall be able to get into a condition to be counted one of the most civilized nations. And as regards two centuries, are they more than a twinkling of an eye in the life of a community ?

M

## PATRIOTISM.

سير<sup>1</sup> خوارلر بشيكنى<sup>2</sup> چوجقلر اكلنديكى<sup>3</sup> يرى كنجلر<sup>4</sup> معيشتكاهنى<sup>5</sup>
اختيارلر<sup>6</sup> كوشهء<sup>7</sup> فراغنى<sup>8</sup> اولاد<sup>9</sup> والدهسنى پدر<sup>10</sup> عائلهسنى<sup>11</sup> نه درلو حسيات<sup>12</sup>
ايله سورسه انسانده وطننى<sup>13</sup> او درلو حسيات ايله سور . بو حسيات ايسه
سببسز<sup>14</sup> بر ميل<sup>15</sup> طبيعتدن<sup>16</sup> عبارت<sup>17</sup> دكلدر . انسان وطننى سور چونكه
مواهب<sup>18</sup> قدرتك<sup>19</sup> اك عزيزى<sup>20</sup> اولان حيات<sup>21</sup> هواى<sup>22</sup> وطنى تنفسله<sup>23</sup>
باشلار .

انسان وطننى سور چونكه عطاياى<sup>24</sup> طبيعتك اك رونقليسى<sup>25</sup> اولان
نظر<sup>26</sup> لمحهء<sup>27</sup> افتتاحنده<sup>28</sup> خاك<sup>29</sup> و طننه تعلق<sup>30</sup> ايدر . انسان وطننى سور
چونكه مادهء<sup>31</sup> وجودى<sup>32</sup> وطنك بر جزئيدر<sup>33</sup> انسان وطننى سور چونكه
اطرافنه<sup>34</sup> باقدقجه هر كوشهسنده<sup>35</sup> عمر<sup>36</sup> كذشتهسنك<sup>37</sup> بر ياد<sup>38</sup> حزيننى<sup>39</sup>
تحجر ايتمش<sup>40</sup> كبى كورر .

(1) P. *Shir*, 'milk;' خوار P. *Khar*, 'one who drinks or eats.' Thus شیرخوار means
'one who drinks milk,' *i. e.* 'a suckling, or babe.'—(2) *Beshik*, 'a cradle.'—
(3) *Eghlenmek*, 'to amuse one's self.'—(4) *Ghenj*, 'young.'—(5) A. *Maïshet*, 'means
of living;' 'a pension.'—(6) *Ikhtiar*, 'old.'—(7) P. *Kiushé*, 'a corner, a place of
retreat.'—(8) A. *Firagh*, 'ease, freedom from work or care.'—(9) A. *Evlad*, 'child,'
often used as a Turkish singular.—(10) P. *Péder*, 'father.'—(11) A. *Aïlé*, 'a family.'
—(12) A. *Hisiyat*, 'feelings.'—(13) A. *Vatan*, 'one's country, the Fatherland.'—
(14) *Sébebsiz*, 'without cause.'—(15) A. *Méil*, 'an inclination, affection.'—(16) A.
*Tabiat*, 'nature.'—(17) A. *Ibaret*, 'consisting.'—(18) A. *Mevahib*, 'gifts.'—(19) A.
*Koudret*, 'might, power, omnipotence;' 'the Almighty.'—(20) A. *Aziz*, 'dear.'—
(21) A. *Hayat*, 'life.'—(22) A. *Hava*, 'air.'—(23) *Téneffus*, 'breathing.'—(24) A.
*Ataya*, 'gifts.'—(25) A. *Revnakli*, 'splendid, glorious.'—(26) *Nazr*, 'the sight.'—
(27) A. *Lemhé*, 'a glance.'—'(28) A. *Iftitah*, 'opening, commencement.'—
(29) P. *Khak*, 'earth.'—(30) *Taaluk etmek*, 'to be attached to, or connected with.'
—(31) A. *Maddé*, 'matter,' 'an article.'—(32) A. *Vujoud*, 'the body,' 'existence,
being.'—(33) A. *Juz*, a part.'—(34) A. *Etraf*, 'sides.'—(35) P. *Kiushé*, 'a corner.'—
(36) A. *Umr*, 'life.'—(37) P. *Ghiugeshté*, 'adventure, event.'—(38) P. *Yad*, 'memory,
remembrance.'—(39) A *Hazin*, 'sad.'—(40) *Téhejjur etmek*, 'to turn into stone' (*v.n.*).

انسان وطننى سور چونکه حربتى ١ راحتى ٢ حقى ٣ وطن سايهسنده ٤
قٓيمدر ٥. انسان وطننى سور چونکه سبب وجودن اولان اجدادينك ٦
مقبرهٴ ٧ سكونى ٨ و نتيجهٴ ٩ حياتى ١٠ اولهجق اولادينك جلوهكاه ظهورى ١١
و طلندر انسان وطننى سور چونکه ابناء وطن آراسنده اشتراك ١٢ لسان
و اتحاد ١٣ منفعت ١٤ و كثرت مٓوانسه ١٥ جهتيله بر قرابت ١٦ قلب ١٧
و بر اخوت ١٨ افكار ١٩ حاصل ٢٠ اولمشدر . . . . . . . .

(1) A. *Hurriyet,* 'liberty.'—(2) A. *Rahat,* 'comfort.'—(3) A. *Hak,* 'right, due,' 'truth.'—(4) P. *Sayé,* 'shadow, protection,' 'auspices.'—(5) A. *Kaïm,* 'upright, standing,' 'existing.'—(6) A. *Ejdad,* 'forefathers.'—(7) A. *Makberé,* 'burial-ground, grave, sepulchre.'—(8) A. *Sukiun,* 'tranquillity, remaining in one place, rest, quiet.'—(9) A. *Netijé,* 'the end.'—(10) A. *Hayat,* 'life.' (11) A. *Zuhour,* 'appearing.'—(12) A. *Ishtirak,* 'community.'—(13) A. *Itihad,* 'unity.'—(14) A. *Menfaat,* 'interest, advantage.'—(15) A. *Mu'anesset,* 'familiar intercourse.'—(16) A. *Karabet,* 'relationship.'—(17) A. *Kalb,* 'the heart.'—(18) A. *Oukhouvvet,* 'brotherhood.'—(19) A. *Efkiar,* 'ideas.'—(20) *Hasil olmak,* 'to arise.'—

## Translation.

A man loves his fatherland with the same feelings, and in the same way, as a babe loves its cradle, children the place they play in, young men where they gain their livelihood, old people their easy corner, a child its mother, and a father his family. These feelings are not a mere inclination of nature without a reason. A man loves his country because the most precious gift of the Almighty, his life, begins by breathing the air of his fatherland.

A man loves his country because the most splendid gift of nature, his sight, at its first glance falls on the earth of his fatherland. A man loves his country because the material of his body is a bit of his country. A man loves his country because, on looking around in it, in every corner he sees some reminiscence embodied as it were.

A man loves his country because his freedom, his rights and his comfort exist only under the auspices of his country. A man loves his country because it is the burial-place of the authors of his being, his forefathers, and the place where his children will come into the world.   A man loves his country because, owing to community of language and identity of interests amongst the sons of the same fatherland, a relationship of the heart and a fraternity of ideas spring up.

## THE ADVENTURE OF ALI BEY.

علی بكك سر كذشتنی حاویدر .

واقعا علی بك پدرينك حياتنده و هله اون درت اون بش يا'شنه كيرد
كدن صكره عالمده معارفدن بشقه سويليه جك - ارزو اولنه حق بر شى
بواه مز اولمشيدى . دنيايى¹ اونودرجەسنه مشغول اولديغى شى وار ايسه
درسلرى ايدى . كوجك مقصد² ايچون بيوك فدا³ كارلق اختيار⁴ ايدرسه
نسخەسى⁵ نادر⁶ بعض كتابلرى بهاسنك قرق اللى مثلنه المقده ايدردى -
خستەلنيرسه⁸ بر بحثده⁹ مغلوب¹⁰ اولديغيچون خستەلنيردى - اغلارسه
اوتوديغى شيلره مشكل مسئلەيه¹¹ تصادف ايدوبده حل¹² ايدەمديكندن
طولايى اغلاردى .

فقط بو عالم انقلاب¹³ كندى كبى ثباتى¹⁴ سونلردن اولمديغندن چوجرق
يكرمى ياشنه¹⁵ كيرر كيرمز - سبب وجودى - مربى ء¹⁶ افكارى اولان - پدرى
اخرتە¹⁷ انتقال¹⁸ ايتمكله علی بكك حالّنده بربرينى متعاقب¹⁹ انواع²⁰ تغير²¹
انواع بلايا²² ظهور²³ ايتمكه باشلادى .

چوجوغك فطرة²⁴ تأثراتى²⁵ غالب²⁶ اولمغله برابر الديغى تربيه²⁷

(1) A. *Dunya,* ' the world.'—(2) A. *Maksad,* ' an object, intention.'—(3) A. *Feda-kiarlik,* ' a sacrifice.'—(4) *Ikhtiyar etmek,* ' to choose, prefer.'—(5) A. *Nuskha,* ' a copy.'— (6) A. *Nadir,* ' rare.'— (7) A. *Missl,* ' a like thing, quantity, or value;' اوچ مثلی *uch misli,* ' three times the quantity or value.' Here *Bahasinin kirk elli misliné almakda idi* means ' He used to buy books at forty or fifty times as much as their real price.'—(8) *Khastalanmak,* ' to get ill.'—(9) A. *Bahss,* ' discussion, discourse.'—(10)A. *Maghloub,* ' conquered, beaten.'—(11) A. *Meselé,* ' a question.'— (12) *Hal etmek,* ' to solve.'—(13) A. *Inkilab,* 'change' (in circumstances), 'a reverse.'—(14) A. *Sebat,* ' firmness, steadiness.'—(15) *Yash,* ' age.'—(16) A. *Murebbi,* ' an educator;' *murebba* (also written مربا), ' preserved, prepared.'— (17) A. *Akhiret,* ' the next world.'—(18) *Intikal etmek,* ' to pass from one place (or subject) to another;' انتقال دار بقا ايتمك, ' to die ' (*i. e.,* to pass to the ' abode of permanence ').— (19) *Muta-akib,* ' following each other.'— (20) A. *Enva,* ' kinds.'—(21) A. *Téghayyur,* ' change.' —(22) A. *Belaya,* ' calamities.'— (23) *Zuhour etmek,* ' to appear.'— (24) A. *Fitret,* ' natural constitution, disposition.'—(25) A. *Té'essur,* ' being effected, effect.'— (26) *Ghalib olmak,* ' to prevail.'—(27) A. *Terbiyyé,* ' education.'

وجداننده‌كى[1] حسياته بر قـات قوت ويرديكندن و پدرى ايسه باعث[2] حياتى اولديغيچون عندنده[3] حياتدن متقدس[4] اولدقدن بشقه هر حال و كارده مربيسى ـ مستشارى[5]ـ رازداشى[6] يار[7] ـ صادق[8] اولديغندن كوكلنده[9] نه قدر قابليات[10] محبت[11] وار ايسه همان جملهسنى اكا حصر ايتمشيدى . اوبله هيچ خاطرنده يوق ايكن ما ملك[13] و جدان و عرفانى[14] اولان بر وجود عزيزى تلافيسى[15] قابل اولهميه‌جق صورتده بغتةً[16] غائب ايدنجه حياتك لذتنى ده[17] برابر غائب ايلدى نديم[18] روحى[19] اولان كندبار ينه باقر ناجنس الفتنه دوشمش قدر صغيليردى . . . . . . ايشى كوچى اوطهنك بر كوشهسنه چكيله‌رك يتيمانه آه اتمكه ـ محزونانه كوز ياشى دوكمكه منحصر اولمشيدى . انك بو حالى ايسه والدهسنه زوجنك[21] وفـتندن[22] زياده انديشه[23] وبرمكده ايدى .

بكك والدهسى بهره‌دار[24] معارف[25] اولان ملتلر[26] قادينلرى[27] كبى دانشلى[28] بر شى دكل ايسهده ذاتاً[29] ذكاسى[30] غالب اولدقدن بشقه يكرمى بش سنه قدر بكنك تربيهسى التنده قالهرق كورديكى ـ ايشتدديكى حادثهلردن[31] انك ارشاد[32] حكيمانه سيله پك چوق حقيقتلر استخراج ايتمش بر قادين ايدى . اكا بناءً[33] كندينىده ياٴس[34] و كدر[35] اوكنه صاليويرمك[36] لازم كلسه سوكيلى زوجندن دور[37] اولديغى كبى برده جكر[38]

---

(1) A. *Vijdan*, 'ecstasy, rapture.'— (2) A. *Baïs*, 'cause.'— (3) *Indindé*, 'in his estimation.'—(4) A. *Mukaddes*, 'holy.'—(5) A. *Mushtéshar*, 'an adviser.'—(6) *Razdash*, 'confidant.'—(7) P. *Yar*, 'a friend.'—(8) A. *Sadik*, 'sincere.'—(9) *Ghiunul*, 'the heart' (the seat of the affections).—(10) A. *Kabiliyah*, 'capabilities.'—(11) A. *Mahebet*, 'affection.'— (12) *Hasr etmek*, 'to confine.'—(13) A. *Ma mélek*, 'what he possessed, possessions.'—(14) A. *Irfan*, 'knowledge.'—(15) A. *Telafi*, 'replacing.'— (16) A. *Baghtéten*, 'suddenly.'—(17) A. *Lezzet*, 'delight, pleasure.'—(18) A. *Nedim*, 'companion.'—(19) A. *Rouh*, 'the soul, spirit.'—(20) *Ish-ghiuch*, 'occupation, business.'— (21) A. *Zevj*, 'husband.'— (22) A. *Vefat*, 'death.'—(23) P. *Endishé*, 'care, anxiety.'— (24) P. *Behrédar*, 'a participator.'— (25) A. *Maarif*, 'knowledge.'— (26) A. *Millet*, 'a nation.'—(27) *Kadin*, 'a lady.'—(28) *Danishli*, 'learned.'—(29) A. *Zatan*, 'personally.'—(30) *Zekia*, 'intelligence.'—(31) A. *Hadisé*, 'an event, accident.'—(32) A. *Irshad*, 'guidance in the right path.'—(33) *Bouna bina'an*, 'in consequence of this.'— (34) A. *Yé's*, 'despair.'—(35) A. *Kéder*, 'grief, sorrow.'— (36) *Salivermek*, 'to let loose.'—(37) P. *Dour*, 'distant.'—(38) *Jighér*, 'the liver;' *Jigher parasi*, 'a piece of one's liver,' means 'a darling.'

پاره‌سنی غالب ایده‌جکنی و کوزلرینی اولورله‌<sup>1</sup> اغلایه اغلایه و دیریلر کورمیه
جك بر حالَه كتيرمك دنياده اونلره مضر<sup>2</sup> ـ اخرتده اولانلره فائده‌سز<sup>3</sup>
اولديغنى بلديكندن مردانه<sup>4</sup> بر اقدام<sup>5</sup> ايله نه قدر حضنى ـ نه قدر كدرى
وارايسه كوكلنده حفظ ايدر و بويله زوجنك فقداننه<sup>6</sup> اغلامق كبى اك
ممدوح<sup>7</sup> اولان بر حالنى قباحت يوللو كتم<sup>8</sup> ايتمكه مجبور<sup>9</sup> اولديغندن
طولايى چهره‌سنه عارض<sup>10</sup> اولان اجى اجى تبسملرى<sup>11</sup> خنده‌ء<sup>12</sup> نشاط<sup>13</sup>
صورتنده<sup>14</sup> كوسترمك ايستردى .

(1) *Eulu*, 'a dead person, dead.'—(2) A. *Muzir*, 'injurious.'—(3) *Faïdésiz*, 'useless.'—(4) P. *Merdané*, ' manly, courageous.'—(5) A. *Ikdam*, 'an effort.'—(6) A.
*Fikdan*, ' loss.'—(7) A. *Memdouh*, 'praised, praiseworthy.'—(8) *Ketm etmek*, ' to
hide.'—(9) A. *Mejbour*, 'forced.'—(10) *Ariz olmak*, ' to come upon, light upon,
happen.'—(11) A. *Tebessum*, 'a smile.'—(12) P. *Khandé*, ' laughter, a smile.'—
(13) A. *Nishat*, 'joy.'—(14) A. *Souret*, ' figure, form.'

## Translation.

### The Adventure of Ali Bey.

Ali Bey, during his father's life-time, and until he was fourteen
or fifteen years of age, had found nothing in the world to talk
about, or to desire, but knowledge. He was so busy with his
lessons that he forgot the world. If he made a great sacrifice for
a small object, it was purchasing rare books at forty or fifty times
their value. If he fell ill, he fell ill because he was beaten in a
discussion. If he cried, he cried because having met with some
difficult question in something he read he could not solve it.

But this world of change, not being so constant as he, when
the young man was about twenty, on his father, the author of his
being and the educator of his mind, dying, a succession of changes
and misfortunes began for him. The education he received
strengthened the poetic tendency of his nature; and, his father
having been not only the author of his being, on which account
he considered him more sacred than life, but also his instructor in
every thing, his counsellor, his confidant, and his sincere friend; all

his capacity for love was confined to him. Thus, on his suddenly losing—when he least expected such a thing—the dear person, who had imparted to him all he knew, and his imagination, in an irreparable way, he lost also all pleasure in living. The companions of his soul, his books, were now as dross to him. . . . . . Withdrawing into a corner of his study he did nothing but sigh and weep. This state of his caused his mother more anxiety than her husband's death.

The Bey's mother, although she was not so erudite as the ladies in more learned lands, was naturally intelligent, and, moreover, she had been cultivated by intercourse with the Bey (her husband) for five-and-twenty years, and had learnt many things under his guidance. Therefore, as she knew that if she gave way to despair and grief she would lose her darling, as she had her husband, and that if she cried so much over the dead till she could not see the living, it would only be injurious to those in this world and useless to those in the next, she made a brave effort, and whatever might be the grief and sorrow she felt, she kept it in her heart, and concealed, as if it were a fault, any condition—however laudable—like weeping for the loss of her husband, and converted into smiles of cheerfulness the bitter smiles which came on her countenance.

# THE FATHERLAND, OR SILISTRIA.*

## (*A Drama.*)

وطن یاخود سلستره .

درت فصل[1] ـ تیاترو .

حضار[2] .

ذكیه خانم

خنیفه خانم

اسلام بك . . . . كوكللی[3] ضابطی

احمد صدقی بك . . . . میر الای[4]

رستم بك . . . . قائممقام[5]

عبد الله . . . . میرالایك چاوشی

بر قائمقام ـ بر بیكباشی ـ برنجی ضابط ـ ایكنجی ضابط ـ
اوچنجی ضابط ـ نفرلر[6] . . . كویلیلر[7] .

---

برنجی فصل .

پرده[8] اچیلنجه سوقاغه ناظر[9] بر اوطه كوریبنور . ذكیه ارناودلغه[10] مخصوص[11]
منتظم قادین البسه‌سیله مندره[12] اوزانمش[13] . النده بر كتاب . اوكنده
بر موم . اسلام بك سوقاقده كزینور :

(1) A. *Fasl*, 'a part, an act.'— (2) A. *Huzar*, 'those present.'— (3) *Ghiunulu zabiti*, 'a volunteer officer.'— (4) *Mir alaï*, 'a colonel.'— (5) A. *Kaïmmekam*, 'a lieutenant-colonel.'—(6) *Neferler*, 'privates.'—(7) *Keuïluler*, 'peasants.'—(8) *Perdé*, 'a curtain.'—(9) A. *Nazir*, 'looking at, on, over.'—(10) *Arnaoudlik*, 'Albania.'—(11) A. *Makhsous*, 'special, peculiar.'—(12) *Minder*, 'a sofa, divan, mattress.'—(13) *Ouzanmak*, 'to lie, lie down at full length,' 'to become longer.'

---

* Published at Constantinople, 1289 *Anno Hejiræ*, by Agop Bey.

برنجی مجلس .¹

ذكيه (كتابی صنديغڭ اوستنه براقه‌رق) — آ‌ه ! . . . . . ننه‌جكم ! ننه‌جكم !² كوكلمه نيچون بو قدر رقت³ ويردك ! فكرمی نيچون بو قدر اچدك ؟ . . . سنده شمدی قزیكی كورسه‌ڭ اوتوتدیغه‌كه پشمان اولوردك . . . . .

بڭم كوكلم اویله بیوك بیوك حیاته نصل طیانه‌سون ! بڭم بیڭم⁴ اویله كڭش⁵ كڭش تصورلره نصل تحمل ایته‌سون :

يوركم نه قدر چارپيور⁶ ! صانكه⁷ كوكسمی یرندن قوپاره‌جقده⁸ طیشاری فرلایه‌جق⁹ . بینم نه قدر صیقلیور! صانكه باشمی پاره‌لایه‌جقده اطرافه طاغیله‌جق . . . . . (اللرینی يوزينه قپایه‌رق)

ننه‌جكم ! ننه‌جكم دائما بابامی دوشنمك ایچون اچدیغك حاضرلادیغك فكرده بشقه‌سی كزیور! دائما سنی سومك ایچون تربیه ايتديگك بيوتديگك كوكلده بشقه‌سی حكم ایدیور!

سنی بابام اوتوتمش . انك يولنه اولدك . بنی سن اوتوتدك . يولكه اولمك دكل اولديكنه اغلامق بیله خاطرمه كلميور .

آه ! . . . . دائما او ! كوزمه او ! خیالمده او ! عقلمده او ! او ! او ! . . . . بر كره سرقاتقده كوردم . . . . . كاشكی يوزینه باقدیغم زمان كوكلمه دوشن اتش اریدیدی¹⁰ . . . .

وجودمده نقدر قوت وارسه طوپلایوبده كوزلرمی بشقه طرفه چویرمك استدم . ایواه ! . . . . . نه وجودمده قوت بولدم نه كوزلرمده حكم كچدی . صانكه عمرمده كوردیكم اشتدیكم اوقودیغم دوشندیكم نه قدر كوزل

---

(1) A. *Mejlis*, 'a sitting, *séance*, a scene.'—(2) *Nené*, or *Niné*, 'a mother, or foster-mother' (used by children); *Nenéjek*, 'little mother' (a term of endearment).—(3) A. *Rikkat*, 'tenderness, compassion.'—(4) *Béyn*, 'the mind.'—(5) *Ghenish*, 'large, wide, full.'—(6) *Charpmak*, 'to strike' (*v.a.*), 'to beat' (*v.n.*).—(7) *Sanki*, 'as if, as though.'—(8) *Koparmak*, 'to tear, or break away.'—(9) *Firlamak*, 'to fly off' (*v.n.*). —(10) *Eritmek*, 'to melt' (*v.a.*).

شی وار ایسه هپسی بریرۀ طوپلانمشده بر انسان چهره‌سی اولمش قارشومه

کلمشیدی . (بر از دوشوندکدن صکره)

حیات نه غریب حال ایمش ! بر قاچ کون اول یانمه بری اغلاسه

کوزینک یاشی صفاسندن دوکیلیور ظن ایدردم . بو کون قرلاشمه قهقهه‌لر [1]

ماتم صداسی کبی کلیور! . . . . بو کون یکی اچیلمش کللرده "چی" [2]

کورسه‌م برینک کوز یاشی دوکلمش ظن ایدیورم ! بر قاچ کون اول یوزم

کولیوردی . . . . . . صانکه هر شیده بنمله برابر کولیوردی ! بو کون کوکلم

اغلیور . . . . صانکه هر شیده کوکلمله برابر اغلیور !

ینه صباح ارلدی . ینه کوزیمه بر دقیقه اوبقو کیرمدی .

(بوبلری سوندیره‌رك) [3]

زواللی [4] موم ! عجبا سنك کبی یانه یانه توکنوب [5] کیده‌جکمی یم ؟

. . . . بش دقیقه جق اوبوبه بیلسیدم . . . .

اللهم ! او مکتوب نه ایدی ؟

اتشله یازلسه انسانك یوره‌کنی او قدر یاقمز . اوقودقجه کوزلریمدن صانکه

یوزیمه کوکسمه طوغری طمله طمله علو پار چه‌اری صاچیلدی . . . . .

بیه‌لم سودننه‌م [6] کتیردیکی زمان نصل عارمدن [7] یره‌ره کچمدم !

انسان سوبجندن اولمیور . لکن چلدیره‌جق ! [8] . . . . مکتوب سوزینی

ایشتدیکم کبی اندن کلدیکنی بیلدم . . . .

سوبیورم . اوده بنی سوبیور . سودیکی مکتوبنده یازیلی . . . . کندی

یازیسیله یازیلی . . . . البته کرجکدر . . . الله اوقدر کوزل بر وجودك

ایچنده خیانت [9] صاقلامز [10] آ؛ . (بر از تأملدن [11] صکره)

کیم بیلور؟ الت کوزل چیچکلرك اراسنده ییلان بولینور .

---

(1) A. *Kahkaha*, 'a burst of laughter.'—(2) *Chi*, 'dew' (generally spelt چی).—
(3) *Moum*, 'a candle.'—(4) *Zéwalli!* 'poor!'—(5) *Dukenmek* (spelt also دوكنمك), 'to
be used up, exhausted,' 'to expire, come to an end.'—(6) *Soud-nené*, 'foster-mother.
—(7) A. *Ar*, 'shame.'—(8) *Childirmak*, 'to go mad.'—(9) A. *Khiyanet*, 'treachery.'
—(10) *Saklamak*, 'to hide, hide away,' 'to keep, protect.'—(11) A. *Té'emmul*,
'deliberation, consideration.'

ایکنجی مجلس

اسلام بك    —    ذكیه خانم

!اسلام بك (پنجرەدن كیرەرك)

ذكیه ـ (اسلام بكی كورنجه نهایت درجه بر تلاش ایله یاننه قوشمق
استر . فقط ینه كندینی طوپلار . بر سكوت متأثرانهدن صكره كندی كندینه
خطاب[1] ایدرك و فقط سوزینی ایشتدیرەرك) یا شمدی هر كون اللهدن
اولومی ایستدیكمده حقم یوقمی ؟   بری كوردیسه بكا نه در ؟

اسلام بك ـ كیمسهنك كورمك احتمالی یوقدر . بو قدر كونلر بو قدر
كیجهلردر كندیمی كوسترمامك ایچون طوپراقلرده یواردلانیورم . . . . صباح
اچیلیور . كوزلر حالا اچیلمغه باشلامدی . كیجه بتیور . هر كیجه بورلری
طولاشیورم تجربهمه اعتماد[2] ایت .

ذكیه (ممنونیتی ستر ایدرك بارد[3] بارد) ـ سزی دعوت ایدنمی
وار ایدی ؟

اسلام بك ـ الله عشقنه اللریكی یوزكه طوتمه . دنیایی طویی بر كون
كوردم .   چونكه بكا دنیادن مراد سنسن . بر دها كورەجكمی یم ؟
اوراسنی الله بیلور .

دمندنبری بر جاسوس[4] كبی پنجرەنك آلتندن سوزلریكی دكلەدم .

(ذكیه اظهار انفعال[5] ایدر)

قباحتمك[6] نه قدر بیوك اولدیغنی بیلورم . انی بری بكا یاپسه
قیامته قدر الچقلقدن قورتیلهمزدی .           (ذكیەنك انفعالی تزاید ایدر)

حیدود[7] كبی پنجرەدن بر اوە كیردم .     (ذكیەنك انفعالی دها تزاید ایدر)

---

(1) *Khitab etmek*, 'to address.'—(2) *Itimad etmek*, ' to trust.'—(3) *A. Barid*, 'cold.'
—(4) *A. Jasous (Shéshid)*, 'a spy.'—(5) *A. Infial*, 'affliction, grief.'—(6) *A. Kiyamet*,
' the Resurrection.'—(7) *Haïdoud*, 'a bandit, robber.'

بنم بورايه كيرديكم كبى برى بزم اوه كيرسه قانفى حلال صايار اولديررردم .

نه ياپهيم كه اختيار¹ المده دكل؟

سنى سوپيورم . . . . . . سندن آيريلهجغم . . .

بو كون اغزكدن بنى سوديككى ايشتدم . . .

بو كون سكا وداع² ايده جكم . . .

ايشته كوكلك بندن قاچنمق³ استدكجه اياقلرك بكا طوغرى كليور . . .

بنده كنديمه مالك اوليدم البته كنديمى ضبط ايدردم . . . البتهسنك ياننده اولسون متهم⁴ اولمامغه چاليشوردم .

مرحمت ! مرحمت كه بويله نوردن دوكلمش⁵ وجوده طاشدن ياپلمش كوكل ياقشمز .

ذكيه (كوكليله دوكوشرجهسنه بر طاقم تـلاش و ترددن صكره) ـ بو قدر زمانلر اولوم⁶ عذابنه⁷ تحمل ايدييورم . ( اسلام بكه خطابا )

مرادك نه در؟ بن كندى حالمه اوغراشوب طورييورم . . . بنى كندمدن الدك . اوبوسهم رؤيامده سن ! اويانسهم خيالمده سن ! يالكز قالسهم قارشمده سن ! دائما سن ! وجودميمى استرسن؟ ايشته اسيركم . جانميمى استرسن؟ آلده . قورتيلهيم⁸

اسلام بك ـ بنى كورديكك زمان كوزلريكى چويرمك استمش سن . . . اويلهمى مرحمتسز بن سنى كورديكم وقت كوكلمدن نه حاللر كچديكنى بيلير ميسن؟ كوز قپاقلرم بر كره يوملوب⁹ اچيلنجه قدر آرهده بتون عمرم غائب اولييور ظن ايدييوردم .

الله بيك شكر اولسون كه سنده بنم كبى اختيارسز سوييورسن . كوكلك سكا غلبه ايديور .

---

(1) *Ikhtiyar*, 'choice.'—(2) *Veda etmek*, ' to say farewell.'—(3) *Kachinmak*, ' to get out of the way, to avoid.'—(4) A. *Muttehim*, 'guilty, culpable.'—(5) *Dukiulmek*, ' to be moulded, cast in a mould.'—(6) *Eulum*, 'death.'—(7) A. *Azab*, 'pain, punishment.'—(8) *Kourtoulmak*, 'to escape, be delivered.'—(9) *Yoummak*, 'to close' (one's eyes tight), *v.a.*

سن بنی بركره كوردك . بن سنی بر كره كوردم ایشته كوكلمز ایكز <sup>1</sup>
یرادلمش . ایشته الله سنی بكا بنی سكا بنی سكه ویرمش . . .

بز بربرمزدن بوراده ایریلدیرسهق اوتهده <sup>2</sup> برلشورز . . . بوكون ایریلدیرسهق
یارین برلشورز . . . ایری كورینورز . . . ینه بولشورز . . . ایری ظن
اولنورز . . . دائما برز . . .

كل . . . یانمه كل . . . بكا بر یمین ایت كه كرك ایریلهلم كرك
ایرلمیهلم . . . دنیاده <sup>3</sup> اخرتده <sup>4</sup> بندن بشقه كیمسهیه یار <sup>5</sup> اولمیهجقس .
ذكیه (كندینی طوتمیهرق) والله <sup>6</sup> . . . . (كندینی طوپلایهرق محجوبانه)
مرامكزی اكلایهمدم                          (اجبار <sup>7</sup> نفس ایله)

بن كندی كندیمه سویلنیوردم . . . سز كورندیكنز . . . بن . . . بن بر
شی . . . . سویلمدم . سویلدمدمی ؟ . . . . یوقسه . . . نه دیهجكم ؟ . . .
(ینه اختیارینی غائبب ایدرك)

هم بنی سویورسن . هم نیچون ایریله جغز ؟
اسلام بك ـ كیدهجكم . چونكه . . . .

ذكیه (حدتله <sup>8</sup> سوزینی <sup>9</sup> كسهرك) ـ ذهنمدن بابامك ننهمك محبتنی
چیقاردك . قرداشمك مزاری <sup>10</sup> كوكلمده ایدی . انیده اونوتدردك .
شمدی خیالی ده كندی كبی قاره طوپراقلرده یاتیور . . . . نه اوبقو قالدی
. . . . نه اختیارم قالدی . . . نه بر شیده ارزوم قالدی . . . . كندكدن
بشقه كوكلمده بر شی براقمدك . . . شمدیده كندیكی المدن الهجقس .
همده مژده <sup>11</sup> سنی كندك كتربیورسن . . .

(كندی كندینه حدتله سویلنوب <sup>12</sup> كزینهرك)

---

(1) *Ikiz*, 'a twin, twins.'—(2) *Eutédé*, 'yonder, far off.'—(3) *Dunya*, 'the world, this world.'—(4) A. *Akhiret*, 'the next world.'—(5) P. *Yar*, 'a lover, a mistress, a friend.'—(6) A. *Wallahi*, 'by God!'—(7) A. *Ijbar*, 'compelling, forcing;' *nefs*, 'one's self.'—(8) A. *Hiddet*, 'violence, impetuosity.'—(9) *Suzini kessmek*, to interrupt any-one.'—(10) A. *Mezar*, 'a grave.'—(11) P. *Muzhdé*, 'glad tidings.'—(12) *Suïlenmek*, 'to talk to one's self, murmur.'

صوكنده نه اوله‌جق؟ او بو مملكتدن كيدر . بنده بو دنيادن كيدرم .
عمرمك هرلذتنى غائب ايتدكدن صكره قره طوپراغك نه‌سى وار؟

اسلام بك ـ كيده‌جكم . . . .

ذكيه (ياننه هجوم ايله لقرديسنى كسه‌رك) ـ ابتدا بنى اولدير .

اسلام بك (ايشتمامش كبى) ـ كيده جكم . . . . . . . . . . . .

بن ادم دكلميم؟ وظيفه‌م[1] يوقمى؟ وطنمى سومه‌يه‌يمى؟ وطننى سو
ميان ادمدن سكا نصل محبت مأمول ايدرسن؟

ذكيه ـ اكر . . . . وطن . . . وطن اولنجه بن . . . . نه ديرم ! كيت !
كيت بكم بندن بريمين[2] استه‌يور ميدك . . . .

عالملر محبت اوزرينه يرادان ربمك بيك بر اسمنه عهد ايدرم كه
دنياده‌ده اخرتده‌ده ذكيه سنكدر سنك توكلدر .

اسلام بك ـ بنده اللهك . . . .

ذكيه (لقردسنى كسه‌رك) ـ صوص ! يمين ايده‌جكسن استه‌م .
اغزكدن بر يلان چيقه‌بيله‌جكنى بر دقيقه دوشونسه‌م او دقيقه‌ده
جلديررم .

---

## دردنجى مجلس

(ذكيه اوطه‌ده * اسلام بكله كوكليلر طيشاريده)

اسلام بك (سوقاقده) ـ ارقداشلر هپ بوراده‌يز دكلمى؟

(ذكيه سسى ايشيدر صيقى صيقى پنجره‌يه قوشار جامك بر
طرفنده صاقلانور.)

بر كوكللى ـ هپ بوراده يز .

اسلام بك ـ قرداشلر بايراغمه طوپلانمشسكز . افتخار ايدرم . لكن

---

(1) A. *Vazifé*, 'a duty.'—(2) A. *Yémin*, 'an oath.'

بیلمم بندن ممنون اوله‌جقمیسکز؟   بن غوغایه کیدیورم .   فقط اولمك
نیتیله کیدیورم .   ایاغم یوق .   استیانلر یانمه کلمسون .   یغما دوشونمم .
دوشونانلر اطرافمدن چکلسون .   راحت ارامم .   ارایانلر .   ارقه‌مه دوشمسون .
قورشوندن کله‌دن قورقمم .   قورقانلر قاریلرینك یاننده اوطور سون . . . . .

سویلدیکم سوزلری اكلیورمیسکز؟   اولوم قورقوسنی بتون بتون کوکلك‌زدن
چیقارمق الیكزدن کلیرمی؟   کوکسکزی وطنك حدودینی محافظه
ایچون یاپلمش استحکام حکمنده بیلمك الیكزدن کلیرمی؟   اولومکزی
ارامغه کیده بیلیرمیسکز . . .   بز وطنی محافظه ایده‌جکز .   الله بزی
محافظه ایده‌جك .   ایتمزسه کندی بیلیر .   کندیکزه بو قدر کوه
نیور میسکز؟ . . .

ارقدا‌شلر!   طونه بوینه کیده‌جکز . . .   طونه بزم ایچون اب حیاتدر .
طونه ارادن قالقارسه وطن یشامز .   وطن یشامزسه و طنده هیچ بر انسان
یشامز . . .   بكله یشایان بولنور . . .   اوت بكله بولنه بیلیر .

یوق . . .   یوق یشایان بولنور .   لكن انسان دکلدر .   انسان وطننك
ایاقلری التنده چیننندیكنی¹ کوررسه یاشامز .   انسان ننه‌سنك ایاقلری التنده
چیننندیكنی کوررسه یشامز .   انسان ولی نعمتنی ایاقلر التنده چیننندیكنی
کوررسه یشامز .   ولی نعمتنی ایاق التنده کوروبده یشایان کوپکدن الچقدر .
برادرلر!   انسان کوپکدن الچق دكلدر .

الله بوطنه محبتی امر ایدیور . بزم و طنمز طونه دیمکدر .   چونکه طونه
الدن کیدنجه وطن قالمیور .

طونه کنارینك نره‌سفی کزرسه فاشدر ایچنده یا باباکزك یا قرداشكزك
بر كمیكی بولنور . . .

طونه‌نك صویی بولاندقجه اوزرینه چقان طوپراقلر محافظه‌سیچون اولان

---

(1) *Chinémek*, 'to chew, to trample on;' *chinenmek*, 'to be trampled on.'

وجودارك اجزاسندندر . عثمانلی نامی ایشیده‌لی طونه کچلدی ! بر
قاچ کره کچلدی . . . .

بر چوق کره کچلدی . . . فقط بر وقت النمدی . . . عثمانلیلر
طوردقجه ینه بر وقت النمز . هله عثمانلیلر عثمانلیلغك نه دیمك
اولدیغنی بیلیرسه هیچ بر وقت النمز . وطنکز ایچون اولمكه حاضر میسکز؟
بز اولمینجه دشمن طونه‌دن کچمیه‌جك کچنلر بزی یا اولمش یاخود یاره‌لی
بوله‌جق .

بن اوله‌جكم دییورم . ایچكزده اولمدن قورتمایان کیمدر؟ ارقه‌مدن
ایرلمامغه اللهله عهد ایدرمیسکز؟

کوکللیلر ــ اللهله عهد[1] ایدرز .

اسلام بك ــ بنی سون بر وقت اردمدن ایرلماز . . . .

---

ایکنجی فصل

(پرده اچیلنجه سلسله قلعه سنك بر طابیه‌سنده[2] ارته‌ده[3] برو‌ده بر طانم
کوکللی اوتورمش ذكیه اركك اثوابیله ایچلرنده کوریفور .)

برنجی مجلس .

کوکللیلر * نفرلر * عبد الله چاوش * ذكیه .

بر کوکللی ــ صوصك . . . صوصك . . .

دیكر بر کوکللی ــ نه وار؟

اولكی کوکللی ــ موزیقه‌یی ایشتمیور میسك؟

ایکنجی کوکللی ــ ای تلاشك نه ؟ ایشته عسکرکلیور .

برنجی کوکللی ــ هوا[4] غوغا هواسی . . .

ذكیه ــ موزیقه غوغا هواسی چالیورسه بزده غوغا تورکوسی[5] سویلرز .

---

(1) *Ahd etmek*, 'to promise solemnly, to undertake.'—(2) *Tabia*, 'a redoubt, a battery, an earthwork.'—(3) *Euté beridé*, 'here and there.'—(4) A. *Hawa*, 'the air,' 'an air in music, a tune.'—(5) *Turkiu*, 'a song.'

ایكنجی كوكللی ـ شونكده چو جوقلغنه باق !

عبد الله چاوش ـ بونك چوجوقلغی نره سنده ؟

برنجی كوكللی ـ جانم صوصك . . . .


(بر قاپچ كشی بردن)

كلك تركی یه كلك تركی یه ؟


(عموم حضار)

امالمز افكار ه زر اقبال وطندر .

سرحدمزه قلعه بزم خاك بدندر .

عثمانلیلرز زینتمز قانلی كفندر .[1]

غوغاده شهادتله[2] بتون كام[3] الورز بز

عثمانلیلرز جان ویررز نام الورز بز

قان ایله قلیچدر كوربنان بایراغه زده

جان قورقوسی كزمز اووه مزده[4] طاغمزده

هر كوشه ده بر شیر یاتار طوپراغمزده

غوغاده شهادتله بتون كام الورز بز

عثمانلیلرز جان ویررز نام الورز بز

عثمانلی ادی هر طویانه لرزه[5] رساندر

اجدادمزك هیبتی[6] معروف جهاندر

فطرت دكیشور صانمه بو قان ینه او قاندر

غوغاده شهادتله بتون كام الورز بز

عثمانلیلرز جان ویررز نام الورز بز


(1) A. *Kefen*, 'a winding-sheet.'—(2) A. *Shehadet*, 'martyrdom.'—(3) P. *Kiam*, 'desire, wish.'— (4) *Ova*, 'a plain, a field.'—(5) P. *Lerzé*, 'a trembling;' *lerzé-resan*, 'who or which bring trembling,' 'terrific.'—(6) A. *Hëïbet*, 'awfulness, dreadness, awe, fear.'

طوپ پاطلاسون اتشلری اطرافه صاچلسون

جنت قپوسی جان ويرن اخوانه¹ اچلسون

دنیاده نه بولدق که اولومدنده قاچلسون

غوغاده شهادتله بتون كام الورزر بز

عثمانلیلرز جان ويربزريز نام الورز بز

---

ايكنجی مجلس

اولكيلر * عسكر * ميرالای *

صدقی بك ـ قلعهده قالمق استيانلر بر طرفه ايرلسون .

بر كوكللی ـ هپ بوراده قالمق استيورز كه بورايه كلدك . بربرمزدن
نيچون ايريله جغز؟

صدقی بك (هيچ كيمسهيه التفات ايتميهرك) ـ اغالر! دشمن
صويی كچدی ......

دولت قلعهسنی كندی عسكر ايلهده محاظهيه قادر در ايچكزدن
هر كيم بوراده بولنمق استمزسه پاشادن اذن وار همان بو كون طيشاری
چيقسون .

بر كوكللی ـ دشمن چوق . عسكر از بزی دها ازالتمقهمی استيور سكز؟

عبد الله چاوش ـ عسكر آز اولمغله قياهتمی² قوپار؟ آزدن از اولور .
چوقدن چوق .

صدقی بك ـ صوصده بر آز شونلر سويلسون .

عبد الله چاوش ـ آی بن ...

صدقی بك (لقردیسنی كسهرك) ـ سبحان الله³ ! ! ! اغالر ..

---

(1) A. *Ikhwan*, 'brethren, comrades.'— (2) *Kiyamet kopmak*, ' to take place' (a
confusion).— (3) A. *Subhana-'llah*, 'Oh, God !' (I sing the praises of God).

محاصره‌ده <sup>1</sup> قورشوندن <sup>2</sup> كله‌دن <sup>3</sup> بشقه آچاق صوسزاه‌ق‌ده وار . . كيم
كندينى قورتارمق استرسه . . . . .

بر كوكللى ـ بك بك بز بورا‌ده كندى ارادتمزله كادك . كاشمز
انجق بو ايچون أيدى بر الكزله بزه دشمنى كوسترييورسكز . بر الكزله
قاچه‌جق قپويى !

بن يشاديغمى كافى كورييورم . كفنمى برينمه شهيدلكى كوزمه آلدم .
بغدادّن بورايه قدر او نيتله كلدم . . . . . .

صدقى بك (هيچ برينه التفات ايتميه‌رك) ـ برادر سوزم سزه دكل .

بر كوكللى ـ هانكيمزه در .

بر ديكر كوكللى ـ هانكيمزى دها غوغا باشلامه‌دن دشمندن يوز چويره
جك قدر الچق ظن ايدييورسكز؟

صدقى بك ـ بك اعلا ! سزده بزم كبى وطن يولنده اولمك
استيورسكز . سعيكز اللّٰه عندنده ضايع اولمز . حياتكز كيدرسه آدكز قالور .
انسان اولانه اولدكدن صكره بر كوزل نام براقمق بلكه هيچ اولمامكدن
خيرليدر . كوكلكزى قوى طوتك الومدن قورقمه‌يك كه قورقسه‌كزده قورقمسه‌كزده
البته بر كون كلور سزى بولور .      (ذكيه‌يه خطابا)

چوجق

ذكيه ـ افندم .

صدقى بك ـ سن كيمه‌سين .

ذكيه (تلاش ايله) ـ آدم .

صدقى بك ـ آدك نه در؟

ذكيه (كندينى طوپليه‌رق) ـ آدم افندم .

صدقى بك (كندى كندينه) ـ نه مناسبتسز خليلا <sup>4</sup> .     (ذكيه‌يه خطابا)

---

(1) A. *Muhaseré*, 'a siege.'—(2) *Kourshoun*, 'lead, bullets.'—(3) *Ghiullé*, 'shot,
a cannon-ball.'—(4) A. *Khulyela*, 'arrogance.'

قلعەدن چیقمغە مأذونسن .

ذكیه ـ بن سزه جانمی عرض ایدییورم . سز بکا یاشمك كو چكلكنی سویلیورسكز .

بورایه ادم اولدیرمك ایچونمی كلدكز؟ اولمك ایچونمی؟ اولدیرمك ایچونسه بنیده اولدیرك . اولمك ایچونسه امین اولك كه سزدن دها قولای دها راحت اولورم . . . . . . . . . . . .

اوچنجی مجلس

اولكیلر * اسلام بك

اسلام بك (كوكسنده بر قاچ یاره اولدیغی حالده قوشەرق) ـ بك! بك! ذكیه ـ آه !

اسلا بك ـ صودن كچدیلر .

اون بیك قدر واردیلر . اوچ یوز كشی ایله قاشولدق . اوچ ساعت اوغراشدق اوچ ساعتده آه! اوچ ساعتده . . . ارقداشلرك هپسی طوپراق اولدی . هپسی اخرته كتدی . لكن اك ادناسی ایكی دشمن اولسون . برابر كتوردی جنازهلری یرده یاتییور . . . . . .

اوچ یوز كشی ایدك . اون بیك سونكی‌یه[1] قارشو طوردق . كله اراسنده سكدك . باشمزه طولو كبی قورشون یاغدی . عاقبت سونكی سونكی‌یه[2] كلدك . عثمانلی‌نه ذیمك اولدیغنی كوستردك . هپمز اولدك . . . آه !

---

(1) *Sunghu,* ‘a bayonet.’—(2) *Sunghu sunghuyé ghelmek,* ‘to cross bayonets.’

هپس اولدی یدی کشی قالدق . اللهده بلورکه بن انلره قاوشمق ۱ استدم . . . اللهده بیلورکه بن هر کسك اوكنده ایدم . جبخانه ۲ توكندی ۳ . قلیچم قرلدی . . . . .

(ذكیه بو سوزلر اراسنده یواش یواش اسلام بکه یاقلاشور . ۴ اسلام بك ذكیهنك قوجاغنه دوشر . هر کس اطرافنه طولاپور .)

اسلام بك ـ عبد الله بورایه كل . شمدی الورسن . طوغری بنم اوطهیه كتوررسن . هر خدمتنه باترسن . جراح چاغررسن . حكیم كتیردیرسن بن . كلنجه یه قدر بر دقیقه یاننده ایرلمزسن . اكلادكمی ؟

(1) *Kawoushmak*, ' to join, meet, come together.'—(2) *Jebkhané*, 'gunpowder, a powder magazine.'— (3) *Dukenmek*, ' to be exhausted.'— (4) *Yaklashmak*, ' to approach.'

## Translation.

### THE FATHERLAND, OR SILISTRIA.

#### A Drama in Four Acts.

---

#### Dramatis Personæ.

ZEKIA HANIM.

KHANIFÉ HANIM.

| | |
|---|---|
| ESLAM BEY . . . . . | A Volunteer Officer. |
| AHMED SIDKI BEY . . . . | A Colonel. |
| RUSTEM BEY. . . . . | A Lt.-Colonel. |
| ABDALLAH. . . . . | The Colonel's *Chawoush*.* |

A Lt.-Colonel.—A Major.—A First Officer.—A Second Officer.— A Third Officer.—Peasants and Privates.

---

\* *Chawoush*, ' a sergeant.'

## ACT I.

*On the curtain rising, a room is discovered, looking into the street. Zekia, dressed in the Albanian national costume, is lying on a sofa, a book in her hand, and a candle before her. Eslam Bey is walking up and down in the street.*

### Scene I.

Zekia [*Leaving the book on a coffer*].—Ah! My dear mother, my dear mother! Why didst thou impart so much tenderness to my heart? Why didst thou develop my intellect so much? If thou couldst see thy daughter now, thou wouldst repent of having taught her . . . . How can my heart bear such a great life? How can my brain bear such great imaginings. My heart beats as if it would tear my breast, and leap forth. My brain aches as if it would break my skull, and be scattered forth.

[*Covering her face with her hands.*]

My dear mother! the mind which thou cultivated and prepared, in order for me to think of my father, is now occupied by another. In the heart which thou cultivated and enlarged, in order that it might love thee, another reigns.

My father educated thee. Thou died for his sake. Thou educated me; but I am not thinking about dying for thee, or even of weeping over thy death.

Ah! It is he always . . . . He is in my eyes, he is in my imagination, in my mind. He! he! he! and I saw him once in the street. . . . . . Would that the fire, which entered my heart when I looked on his face, had melted it! . . . .

Collecting all the strength I had in my body, I wished to turn my eyes in another direction. Alas! I neither found strength in my body, nor did my will appear in my eyes. It was as if all the beautiful things I had seen or heard of, or thought of in my life, were collected in one man's face, and stood before me.

[*After some reflection.*]

What a strange thing is life! But a few days ago, if any one near me wept, I thought his tears arose from pleasure. To-day, peals of laughter seem to me like sounds of mourning. To-day, if I see dew on roses just in full blossom I think some one has shed tears! A few days ago my face smiled, as if everything smiled with me. To-day my heart weeps as if everything wept with my heart.

It is morning again! Again, I have not had a moment's sleep.

[*Extinguishing the lights.*]

Poor candle! I wonder whether I shall gradually be consumed like thee, and perish. . . .

If I could only sleep five small minutes!

My God! What was that letter?

If it were written in fire it could not burn so much!

As I read it, it seemed as if drops of fire were scattered on my face and in my breast.

When my foster-mother brought it I nearly sank into the ground with shame!

One does not die of joy, but one goes mad. As soon as I saw the words of the letter I knew he would come. I love him, and he loves me! It is written in his letter. It is written with his own writing. . . . . It is certain it is true. . . . . Oh, God! Such a handsome body does not conceal treachery. Ah!

[*After meditating awhile.*]

Who knows? Snakes are found in the most beautiful flowers.


SCENE II.

ESLAM BEY. ZEKIA KHANIM.

ESLAM BEY [*Entering through the window*].

ZEKIA [*On seeing Eslam Bey, in great excitement, is impelled to run towards him, but collects herself; after an affecting silence, speaks to herself, but audibly*]. . . . Was I not right in wishing every day for my death? What would happen to me, if any one saw this?

ESLAM BEY.—There is no probability of any one seeing us. How many days and nights have I crept along the ground in order not to be seen. Day is breaking. People's eyes are not yet open, as night is only ending. I have been wandering round here every night. Trust to the trial I have made.

ZEKIA [*coldly, concealing her pleasure*].—Did any one invite you?

ESLAM BEY.—For God's sake do not cover your face with your hands. I saw all the world once, for you are the whole world to me. Shall I see it again? God only knows.

From that moment, like a spy under your window, I have been listening to your words.         [*Zekia appearing grieved.*]

I know how great my fault is. If anyone acted so towards me, I should despise him till the Day of Judgment.

        [*Zekia appears still more afflicted.*]

I have entered a house by the window like a robber.

If anyone entered our house, as I have entered here, I would consider it lawful to take his blood, and would kill him; but what am I to do, as I have no control over my will.

I love you . . . . . I am going to be separated from you . . . . .

To-day I heard from your own mouth that you love me . . . . .

To-day I bid you adieu . . . . .

See, the more your heart wishes to avoid me, the more thy feet approach me.

I too, if master of myself, would certainly control myself . . . . I would certainly strive not to be guilty towards you.

Mercy! mercy! For a stony heart would ill befit such an angel's body.*

ZEKIA [*struggling with herself, excitedly and hesitatingly*].—How long have I been suffering the pain of death?

        [*Addressing Eslam Bey.*]

What is your purpose? I am struggling with myself. You have taken me from myself. If I sleep, you are in my dreams. If I wake, you are in my imagination. If I am alone, you are before me. Always you! If you wish for my body, I will be your slave. If you wish for my soul, take it! that I may be delivered (from this state).

ESLAM BEY.—When you saw me, you tried to avert your eyes. . . . Was it not so, cruel one? When I saw you, do you know what a state my heart was in? If I closed my eye-lids for one moment, until they opened again it seemed to me as if I had lost my whole life-time!

---

* Literally, a body 'made of light.'

Thanks be to God that you love, like me, involuntarily, and that your heart overcomes you.

You have only seen me once and I you only once. Our hearts were created twins! God has given you to me and me to you.

If we are parted here, we shall be united yonder. If we are parted to-day, to-morrow we shall be united. We may appear separated, but we shall find each other. We may be supposed to be separated, but we are one.

Come! ... Come near to me! ... Swear to me that whether we be separated, in this world and the next, you will love none but me.

ZEKIA [*not able to control herself*].—By God ......

[*After collecting herself—shyly.*]

I do not understand what you mean ...   [*Forcing herself.*]

I said to myself .... you appeared .... I .... I .... I said .... nothing .... Did I say anything? .... What shall I say? ....

[*Again losing command over herself.*]

If you love me, why shall we separate?

ESLAM BEY.—I will go .... for ....

ZEKIA [*interrupting him impetuously*].—You have driven the love for my father and mother out of my mind. My brother's grave was in my heart. You have caused me to forget it. Now his image, like his body, is buried in the dark earth .... I have no sleep .... no will .... no desire for anything. You have left nothing in my heart but yourself .... And now you wish to take yourself away from me; and you bring the glad tidings yourself!

[*Pacing up and down and talking to herself excitedly.*]

In the end what will happen? He will leave this country, and I shall quit the world. After losing all pleasure in life—what is the grave!

ESLAM BEY.—I must go ....

ZEKIA [*rushing towards him, and interrupting him*].—First kill me!

ESLAM BEY [*as if he had not heard*].—I must go ..........
Am I not a man. Have I not a duty to perform. Shall I not love my country? How can you expect affection for you from a man who does not love his country?

ZEKIA.—If .... the country. When you speak of country, what

am I to say? Go! Go! Boy . . . . . . . . Did you not wish an oath
from me? . . . . . I solemnly promise, by the thousand and one names
of the Lord, who created the world in love, that Zekia is yours in
this world and the next, that Zekia is your slave.

ESLAM BEY.—I also swear by God . . . . .

ZEKIA [*interrupting him*].—Silence. I do not wish you to take
an oath. If I think for one moment that a lie can come from your
mouth, that moment I shall go mad . . . . . . . . . . . . . . . . . . . . . . .

## SCENE III.

ZEKIA in the room. ESLAM BEY and Volunteers without.

ESLAM BEY [*in the street*].—Comrades, we are all here.

[*Zekia hears his voice, runs frequently to the window, and conceals
herself near the glass.*]

A VOLUNTEER.—We are all here.

ESLAM BEY.—Comrades! You have rallied round my flag, and I
am proud of it, but I do not know whether you will be pleased with
me. I am going to the war, but I go intending to die. I have no
pay. Let those who wish for pay come not with me. I do not think
of booty. Let those who think of it, retire. I do not seek comfort.
Let those who seek it, not follow me. I do not fear cannon-balls or
bullets. Let those who do, stay with their wives. Do you com-
prehend my words? Are you able to expel all fear of death from
your hearts? Are you capable of looking upon your breasts as a
fortification made to defend the frontiers of your country? Can
you go and seek your death? . . . . We shall defend our country,
and God will defend us; but if he does not, He knows best. Have
you so much confidence in yourselves? . . . .

Comrades! we are going to the banks of the Danube. The Danube
is life to us. If the Danube be lost, the country cannot live; and
no one in the country can live . . . . . Perhaps there may be one
who could live . . . . . yes, perhaps.

No! . . . No! There may be one who could live, but he is not a
man. A man, when he sees his country trampled under foot, cannot
live. A man cannot live if he sees his mother trodden under foot.
A man cannot live if he sees his benefactor trampled on. Anyone

who sees his benefactor trampled on, and lives, is viler than a dog: and,—brethren ! a man is not viler than a dog.

God commands us to love our country. Our country means the Danube; for if the Danube goes, our country will not remain.

Wherever you go on the banks of the Danube, the bones of your fathers or comrades are to be found. If the waters of the Danube be stirred up, the mud which rises to the surface is compounded of the bodies of those who defended it.

The Danube has been crossed, since the name of the Turks was first heard. It has been crossed several times, many times, but it has never been taken. As long as the Turks remain it never will be taken. Are you ready to die for your country ? Until we die, the enemy will not cross the Danube. Those who do cross will find us either dead or wounded.

I tell you I shall die. Who of you do not fear death ? Do you swear to God you will follow me ?

VOLUNTEERS.—We swear by God.

ESLAM BEY.—Let him who loves me follow me ! . . . . . . . . . . .

---

## ACT II.

[*On the curtain rising a number of Volunteers are seen sitting here and there in a redoubt of the Castle of Silistria, and Zekia disguised in male attire*].

### SCENE I.

VOLUNTEERS. SOLDIERS. SERJEANT ABDALLAH. ZEKIA.

A VOLUNTEER.—Silence . . . . Silence !

ANOTHER VOLUNTEER.—What is the matter ?

1st VOLUNTEER.—Do you not hear the band ?

2nd VOLUNTEER.—Well, why such a fuss ? The troops are coming.

1st VOLUNTEER.—The tune is a martial air.

ZEKIA.—If the band is playing a martial air, let us also sing a war song ?

2nd VOLUNTEER.—See ! What childishness !

Sergeant Abdallah.—Where is the childishness?

1st Volunteer.—Silence, my dear fellow!

[ *A number of people together.*]

Come, let us have the song! [*All together.*]

Our hopes and our thoughts are for the Fatherland,
And our bodies are a bulwark for the Turkish frontierland.
We are Turks, and our pride is a bloody winding-sheet.
We desire nothing else but a martyr's death in war;
We are Turks, who will pay for fame with our gore.

Our flag is a sword upon a bloody ground;
In our valleys, on our mountains, no fear of death is found,
And, in every corner of our land, a lion lurks unbound.
We desire nothing else but a martyr's death in war;
We are Turks, who will pay for fame with our gore.

The name of the Turks makes every hearer shake, [quake.
And the terror of our fathers' name once made the whole earth
And, think not we are altered, our blood is just the same.
We desire nothing else but a martyr's death in war;
We are Turks, who will pay for fame with our gore.

Then let the cannons roar, and around the bullets fly,
For Heaven's gate is open for those who bravely die;
And what does earth us offer, that we should dying shy?
We desire nothing else but a martyr's death in war;
We are Turks, who will pay for fame with our gore.

## Scene II.

### The same persons. Soldiers. The Colonel.

Sidki Bey.—Let those who wish to stay in the castle step on one side.

A Volunteer.—We all wish to remain here; for we have come here, and why should we separate?

Sidki Bey.—Gentlemen! the enemy has crossed the river. The government is capable of defending its castle with its own soldiers.

Whoever among you may not wish to remain, has permission to go out to-day.

A Volunteer.—The enemy are numerous. Our soldiers are few. Do you want to decrease them still more?

Sergeant Abdallah.—If the soldiers are few does that matter? If they are few, few will die. If there are many, many will die.

Sidki Bey.—Silence! Let them speak!

Sergeant Abdallah.—Oh! I . . . . .

Sidki Bey [*interrupting him*].—Oh God! Gentlemen! . . . . . In a siege, besides bullets and cannon balls, there are hunger and thirst. Whoever wishes to save himself . . . .

A Volunteer.—Bey! Bey! We came here of our own free will. Our coming was only for this. With one hand you show us the enemy, and with the other you show us the door to escape! I consider I have lived long enough. I have my shroud with me, and am ready to die. I have come from Bagdad here with that intention.

Sidki Bey [*not looking at any one*].—Comrade! I am not speaking to you.

Another Volunteer.—Which of us do you think mean enough to turn his back to the enemy before the fight begins?

Sidki Bey.—Very good. You also, like us, desire to die for our country. Your efforts will be appreciated by God. If you lose your life, your name will remain. For him who is a man, leaving a glorious name after dying, is better than not dying. Keep a bold heart. Fear not death: for whether you fear it or do not fear it, one day it will assuredly find you.          [*Addressing Zekia.*]

Boy!

Zekia.—Sir!

Sidki Bey.—Who art thou?

Zekia [*embarrassed*].—A man!

Sidki Bey.—What is thy name?

Zekia [*collecting herself*].—A man, Sir!

Sidki Bey [*to himself*].—What impertinence! [*Addressing Zekia.*] Thou art permitted to leave the castle.

Zekia.—I offer you my life. You talk to me of my youth. Did you come here to kill men, or to die? If you came to kill, kill me also.   If you came to die, be assured I shall die more easily and contentedly than you................

## Scene III.

### The same persons, and Eslam Bey.

Eslam Bey [*running, with several wounds in his breast*].—Bey, Bey.

Zekia.—Ah !

Eslam Bey.—They have crossed the river.   Ten thousand of them came ; we opposed them with three hundred.   We struggled for three hours.   In three hours . . . Ah ! in three hours . . . all our comrades fell.   All have gone to heaven ; but each one took two of the enemy with him at least ; their bodies are lying on the ground. . . . . . .   We were three hundred ; we stood against three thousand bayonets.   We rebounded between the cannon-balls.   We let them see what the Turks are like ; we all died . . . Ah ! all died ; seven only remained.   God knows I wished to die also.   I was in front of all of them.   But our powder was exhausted, and my sword broke.

[*Zekia, while hearing these words, draws closer and closer to Eslam Bey.   Eslam Bey falls into Zekia's arms.   Everybody collects round them.*]

Eslam Bey.—Abdallah, come here !   Take her at once to my room ; look to all her wants.   Call a surgeon ; send for a doctor. Do not leave her a moment till I come..............................

## JEZMI.

*Jezmi's feelings on first going into action.*

هر نه مسلكده[1] اواورسه اولسون برنجى تشبث[2] برنجى حركت وجداننده
نه درلو تأثرلر فكرده نه يولده تصورلر[3] حاصل ايلديكى هر كسك نفسنده
تجربه[4] ايله بيلديكى حالكردندر .

جزميلك طريقى اولان عسكرلكده برنجى تشبثدن ظهور ايده جك
تأثيرات تصوراتك شدتى ايسه هيچ بر حاله قياس[5] قبول ايتمز . فطرتده[6]
نه قدر لاابالیلك[7] مشربده[8] نه قدر قيدسزلق[9] كوكلده نه قدر فداكارلق[10]
اولورسه طبيعتك[11] حاسهء[12] غالبه سى اولان حفظ[13] نفس انهماكى[14]
اردن زائل[15] اولمق ممكن دكلدر . هله اعتيادسزلق[16] تجربه سزلك
دنيانك اك زكى اك جرأتلى اولان اصحاب تمييزنده[17] بيله ذهناً[18] بر
تردد[19] قلباً بر خلجان[20] حاصل ايتمامك احتمالك[21] خارجنده كورينور .
كيد يله جك ميدان[22] حرب ايسه بر موقع[23] امتحاندر[24] كه آخرة اك
اوزاق مسافه سى[25] بر كله[26] منزلندن عبارتدر[27] . ائتلاف[28] ايتميانلر ايچون
هادم[29] اللذاة اولان موت[30] بالطبع[31] دشمنك افرادنده دكل افرادينك

(1) A. *Meslek,* 'a road, path, a career.'—(2) A. *Téshebbus,* 'setting about a thing.'
—(3) *Tésavvur,* 'picturing to one's self, forming an idea.'—(4) A. *Tejribé,* 'experience, an experiment, a trial.'—(5) A. *Kiyas,* 'measuring, judging of;' *kiyas
etmek,* (v.a.) 'to liken, compare;' (v.n.) 'to think, suppose.'—(6) *Fitret,* 'disposition, nature.'—(7) *La-ubali-lik,* 'carelessness.'—(8) A. *Meshreb,* 'temperament,
character.'—(9) *Kaïdsizlik,* 'recklessness.'—(10) *Fedakiarlik,* 'self-sacrifice.'—
(11) A. *Tabiat,* 'nature.'—(12) A. *Hasé,* 'a feeling, a sense.'—(13) A. *Hifz-i-Nefs,*
'self-preservation.'—(14) A. *Inhimak,* 'diligent application;' 'setting about a thing
with heart and soul;' 'being urged or pressed to do something.'—(15) *Zaïl olmak,*
'to disappear.'—(16) *Itiyadsizlik,* 'being unaccustomed to a thing.'—(17) A. *Tem-
yiz,* 'distinction.'—(18) *Zihnan,* 'mentally.'—(19) A. *Téreddud,* 'hesitation.'—(20) A.
*Khalejan,* 'agitation, or tremor.'—(21) A. *Ihtimal,* 'probability.'—(22) A. *Méidan,*
'an open space, a square;' *méidan-harb,* 'a battle-field.'—(23) A. *Mevki,* 'a place,
position.'—(24) A. *Imtihan,* 'trial, testing, examination.'--(25) A. *Mesafé,* 'distance.'—(26) *Ghiullé,* 'a cannon-ball.'—(27) A. *Ibaret-olmak,* 'to consist of.'—
(28) *Itilaf etmek,* 'to be accustomed to.'—(29) A. *Hadim,* 'who demolishes;' *hadim-
u-lezzat,* 'the destroyer of pleasures' (death).—(30) A. *Mevt,* 'death.'—(31) A.
*Bittali,* 'naturally.'

كولسكەلرندە ¹ بیله تجسم² ایتمش كبی كوریپنور . انسان كـزندیكی
طویراقلرك هر طرفنی كندی ایچون حاضرلنمش بر مزار³ قیاس ایدر .
دنیانك نه قدر بدایعی⁴ عمرك⁵ نه قدر لذایذی⁶ قلبك نه قدر آمالی⁷
وار ایسه جملهسی بر یرە طویلانیردە عرض اشتیاق⁸ ایلرجەسنه كوز اوكندە
دور ایتمكە⁹ باشلار .

ایشتە جزمی حربه كیتمكە او درجەاردە ارزوكش¹⁰ ایكن ینه آتنه
بنوب دە آلایه¹¹ كیرنجه بو انفعالات¹² طبیعیەدن¹³ بر درلو كندینی
قورتارەمدی . بوندن بشقه عاقل¹⁴ نه قدر كندینه اعتماد¹⁵ ایتسه طالعنه¹⁶
اعتماد ایدەمز . بناء علیه اوصولمدق¹⁷ یردن بر بادرە¹⁸ ظهور ایدوب دە
مهارت¹⁹ ویا شجاعتنه²⁰ شئن²¹ ترتب²² ایدە بیلمك و او صورتله كرك
حامیلری²³ كرك ارقداشلری نظرندە الچقلقله معروف²⁵ اولەمق واهمه²⁶
سیدە كوكلندەكی اضطراب²⁷ خیلیدن خیلی قوت ویرمكدە ایدی .

فقط فطرتندەكی²⁸ شجاعت عزمندەكی²⁹ قوت خصوصیله كبر نفسنك
مزیتندن³⁰ اولان داعیهء³¹ ناموس و سائقه³² غیرت یوقاریدە بحث
ایتدیكمز حسیاته تمامیله مقابله³³ ایدردی .

جزمی بو كشاكشار³⁴ بو تردداره³⁵ دشمك قارشیسنه كلوب دە تفك
علوی³⁶ قلیج پارلدیسی³⁷ نظرندە جولان³⁸ ایتمكە باشلاینجه محاربەیی³⁹ نه

(1) *Ghieulghé*, ' a shadow.'— (2) *Tejessum etmek*, ' to take bodily form.'—
(3) A. *Mézar*, ' a burying-ground.'—(4) A. *Bedaï* (pl. of بدیعه *bedia*, ' wonderful or
beautiful things.'—(5) A. *Eumr*, ' life-time.'—(6) A. *Lezaïz*, ' enjoyments.'—(7) A.
*Amal*, ' hopes.'—(8) A. *Ishtiyak*, ' longing to see anyone.'—(9) A. *Devr etmek*, ' to
revolve.'—(10) *Arzoukesh*, ' desirous.'—(11) *Alaï*, ' a regiment.'—(12) A. *Infialat*,
' afflictions.'—(13) A. *Tabi'i*, ' natural.'—(14) A. *Akil*, 'sensible.'—(15) *Itimad etmek*,
' to trust.'—(16) A. *Tali*, ' luck.'—(17) *Oumak*, ' to hope, expect.'—(18) A. *Badiré*,
' what happens suddenly.'— (19) A. *Méharet*, ' skill.'— (20) A. *Shejaat*, ' valour,
courage.'—(21) A. *Shéin*, ' disgrace.'— (22) *Térettub etmek*, ' to result, proceed, to
take form and being.'—(23) A. *Hami*, ' a protector.'—(24) *Alchaklik*, ' meanness,
baseness.'—(25) A. *Marouf* ' known.'—(26) *Vahimé*, ' a fear, fancy.'—(27) *Iztirab*,
' disturbance, perturbation.'—(28) A. *Fitret*, ' disposition, nature.'— (29) A. *Azm*,
' determination.'—(30) A. *Meziyyet*, ' a virtue.'— (31) A. *Daïyyé*, ' an incentive,
cause.'—(32) A. *Saïké*, ' what urges.'—(33) *Mukabelé etmek*, ' to counterbalance.'—
(34) P. *Keshakesh*, ' discord, pulling in various directions.'—(35) A. *Tereddud*,
' hesitation.'—(36) *Alev*, ' a flame, a flash.'—(37) *Parladi* (n.), ' shining, flashing.'—
(38) *Jevelan etmek*, ' to move, circulate.'—(39) A. *Mouharebé*, ' war, a battle.'

O

دها ارزوسی قوهده <sup>1</sup> ایکن تصور ایتدیکی کبی صفا و اقبال مسیرهسی <sup>2</sup>
حالنده کوردی نه ارزوسی فعله <sup>3</sup> کلدکدن صکره توهم <sup>4</sup> ایلدیکی کبی بر بلای
مبرم <sup>5</sup> جولانکاهی <sup>6</sup> حکمنده <sup>7</sup> بولدی .

## The Battle with the Persians.

درویش پاشا قهرمانلغی <sup>8</sup> ایله برابر ذاتاً <sup>9</sup> پك كنج و فطرة متهور <sup>10</sup> بر
ذات اولهرق دشمنی کوردیکی کبی طبیعتنده اولان صولت <sup>11</sup> شیرانه <sup>12</sup>
كافة حواس <sup>13</sup> و قواسنه <sup>14</sup> غلبه ایلدیکندن ایکی طرفك مقدارنجه اولان
تفاوته <sup>15</sup> هیچ اهمیت <sup>16</sup> ویرمدی . رایت <sup>17</sup> افبالی التنده بولنان اوچ درتدیوز
دلیر <sup>18</sup> ایله قوجه بر اردونك قلبکاهی <sup>19</sup> اوزرینه هجوم ایلدی کویا که
پاشانك فرقهسی بر زبانه <sup>20</sup> جهانسوز <sup>21</sup> مقابله سنه کلان دشمن ایسه بر
ییغین <sup>22</sup> خاشاك <sup>23</sup> ایدی . برنجی صفده <sup>24</sup> بولنان ایران آلایلری صدمة <sup>25</sup>
اولیسنده محو <sup>26</sup> اولندی . بو صولت طاقت <sup>27</sup> براندازانه <sup>28</sup> ایله دشمن اردوسنك
عمومی <sup>29</sup> ترلزله و حتی بعض فرقهلری انهزامه <sup>30</sup> باشلادی ایسه ده طوقمان
خان او قدر کوچك بر فرقه اوکندن فرار ایتمك رذالتنی <sup>31</sup> موتدن
شنیع <sup>32</sup> عد ایدهرك نهایت درجهلرده غیرتلرله عسکرینی ینه موقع ثباته
کتیرمش و هر جهته عثمانلیلرك عمومندن غلبهلك بر فرقه سوق

---

(1) *Kuvvédé*, 'in posse.'—(2) A. *Mésiré*, 'a place of promenade.'—(3) *Filé ghetir-mek*, 'to execute, perform;' *filé ghelmek*, 'to be realised.'—(4) *Tévehhum etmek*, 'to surmise, dread.'—(5) A. *Mubrem*, 'irresistible, urgent.'—(6) P. *Jevelanghiah*, 'the place where any thing moves or happens' (theatre).—(7) *Hukmindé*, 'like.'—(8) *Kahramanlik*, 'might, valour.'—(9) *Zatan*, 'personally.'—(10) A. *Mutehavvir*, 'impetuous.'—(11) *Savlet*, 'a rush, impetuosity.'—(12) *Shirané*, 'lion-like.'—(13) A. *Héwas* (pl. of حاس), 'senses, faculties.'—(14) A. *Kuva* (pl. of قوت *kouvvet*), 'powers, faculties.'—(15) A. *Téfavout*, 'the difference, surplus, remainder.'—(16) *Ehemiyyet*, 'importance.'—(17) A. *Rayét*, 'a flag, standard.'—(18) P. *Dilir*, 'a hero.'—(19) P. *Kalbghiah*, 'the place of the heart.'—(20) P. *Zebané*, 'a flame.' —(21) P. *Jihansuz*, 'which burns or consumes the world.'—(22) *Yighin*, 'a heap.' —(23) P. *Khashak*, 'sticks or straws blown about.'—(24) A. *Saf*, 'a rank, row.'—(25) A. *Sadamé*, 'a shock.'—(26) *Mahv olounmak*, 'to be annihilated.'—(27 & 28) P. *Taket ber-endazané*, 'strong enough to overthrow,' 'tremendous.'—(29) A. *Tézelzul*, 'quaking, shaking.'—(30) A. *Inhizam*, 'a defeat, rout.'—(31) A. *Rezalet*, 'base-ness.'—(32) A. *Sheni*, 'odious, shameful.'

ایدهرك پاشانك اطرافنی بر دائیرة صورتنده احاطهیه قالقشمش
ایدی . . . .

ایرانلیلر مهاجمات[1] متوالیه[2] ایله بزم عسکری احاطه ایتدیلر و بر خیلی
آدم ده تلف ایلدیلر . درویش پاشا یانننده بولنان بقیهء شهدا[3] ایله ایکی
اوچ ساعت قدر قلیچ قلیچه بر جنك رستمانه ایله یذه دشمنی لرزهناك[4]
ایتمشکن طوقمان خان طرفندن اوزرینه برمکمل[5] سواری فرقهسی دها سوق[6]
اولندیغندن بو تازه قوت بر صولت شدیده ایله پاشانك توابع[7] جلادتندن[8]
اوتوز قدر دلاوری قربان ایلدکدن صکره کرز[9] و قلیچ ضربهلر[10] یله کندیسنی
اتدن اشاغی المشدی .

مجاهد[11] حیدر[12] اقتدار پیاده بولندیغی حالده تك باشنه قوجه بر
اوردو ایله بر خیلی زمان اوغراشدی[13] . و بربرینی متعاقب اوزرینه هجوم
ایدن اوچ عجم فدائیسنی[14] برر قلیجده ایکی پاره ایلدی. بو مدافعه[15] رستم[16]
پسندانه صرهسنده شاکرد جلادتی[17] اولان دائرهسی طاقمی بر غیرت فوق[18]
العاده ایله هر بری اطرافنی صاران[19] عجم الینی یارارق[20] سلحدارینك[21]
یاننده اجتماع[22] ایتدیلر و ولی نعمتلرینك[23] شان مربیانهسنی[24] اعلا[25]
ایدهجك بر صولتله پاشانك اطرافنی صاران عجملر تارمار ایدهرك کند
یسنی ینه تخت[26] روان[27] اجلالی[28] اولان زین[29] سمندینه[30] اصعاد[31] ایلدیلر.

(1) A. *Muhajemat*, 'attacks.'— (2) *Mutévali*, 'successive.'— (3) A. *Shuheda*, 'martyrs.'—(4) P. *Lerzénak*, 'seized with trembling.'—(5) A. *Mukemmel*, 'complete.'— (6) *Sevk olounmak*, 'to be urged, pushed, driven.'—(7) A. *Tévabi*, 'dependents.'—(8) A. *Jeladet*, 'intrepidity.'—(9) P. *Ghiurz*, 'a mace.'—(10) A. *Darbé*, 'a blow.'—(11) A. *Mujahid*, 'a champion of the faith.'—(12) P. *Haïdar-iktidar*, 'having the might of a lion.'—(13) *Oghrashmak*, 'to struggle.'—(14) *Fedaï*, 'one who risks his life desperately.'—(15) A. *Mudafaa*, 'defence.'—(16) P. *Rustem*, a famous hero; *Rustem-pésendané*, 'heroic.'—(17) A. *Jeladet*, 'intrepidity.'—(18) A. *Fevk-él-adé*, 'extraordinary.'— (19) *Sarmak*, 'to bind or twine round' (a thing).—(20) *Yarmak*, 'to cleave.'— (21) *Silahdar* (*silihdar*), 'an esquire, a sword-bearer.'—(22) *Ijtima etmek*, 'to assemble.'—(23) A. *Veli-nimet*, 'a benefactor.'—(24) P. *Murebbiané*, *Murebbi*, 'an educator;' *Murebbiané*, pertaining to an educator (exemplary).—(25) A. *Ila*, 'elevating.'—(26) P. *Takht*, 'a throne.'—(27) *Takht-i-rewan*, 'a palanquin.'—(28) A. *Ijlal*, 'glory.'—(29) P. *Zin*, 'a saddle.'—(30) P. *Semend*, 'a horse.'—(31) *Isaad etmek*, 'to raise.'

جزمی هر نه قدر سپاهی¹ ایسهده درویش پاشا معیتنه² الیندن ایریلهرق

کیتمش اولمق و الّنده سردار طرفندن توصیهلر بولنمق جهتلریله پاشانك

دائرهسی خلقنه قارشمش و بناء علیه بو صولت قهرمانییه اشتراك³

ایتمشیدی . مخاطرهٔ⁴ بو بادرهٔ⁵ ایله ختامهٔ⁶ ایرمدی درویش پاشا دوشدیکی

مهلکهدن⁷ قورتیلوبده بنهجك بر حیوانه مالك اولنجه ینه فرقهسنی

احاطه ایدن دشمن آلایلرینی سوندیرمك⁹ امیدینه دوشهرك شدتلی

شدتلی حملهلرٔ⁰ قیام¹⁰ ایلدی و حتی امید غالبیتنیده قوهٔ قریبهیه

کتیردی . فقط طوغمان خان پیدرپی¹¹ یکی فرقهلر سوقیله حرب اوزرنده

بولنان قوّتنی تزیید¹² و تأیید¹³ ایتدیکندن اوچنجی دفعه اولهدق محاربه

علولنمکه باشلادی .

عثمانلیلر نه قدر ازالدیسه ایرانلیلر انك بر قاچ قاتی چوغالدیغیچون بو

دفعه کی مصادمه اولکیلره نسبت قبول ایتمیهجك درجهلرده شدید ایدی .

عثمانلیلرك هر نفری سکز اون کشی ایله اوغراشیر و اوغراشانلرك هر بری

قاننك هر طمله سنی بر جوهر جانه بدل¹⁴ ویرر ایدی . بقیهٔ شهدا ایچنده

مجروح اولمدق کیمسه قالمدی او زمانك سلاحنده شمدیکی تأثیر

اولمدیغندن اکثرینك جریحه¹⁵ سی خفیف ایدی عاقبت کندی نفسلرینی

ولی نعمتلرینه سپر¹⁶ ایتمکده اولان توابعك سیرکلنمسی¹⁷ جهتله عجمار بر

مهاجمهٔ شدیده ایله پاشانك صاغ طرفنده بولنان بر قاچ سوارییی عموماً

شهید ایتدکدن صکره بر اوق ایله اتنی تلف و بر دیکر اوق ایله کندیسنی

مجروح ایدهرك ینه او پرتو¹⁸ رخسان¹⁹ حمیتی²⁰ زمینه دوشورردیلر . . . . .

---

(1) *Sipahi*, 'a Spahi.'— (2) A. *Maïyyet*, 'a suite.'— (3) *Ishtirak etmek*, 'to participate in.'— (4) A. *Mukhateré*, 'danger.'— (5) A. *Badiré*, 'an unexpected event.'— (6) A. *Khitam*, 'completion, conclusion.'— (7) A. *Mehleké*, 'peril.'—(8) *Seundurmek*, 'to extinguish.'—(9) A. *Hamilé*, 'a charge, an effort, a pull.'—(10) *Kiyam éilémek*, 'to set about diligently.'— (11) *Péï-der-péï*, 'by degrees, continuously.'— (12) A. *Tezyid*, 'increasing.'—(13) A. *Téyid*, 'strengthening.'—(14) A. *Bédel*, 'a substitute, equivalent.'—(15) A. *Jeriha*, 'a wound.'—(16) P. *Siper*, 'a protection, shield;' 'parapet, peak of a cap.'— (17) *Séïreklenmek*, 'to get thinned.'— (18) P. *Pertev*, 'a ray, light.'— (19) P. *Rakhsan*, 'brilliant.'— (20) A. *Hamiyyet*, 'patriotism.'

جزئی بولنديغی بر قاچ يوز آديم¹ مسافهدن² پاشانك دوشديكی مهلكهيی
كورنجه وجودنده نه قدر حرارت غريزيه³ وار ايسه بردنبره⁴ التهاب⁵
ايدهرك بهار كونشه اوغرامش اغاجلر كبی درلو درلو رنكلر ايچنده قالمغه باشلادی .
كوزلرينی قان بوريدی⁶ . هر بری يكی اچلمش بر غنچهيه بكزهردی . تويلری⁷
اوپردی⁸ برر ديكن شكلی باغلادی . كندندن كچمش دينيلهجك بر طرز⁹
مهيب¹⁰ ايله

"سر كشلك ايتدی توسن بخت ستيزكار
دوشدی زمينه سايهٴ الطاف كردكار"

بيتنی¹¹ اوقويهرق "پاشا يرارا ياتيور دينلنی دولتنی سون ارقهمدن
كلسون ! " ديهرك قليجنی اغزينه قارغيسنی الينه الدی . فرهاد پاشا
يادكاری¹² اولان كحيلانك ديزكيننی¹³ بربننه اتدی . باشنی دشمن اوزرينه
چويردی "كسكين¹⁴ " اوزنكی پاشانك بولنديغی طرفه هجوم ايلدی . دائره
طاقمندن يانننده اولانلارده مسلك غيرتنده جزئی يه مرافقتدن¹⁵ چكنمديلر .
بلكه ولی نعمتلرينك خلاصنه اندن زياده اقدام ايتديلر انجق جزمينك
كحيلانی زور كار ايله مسابقه¹⁷ ايدهجك بر سرعته مالك اولديغندن پاشانك
اطرافنی احاطه ايدن دشمن عسكرينه هر كسدن اول او يتشدی و بربرينی
متعاقب بر قاچ عجم تلف ايدهرك سلاح قوتيله اچديغی شهراه¹⁸
جلادتدن ملك¹⁹ مؤكل²⁰ كبی مجروحك²¹ ياننه ورود²² ايلدی همان يره
ايندی پاشايی كندی آتنه سوار ايلدی . . . . . تعظيماً اوزنكيسنی²³ اوپديكی²⁴

---

(1) *Adim*, 'a pace.'— (2) A. *Mesafé*, 'distance.'— (3) A. *Gharizi*, 'innate.'—
(4) *Birdenbiré*, 'all at once.'—(5) *Iltihab etmek*, 'to flame up.'—(6) *Bouroumek*, 'to
cover up, wrap up.'—(7) *Tuï*, 'a feather, soft hair, down.'—(8) *Eupermek*, 'to stand
on end.'—(9) A. *Tarz*, 'way, fashion, manner.'—(10) A. *Muhib*, 'terrific.'—(11) A.
*Beït*, 'a couplet, verse.'—(12) P. *Yadighiar*, 'a souvenir, a memento.'—(13) *Dizghin*, 'the reins, a rein;' طولو ديزكين *dolou dizghin*, 'at full gallop.'— (14) *Keskin*,
'sharp, swift.'—(15) A. *Murafakat*, 'accompanying.'—(16) *Chekinmek*, 'to be loth,
to scruple, to hang back, to be bashful.'—(17) *Musabaka etmek*, 'to race with, com-
pete with.'—(18) P. *Shah-rah*, 'a public road.'— (19) A. *Mélek*, 'an angel.'—
(20) A. *Muvekkel*, 'charged, appointed as an agent.'—(21) A. *Mejrouh*, 'wounded.'—
(22) A. *Vuroud éïlémek*, 'to arrive.'—(23) *Uzenghi*, 'a stirrup.'—(24) *Eupmek*,
'to kiss.'

صرّده ایدی که سلاح ارقداشلرینده بربربنی متعاقب یانلرینه واصل
اولدیلر .

یو فرقهٔ ناجیه¹ اقدامات متوالیه ایله ینه دشمن مهاجملرینی² اطرافدن
دفع ایتمکه باشلامشدی حیوانفی پاشایه تقدیم ایلدیکی جهتله پیاده قلان
جزوی‌ده بر عجم سواریسنك دیزكیننه صاریلهرق و چیره دستانه³ بر
مهارتله اعدام ایدهرك التندهكی شاه‌بكندیه⁴ سوار اولدی . و اومجاهدارك
ارهسنه قارشدی . . . . . . . آرهدن بر از وقت کچرکچمز دشمن عسکرینك
ارقه سنده هوادن بر سیاه دومان⁵ پیدا اولدی و بزم عسکرك ارقه‌سنده
بر قزل توز قالقدی .

دشمن طرفندن كوریغان دومان فورتنهلی⁶ بر یاغمور بلوطی بزم طرفدن
قالقان توزده سردار پاشانك درویش پاشا امدادینه⁷ كوندردیكی اوز تیمور
اوغلی عثمان پاشا فرقهسی ایدی . . . . . . بلوط حامل⁸ اولدیغی یاغمور
طمهلرینی⁹ اردوارك اوزرینه صاچمغه عثمان پاشاده دشمنه او طمهلارله
یاریشیرجه‌سنه قورشون یاغدیرمغه باشلادی .

عثمانلیلرك آتشی بریارم ساعت دوام¹⁰ ایتمش اولسه عجم اردوسنك
بتون مضمحل¹¹ اولمسی مقرر¹² ایدی نه نهأكده كه او وقتك سلاحی صودن
محافظه اولنور شیلردن اولهدیغی ایچون یاغمورك شدتله اون اون ایکی
دقیقه ایچنده طوپلر تفكر بتون بتون استعمالدن قالمش و ینه ایش فلیجه
طیانمش ایدی .

عجم عسکری ایسه درویش پاشا و حتی مؤخراً¹³ امدادارینه کلان
فرقهلرینك مجموعلدن یوزده یتمش نسبتنده زائد اولدیغی ایچون —
او زمانلر حکمنجه حسن استعمالی عثمانلیلرك مخصوصاتندن اولان —

---

(1) *Naji,* 'saving, rescuing.'—(2) A. *Muhajim,* 'an assailant.'—(3) P. *Chiré-dest,*
'adroit.'—(4) *Shah-béyendi,* 'a kind of horse.'—(5) *Doman,* 'a fog, mist.'—(6) *Fir-
linali,* 'stormy.'—(7) A. *Imdad,* 'assistance.'—(8) *Hamil olnak,* 'to bear, carry.'—
(9) *Damla,* 'a drop.'— (10) *Déwam etmek,* 'to continue.'— (11) A. *Mouzmahil,*
'destroyed, annihilated.'— (12) A. *Mukarrer,* 'sure.'— (13) A. *Mouakhkheran,*
'latterly.'

اتشلی سلاح معطل' اولانجه کثرتلرینه کروندیلر. قلیجمزه مقاومت ایده
بیلمك امیدینه دوشدیلر اردومزله کوکس کوکسه' کلمكدن چکنمدیلر .

عثمان پاشا درویش پاشایه بکزمزدی درویس پاشا انسان قیافتنده'
غضنفر' ایسه عثمان غضنفر صولتنده بر انسان اولهرق ترتیبات حربیهجه
زمانندهکی اصحاب سیفك عمومنه فائق' ایدی او جهتله ایش قلیجه
دوشدیکی صرهده دخی ابراز ایتدیکی مهارت فوق العاده دشمنك کثرتنی
حکمدن اسقاط' ایلدی .

اویلهدن' غروبه' قدر امتداد'[10] ایدن محاربهده عثمان پاشا تعدد'[11] ایدر
جهسنه بر سرعتله'[12] هر مخاطره محلنه یتیشهرك جبر'[13] ما فات ایدردی
هرفرصت غالبیتك موقع ظهورنده بولنهرق تمامیله اغتنامه'[14] موفق'[15] اولوردی .
درویش پاشا اویله کندندن قدملی'[16] کندندن اقتدارلی'[17] بر ذاتك میدان
حربه وروردی اوزرینه یارهسنه باقدیرمق ایچون بر چادره'[18] چکلدی'[19] مع
مافیه'[20] حربك او فصلندهده'[21] ینه دشمنك هجومنه قارشی مقاومت'[22]
مقاومتنه قارشی هجومده عثمانلی عسکرینك ممتازی'[23] درویش پاشا فرقهسنك
بقیهسی و او بقیهنك اك ممتازیده جزمی ایدی . . . . . . . . .

غروب زمانلرینه یقین ایکی عسکر صوك دفعه'[24] اولمق اوزره ینه تمامیله
بربرینه قاریشهرق عثمانلیلرك رنکارنك'[25] بایراقلری عجملرك ظلام'[26] تحشد'[27]
ایچنده متعدد'[28] قوس'[29] قزحلر پیدا اولمش کبی بر شکل غریب حاصل

---

(1) *Mouattal*, 'useless, idle, inactive.'— (2) *Ghiuwenmek*, 'to put faith in, to trust.'—(3) *Ghieuks*, 'the chest;' *ghieuks ghieuksé ghelmek*, 'to fight hand to hand.' —(4) A. *Kiyafet*, 'costume, form, appearance.'—(5) *Ghazanfer*, 'a lion.'—(6) A. *Faïk*, 'excelling.'— (7) *Iskat etmek*, 'to lower, cause to fall.'— (8) *Evilé*, 'noon.'— (9) A. *Ghuroub*, 'sun-set.'—(10) *Imtidad etmek*, 'to extend' (*v.n.*).—(11) *Taadud*, 'exceeding calculation.'—(12) A. *Surat*, 'swiftness.'—(13) *Jebr-ma-fat etmek*, 'to repair what has happened, to restore, retrieve.'—(14) *Ightinam*, 'taking advantage of.'—(15) *Muwafak olmak*, 'to succeed.'—(16) *Kademli*, 'one whose approach brings good luck;' 'lucky, fortunate.'—(17) *Iktidarli*, 'capable.'—(18) *Chadir*, 'a tent.'—(19) *Chekilmek*, 'to retire, withdraw' (*v.n.*).—(20) A. *Ma-ma fih*, 'however.' —(21) A. *Fasl*, 'a division, section, chapter, season.'—(22) A. *Mukavémet*, 'Resistance.'—(23) A. *Mumtaz*, 'distinguished.'—(24) A. *Defa*, 'a time.'—(25) P. *Renghiareng*, 'of various colours.'—(26) A. *Zilam*, 'darkness.'—(27) A. *Tehashshad*, 'congregating, collecting together.'—(28) A. *Mutaadid*, 'numerous.'—(29) A. *Kavsi-Kouzah*, 'a rainbow.'

ايتمشدى . ايرانليلر هوا بتون قرارجمهيه ¹ قدر ايستر ايستمز
موقعلرنده ثبات ² ايدهرك نهايت قراكلقدن استفاده ³ ايله محاربه ميداننه
بش بيك بو قدر مقتول ⁴ و بر او قدر اسير براقدقدن و چادرلرينى قطارلرينى ⁵
و سائر هر درلو مهمات حربيهلرينى عثمانليلرك دست اغتنامنه ترك
ايلدكدن صكره مقتدر اوله بيلدكلرى قدر اوزاغه فرار ايله اردولرينك بقيهسنى
بتون يتون اضمحلالدن قورتارديلر .

عثمان پاشا ميدان محاربهدن عودت ايدنجه اولكى ايشى درويش
پاشانك خاطرينى سؤاله عزيمت اولدى . درويش پاشاده عثمان پاشايى
كورور كورو زجزمى ماجراسنى ⁶ نقل ايله حقنده نياز مكافات ايلدى . عثمان
پاشا بو سوزه قارشى '' بنده بو كون قوله ⁷ آتلى بر سپاهى كوردم پاشالر مزدن
زياده ايشه يارامشدى ان شا اللّه ايكيسنه بردن مكافات ايدرز'' دينجه
درويش پاشا عسكر ايچنده قوله آتلى بر آدم اواهرق كنديسنه قورتاراندده
ينه او سپاهى اولديغنى بيان ايتديكندن عثمان پاشا چوجوغك ايكى صورتله
مكافاته لايق بيان ايله درويش پاشا توابعنه جزمينك بولديريلهرق كندى
ياننه كوندرلمسنى تنبيه ايتدكدن صكره چادرينه عودت ايلدى .

و قتا كه جزمى يى بولوب ياننه كو تورديلر پاشا همان يرندن قيام ايدهرك
و اويله تك ⁸ آتلى بر سپاهىيسى '' كل اوغلم '' حطابيله ⁹ قوجاقلايهرق
تلطيفاتنه ¹⁰ مستغرق ¹¹ ايلدى . باشنه انيله ايكى چلنك ¹² طاقدى ¹³ . ارقاسنه
بر كوزل خلعت كيدردى . كنديسنه بش يوز التون بر التون قبضه ¹⁴ قليج
بر زمردلى ¹⁵ خنجر ¹⁶ احسان ¹⁷ ايلدى .

---

(1) *Karamak*, 'to get dark, black.'—(2) *Sebat etmek*, 'to be firm.'—(3) *Istifadé*
'taking advantage of.'—(4) A. *Maktoul*, 'killed.'—(5) A. *Katar*, 'a string of mules,
horses, or camels.'—(6) A. *Ma-jera*, 'what has happened.'—(7) *Koulé*, 'bay-
coloured.'—(8) *Tek*, 'merely.'—(9) A. *Khitablé*, 'addressing.'—(10) A. *Teltifat*,
'kindnesses and attentions.'—(11) A. *Mustaghrak éilemek*, 'to overwhelm with.'—
(12) *Chélenk*, 'an ornament worn on the head-dress, which was in the olden times
conferred as an honour.'—(13) *Takmak*, 'to put on.'—(14) *Kabzé*, 'the handle of a
sword.'—(15) A. *Zumurrud* (*Zumrud*), 'an emerald.'—(16) P. *Khanjer* (*Hancher*),
'a large curved dagger.'—(17) *Ihsan etmek*, 'to confer.'

Everybody knows, from his own experience, what effects the first step, the first act, in any path in life has on one's feelings, and the reflections it produces on one's mind.

The effects the first step in Jezmi's career—soldiering—had on him, and how it excited his imagination, cannot be described. However reckless and careless he might be by nature, or whatever self-sacrifice there was in his heart, it was impossible to suppress the predominant feeling of nature—self-preservation—and it is improbable that want of experience and practice does not produce hesitation in the mind, and agitation in the heart, of even most distinguished people (on such an occasion).

A battle-field one has to go to is a place of trial between which, and the next world, the greatest distance is only the range of a cannon-ball. Those who are unaccustomed to it naturally see the incarnation of death, the "destroyer of all delight," not merely in the soldiers of the enemy but even in their shadows. One looks upon every part of the ground he walks on as burying-ground prepared for him. All the beauties of the world, all the pleasures of life, all the hopes of one's heart, are collected together in one place, and present themselves enticingly before one's eyes.

Hence, however eager Jezmi had been to go to the war, still, when he mounted his horse, and entered his regiment, he could not free himself from these natural anxieties. Moreover, however much a sensible man may have confidence in himself, he cannot be confident about fortune. Therefore, the dread that an unexpected accident might bring discredit on his valour and skill, and make him contemptible in the eyes of his patrons and friends, greatly increased the perturbation of his heart; but the courage and determination in his nature, and the pride and ambition he possessed, counterbalanced the feelings spoken of above.

On Jezmi coming against the enemy with this agitation, and this mental struggle going on in him, and muskets began to be fired, and swords to flash, he neither found war such a pleasant agreeable promenade as he had imagined it while his desire for it was *in posse*, nor the theatre of irresistible calamity as he had dreaded it might be after his desire for it had been realised.

### The Battle with the Persians.

Dervish Pasha being a young courageous man, and of an impetuous disposition, as soon as he saw the enemy, the "lion-like" impulse of his nature prevailed over all his senses and faculties, and he attached no importance to the difference in numbers between the two armies. With three or four hundred heroes who were under his fortunate flag he attacked the centre (the heart) of a large army. The Persians, as it were, were like a heap of straw opposed to the "world-consuming" flame of the Pasha's detachment. The Persian regiments which were in the front rank were annihilated at the first shock. Although this terrific rush shook the whole of the enemy's army, and some of their regiments even began to retreat, Tokman Khan, looking upon the disgrace of flying before such a small detachment as more odious than death, by dint of great exertion got his army to stand steady again, pushed a detachment stronger than the whole of the Turks in every direction forward, and surrounded the Pasha. . . . . .

The Persians, by successive attacks, surrounded our soldiers, and killed many men. Dervish Pasha, with the remainder of the heroes who were with him, by valiantly fighting hand to hand for two or three hours, again having shaken the enemy, Tokman Khan sent a whole detachment of cavalry more forward. This fresh force, by a violent rush, killed thirty of the Pasha's intrepid companions, and by blows of the sword and the mace, brought him down from his horse.

The lion-like "Champion of the Faith," when dismounted, struggled by himself against a whole army for a long time, and cut in two three desperate self-sacrificing Persians who successively attacked him. After this heroic defence, his suite, who were his pupils in valour, with a supreme effort, cleaving the crowd of Persians hemming them in on all sides, collected near his standard-bearer, and with a rush, "calculated to enhance the exemplary glory of the Pasha," scattered the Persians who surrounded him in every direction, and again mounted him in his horse's saddle, the palanquin of his glory. Jezmi, although he was a Spahi, having separated from his regiment and joined the Pasha's suite, and having mixed with the Pasha's attendants (as he had letters of recommendation from the Commander-in-Chief), took part in this valiant charge. The danger, however, did not terminate with this episode. The Pasha having been rescued from the peril into which he had fallen, as soon as he had a horse to ride, set about violently charging in the hope of extinguishing the enemy's regiments, and he nearly succeeded in realising his hopes of victory. But Tokman Khan, continually pushing forward fresh detachments, increased and strengthened his forces engaged in the fight, and the combat flamed up again for the third time. As the more the Turks decreased the more the Persians increased several fold, this last collision was more violent and irresistible than the preceding ones. Every man amongst the Ottomans struggled with eight or ten persons, and for every drop of their blood they took a life in exchange. Amongst the remnant of the heroes not one remained unwounded ; but, as the arms of that period had not the same effect as those used at present, the wounds of most of them were slight. At last, as the ranks of the followers of the Pasha who shielded their benefactor with their bodies became thinned, the Persians, with a violent charge, killed the whole of some horsemen on the right side of the Pasha, and then, destroying his horse with one arrow and wounding him himself with another arrow, they brought that " brilliant light of patriotism " to the ground.

Jezmi, who was a few hundred paces distant, seeing the peril the Pasha had fallen into, all the innate ardour of his nature was at once kindled, and he changed colour "like the trees when in contact with the sun of Spring." His eyes became blood-shot ; and each one looked " like a newly opened rose-bud." His hair stood on end, like thorns, and, beside himself, he recited, in a terrific manner, the couplet,—

*" Serkeshlik etdi tersén bakht sétizkiar,*
*Dushdou zeminé sayé-i-eltaf-i-kerdighiar,"*

and cried : "The Pasha is on the ground ! Let him who loves his religion and his country follow me ! " He took his sword in his mouth and his " karghi " in his hand, and threw the reins on the neck of the horse which Ferhad Pasha gave him as a keepsake, and turned his head towards the enemy, and, at full gallop, charged in the direction where the Pasha was.  Those belonging to the Pasha's *suite* who were near did not hesitate to accompany Jezmi in the path of valour, and perhaps they exerted themselves more than he to rescue their benefactor, but as Jezmi's horse possessed a swiftness equal to that of the wind, he reached the enemy's troops who surrounded the Pasha before anybody else; and, after killing several Persians, one after another, came to the side of the wounded man like a guardian angel by a path which he bravely opened by arms.  He at once alighted, and mounted the Pasha on his horse. . . . . . When he was kissing his stirrup respectfully, his companions in arms came up one after another.

By the continued charges of this troop, which came to the rescue, our assailants were again repelled.  Jezmi, who, after giving his horse to the Pasha, remained on foot, caught hold of the reins of a Persian horseman, killed him, mounted his steed, and then joined our champions.  After a short interval, a black mist appeared behind the enemy's troops, and red dust arose behind our soldiers.

The mist in the direction of the enemy's army was a stormy rain-cloud, and the dust which arose on our side was raised by the detachment of Osman Pasha, son of Uz Timour, whom the Commander-in-Chief had sent to the assistance of Dervish Pasha . . . .

Osman Pasha began to pour bullets on the enemy, so that they vied with the way in which the drops of the rain, which the cloud contained, fell on the armies.

If the fire of the Turkish troops had continued half an hour, it is certain that the Persian army would have been entirely destroyed. But of what avail was it that—as the arms of that period were not proof against wet—owing to the violence of the rain, in ten or fifteen minutes, muskets and cannon were entirely unserviceable, and the matter again rested with the sword ?

As for the Persian army, as they were seventy per cent more numerous than Dervish Pasha's division, and to all the divisions which had come to his help, all put together, on fire-arms (the skilful use of which was one of the specialities of the Turks in those days) becoming useless, they trusted to their numbers, and fancying they could resist our swords, did not hesitate to come to hand to hand fighting with us.

Osman Pasha did not resemble Dervish Pasha. Dervish Pasha was like a lion in the form of a man, but Osman Pasha, being a man with the impulses of a lion, was superior to all his contemporary warriors in military tactics. This being the case, when the matter rested with the sword, the skill he displayed materially counter-balanced the numerical superiority of the enemy.

In the battle, which lasted from noon till sunset, Osman Pasha rushed to every place of danger with extraordinary rapidity, re-paired what had happened, and succeeding in turning to advantage every opportunity for victory.

Dervish Pasha, on the arrival of such a person on the battle-field superior to himself in luck and capacity, retired to his tent to have his wound attended to. However, at this stage of the battle, still the most distinguished of the Ottoman troops in resisting the assault of the enemy, and in assaulting them where they resisted, was the remnant of Dervish Pasha's division, and the most distinguished one of them was Jezmi.

Towards sunset the whole of the two armies met again for the last time, and the variously coloured flags of the Turks amongst the black mass of the Persians presented a strange scene, as if several rain-bows had appeared. The Persians, *nolens volens*, stood firm until it became quite dark, and then took advantage of the darkness to save the rest of their army from total destruction, by flying away as far as possible, after leaving five thousand killed, and as many prisoners, on the battle-field, and abandoning their tents, their animals, and all kinds of military stores to be plundered by the Ottomans.

The first thing Osman Pasha did on returning from the battle-field was to inquire after Dervish Pasha. Dervish Pasha, also, immediately he saw Osman Pasha, related all that Jezmi had done, and asked for him to be rewarded. Osman Pasha replied : " I have also to-day seen a Spahi on a bay-coloured horse, who was more useful than our Pashas. I hope to reward both of them at once." On Dervish Pasha explaining that there was only one man in the army with a bay-coloured horse, and that he was the same Spahi who had rescued him, Osman Pasha said the youth deserved to be doubly rewarded, and after giving orders to the followers of Dervish Pasha to find Jezmi and send him to him, returned to his tent.

When they found Jezmi, and brought him, the Pasha at once rose from his seat, and addressing this simple Spahi with the words: "Come, my son!" embraced him and overwhelmed him with kindnesses.   He then fixed two "Chelenk"* (ornaments) on his head with his own hand, invested him with a robe of honour, gave him five hundred pieces of gold, a sword with a gold hilt, and a dagger studded with emeralds.

---

* A reward for bravery and a kind of decoration, much prized in those days by the Turks.

## MEHEMET TEVFIK.

### ISHTIYAK.—A NOVEL.

اشتیاق .

\* \* \* \* سنۀسنه مصادف اغستوسك ۱۳ نجی کونی ایکندییه یقین
بر ساعتده سلطان محمود تربهسندن باب عالییه¹ کیدن جاده³ اوزرنده²
سزه دلالت⁴ ایدرسهك کلن کچنلر میاننده⁵ ایکی کنج⁶ ارقداشك⁷
یکدیکربنه⁸ ملاقی اولدقلرینی کوررسکز بونلردن بری یوقاری طوغری چیقیور
دیکری اشاغی طوغری اینیور ایدی ایکیسیده هنوز⁹ یکرمی یاشلرنده اونوب
یوقاری طوغری چیقان صاریشین سیمالی اچیق مای¹⁰ کوزلی ایدی
اینجه بیقلری¹¹ صاریلغی¹² جهتله¹³ اول قدر حس¹⁴ اولنمیور ایدی دیکری
قومرال¹⁵ صاچلی¹⁶ اچیق¹⁷ الا¹⁸ کوزلی ایدی دقت اولنسه صاریشین¹⁹
کنج یوزنده بر نور بشاشت²⁰ لمعان²¹ ایتمکده اولدیغی اکلاشیله بیلیر
یوقاریدن کلن دلیقانلی یی کورنجه وجهنده²²کی سرور²³ بر قاندها²⁴ تجلی²⁵
ایتمکه باشلادی بو حال دیکرنده دخی حس اولنیور ایدی بر بربنه ملاقی
اولدیلر صاغ²⁶ اللرینی چاپرازواری²⁷ یقلایوب²⁸ صمیمی²⁸ بر حس²⁰ محبت³¹
ایله³² صیقدیلر .

---

(1) A. *Turbé*, 'a grave.'—(2) A. *Bab-i-ali*, 'the Sublime Porte.'—(3) A. *Jadé*, 'a highway.'—(4) A. *Delalet*, 'to conduct.'—(5) *Miyaninde*, 'amongst.'—(6) *Ghenj*, 'young.'— (7) *Arkadash*, 'companions.'—(8) P. *Yekdigher*, 'one another.'—(9) P. *Henouz*, 'only just this moment,' (with a negative) 'not yet.'—(10) A. *Maï* (generally pronounced by the Turks *Mavi*), 'light blue.'—(11) *Biyik*, 'the moustache.'—(12) *Sarilik*, 'yellowness.'—(13) *Jihetlé*, 'by reason of.'—(14) *Hiss olounmak*, 'to be felt, perceived.'—(15) *Koumral*, 'auburn.'—(16) *Sachli*, 'haired.'—(17) *Achik*, 'light.'—(18) *Ala*, 'reddish.'—(19) *Sarishin* or ماروشین, 'yellowish, reddish.'—(20) *Beshashet*, 'hilarity, joy.'—(21) *Leman etmek*, 'to shine, flash.'—(22) A. *Vej*, 'a face.'—(23) *Surour*, 'joy, pleasure.'—(24) *Bir kat daha*, 'still more, doubly.'—(25) A. *Tejelli etmek*, 'to become manifest.'—(26) *Sagh*, 'right.'—(27) *Chapraz*, the braidings on military coats with loops and buttons.—(28) *Yakalamak*, 'to lay hold of, to collar.'—(29) A. *Samimi*, 'sincere.'—(30) A. *Hiss*, 'feeling.'—(31) A. *Mahabbet*, 'affection, friendship.'—(32) *Sikmak*, 'to squeeze.'

صاریشین صوربیور<sup>1</sup> ایدی که .

قرداش نرهده قالدك ؟    بر هفتهدر عودتکه اتنظار ایدیورم حالبوکه کهلی اوچ کون اولمش ده کوروشهمدك .

اوت بنده سنی چوق آرادم<sup>2</sup> نقط بعض مستعجل<sup>3</sup> ایشلرك تسویهسی<sup>4</sup> کوروشمکه مانع<sup>5</sup> اولمدی دکل بو کون بورادہ قرائتخانهده<sup>6</sup> بولیشه بیله جکهزی خبر<sup>7</sup> براقمشسك کلیوردم تشکر ایدرم که بکلتمدك<sup>8</sup> کلدك .

صاریشین دلیقاتلی هم محبنك<sup>9</sup> بو سوزلرینی دیکلیور همده<sup>10</sup> ذهناً<sup>11</sup> <sup>12</sup> بشقه بر مشغولیتده<sup>13</sup> اولدیغی طالغینلغندن اکلاشیلیور ایدی .

دیکری بونی حس<sup>14</sup> ایتدیده دیدی که .

سکا بویله نه اولمش !    بو کون شاقراقلغك یرنده دکل .

سنی کوردمده سونجمدن<sup>15</sup> . . . .

هلههله<sup>16</sup> . . . مزورلك<sup>17</sup> ایتمه طوغری سویله .

شفیق بیلسهك بو کون پك بختیارم<sup>18</sup> هم سنی کوردم همده . . . . .

ای هم ده . . . .

بورایه کلیرکن یانکدن سرعتله<sup>19</sup> کچن عربهیی کورمدكمی ؟

خیر دقت<sup>20</sup> ایتمدم . سکا طالمش<sup>21</sup> ایدم .

شفیق کورملی ایدك . سکا هروقت سویلمزمی ایدم .

ایشته او ملك<sup>22</sup> . بو کون بکا شونی عنایت<sup>23</sup> ایتدی .

---

(1) *Sormak*, 'to ask.'—(2) *Aramak*, 'to seek, look for, to miss, inquire for.'—(3) *Mustajel*, 'urgent.'—(4) A. *Tesvíyé*, 'arranging, settling.'—(5) A. *Mani*, 'an obstacle.'—(6) *Kira'et-Khané*, 'a reading-room.'—(7) A. *Khabr*, 'news;' *Khabr brakmak*, 'to leave word.'—(8) *Bekletmek*, 'to keep anyone waiting.'—(9) A. *Muhib*, 'a friend.'—(10) *Dinlémek*, 'to listen.'—(11) *Hem . . . . hemdé*, 'both.'—(12) A. *Zihn*, 'the intellect, mind;' *Zihnan*, 'in his mind, mentally.'—(13) A. *Meshghouliyet*, 'occupation, business.'—(14) *His etmek*, 'to feel.'—(15) *Sevinj*, 'joy.'—(16) *Helé! helé!* 'now! now! did you ever!'—(17) *Muzevver* is an Arabic word meaning 'concocted, made up,' and *Muzevverlik* is a Turkish noun made from it, meaning 'fibs, humbugs, nonsense.'—(18) P. *Bakhtiar*, 'lucky.'—(19) *Suratilé*, 'rapidly.'—(20) *Dikkat etmek*, 'to pay attention.'—(21) *Dalmak*, 'to plunge, dash.'—(22) *Melek*, 'an angel.'—(23) *Inayet etmek*, 'to do a favour.'

ديەرك تقريرلك<sup>1</sup> كاغدن قوپارلديغى<sup>2</sup> ايكى طرفنك يالديزلى اولوب دە
ديكر ايكى كنارينك يىرتيقلغندن بللى اولان ال قدر بركاغدى شفيقە ويردى
و " هايدى كيدەلم شورادە قرائتخانەدە اوقورسك " دیە رفيقنك<sup>3</sup> قولندن<sup>4</sup>
چكدى<sup>5</sup> برلكدە<sup>6</sup> اورادە بولنن قرائتخانەيە كيرديلر.<sup>7</sup>
عرفان دييور ايدى كە .

عفو<sup>8</sup> ايدرسك قرداشم باق نە قدر طالميشم كە تلاش<sup>9</sup> ايلە صحتكنى<sup>10</sup>
صورەمدم .

شمدىدە شفيق كاغدە<sup>11</sup> طالمش ايدى عرفانە جواب<sup>12</sup> و يرەبيرر دقتلى
دقتلى مينى مينى كاغدى اوقيور ايدى .

كاغد قورشون<sup>13</sup> قلميلە حرفار<sup>14</sup> اينجى كبى دوكلمش ايدى دقت ايدنلر
اونك قادين يازيسى اولديغنە شبهە<sup>15</sup> ايتمزلر . بو قادينارك هر شيئى
هر حالى اركككلردن<sup>16</sup> فرقليدر . . . .

و الحاصل<sup>17</sup> شفيقك اللندەكى كاغك خطندن<sup>18</sup> افادەسندن<sup>19</sup> بر قادين
يازيسى فقط<sup>20</sup> بزم مملكتنجە<sup>21</sup> تربيە<sup>22</sup> و تحصيل<sup>23</sup> كورمش بر قادين يازيسى
اولديغى اكلاشيلير ايدى شفيق كاغدى كمال<sup>24</sup> دقتلە اوقودى كە محتوياتى<sup>25</sup>
شودر :—

" مظهر<sup>26</sup> التفات<sup>27</sup> و نوازش<sup>28</sup> عاليلرى اولمغى سرمايە<sup>29</sup> حيات<sup>30</sup> بيلورم تأثير<sup>31</sup>
عشقلە<sup>32</sup> زخملى<sup>33</sup> اولان كوكلمك<sup>34</sup> محتاج<sup>35</sup> التفات بولنديغنى هر دقيقە<sup>36</sup>

(1) A. *Takrir*, 'an official report or diplomatic note.'—(2) *Koparmak*, ' to tear off,
break off, pluck off.'—(3) A. *Refik*, 'companion.'—(4) *Kol*, 'the arm.'—(5) *Chekmek,*
' to pull, draw.'—(6) *Birlikdé*, 'together, in unity.'—(7) *Ghirmek*, ' to enter.'—(8) *Afv
etmek,* 'to pardon.'—(9) *Telash*, 'a hurry, fuss.'—(10) A. *Sihat*, 'health.'—(11) *Kiaghid,*
' paper, a card.'—(12) *Jawab vermek*, 'to answer.'—(13) *Kourshoun-Kalemi,* 'a lead-
pencil.'—(14) A. *Harf*, 'a letter.'—(15) *Shuphe etmek*, 'to doubt.'—(16) *Erkek,* 'a male.'
—(17) A. *Elhasil*, 'in short.'—(18) A. *Khat*, 'writing.'—(19) A. *Ifadé,* ' expression.'
(20) *Fakat*, 'only.'—(21) A. *Memleket*, 'a country.'—(22) A. *Terbiyé*, 'education.'—
(23) A. *Tahsil*, 'study.'—(24) A. *Kémal*, 'perfection.'—(25) A. *Muhteviat*, 'the
contents.'—(26) A. *Mezher*, 'an object.'—(27) A. *Iltifat*, 'attention, notice.'—
(28) P. *Nuwazish*, 'treating with kindness, a caress.'—(29) P. *Sermayé*, 'capital,
stock, material.'—(30) A. *Hayat*, 'life.'—(31) A. *Te'sir*, 'effect.'—(32) A. *Ashk,*
'love.'—(33) *Zahmli*, 'wounded.'—(34) *Ghiunul*, 'the heart.'—(35) A. *Mouhtaj,*
'needing.'—(36) A. *Dukika*, 'minute?

حس ایتمكدءیم ٰ . فكرم ٰ خیالكزله ٰ مشغول ٰ آرزو ٰ و املم ٰ زیارت ٰ
جمالكزله ٰ مشرف ٰ اولمغه معطوفدر ٰ . احتمال خاطرهده ٰ نام ٰ و نشانم ٰ
دخی قالمامشدر بویله ایكن ینه توجهات ٰ كرانبهای ٰ عالیلرینك حق ٰ
جاریارنهمده ٰ اسیركنمیهجكنی ٰ امید ایدرك تصدیعه ٰ جسارتلندم ٰ بو
جرأت ٰ قباحت ٰ ایسه عفوكنی ٰ مروتكزدن ٰ بكلرم باقی لطف ٰ و عنایت ٰ
افندمكدر"

مكتوبی نهایتنه ٰ قدر اوقویوب اتمامدن ٰ صكره بر قاچ دفعه ٰ دها
تكرارلدی ٰ كوكلی هنوز اقربا محبتندن بشقه بر محبته ٰ مقر ٰ اولمامش . . .
بو قبیلهدن اولهرق شفیقده مكتوبی ٰ كندینه تعلقی ٰ اولمدیغی حالده
دخی ـ قلبی حوپلایه حوپلایه اوقیور ایدی . بر قاچ دفعه اوقودقدن صكره
كاغدك ارقهسنده دخی بر قاچ سطر ٰ یازی بولندیغنی كوردی بو سطرلرك
كلمهلری مكتوبك كیلر كبی اینجه ٰ و مرسّم ٰ دكل ایدیلر تلاش ٰ ایله و
عربهده یازلدیغی حرفلرك ایریلكندن و انتظامسزلغندن بللی اولیور ایدی
ظاهر ٰ مكتوبی یازان خانم قز اولچه محبتنامهسنی حاضرلمش صكرهده
سودیكنه تصادف ٰ ایدنجه مكتوبی ویرهبیلهجكم دیو سرور ٰ و تلاش ایله
او سطرلری یازمش . صكرهكی سطرلر: ـ " نه وقتدنبریدر سزی ارایپیورم ده

---

(1) A. *Fikr*, 'thought, idea.'—(2) A. *Khayal*, 'an idea, fancy, a vision, imagination.'—(3) A. *Meshgoul*, ' busy, occupied.'—(4) A. *Arzou*, ' wish.'—(5) A. *Eml*, ' hope.'—
(6) A. *Ziaret*, ' a visit.'—(7) A. *Jimal*, ' beauty.'—(8) *Mushérref*, ' honoured.'—
(9) A. *Matouf*, ' inclined, turned.'—(10) A. *Khatiré*, ' a thought.'—(11) P. *Nam*,
' name.'—(12) P. *Nishan*, ' a sign, signal, trace.'—(13) A. *Tévejjuhat*, ' favours.'—
(14) P. *Ghiranbaha*, ' valuable.'—(15) A. *Hak*, ' truth;' *hakimdé*, ' with respect to me.'
—(16) P. *Jariané*, ' humble.'—(17) *Esirghémek*, ' to spare, to be chary of ;' *esirghen-
mek*, ' to be spared.'—(18) A. *Tasdi*, ' giving a headache, bothering.'—(19) *Jessaret-
lenmek*, ' to have the boldness.'—(20) A. *Jera'et*, ' boldness, audacity.'—(21) A. *Kabahat*,
' a fault.'—(22) A. *Afv*, ' pardon.'—(23) A. *Murouvvet*, ' magnanimity, generosity.'—
(24) A. *Loutf*, ' kindness, amiability.'—(25) A. *Inayet*, ' grace.'—(26) *Nihayet*, ' end.'—
(27) A. *Itmam*, ' completing.'—(28) A. *Defa*, ' a time.'—(29) *Tekrarlemek*, ' to repeat.'—
(30) A. *Mahabbet*, ' affection.'—(31) A. *Makar*, ' abode.'—(32) A. *Taaluk*, ' connection.'
— (33) A. *Setr*, ' a line.'—(34) *Injé*, ' thin, fine.'—(35) A. *Murassam*, ' drawn.'—
(36) *Telash*, ' haste, flurry.'—(37) A. *Zahir*, ' evident.'—(38) A. *Tésadduf*, ' meet-
ings.'—(39) A. *Surour*, ' pleasure.'

تصادف ایده‌میورم بو كون نائل¹ اولدیغم ایكی موفقت بنی نه قدر مسعود²
ایتدی بیله‌سك‘‘ . . . . سوزلرینی مشتمل ایدی .

شفیق بو سطرلری دخی اوقودقدن صكره كاغدی عرفان بكه اعاده³
ایتدی . . . . عرفان بك كندینه اعاده اولنان كاغدی الهرق صوردی كه
ای نصل بولدك باقه‌لم ؟

پك اعلا سزی تبریك ایدرم⁴ یازیسی افاده‌سی كبی كندیسی كوزل
ایسه سزه كوسترمكه باشلادیغی محبتده ثبات ایدرسه بختیار اولوسك
اكر تصادفمزده یانكدن كچن عربه‌یه دقتلی باقسه‌یدك بو مكتوبی یازانك
نه قدر كوزل بر خانمجغز اولدیغنی كورردك .

كاشكی ! فقط كوره‌دم بو قدر بكندیككز خانمك كیمك نه‌سی اولدیغنی
اوكرنه بیلیرمی‌یز ؟

سن‌ده نه اونوتقان چوچقسك سكا هر وقت سویلمزی‌ی ایدم . . . . بیوك
مأمورارندن⁵ سرمد افندینك قزی خاطرلمیورمیسك⁶ ؟ هانی بو سنه
قیشین بر صغوق هواده ایوبه كیتمك اوزره عزب تپوسنه اینمش ایدك‌ده
حضرت خالده طوغری قایقله بر جنازه⁷ كوتورلدیكنی اوزاقدن كورمش ایدك
اوت اوت خاطرلیودم او كون‌ده هوا نه قدر مظلم⁸ نه قدر قسوتلی⁹
ایدی . . . . حتی یاننده‌كی غلبه‌لكدن بو جنازه‌نك بر بیوك ذاته متعلق¹⁰
برلندیغنی استدلال¹¹ ایدوب كیم اولدیغنی مراق¹² ایدرك صورشدیریه‌مغه
باشلادقده اوراده بولنان یاشلیجه¹³ بر آدم ‘‘سرمد افندینك بر كنج قزی
اولمش جنازه او در‘‘ دیمش ایدی . . . . ایشته او جنازه‌سنی كوردیكك
مرحومه بو قزك همشیره‌سیدر¹⁴ .

---

(1) *Naïl olmak,* 'to attain.'— (2) A. *Mesoud,* 'happy.'— (3) *Iadé etmek,* 'to
return, give back.'— (4) *Tebrik etmek,* 'to congratulate.'— (5) A. *Mé'mour,* 'an
official.'— (6) *Khatirlamak,* 'to remember.'—(7) *Jenazé,* 'a funeral.'—(8) A. *Mouz-lim,* 'dark.'—(9) *Kasvetli,* 'severe.'—(10) A. *Mutaalik,* 'belonging to.'—(11) *Istidlal
etmek,* 'to infer.'— (12) *Merak etmek,* 'to be curious.'— (13) *Yashlijé,* 'elderly.'—
(14) P. *Hemshiré,* 'a sister.'

*Translation.*

## The Two Friends.

If you went back under our guidance to the year ——, and to the afternoon of the 13th of August, in the street leading from the tomb of Sultan Mahmoud to the Sublime Porte, amongst the passers by you would see two young friends meet one another. One of them was going straight up the road, and the other was coming straight down. Both of them were only just about twenty years of age. The one going up was fair, and had light blue eyes. His slight moustache was so fair that it was scarcely perceptible. The other had auburn hair and light brown eyes. The face of the fair youth was radiant with joy. On his seeing the young man who was descending, the pleasure on his face became still more manifest. The other perceived this. They met, shook hands, and embraced each other with sincere affection.

The fair youth asked: "Where have you been, my friend, I have been expecting you to return for a week, and now it is three days since you came back, and yet we have not met each other."

"Yes, I have wanted to see you also, but I had pressing affairs to attend to which prevented me. You left word that we could meet to day in the reading-room, and I have come, and I thank you that you have not kept me waiting."

The fair youth listened to the words of his friend, but it was clear, from his excitement, that his mind was occupied by something else.

The other, noticing this, said: "What has come to you! You are not yourself to day?"

"My joy at seeing you."—

"Come, come, no humbug, speak plainly."

"Shefik, you must know that I am in luck's way to day, I have seen you and also,"—

"And also?"—

"As you were coming here did you not see a carriage pass quickly by?"

"No, I did not pay attention, I was rushing towards you."

"Shefik, you ought to have seen it. Was I not always talking to you about her? That angel to-day favoured me with this." So saying he gave Shefik a paper, which it was evident from two of the edges being gilt and the two others torn, had been torn from a piece of official paper (on which diplomatic notes are written). "Come, let us go, you can read it here in the reading-room." So saying, he pulled Shefik by the arm, and they entered the reading-room, which is there together.

Arfan said : "Pardon me, my friend, I was in such a flurry that I did not ask you how you are."

Shefik was now so absorbed in the letter that he gave Arfan no answer. He was most attentively reading it. It was written in pencil, and the letters looked like scattered pearls. Anyone who looked at it attentively would have known it was a lady's handwriting. These ladies—everything about them, and everything they do is different from what belongs to a man.

In a word, it was evident from the style of the writing on the piece of paper in Shefik's hand that it was a lady's writing, but the writing of a lady educated and brought up in our country's way.

The paper which Shefik read so attentively ran thus: "To be the object of your attentions and favours is the only aim of my life. That my heart, which has been pierced by love, needs your notice, I feel every minute. My thoughts are busy with your image, and my desire and hope is to be honoured by the sight of your beauty. Probably you have forgotten my name and appearance. As I trust you will not be chary with your favours to your slave, I have troubled you with this foolish letter. If this boldness of mine be a fault, I expect your magnanimity will pardon it. For the rest, you must bestow favours as you think fit."

After reading the letter through, he read it several times again.

Hitherto his heart had been a stranger to all love but that for his relations . . . . .

This kind of letter, although it did not belong to him, he read with a palpitating heart. After having read it several times, he saw there were a few lines of writing on the back. The words of these lines were not so fine or so carefully written as those inside the letter. It was clear from the irregular and scattered way in which they were written that they had been penned in the carriage.

It was evident that the young lady who wrote the letter had first prepared her *billet-doux*, and then, on happening to meet him, saw she could give it him, and added the other words in joy and haste. They were as follows : " What a long time I have been looking for you and could not meet you ! How happy the double luck I have had to-day has made me ! " . . .

Shefik, after reading these lines also, returned the paper to Arfan Bey.

Arfan Bey, on taking the paper returned to him, said : " Well, what do you think of it, eh ! "

" Very good ! I congratulate you. If she be as beautiful as the writing and the style, and be constant in the love she has begun to show you, you are lucky."

" If you had looked attentively at the carriage which passed close by you when we met, you would have seen how beautiful she is."

" I wish I had ! But I could not see her. May I ask who is the lady you like so much ? "

" What a forgetful boy you are ! Was I not always talking about her ? . . . Do you not remember the daughter of Sermed Effendi, one of the great officials ? One day in winter, in cold weather, we went to ' Azeb Kapousou,' in order to go to Eyoub. From there, in the distance, we saw them bringing a corpse in a boat."

" Yes, yes, I remember. How dark and severe the weather was that day ! . . . We thought, from the number of persons who followed the corpse, that it must be the funeral of some great person, and, being curious to know, we began to inquire. An elderly man who was there told us it was the funeral of a young daughter of Sermed Effendi. Well, the lady whose funeral you saw was the sister of this lady." . . . .

## MAHMOUD EKREM.

MAHMOUD EKREM is a modern Turkish writer, whose style is as remarkable for its elegance as his ideas are for their refinement. It will be seen from the following extract that he is one of the new authors, like Kemal Bey, who have introduced the European system of punctuation. Formerly Turkish was written without any stops whatever, which rendered its perusal extremely difficult, and gave rise, sometimes, to great ambiguity. In this respect, at any rate, the Turks have progressed of late years.

## LOVE.

عشق¹ ندر حياتك² لذتى³ . روحك⁴ صفاسى⁵ كوكل كه بر سمادر⁶ .
كنار افقندن⁷ محبت كونشى طوغنجه⁸ نه قدر لطيف اولور . عشقله محبت
ايسه كوكل عالمنك سحر⁹ وتنيدر . وقت سحر نه قدر حزين¹⁰ اولسه ينه
نظره رونق¹¹ ينه روحه صفا ويرر . . . . .

اى عشق ! بندن النى چكمهده استرسن كوكلمى حزن¹² ايله طولدر . . . .
؟ه نه غريبدر كه عشق عقلى فكرى بر باد¹³ ايدر جسمى جانى ياقار
قلبى دائما بر خلجان¹⁴ ايچنده براقار . اوبقو اوبوتمز يمك يدرمز . بو حاللرله
دائما انسانك حياتنه قصد¹⁵ ايدر طوررده ينه حياتك لذتى عشق ايله بيلنور
ينه وارلق¹⁶ عشقدن عبارت¹⁷ كوريفور .

" وارلغك عشقدن عبارت اولديغى صحيحدر."

عشق اولامسه موجودات اولورميدى ؟ جهان عشق ايله يرادلدى . جهان
عشق ايله قائمدر عشق اولامسه سحر اولمز . سحر اولامسه كونش طوغمز . عشق
اولامسه كيجه اولمز . عشق اولامسه ييلدزلر پارلامز¹⁸ . اى¹⁹ طالغملى دكزا!
سنكده جوش²⁰ و خروشك عشقنى اعلان ايچون دكلمى ؟ . . . . .
جان كوز نورينه نصل قاويشور²¹ يورك ده آغزه نه درلو كلير كورمدكسه

(1) A. *Ashk*, 'love.'—(2) A. *Hayat*, 'life.'—(3) A. *Lezzet*, 'taste, enjoyment.'—
(4) A. *Rouh*, 'the soul, spirit.'—(5) A. *Safa*, 'pleasure.'—(6) A. *Sema*, 'the sky.'—
(7) A. *Oufouk*, 'the horizon.'—(8) *Doghmak*, 'to be born, to rise.'—(9) A. *Sihr*,
'enchantment;' *sahr*, 'early morning.'— (10) A. *Hézin*, 'sad.'— (11) A. *Revnak*,
'splendour, beauty, glory.'— (12) A. *Huzn*, 'sadness.'—(13) *Ber-bad etmek*, 'to
send flying, send into the air;' 'to destroy, ruin.'—(14) A. *Khélejan*, 'agitation.'—
(15) *Kasd etmek*, 'to intend;' 'to make an attempt on anyone's life.'—(16) *Varlik*,
'property, possessions, wealth.'— (17) *Ibaret, olmak*, 'to consist of.'— (18) *Par-
lamak*, 'to shine.'— (19) *Ey*, 'oh !'— (20) P. *Joush-ou-Khouroush*, 'commotion,
ebullition.'—(21) *Kawoushmak*, 'to bring together.'

عاشق ¹ نكاه نصب جمالله بربرينك محزون محزون
معشوقترك ² ايدن
حالاربنه دقت ايت . روحلرينك كوزلرنده اوپنادىغنى يورکلرپنك و دوداقلرى ⁴
اوزرنده ترترترهدىكنى كورسين . سويلمك نه قدر لذيذ ⁵ در . هله سومك
اندن نه درجه دها طاتليدر . نه بختيار ⁶ در انلر كه بو ايكى لذتله متلذذ ⁷
اولورلر . يا نه بيچاره ⁸ در انلر كه بو لذتى طاتمدن دنيادن كيدرارا !!

(1) P. *Nighiah*, 'a glance.'— (2) A. *Ashik*, ' a lover.'— (3) A. *Mashouk*, 'beloved,
a beloved one.'— (4) *Doudak*, 'a lip.'— (5) A. *Léziz*, 'pleasant, delightful.'—
(6) P. *Bakhtiar*, 'fortunate.'— (7) A. *Mutélezziz*, 'enjoying.'— (8) P. *Bi-charé*,
'wretched.'

## Translation.

What is love? It is the enjoyment of life. The pleasure of the
spirit, an affection which is heaven. When the sun of love appears
on the horizon how lovely is it! When love is combined with affection it is the dawn of the heart's world. However sad dawn may
be, it yields beauty to the sight and pleasure to the soul. . . . .

Oh! love, withdraw not thy hand from me! If thou wilt, fill my
heart with sadness . . . Ah! how strange it is that love scatters
sense and thought to the winds. It consumes the body and the
soul, and leaves the heart continually in a state of agitation. It
drives away sleep and deprives one of appetite. In this way it
attacks one's life, yet the pleasure of life is only known through
love; all one possesses consists of love.

"It is true that all one possesses comes from love." If there were
no love, would there be anything existing? The world was created
by love. The world lives by love. If there were no love, there
would be no dawn (for us). If there were no dawn, the sun would
not rise. If there were no love, there would be no night and the
stars would not shine (for us).

Oh! stormy ocean! Is not thy commotion to show thy love? . . . .

How the soul comes into the light of the eye! How the heart
comes into the mouth. If thou hast never seen the condition of lovers
glancing at each other's beauty, mark it well. See how their souls
flash in their eyes, see the trembling on their lips! How sweet it is
to be loved! Well! to love is still sweeter. How fortunate are
they who have tasted these two delights! How wretched are those
who go from the world without tasting them!

## MEHEMET HILMI.

### THE TWO SERGEANTS.*

ایکی احباب چاوشلر .

درام ۳ پرده

(اشخاص)

| | |
|---|---|
| مارشال | |
| والمور . . . . . قائممقام |
| کیروم . . . . . چاوش |
| روبرط . . . . . دیکر چاوش |
| والانتن . . . . . زنداننجی |
| کوستاو . . . . . بحریه ضابط |
| طوما . . . . . مسن¹ بر ادم |
| ترهزا . . . . . کیروملك زوجهسی |
| لاورا . . . . . روبرطك معشوقهسی |
| اندرا . . . . . بر کمیجی |

برنجی و اوچنجی فصلی پورطو اندرهده وایکنجی فصلی روزا
اطهـنده وقوعبولمشدر .

---

بـرنجی فـصـل

برنجی فقره

(بر قلعهنك حولیسی مشاهده اولنور)

والانتن * لاورا

والانتن ـ و الحاصل پك كوزل سویلهیورسین . کوستردیك سبدلرهده
دیهجك یوق فقط بنی قاندیرهمزسین .

(1) *Mussin*, 'aged, old.'

* Constantinople, 1301 *Anno Hejiræ*, published by Arakil.

لورا ـ افندم هیچ اولمزسه باری . . . .

والانتن ـ خیر خیر . اویله شیلره دکلمك بڭم ایشمه کلمز .

لورا ـ عموجهٔجغم . سز دائما بڭم ایولکمی استرسکز دکلمی ؟

والانتن ـ اوت . بن سنڭ عموجهك اولدیغم حالده دائما ایولككی
ایسترم . لکن او صاچمه صاپان سوزلرینه ده قولاق وبرهٔم .

لورا ـ واه زوالّی¹ جوان بیچاره روبرباو!

والانتن ـ اه دیوانه² . سن روبرباودن نه اوکرنهٔجکسن !

لورا ـ نهٔیی اوکرنهٔجکم . او بنی سویور . همده بڭا الاجغنی وعد ایتدی .
بڭم ایچون بو بر سعادت دکلمی ؟

والانتن ـ دیوان حربده محکوم اولهٔرق حبسه قونلدیغنی بیلمیورمیسن ؟

لورا ـ اوت رفیقی قهرمان کیومم ایله برابر فقط . . . .

والانتن ـ جزالرینك ترتیب اولنه جغنی بیلمیورمیسن ؟

لورا ـ افندم بویله بر جزؤی³ قباحت ایچون ویریلهٔجك قرار اولسه اولسه
انجق برقاچ هفته حبس جزاسی . بشقه نه اوله بیلور؟

والانتن ـ بو مسئله بکا پك اغر کلیور . قورقارم حیاتلرینی تهلکهدن
قورتارهٔمیهٔجقلر .

لورا ـ ها !⁴ . . .

والانتن ـ وای⁵ سن قانون عسکریهٔیه مغایر حرکتده بولنهٔمغی از بر شیمی
ظن ایدیورسن ؟

لورا ـ مخالفت مرحمتلرندن ایلرو کلدیکیهٔجون .

والانتن ـ عسکر قانونی بویله شیلری دکله مز . شفقت قلبیهٔلری اقتضاسنجه
ایستر مرحمت ایتسونلر ایستر شفقت ایتسونلر . نظر قانونده متهمدرلر و
السلام . انك ایچون صاغ قالهٔجقلرینه هیچ امید یوقدر .

---

(1) *Zewalli*, 'poor!'— (2) *Diwané*, 'a lunatic.'— (3) *Juzvi* (or جزئی *juzi*), 'in-
significant, partial, trifling.'—(4) *Ha!* 'Oh, ho!'—(5) *Vaï*, 'Alas!' 'Holloa! oh!'

لاورا ـ سبحان اﻩ .

والانتن ـ بلكه بو اقشام شوراجقده[1]

لاورا ـ امان يا ربم !

والانتن ـ يا سكا بر عسكره كوكل وير ديه كيم ديدى؟ واقعا بر قهرمان[2]
اپيده حسنه[3] مالك[4] ايسهده عاقبت[5] چاوش[6] پايه‌سنده[7] بر عسكردر .

لاورا ـ اويله افتخار نشاننى كوكسنده طاقمش . يپوكلرينك حسن[8]
توجهنى[9] قزانمس بتون الينك محبتنى جلب ايتمش برچاوشدر . درت
سنه اول واندره ليمانى محافظه ايتمك اوزره بورايه كلديكنده كنديسنى
كورر كورمز طور و اطواربنه[10] قاپيلوب[11] محبت ايتدم . نه پيامم سويورم .
اونسز دنيا بكا حرام اوليور . اﻩ يوركم طيانه‌ميور .

والانتن ـ سوزلرم قلبكزه تأثيرى ايديور؟

لاورا ـ بنمى ! خير . اصلا !

والانتن ـ اوت ايشته كوزلرندن ياش آقيور .

لاورا ـ آﻩ . آﻩ عموجه‌جغم بويله فنا خليارله بنى محزون ايتمه . روبرطك
قورتيله‌جغنه قلبم شهادت ايديور . انشا اﻩ[12] ياتينده بو غائله[13] دفع اولورده
سزده محبتكز ايجابنجه ازدواجمزه[14] معاونت ايدرك سعادت حالمزه
سبب اولورسكز .

والانتن ـ چكيل . چكيل . بريسى كليور .

ايكنجى فقره

اولكيلر . . . . بر نفر ايله تبديل قيافتنده (مارشال)

نفر ـ مير الاى افندمز امر بيوردى بو مسافر افندى يه قلعه و ابنيه‌ارك[15]
هر طرفنى كزديره‌جكسك .

---

(1) *Shoura*, 'this place, this spot.'— (2) *Kahraman*, 'a hero.'— (3) A. *Husn*,
'beauty.'—(4) A. *Malik*, 'a possessor.'—(5) A. *Akibet*, 'after all.'—(6) *Chawoush*,
'a sergeant.'— (7) P. *Payé*, 'rank, grade.'— (8) A. *Hasan*, 'beautiful, good.'—
(9) *Tévejjuh*, 'favour, attention, countenance.'—(10) A. *Tavr* (pl. *etvar*), 'manners,
behaviour.'—(11) *Kapmak*, 'to snatch, catch, seize;' *Kapilmak*, 'to be caught,
taken, smitten.'—(12) Abbreviation for الله, 'God.'—(13) A. *Ghailé*, 'a difficulty.'—
(14) A. *Izdivaj*, 'marriage.'— (15) A. *Ebniyé* (pl. of بنا *bina*), 'a building.'

والانتن ـ باش اوستنه اعدرارينى اجرايه حاضرم
نفر ـ مساعده كزله¹ (كيدر) .

مارشال ـ سن بيلورسن .

لاورا ـ (والانتنه) نه كوزل دايقانلى .

والانتن ـ اوت كوزلدر .

مارشال ـ بو قلعه يك اسكى يه بكزيور .

والانتن ـ افندم باروتك ايجادندن² اوچيوز سنه اول ياپلمش اولملى .
چوقدنبرو خراب طوريور ايدى . فقط شو خستهلك سببيله قوردونلر ترتيب
اولمهلى بهر از تعمير³ ايتديلدى اردونك برنجى بلوكنه⁴ حبسخانه
ياپديلر . بيورك كيدهلم .

مارشال ـ يك يورغونم . ازاجق نفس الايمده صكره . . .

والانتن ـ امر سزك افندم .

لاورا ـ (عموجهسنه) بن كيديورم (كندى كندينه) وارايم روبرطونك
حالندن بر خبر الهيم (مارشاله) مساعده كزله .

مارشال ـ بو ماده موازال قزكز ميدر؟

والانتن ـ بندهكز اولى⁵ دكلم . بزم رحمتلو برادرك قزيدر . قرنداشم
جسور بر عسكر ايدى . بوندن اون ايكى سنه مقدم ميدان محاربهده باشنه
بر كله اصابت⁶ ايتدى .

مارشال ـ اسمكزنه در .

والانتن ـ والنتن مخلصمده غمسز . طوپچيلر بلوكنده اونباشى ايدم .

مارشال ـ نه قدر وقتدر عسكرلك ايديورسكز؟

والانتن ـ چوق دكلدر . اوتوز ايكى سنه دنبرو . همده بو خدمتى مع⁷
الافتخار ايديورم . نه چاره كه كچن محاربهده بر كله كلدى . شو قولمى الدى

---

(1) A. *Musaadé*, 'permission, assistance;' مساعده كزله , 'by your leave.'—(2) A. *Ijad*,
'invention.'—(3) *Tamir etmek*, 'to repair.'—(4) *Beuluk*, 'a division, a company (cf
infantry), squadron (of cavalry).'—(5) *Evli*, 'married.'—(6) *Isabet etmek*, 'to hit.'—
(7) A. *Ma eliftikhar*, 'with pride.'

كوتوردى . اول وقتدنبرو تقاعد¹ اولدم . بونكله برابر دليقانلیلر كبى حالا
قائم طمرمده² قاپنیور . شو عالمده عسكرلك كبى ايو خدمت یوقدر . واقعا
چوق تهلكه‌لرى وار ايسه‌ده اولقدرده مسرّتلرى وار در كه تهلكه‌لرينى
اونوتدیرر . بر ادم اوپله زمانلرى در خاطر ايتدكجه زياده سيله محظوظ اولور .
ايشته بنده كچمش زمانلرى در خاطر ايدرك متسلّى اولوب كيدیورم !

مارشال ـ تعیشكز³ نصل ؟ . . .

والانتن ـ اى ايشته . اورته⁴ حالى . ايتدیكم خدمتلره مكافات اولمق
اوزره جزئى بر تقاعد معاشمله وطنم بولنان بو قریه‌ده اخر عمرمى
كچرمكه رخصت ويرديلر . بو قاعده‌نك محافظلغنى بكا ويردكلرى ايچون جزئى
بر شيده اوته‌دنبرودن قوپاره‌جق⁵ اواورايسه‌م قناعتله كچنور كيدرم . عفو
ايدرسكر سزده سلك⁶ عسكريه‌ده میسكز .

مارشال ـ اوت !

والانتن ـ لكن رتبه‌ایچه ؟

مارشال ـ سكا مساوى بر عسكر !

والانتن ـ (روبالرينه دقت ايدوب) مأمول ايتمم پارسدنمى كلیورسكز .

مارشال ـ اوت !

والانتن ـ اردوبز قوماند'نلغنى در عهده ايدن مارشال جنابلرى نه زمان
بورايه كله‌جكلر خبركز وار مى ؟

مارشال ـ ذاتاً⁷ كلمشدر .

والانتن ـ صحیحمى ؟

مارشال ـ اوت يالانمى سوبليه‌جكم ؟

والانتن ـ غالبا سزده ؟ . . . . .

مارشال ـ اوت كندى⁸ ياورلرندن بریسى يم !

والانتن ـ عصرمزك⁹ اك مشهور¹⁰ و حميتلو¹¹ بر مارشالنك خدمتنده

---

    (1) *Tcka'ud olmak*, 'to be pensioned off.'—(2) *Damar*, 'a vein, artery, nerve.'—
(3) *Téayyush*, 'living,' 'maintaining one's self.'— (4) *Orta*, 'middling.'—(5) *Koparmak*, 'to pluck, gather,' 'obtain by pertinacity.'—(6) A. *Silk*, 'a career, road.'
— (7) A. *Zatan*, 'in person.'—(8) *Yaver*, 'an aide-de-camp.'—(9) A. *Asr*, 'a century, ago.'—(10) A. *Meshhour*, 'celebrated.'—(11) *Hamiyetli*, 'patriotic, zealous.'

استخدام [1] اولنمق شرفنه نائل [2] اولديغكز ايچون بنده سزك ايله برابر ممنونم .

مارشال ـ (تبسم [3] ايله) نه سويلەيورسكز؟

والانتن ـ اويله شجيع [4] اويله عالى [5] جذاب بر ذاتكه . . . .

مارشال ـ پك مبالغه [6] ايديورسكز .

والانتن ـ مبالغه دكلدر . هر وجهله مدحه [7] شاياندر . حتى كرك وطننه كرك ايمپراطور حضرتلرينه بيوك خدمتلر ايتمشدر . واقعا بن كنديلرينى * شخصاً كورمدم . لكن روايته [8] كوره سلك عسكريه‌ده بولنانلر حقنده شفقتى چوق وعادل بر ذات ايمش . اكثريا تبديل كزر . وهر شيئى كوزيله كورير . اكلار تحقيق و تجسس ايدر . مظلوملرى عدالتله كامياب ايتديكى كبى خائنلريده تأديب و تربيه ايدر ايمش ايشته ضابط ديديككده بويله اولمليدر . . . . . . . . . . . . . .

مارشال ـ پك اعلا . مسموعاتمه كوره بو قلعه‌نك محافظلق خدمتى كمال دقتله اجرا اولنديور .

والانتن ـ حقكز وار تجربه سيده ميدانده . يالكز كچن هفته زواللى محبوسك برى وار ايدى . البسه‌لرينى سلاحلرينى الوب تيمور پنجره‌لرك بر يسنى قيره‌رق قاچديغى ايچون طوتوب قورشونه ديزديلر . بو كونده ايكى بيچاره چاوشلر وار . عين جزايه اوغرايه‌جقلر كبى اكلاشيلور . براز اول ديوان حربه كوتورديلر . . . .

مارشال ـ ايكى چاوشمى ؟

والانتن ـ اوت . عالم آه ايكيسيده بابا [9] يكيت . همده اردومزده بولنان عسكرك اك كوزللريدر . بونك ايچون اردو خلقى كنديلرينه اجيورلر . [10]

---

(1) *Istikhdam olounmak*, ‘ to be employed.’— (2) *Naïl olmak*, ‘ to attain.’— (3) A. *Tébessum*, ‘ smiling, a smile.’—(4) A. *Sheji*, ‘ valiant.’—(5) *Ali-jenab*, ‘ magnanimous.’ — (6) *Mubalagha etmek*, ‘ to exaggerate.’— (7) *Medhé-shayan*, ‘ praiseworthy.’— (8) *Rivayeté ghieure*, ‘ according to report.’— (9) *Yighit*, ‘ a young man, a brave fellow ;’ *Baba yighit*, ‘ a full-grown young man.’—(10) *Ajimak*, ‘ to pity, to hurt.’

---

\* The 3rd person plural is often used for the 3rd person and the 2nd person singular, to show respect either for a person spoken of or to whom one is speaking.

مارشال ـ قباحتلرى نه ايمش ؟

والانتن ـ آه نـه ديهيم ؟ نصل سويلهيم ؟ مرحمتلرندن . هـر نصل
ايسه بر خطا [1] ايتمشلر . ايشته كليورلر كنديلرندن سؤال ايدكده باقين !


اوچنجى فقره .

كيوم * روبرطو * برچاوش * درت نفر و اولكيلر .

چاوش ـ غمسز اون باشى . ايشته محبوسلرى تكرار كتوردم . ديوان
حرب بو بيچارهلره خوش كچنسون هيچ بر كونا [2] بد معاملهده بولنمسون
ديو تنبيه ايتدى . بالجمله عسكرده بونك ايچون سكا رجا ايديورلر .

والانتن ـ باش اوستنه . هيچ قساوت [3] ايتميك . . . . .

روبرطو ـ ياهو . ايكيكنزهده تشكر ايدرز . ارقداشلرهده تشكرمزى بيان
ايت حقمزده نه كونا جزا [4] اولورسه اولسون قلبمز پاكدر [5] . وجدانمز بزى
تضييق ايتمز .

والانتن ـ (مارشاله) ايشيديورمـيسك ؟

مارشال ـ اوت .

روبرطو ـ كيوم برادر!

كيوم ـ روبرطو ارتق هيچ بر اميدم قالمدى . ديوان حرب [6] رأى طوپلايور .
قتل امرى شمدى چيقار .

روبرطو ـ بزم ايچون ارتق اميد قالمدى . بيچاره لاورايه اجيورم . بيچاره
قزجغز نقدر دلبر نقدرده صافدر! نه مرتبه حزين عجبا بو قره خبرى
الورسه نه حاللره كرفتار اولهجقدر؟

كيوم ـ (كندى كندىسنه) يا بنم زوجهم . يا زواللى چوچقلرم آه كنديلرينه
اول قدر ياقين ايكن وداعلشمقسزين اجل شربتنى ايچهجكم . (يوزينى اورتر)


(1) A. *Khata*, 'error, fault, mistake.'— (2) Or كونه (P.), *Ghiuné*, 'sort, kind.'—
(3) *Kasavet etmek*, 'to grieve, be frightened.'—(4) A. *Jeza*, 'punishment.'—(5) P.
*Pak*, 'pure, clean.'— (6) A. *Divan-i-harb*, 'a court-martial.'

روبرطو ـ (باشنى صاللايه‌رق<sup>1</sup>) دوشنمك كار ايتمز كبوم . واريم بن اوطه‌مه چكيله‌يم .

كبوم ـ بنده<sup>2</sup> اويله (وداعلشوب ايريلورلر) .

والانتن ـ طورك بو افندى سزكله ازاجق قوكشمتق ايستيور . . . .

كبوم ـ براق كيده‌لم پك مكدر بر حالده بولنديغمزدن بورادە طور ماهنز كنديلرينى متأثر<sup>3</sup> ايتمكدن بشقه شىء مفيد اولمز .

مارشال ـ حاشا سزك برر قهرمان اولديغكز سيماكزدن اكلاشيليور .

روبرطو ـ حسن نظركزه تشكر ايدرز .

والانتن ـ بو افندى مارشال جنابلرينك ياورلرندندر .

كبوم ـ سز او عادل ذاتك معيتنده ميسكز؟

روبرطو ـ او جسور او قهرمان ذاتك . . .

والانتن ـ (مارشاله) ديكله‌يورميسكز! باقكز نه درلو ستايشلرده بولنيور .

مارشال ـ ايشيديورم .

كبوم ـ اكر كنديلرى بورادە بولنسه ايدى . اكر ايشلديكمز فضيلتك موتمزه سبب اولديغنى كوره ايدى . . .

روبرطو ـ كيم بلور حالمزه نه قدر اجيه‌جقدى . . .

والانتن ـ ذاتاً كنديلرى بورايه كلمش .

روبرطو ـ كلمشمى ؟

مارشال ـ اوت همده كيم بيلور بلكه . . . . نقل ايدك بقايم نه ياپديكزده مجازات قانونه مستحق اولديكز؟

كبوم ـ افندم ايشى سزه مختصرجه بيان ايده‌يم . دون بزم روبرطو ايله برابر قورتون حدودنده نوبت<sup>4</sup> بكليور ايدك . بو برنجى بنده‌كزده ايكنجى قولدە بولنيور ايدم . روبرطو ياننه ياقلاشوب برابر سويله‌شور ايكن . بر قطر<sup>5</sup> اوزرينه بنمش اسپانياولنك بريسى كوزمزه اياشدى<sup>6</sup> . بزى كورنجه

---

(1) *Sallamak*, ' to shake, nod, wag, wave.'—(2) *Bendé euilé*, ' and I too.'—(3) A. *Mutéessir*, ' affected.'—(4) *Neubet beklemek*, ' to stand sentry, to be on guard ;' *neubetji*, ' a sentry.'—(5) Or قاطر *Katir*, ' a mule.'—(6) *Ilishmek*, ' to catch, adhere to.'

Q

حیواندن ایندی . بزه یاتقلاشدی . قوردوندن کچمك ایچون بزدن مساعدة

ایستدی . بخشیش اولهرق اوکمزه ٣٠ التون اتدي . بزه ویردیكی پارهیی

قبول ایتمیوب کیرو چکلمسنی اخطار[1] ایتدك . واقعا بر قاچ دفعه

ابرام ایتدی ایسهده ینه مساعدة ایتمدك . نهایت تف‌نکلرمزی کندیسنه

چویرهرك . اطاعت ایتمزسك شمدی سنی تلف ایدرز دیه تهدید[2] ایتدك

بونك اوزرینه مرلدانهرق[3] اقجهلرینی طوپلایوب حیواننه بندی . و قیالقلر

اراسنه طوغری غیبب اولوب کیتدی . بردە کونش باطمسی راده‌لرنده بر

اغلامه بر ایکلتی[4] ایشتدك . بردە نه بقارسك قادینك بری مرحمت

ایدك عنایت ایلیك دیهرك یواش یواش بزه طوغری کلدی . اویله بر

حالده که انسان طاشدن اولسه تحمل ایده مز . . . . .

روبرتو – بیچاره قادین هنوز[5] التي یاشنده بر چوجغك الذن طوتمش

درت بش ایلق بر معصرمده[6] قوجاغنه المش اچلقدن سفالتدن[7] او

درهجهره کلمشكه اغزینی اچوبده چوجقلرینه واه اولادم دیمكه بیله اقتداری

قالمامشدی . دستور دیهرك کیرو چکلمسنی اشارت ایدر ایتمز . بردن

برە اویله بر فریاد و فغان ایتمكه باشلادی که یورکمزه صانكه بر اوق

صاپلاندی[8] . . . . . زواللی کادی . چوجقلریله برابر ایاغمزه قپاندی[9]

هپسی بردن قوللرینی بزه طوغری اوزاتوب مرحمت ایدك دیو اغلامغه

باشلادیلر . کوزلریمی کیومه چویردم . باقدمكه کوزلرندن ایرمق[10] کبی

یاش[11] اقیور . . .

کیوم – سنكده کوزلرکدن اقان یاش لاتردی سویلمكه مانع اولیوردی .

روبرتو – بو بورك پاره‌لایجی منظرهیه ایکیمزده بر مدت حیرتله نظر

ایتدكدن صكره . . . . .

---

(1) *Ikhtar etmek*, 'to warn.'—(2) *Tehdid etmek*, 'to threaten.'—(3) *Mirildanmak*,
'to murmur, mutter.'— (4) Or اینلدی *Inildi*, 'a moaning;' *Inlémek*, 'to moan.'—
(5) P. *Henouz*, 'scarcely, only, just.'— (6) A. *Masoum*, 'an innocent, a young
child.'— (7) A. *Sefalet*, 'lowness, indigence.'— (8) *Saplamak*, 'to stick in;'
(*v. a.*) *saplanmak*, 'to be stuck in.'—(9) *Kapanmak*, 'to stumble, trip.'—(10) *Irmak*,
'a river.'—(11) *Yash*, 'moisture,' 'tears.'

كيوم ـ بربريمزك بويونكه صارلدق .

روبرطو ـ صكره بيچارهلری يردن قالدردق .

كيوم ـ كيزلی بر يول كوستروب برنجی خطه كلنجهيه قدر برابر كيتدك .

روبرطو ـ يانمزده نه قدر پاره وار ايدی ايسه كنديلرينه ويردك .

كيوم ـ بيچاره قادين مسروريتندن درترهيه درترهيه كچوب كيتدی .

والانتن ـ بنم قوچ يكيتلرم كليك . كليك . سزی بر دفعه در اغوش[1] ايدهيم الكزدن اوپهيم . مأموريتم اقتضاسنجه سرت طوراننمليم[2] . لكن سر كذشتكری ايشيدندجه يوركم پارچه پارچه اولدی . ارتق[3] تحمل قالمدی . اغلايهجغم . ايو ايتدكز پك كوزل طوراندیكز .

مارشال ـ طورك . نصل اولديده ايش ميدانه چيقدی ؟

روبرطو ـ ويرديكی رشوتی[4] يوزينه اتديغمز او خائن[5] اسپانيالی مكر بر قيانك ارقهسنده كيزلنوب بو حالی كورمش ايمش . بزدن انتقام[6] الق ايچون . كيتمش حكومته خبر ويرمش .

والانتن ـ الجق خائن !

روبرطو ـ ايشته بو صباح بزی در دست[7] ايدهرك ديوان حرب حضورينه چيقارديلر . شمدی مجلس مضبطهمزی[8] تنظيم ايديور .

كيوم ـ البته قتلمز حكم ايدهجكلر . كونش باطهجق رادهلرده شوراجه متهم[9] ادملر كبی قورشونه[10] دبزهجكلر .

روبرطو ـ اولقدر دشمنلره قارشو جنكشدم . يكرمی دفعه ميدان محاربهيه كيردم چيقدم . فقط شمدی ارقهداشلرمك بنی اولديرهجكلرينی دوشندكچه يوركم پارچهلنيور . . . . .

مارشال ـ بونده بتون بتون قطع اميد ايدهجك بر شی يوقدر . اكرچه

---

(1) *Der aghoush etmek*, 'to embrace.'—(2) *Dawranmak*, 'to assume an attitude,' 'behave.' — (3) *Artik* (with a negative), 'no longer, never again;' (with an affirmative), 'now, at last.'—(4) A. *Rishvet*, 'a bribe.'—(5) A. *Khaïn*, 'a traitor.'—(6) A. *Intikam*, 'vengeance, revenge.'—(7) *Der dest etmek*, 'to take, arrest.'—(8) A. *Mazbata*, 'a report,' '*procès-verbal*.'—(9) A. *Muttehim*, 'guilty, culpable.'—(10) *Kourshouné dizmek*, 'to shoot.'

بو احتياط قورّدونى محافظه‌سى الزمدر . لكن الحمده اطرافده اشورى خسته‌لك
قالمدى . مغ ما فيه ' بونى برنيت فاسده ياخود طمعكارلقله ياپماءشسكز .
مرحمتكزدن ناشى ياپمشسكز . بونى ديوان حرب اكلاير . شو نقل ايتديككز
حكايه بكا تأثير ايتدى . . . . . . مارشاله طوبديره‌يمده انشا الله بر چاره‌سنه
باقرز .

كيوم ـ صحيح‌مى سويليورسين ؟

والانتن ـ هاى الله عمركزه بركت ويرسون . صحيح بو بيچاره‌لره معاونت
ايدك . عجبا احتمالى وارمى ؟

مارشال ـ دمينجك<sup>2</sup> مرحمتى مسلمدر ديورايدكز . شمدى شبهه
ايديورسكز ؟ . . . . . .

روبرتو ـ آمان اياق سببى وار . لاورا كليور بيچاره قزبده محزون ايتميه‌لم .
بن اوطه‌مه چكيله‌يم .

كيوم ـ بنده كيدرم . ارقه‌داش .

روبرط ـ اه اصمرلدق (وداعلشوب قارشو قارشويه اولان زندانلرينه كيررلر) .

والانتن ـ (زندان قپولرينى قپايوب) (مارشاله) اى نه ديرسك بوكا ؟

مارشال ـ طوغريسى ايكيسيده‌ برى برندن بكيت قهرماندر . نه ايسه
هايدى بكا شو قلعه‌يى كزدر . بقالم . . . . .

والانتن ـ قلعه‌يى بر بشقه وقتده كزه بيلورسكز . كيدوب مارشاله ايشى
اكلاتمكزى رجا ايدرم .

مارشال ـ دها وقتى وار .

والانتن ـ دها وقتى وار نه ديمك ؟ وقتك قيمتنى بيلن وقتى
غيب ايتمز .

مارشال ـ عجله ايده‌جك نه وار ؟

والانتن ـ ايكى كشينك جانى تهلكه‌ده در . . . . . . . . .

---

(1) *Ma ma fih,* 'however.'—(2) *Demin. Deminjek,* 'Just this moment.'

بشنجی فقره

(لورا ایله کستاو) .

کستاو ـ ها[1] دلبر[2] لورا .

لورا ـ خوش کلدیکز موسیو کستاو . شو ایکی چاوشلره نه جزا ویردیله جکـنی ایشتدکمی ؟ بنم ایشتدیکم یالکز ایکی اوچ هفته ‹محبوس›[3] اوله جقلر ایمش . عجبا اصلی[4] وارمی . . . . .

کستاو ـ هرکسده اویله ظن ایدیور!

لورا ـ آه نه قدر ممنونم . . . .

کستاو ـ روبرطو ایچون دکلمی !

لورا ـ شبهه‌می وار!

کستاو ـ بنده‌کزده کیوم ایچون .


التـنجی فقره .

(ساعت ای اوور . یوارلق[5] پرمقلغك[6] طیشاروسنده قره‌ول[7] دکیشیلور) .

کوستاو ـ ساعت اون براز قالدی .

لورا ـ بریسنی بکلیورسکز؟

کوستاو ـ جنرالك برنجی معاوننی[8] بکله‌یورم . روز اطه‌سنده بولنان بلوکه ویریله‌جك نعلیماتی[9] کوتیره‌جکم .

لورا ـ روز ‹صه‌سنه‌می کیده‌جکسکز؟

کوستاو ـ برساعتدن صکره

لورا ـ ماشا اللہ . بو کون هوا پك کوزل یولده صیقندی[10] چكمزسكز .

_____

(1) Ha, ' oh ! '— (2) P. Dilber, 'charming.'— (3) A. Mahbous, 'imprisoned.'— (4) A. Asl, 'origin, foundation.'— (5) Yiwarlak, round.'— (6) Parmaklik, ' a grating, railing, banister.'—(7) Or قراول Karaol, 'a guard of soldiers or police.'— (8) Mouavin, 'an assistant.'— (9) A. Talimat, 'instructions.'— (10) Sikindi, 'un-pleasantness, trouble.'

كستاو ـ انشا الله . دكزدن اوچ ميل مسافهسى¹ وار . هوا ايو اولو

ايسه بر ساعتده كيديلور . على الخصوص شمدى ياز هوالرى دائما دوزكون .

روز اطهسنه دها برنجى دفعه اولهرق كيده‌جكم . فقط بوندن بويله² انشا الله

چوق كيدرم . چونكه هفتهده اوچ دفعه صندال³ كيتمهسنه قرار ويرلدى .

لورا ـ شو يمورجق⁴ خستهلكىده بتون اطراف اهاليسنى قورقوتيور .

تكرار بولشمامق⁵ لازم كلان تدبيرلرى اله الملى .

كستاو ـ اوت . بولاشق⁶ طرفدن تهلكه كلمامك ايچون اطه نه قدر

صندال وار ايسه جملهسنى قالدردك . شمدى اطهنك ساحله تعلقى

قالمدى . لكن اهالى حكومتى چوق تعجيز ايتديكيچون بزم ليماندن

هفتهده اوچ دفعه صندال كيتمهسنه قرار ويرلدى . بنده قپودانى

اولهجغم . . . . . . . . . .

لورا ـ اياق سسى وار . موسيو والمور كليور .

يدنجى فقره .

اولكيلر ٭ والمور

والمور ـ كيت چابوق عموجهكى بكا چاغر .

لورا ـ بر مسافر⁷ ايله قوكشيور .

والمور ـ كندى خدمتلرينه باقملى . اويله بر طاقم طالقاوقلقله⁸ وقت

غيب ايتمك اولمز⁹ . چابوق بورايه كوندر . يوقسه ارقهسى صره ضابط

يوللر اويله كتورتديريرم .

لورا ـ كى . . . كى . . . كى . . . كيديورم . افندم . امركز يربنى

بولسون . (بر طرفه¹⁰) نه قدر غرور¹¹ . شو حريفدن هيچ حظ¹² ايتمه‌يورم . . . .

---

(1) A. *Mesafé*, 'distance.'— (2) *Boundan beuilé*, 'henceforth.'— (3) *Sandal*, 'a large boat, a ship's boat.'— (4) *Yimourjak*, 'the plague.'— (5) *Boulashmak*, 'to spread by contagion.'—(6) *Boulashik*, 'contaminated.'—(7) A. *Musafir*, 'a traveller.' —(8) دالقاوق *Dalkawouk*, 'a buffoon;' *Dalkawouklouk*, 'buffoonery, foolery.'—(9) *Olmaz*, 'It won't do!'— (10) P. *Bér taraf*, 'aside, on one side.'— (11) A. *Ghourour*, 'presumption, vanity.'— (12) *Haz etmek*, 'to like.'

والمور ـ بو قدر وظيفهسزلك[1] . بيلمم ديوان حرب نيچون بو درجه كوشك[2] طورانيور .

كستاو ـ افندم مير الاى روز اطهسنه دائر بندهكزه بعض تعليماتلر ويردى خاكپايكزكده بر امرى وار ايسه . . . .

والمور ـ كيدك محافظ عسكرى مركزنده[3] بنى بكلهيك بر از صكره كلور سزى كوررم .

كستاو ـ عفو ايدرسكز . افندم . او ايكى چاوشلر حقنده نه قرار ويرلدى .

والمور ـ ايشته اعلاملرى[4] .

كستاو ـ اعلاممى ؟

والمور ـ مير الاى بو كون بتون بلوكه كوزل بر عبرت كوسترمك ايستدى .

كستاو ـ ايكيسيده قتل اولنهجقلر .

والمور ـ خير . يالكز بريسى قتل اولنهجق .

كستاو ـ اه ويرهده ولى نعمتم كيرم قورتيله ايدى .

والمور ـ بنده سنك كبى انك قورتلمسنى ارزو ايديورم .

كستاو ـ اوت . بيلورم . چونكه روبرطو شمدى يه قدر سزك حسن توجهكزى قزانمامش در .

والمور ـ كيدك سزه تعريف ايتديكم يرده بنى بكلهيك .

كستاو ـ پكى افندم (كيدر) .

والمور ـ (كندى كندينه) خير احتمالى يوقدر . روبرطو ايچون كوكلمده يانان كين[5] و غرض[6] اتشى هيچ بر وقت سونميه جكدر . زيرا او محاربهده كى وقوعات حالا خاطرمده در . اردويه قاوشمق ايچون اقنتيلى[7] بر چايدن[8] كچمكه بن جسارت ايتميوب طورر ايكن . او بر قاچ ارقهداشلربنى باشنه

---

(1) *Vazifésizlik*, ‘ neglect of duty.’— (2) *Ghevshek*, ‘ lax, loose, slack, lukewarm.’
(3) A. *Merkez*, ‘ a centre, head-quarters.’—(4) A. *Ilam*, ‘ an official report, declara-
tion ;’ ‘ a sentence of a court given in writing.’— (5) P. *Kin*, ‘ rancour, ill-will,
malice.’—(6) A. *Gharaz*, ‘ spite,’ ‘ a motive.’—(7) *Akindi*, ‘ a current ;’ *Akindili*,
‘ having a strong current ;’ ‘ rapid.’—(8) *Chaï*, ‘ a brook, stream, rivulet.’

طوپليوب اتندىيه اتلدى قارشو ياقهيه[1] چيقدى . صكره قورقاقدر ديو
كيتدى . مير الايه بنى شكايت ايتدى بن درت آى محبوس اولدم ٠٠ او
نشان آلدى ٠ افرين ديو هر كس طرفندن تحسين اولندى . شمدى حكم
قدر كنديسنه ياردم ايدوبده كيوسى چيكنهيهجك اولسه بن ينه المدن
كلان ظلمى كندوسنه ياپه جغم . مطلق اوجمى[2] المغه بر چاره بولهجغم .

سكزنجى فقره .

والمور ايله والانتن .

والانتن ـ افندم . بندهكزى ايستهمهشسكز .

والمور ـ سن بو قلعهنك محافظى بولنديغندن دائما بيوكلرينه اطاعته
بورجليسكز . كلان مسافرلرك اكرا ملرى ايله اوغراشماملىسك . سنى چاغر
ديغم بر دها بويله بكلته جك اولورايسهك سنى قورى اتمكله تمام بر اى
حبس ايدرم .

والانتن ـ (كندى كندينه) بويله اولور ايسه دها ضعيفلنئيرم .

والمور ـ ايشتدكمى ؟

والانتن ـ ايشتدم افندم لكن بيلمش اولك كه . . . .

والمور ـ الويرير .

والانتن ـ نه امركز وار .

والمور ـ شو محبوسده[3] اولان ايكى چاوشلرى حضورمه[4] كتور . . .

والانتن ـ باش اوستنه افندم . (كندى كندينه مغرور[5] شيطان (محبو
سلره) طيشارى چيقكز .

طقوزنجى فقره .

اولكيلر * روبرطو * كيوم .

روبرطو ـ شكر كورشدىكمزه . . . موسيو والمور . مطلقا سن بزه بر قره خبر

_____
(1) *Yaka,* 'the shore, coast, bank.'—(2) *Evj,* 'revenge.'—(3) A. *Mahbous,* 'imprisoned,' 'a prisoner.'— (4) *Huzour,* 'presence.'— (5) A. *Maghrour,* 'haughty, proud.'

كنتروبيورسك . همده بويله بر حال سفالتده كورنجه البته جان و كوكلدن
ممنون او ليورسكـز . دكلمى ؟

والمور – نه سويليورسين روبرطو ؟

روبرطو – بكا اولان عداوتكى ` پك اعلا بيلورم . قانمى ايچمينجه غرضكى
تسكين ` ايدهميهجكسن . فقط ايشته بنده يوزكه قارشو سويلارمكه . شمدن
صكره ارتق قورقهجق يرم يوقدر .

كيوم – (ايلرو كلهرك) امركزه منتظرم .

والمور – اعضالر` طرفندن ديوان حربك ويرديكى قرارى سزه قرائت
ايتمك وحكمنى اجرا ايتدرمك خدمتى بكا سپارش` اولندى .

روبرطو – ايكيمزده قورشونهمى ديزيلهجكـز .

والمور – خير ايكيكزدن بريكز قورتيلهجق .

كيوم – نه كبى ؟

والمور – (اعلامى اوقريهرق) اويله ايسه دكلهيك .


كيوم ايله روبرطو نامان چاوشلر احتياط قوردونى حققنده موضوع اولان
قانونه مغاير حركتده بولنمش اولدقلرى جهتله ديوان حرب هيئتى بالاتفاق`
ايكيسنك دخى اعدامنه` قطعياً حكم ايتمش ايسهده مرقومانك بو حركتى
مرحمتلرندن ناشى اولهرق و حكم قانونك عدم اجراسيده قابل اولهمامق
ملابسه سيله هم قانون عسكريهيه رعايت و همده عموم اهاليهيه عبرت
قصديله ايكـيسنده حكم قانونه اوغراتلميوب يالكز بريسنك اعدامى
و ديكرينك سلك عسكريده عدم استخدامى بالتنسيب` عادات قديمه
عسكريه موجبنجه مرقومانه زار` اتديريلهجق بيوك زار كيمه اصابت
ايدرسه انك طردى` . و ديكرينك اخشام ساعت يديسنده قورشونه دب

---

(1) A. *Adavet*, 'enmity.'— (2) *Teskin etmek*, 'to calm.'— (3) *Aza*, 'a member.'—
(4) *Siparish olounmak*, 'to be entrusted to.'—(5) A. *Bil itifak*, 'unanimously.'—
(6) A. *Idam*, 'killing, destroying.'— (7) A. *Bil tensib*, 'approving, deeming fit and
proper.'—(8) *Zar*, 'a die' (for playing dice).—(9) A. *Tard*, 'expulsion.'

لمسى إيجاب حالدن بو لنمش و اول وجهله اشبو اعلامك احراى احكامى

قائممقام والموره احاله قلنمش اولمغله . . . . . . . . . .

روبرطو ـ اوقدرى كافيدر .

والانتن ـ ديمك بو بيچارهلر جانلرينه قمار[1] اوينايهجقلر .

(1) *Koumar oïnamak,* ' to gamble.'

*Translation.*

### The Two Sergeants.

*A Drama in Three Acts.*

———

*Dramatis Personæ.*

Marshal ——
Lt-Colonel Valmour.
Sergeant William.
Sergeant Robert.

| | |
|---|---|
| Valantine | A Jailor. |
| Gustave | A Naval Officer. |
| Thomas | An aged man. |
| Theresa | William's wife. |
| Laura | Robert's sweetheart. |
| Andrew | A Sailor. |

The 1st and 3rd Acts take place in Porto Andera ; the 2nd in the island of Ruza.

———

### ACT I.

#### Scene I.

*The Court-yard of a Castle.*

Laura   .  .   Valantine.

Valantine.—What you say is all very fine ; and there is nothing to be said to your arguments, only you cannot convince me.

Laura.—At any rate, Sir . . . . . .

VALANTINE.—No, no, it is not my business to listen to such things.

LAURA.—Dear uncle! You always wish for my good; don't you?

VALANTINE.—Yes, as I am your uncle, I always wish for your good; but I cannot listen to your nonsensical words.

LAURA.—Oh, poor young man! poor Robert!

VALANTINE.—Ah, silly girl! What will you learn from Robert?

LAURA.—What shall I learn from Robert? He loves me, and has promised to marry me. Is not that happiness for me?

VALANTINE.—Do you know that he has been sentenced by a Court-martial and put in prison?

LAURA.—Yes, along with his brave comrade William, only. . . . .

VALANTINE.—Do you know that they are preparing to punish them?

LAURA.—If they decide on punishing them for such a trivial fault, it will be a few weeks imprisonment. What else can it be?

VALANTINE.—This matter appears to me very serious.

LAURA.—Ah!

VALANTINE.—What! You think it a trifle to commit an act contrary to military law?

LAURA.—That came from their being merciful.

VALANTINE.—Martial law does not listen to such things. Whether they had mercy or compassion, out of kindness, in the eyes of the law they are guilty, and there's an end of it. Therefore, there is no hope for their lives.

LAURA.—My God!

VALANTINE.—Perhaps, here, this evening. . .

LAURA.—Mercy. Oh, Lord!

VALANTINE.—Who told you to give your heart to a soldier? If he is a brave, handsome young fellow, after all he is only a soldier, with the rank of sergeant.

LAURA.—He is a sergeant, who wears the Legion of Honour on his breast, who has gained the favour of his superiors, and the love of the whole regiment. When he came here, four years ago, for the defence of the harbour of Audera, as soon as I saw him, I was smitten by his manners and fell in love with him. What can I do? I love him. Without him the world is a desert to me. Ah! my heart cannot bear it.

VALANTINE.—Do my words affect your heart?

LAURA.—Mine? No; not at all.

VALANTINE.—Oh, yes they do. There are tears in your eyes.

LAURA.—Oh, dear uncle, do not make me wretched with your dismal imaginings. My heart tells me Robert will be saved. Please God, this difficulty will soon be got over, and you will help us to get married, as you love me, and be the cause of our happiness.

VALANTINE.—Retire! Retire! Some one is coming.


## SCENE II.

THE SAME PERSONS. THE MARSHAL [*in disguise*] with a PRIVATE.

PRIVATE.—The Colonel has given orders for you to show this gentlemen, a traveller, over all parts of the castle and the building.

VALANTINE.—Certainly. I am ready to carry out his orders.

PRIVATE.—By your leave [*exit*].

THE MARSHAL.—You know.

LAURA [*to Valantine*]. What a handsome young man?

VALANTINE.—Yes, he is handsome.

THE MARSHAL.—This castle seems very old.

VALANTINE.—Yes, Sir, it must have been built three hundred years before the invention of gunpowder. For a long time it was standing in ruins; but since a cordon has been drawn, owing to this illness, it has been repaired a little. They have made it the prison of the first division of the army. If you please, let us go.

THE MARSHAL.—I am very tired. Let me take breath a little. Then . . .

VALANTINE.—As you please, Sir.

LAURA [*to her uncle*].—I shall go. [*To herself*] I will go and inquire about Robert. [*To the Marshal*] By your leave.

THE MARSHAL.— Is this young lady your daughter?

VALANTINE.—I am not married. She is the daughter of my late brother. My brother was a bold soldier. Twelve years ago a cannon-ball struck him on the head, on the field of battle.

THE MARSHAL.—What is your name?

VALANTINE.—Valantine; and my surname, Sergeant Ghamsiz, of the artillery.

THE MARSHAL.—How long have you been a soldier?

VALANTINE.—Not long. For thirty-two years; and I am proud of being in the service. What matters, if a cannon-ball came during the last war and carried away this arm? Since then I have been pensioned. Notwithstanding that, my blood boils in my veins like a youth. There is no profession in the world like the army. In fact, if there be many dangers in it, there are so many joys that they make us forget the dangers. When a man remembers such times, he is happy. So, when I think of by-gone times I am consoled.

THE MARSHAL.—How do you live?

VALANTINE.—Pretty middling. They have given me a small pension for my services, and permission to spend the rest of my days here, in my native village. As they have given me the care of this castle, I live contentedly, if I can occasionally obtain a trifle. I beg your pardon; are you also in the military profession?

THE MARSHAL.—Yes.

VALANTINE.—But what is your rank?

THE MARSHAL.—Equal to yours.

VALANTINE [*looking at his clothes carefully*].—I dont expect it. Do you come from Paris?

THE MARSHAL.—Yes.

VALANTINE.—Do you know when His Excellency, the Marshal, who has undertaken the command of our army, will come here?

THE MARSHAL.—He has come himself.

VALANTINE.—Really?

THE MARSHAL.—Do I tell lies (do you think)?

VALANTINE.—Probably you also? . . . . .

THE MARSHAL.—Yes, I am one of his *aides-de-camp!*

VALANTINE.—I rejoice with you that you have the honour of being employed in the service of the most famous and glorious Marshal of our age.

THE MARSHAL [*smiling*].—What do you say?

VALANTINE.—Such a gallant, magnanimous man . . . . .

THE MARSHAL.—You exaggerate very much.

VALANTINE.—It is not exaggeration. He is deserving of praise in every way, for he has done great service both to his country and to His Majesty the Emperor. It is true, I have not seen him, himself, but, according to report, he is very kind to all in the military profession, and a just man. He very often goes about in disguise, sees things with his own eyes, and investigates and inquires into them. He rights the oppressed and punishes traitors. That is something like an officer!

THE MARSHAL.—Very good. According to what I hear, you attend very carefully to this castle.

VALANTINE.—You are right ; but it is also very trying. Only last week, there was a poor prisoner, who took his clothes and his arms and broke a window, and ran away; and they shot him for it. To-day there are two poor prisoners who will suffer the same punishment, they have just brought them before a Court-martial.

THE MARSHIAL.—Two sergeants ?

VALANTINE.—God Almighty ! They are two young men, and the finest soldiers in our army, and for that reason the army pities them.

THE MARSHAL.—What is their offence ?

VALANTINE.—What shall I say ? How shall I say it ? Mercy. Anyhow they have committed an error. But here they come, you can ask them themselves.

## SCENE III.

### THE SAME PERSONS. WILLIAM. ROBERT. A SERGEANT.
### FOUR PRIVATES.

SERGEANT.—Corporal Ghamsiz. Here, I bring you the prisoners again. The Court-martial directs you to deal kindly with these poor fellows. They are not to be ill-treated in any way, and the whole army request you to act thus.

VALANTINE.—Certainly ! Never fear !

ROBERT.—Oh ! I thank you both. And give our thanks to our comrades. Whatever punishment we may receive our consciences are clear. We have no remorse.

VALANTINE [*to the Marshal*].—Do you hear ?

THE MARSHAL.—Yes.

ROBERT.—William, my friend !

WILLIAM.—Róbert ! I have no longer any hope. The Court-martial are here, consulting together. The sentence of death will soon be issued.

ROBERT.—There is no longer any hope for us. I pity poor Laura. Poor girl, how attractive, how good she is! How sad! When she receives this bad news what a state she will be in!

WILLIAM [*to himself*].—Oh, my poor wife! Oh, my poor children! Ah! although so near to them, I shall die without wishing them good bye [*he covers his face*].

ROBERT [*shaking his head*].—Thinking about it is useless. I will go. I will go to my room.

WILLIAM.—And I, too. [*Taking leave of each other and separating.*]

VALANTINE.—Stop. This gentleman wishes to speak with you.

WILLIAM.—Let us go. As we are in a very sad state, our stopping here will be of no use, but affect him and make him sorrowful.

THE MARSHAL.—Oh, no. One can see from your physiognomy that you are two brave fellows.

ROBERT.—I thank you for your good opinion.

VALANTINE.—This gentlemen is an *aide-de-camp* of the Marshal's.

WILLIAM.—Are you in the suite of that good gentleman?

ROBERT.—That brave, valiant gentleman. . . . . . . .

VALANTINE [*to the Marshal*].—Listen! See, how they praise him.

THE MARSHAL.—I hear.

WILLIAM.—If he were here himself, if he saw that the good action we did is the cause of our death.

ROBERT.—Who knows how he would pity us?

VALANTINE.—He has come here himself.

ROBERT.—Has he come?

THE MARSHAL.—Yes; and who knows? . . . . Tell me about it. Let me see. What have you done? Have you deserved the punishment of the law?

WILLIAM.—Sir, I will explain to you briefly. I was standing sentry, yesterday, with Robert, on the "Cordon" boundary. He was in the first, and I in the second, patrol. I had approached him, and while we were talking together we caught sight of a Spaniard, mounted on a mule. As soon as he saw us he dismounted, and came towards us. He wanted us to permit him to cross the *Cordon*. He threw twenty pounds before us as a bribe. We did not accept the money offered to us, and warned him to retire. He persisted several times, but we did not allow him. At last we pointed our guns at him, and threatened to kill him if he did not obey. Whereupon he muttered to himself, picked up his money, mounted his horse and went away, and was lost amongst the rocks. Again, about sunset, we heard some crying and moaning, and a woman came slowly towards us, saying: "Have pity on me! Have compassion!" She was in such a state anyone would have pitied her, even if he had been of stone.

Robert.—The poor woman led a child, scarcely six years of age, with one hand, and carried a baby six months old, and was in such a state of starvation and misery that she had scarcely strength to speak. On her asking permission to pass, and our motioning to her to go back, she uttered a heart-rending cry. To be brief, Sir, the poor thing came and fell, with her children, at our feet; and they all stretched out their arms and cried for mercy. I looked at William, and saw his eyes were streaming with tears.

William.—The tears from your eyes, too, prevented you speaking.

Robert.—After we had looked at this heart-rending sight. . . . .

William.—We threw ourselves on each other's neck.

Robert.—Then we raised the poor things from the ground.

William.—We showed them a secret road, and accompanied them to the first line.

Robert.—We gave them all the money we had about us.

William.—The wretched woman trembled, passed the Cordon, and went away.

Valantine.—Come, my brave boys, Come! Let me embrace you once. Let me kiss your hands. In my position I ought to be severe, but when I hear what you have gone through, my heart is broken. I can stand it no longer, I shall cry. You did right. You behaved well.

The Marshal.—Stop! How came it that the matter came out.

Robert.—The treacherous Spaniard, whose bribe we threw in his face, hid behind a rock, saw what happened, and gave information to the government, in order to be revenged on us.

Valantine.—The mean traitor!

Robert.—This morning they arrested us, and brought us before a Court-martial. And they are now drawing up the report.

WILLIAM.—Of course they will sentence us to death, and towards sunset they will shoot us, like criminals.

ROBERT.—I have fought with so many enemies, I have been in the battle-field twenty times; but now that I think that my comrades will kill me, my heart is broken.

THE MARSHAL.—You need not despair entirely. It is most necessary to guard the "Cordon" but, thank God, the disease is not so very bad in the neighbourhood now. You did not do this from a corrupt motive, or through avarice. You acted so from pity; the Court-martial understand that. Your tale has affected me. I will let the Marshal know, and I hope we shall find a remedy.

WILLIAM.—Will you, really?

VALANTINE.—To be sure! God bless you! Right. Help these poor fellows. Is there any probability?

THE MARSHAL.—Just this moment you thought mercy was certain, and now you doubt.

ROBERT.—There is a sound of footsteps; Laura is coming. Let me go to my room, and not make her sad.

WILLIAM.—I will go, too, comrade!

ROBERT.—Good bye! [*They take leave of each other, and enter their cells, which are opposite to each other.*]

VALANTINE. [*closing the doors of the cells. To the Marshal*].—What do you say to this?

THE MARSHAL.—Well, to tell the truth, they are brave boys. However, come, show me over the castle. I will see.

VALANTINE.—You can look over the castle another time. Go, I beg of you, and explain the matter to the Marshal.

THE MARSHAL.—There is plenty of time.

VALANTINE.—What do you mean by saying there is plenty of time? He who knows the value of time does not waste it.

THE MARSHAL.—What is there to hurry about?

VALANTINE.—Two people's lives are in danger.

SCENE V.

LAURA AND GUSTAVE.

GUSTAVE.—Ah, charming Laura!

LAURA.—I am glad to see you, Gustave. Have you heard what punishment will be given to those two sergeants? What I have heard is that they will only be imprisoned for two or three weeks. Is there any foundation for that?

GUSTAVE.—Everybody thinks so.

LAURA.—Ah! How glad I am.

GUSTAVE.—For Robert's sake, is it not?

LAURA.—Is there any doubt?

GUSTAVE.—I, for William's sake. . . . . . .


SCENE VI.

[*Eleven o'clock strikes. The guard is relieved outside a round grating.*]

GUSTAVE.—It is near eleven o'clock.

LAURA.—Are you waiting for some one?

GUSTAVE.—I am waiting for the general's head-assistant. I shall carry instructions to the company in the island of Rouz.

LAURA.—You will go to the island of Rouz?

GUSTAVE.—In an hour.

LAURA.—Dear me! As the weather is very fine to-day you will not have any unpleasantness on the road.

GUSTAVE.—Please God. It is a distance of three miles by sea. If the weather is good it is done in an hour, especially as now, in summer, the wind is always favourable. I shall go to the island of Rouz for the first time, but, henceforward, I hope to go often, as it has been decided that a boat shall go three times a week.

LAURA.—The plague frightens the people in all parts. It is necessary to take measures for its not spreading again.

GUSTAVE.—Yes. In order that there may be no danger from the infected district we have taken off all the boats in the island. Now there is no connection between the island and the shore; but, as the inhabitants of the island have worried the government very much about it, it has been decided that a boat shall go from our port three times a week; and I shall be the captain of it.

LAURA.—I hear footsteps. Monsieur Valmour is coming.

### SCENE VII.

#### THE SAME PERSONS. VALMOUR.

VALMOUR.—Quick! Go and call your uncle to me.

LAURA.—He is speaking with a traveller.

VALMOUR.—He should attend to his own duty. It won't do for him to waste his time with such tomfoolery. Send him here directly, or I will send an officer after him to fetch him.

LAURA.—I.... I.... I'm going, Sir. Your orders will be executed. [*Aside*] How presumptuous! I don't like this fellow. . . .

VALMOUR.—Such neglect of duty. I do not know why the Court-martial behaves so weakly.

GUSTAVE.—Sir! The Colonel has given me instructions about the island of Rouz. If you have any orders . . . . . .

VALMOUR.—Go! and wait for me at the head-quarters of the protective force. In a little while I will come and see you.

GUSTAVE.—I beg your pardon; what has been decided respecting the two sergeants?

VALMOUR.—Here is their sentence.

GUSTAVE.—Their sentence!

VALMOUR.—To-day the Colonel wished to give the whole division a good lesson,

GUSTAVE.—Both will be executed.

VALMOUR.—No; only one of them will be executed.

GUSTAVE.—God grant that my benefactor, William, may be saved!

VALMOUR.—I, too, hope he may be saved.

GUSTAVE.—Yes, I know; because Robert, hitherto, has not won your favour.

VALMOUR.—Go! Wait for me at the place I told you.

GUSTAVE.—Very good, Sir. [*Exit.*]

Valmour [*to himself*].—No, there is no probability of it.   The rancour and spite I feel against Robert will never be extinguished; for the events of that war are still in my mind.   It was requisite, in order to rejoin the army, to cross a rapid stream, and, while I stood hesitating, he collected a number of his comrades round him and threw himself into the current, and reached the opposite bank. Then he went and said I was a coward, and complained of me to the Colonel.   I received four months imprisonment, and he got a decoration.   Everybody said, " Well done! " and applauded him. Now, if chance helps him, and he tramples on William, I will oppress him as much as I can.   I must find a means to get my revenge.

## Scene VIII.

Valantine.—You wanted me, Sir!

Valmour.—As you are the keeper of this castle you ought always to obey your superiors.   You ought not to strive to do honour to travellers.   If you keep me waiting so again, when I call you, I will give you a month's imprisonment on bread and water.

Valantine [*to himself*].—If so, I shall get still thinner.

Valmour.—Did you hear?

Valantine.—I heard, but you must know that. . . . . . .

Valmour.—That will do.

Valantine.—What are your orders?

Valmour.—Bring the two sergeants, who are in confinement, before me.

Valantine.—Certainly, Sir.   [*To himself*] The proud devil! [*To the prisoners*], Come out.

## Scene IX.

### The same Persons.   Robert.   William.

Robert.—Thanks for seeing you again. . . . Monsieur Valmour, no doubt you bring us bad news.   You rejoice too, heart and soul, at seeing me in such a wretched position.   Don't you?

Valmour.—What do you say, Robert?

ROBERT.—I know very well the hatred you have for me. You will not be satisfied till you have drunk my blood. But I tell you, to your face, that I henceforth have no reason to fear you.

WILLIAM [*coming forward*].—I await your orders.

VALMOUR.—I come on behalf of the members of the Court-martial to read to you the decision they have arrived at; and they have entrusted the carrying out of it to me.

ROBERT.—Shall we both be shot?

VALMOUR.—No, one of you will be saved.

WILLIAM.—How?

VALMOUR [*reading the sentence*].—Then listen. The Court-martial condemned both the Sergeants, called William and Robert, to death, for having violated the law laid down with regard to the sanitary " Cordon; " but, considering that the conduct of the aforesaid arose from pity, and yet it is impossible for the law not to be carried out, with a view to showing respect for the military law, and making an example, the Court have approved of the law not being put in force in the case of both, and one only will be executed; the other will be expelled from the army. According to ancient military custom, the aforesaid will cast lots. Whichever gets the big die will be expelled, and the other be shot at seven o'clock in the evening. The carrying out of the terms of this sentence has been entrusted to Lt.-Colonel Valmour. . . . . . .

ROBERT.—That is enough of it.

VALANTINE.—That is to say these poor fellows are to gamble for their lives! . . . . .

## ABOU 'L ZIA.

ABOU 'L ZIA is a living Turkish writer of considerable ability, who has published several useful works.  He is the Editor of a Turkish Magazine called " Abou 'l Zia's Magazine," which appears monthly, and which is very creditably written, from which we have taken the following extracts.

## ABOU 'L ZIA'S MAGAZINE.

(مجموعه ابو الضيا)

---

*Historical Anecdotes.*

عثمانلیلرك میاننده¹ تیمور² باش دیه مشهور اولان اسوه‌چ قرالی اون ایکنجی شارل بر کون پك زیاده مست³ اولدیغی صره‌ده والده‌سنه ایفاسی لازم کلان حرمته⁴ بدل⁵ مخل⁶ رعایت⁷ حرکتده بولنور . والده‌سی مشار الیهك بو معامله‌سندن فوق الغایه مکدر اولمغله دائره‌سنه چکیله‌رك اوچ درت کون طیشاری چیقمز .

شارل والده‌سنك سبب احتجابنی⁸ مراق⁹ ایله قرناسندن¹⁰ استفسار¹¹ و حقیقت حاله اطلاع¹² ایلدکده در حال الله بر قدح شراب الهرق والده‌سنك نزدینه شتاب ایدر و دیر که :—

"مادام ! سرخوشلق ایله سزه لازم کلان احترامده قصور ایتمش اولدیغمی خبر آلدم . سزدن استدعای عفوه کلدم . بر دها سر خوش اولمامق اوزره بو قدحی دخی سزك صحتكزه ایچییورم . عمرمده ایچه جکم اك صوك قدح¹³ بو در ."

---

(1) *Miyaninde,* 'among.'— (2) *Démir-Bash,* 'a pensioner, or old servant.'— (3) P. *Mest,* 'tipsy, intoxicated.'— (4) A. *Hurmet,* 'respect.'— (5) A. *Bedel,* 'a substitute,' 'instead of.'—(6) A. *Moukhil,* 'injurious, detrimental.'—(7) A. *Riayet,* 'respect.'—(8) A. *Ihtijab,* 'retirement.'—(9) A. *Merak,* 'curiosity.'—(10) A. *Kourena,* 'associates,' 'the suite of a Sovereign.'— (11) A. *Istifsar,* 'enquiring.'— (12) *Ittila etmek,* 'to be informed.'—(13) A. *Kadeh,* 'a glass.'

فى الحقيقة مشار اليه او كوندن وفاتنه[1] قدر بردها هيچ بر وسيله ايله
اغزينه برقطره شراب[2] قويمامشدر .

___

پروسيا قرالى بيوك فردريقك وفاتنده ترك[3] ايلديكي البسهسى[4] انجق[5]
ايكى يوز فرانق قيمتنده ايمش . صندوقنده يالكز اوچ قات[6] البسهسى
ظهور ايدهرك بونلردن بريسى بيوك اونيفورمهسى ايدى كه مدت[7] عمرنده[8]
۳ دفعه كيمش ايدى .

ديكر ايكى قاتى او درجهلرده پيرايوب[9] كهنهلشمش[10] ايدى كه قرالك
انلرى كيمش اولديغنه كورنلر اينانهجغى كلمز ايدى . شابقهلرى چزمهلرى[11]
و كوملك[12] و مندیل تبدیلندن اولان چماشيرلرى[13] البسهسيله متناسب[14] بر
حالده ايدى . حتى مشهوردر كه بر كون كبراى[15] اجنبيهدن[16] بريسى
پوتسدامدهكى سانسوسى سراينى كزديكى صرهده دائره مديرندن " قرالك
البسه[17] اوطهسى نرهدهدر؟ ديه سؤال ايلديكنه مدير مومى اليه جواباً
" قرالك صرتنده درا"[18] ديمشدر .

___

روسيه ايمپراطوريچهسى (الیزابت)ك البسهاوطهسنده ۸۷۰۰ قات البسه
و ۱۵۰۰ كيجهلك[19] كوملكى موجود ايدى .

___

### Friends.

لياقت[20] سايه سنده قزانيلان دوستلر ثروت سايهسنده قزانيلان دوستلره

(1) A. *Vefat,* 'death.'—(2) *Sherab,* 'wine.'—(3) *Terk etmek,* 'to leave.'—(4) A.
*Elbisé,* 'clothes.'—(5) *Anjak,* 'only.'—(6) *Kat,* 'a suit.'—(7) A. *Muddet,* 'a space' (of
time).— (8) A. *Umr,* 'life.'—(9) *Piramak,* 'to grow old.'—(10) P. *Kiuhné,* 'old;'
*Kiuhnéleshmish,* 'worn out, old.'—(11) *Chizmé,* 'a boot.'—(12) *Ghiumlek,* 'a shirt.'
—(13) *Chemashir,* 'linen.'— (14) A. *Muténasib,* 'in proportion, corresponding.'—
(15) A. *Kiubera* (pl. of كبیر *kébir*), 'grandees.'— (16) A. *Ejnébi,* 'foreign.'—
(17) *Elbisé odasi,* 'a wardrobe.'—(18) *Sirt,* 'the back (of a man or animal),' 'a
ridge.'—(19) *Géjélik ghiumléyi,* 'a night-dress.'—(20) A. *Liyakat,* 'merit.'

مرجحدر ١ . چونکه ثروت اکثریا ضایع ٢ اولور . لیاقت ایسه ضیاعدن ٣ مصون ٤
اولدیغندن او سایهده قزانیلان دوستلر دخی ابدیدر ٥ .

(1) *Murejjah*, 'preferable.'—(2) *Zaï olmak*, 'to be wasted, lost.'—(3) *Zaya*, 'destruction.'—(4) A. *Masoun*, 'preserver, protected, safe.'—(5) *Ebedi*, 'eternal.'

## Translation.

Charles XII. of Sweden, well known among the Turks by the name of *Démir Bash* (the Pensioner),* being tipsy one day, did not, show his mother the respect which was due to her. His mother, being extremely pained by this treatment, retired to her apartments, and did not come out for three or four days.

Charles, being curious to know the reason of this retirement, inquired of one of her *suite,* and was informed of the real state of things. He at once took a glass of wine in his hand, hastened to his mother and said:—"Madam, I have heard that owing to intoxication I have been wanting in the respect due to you. I drink this glass of wine to your health, intending never to be intoxicated again. It is the last glass I shall drink in my life."

And, in reality, from that day, till his death, he never put a drop of wine in his mouth in any way.

---

On the death of Frederick the Great, King of Prussia, the clothes which he left were only worth two hundred francs. Only three suits of clothes appeared in his box, one of these was his full dress uniform, which he had only worn three times in his life.

The other two suits were so old and worn out that anyone who saw them would not have believed that the king had worn them. His hat and boots, and his linen, such as shirts and handkerchiefs,

---

* Charles XII. of Sweden was thus called by the Turks, as he took refuge from the Russians, after his defeat, in Turkey, and was kept by the Turks.

were in a corresponding condition. Then, it is well known that one day a foreign personage, while walking about the palace of Sans Souci, at Potsdam, asked the keeper of the royal apartments where the king's wardrobe was, and the keeper replied, "It is on the king's back."

---

In the wardrobe of Elizabeth, Empress of Russia, there were 8700 costumes and 1500 night-dresses!

---

### *Friends.*

Friends made by one's merit are preferable to friends made by one's wealth; because wealth, generally, is wasted and lost; but merit, being safe from waste, friends made through it are everlasting friends.

## SIRI PASHA.

Siri Pasha, Governor of Angora, in recent times, distinguished himself by his eloquence as a public speaker, his elegant letters, and powerfully written official despatches. His letters, speeches, and articles in newspapers, being considered models of good Turkish composition, have lately been collected in a volume called *Mektoubat-i-Siri Pasha* (Letters of Siri Pasha).

## SIRI PASHA.

### *A Letter to a Writer.*

قیمتدار<sup>1</sup> قلمکزله بو کون یالکز دولت علیهٴ عثمانیهیه دکل بلکه هیئت
عمومیهٴ اسلامیهیه ایتدیککز خدمتی عالمده تقدیر<sup>2</sup> ایتمین وار ایسه
قطعیا عرض ایلرم که یا غافل<sup>3</sup> یا متغافلدر<sup>4</sup> .

حقاکه<sup>5</sup> مداد<sup>6</sup> خامهکزك<sup>7</sup> هر قطرهسی<sup>8</sup> میزان<sup>9</sup> عدل<sup>10</sup> وحقده برغازینك
قلیجندن آقان قان برابر در .

اك مکمل اك منتظم بر اوردو قوماندانی دخی بو کون بلکه خدمت
قلمیهکزه معدل<sup>11</sup> بر ظفری<sup>12</sup> تأمین<sup>13</sup> ایدهمز .

خامهٴ سحرآفرینکزه<sup>14</sup> بو شرف<sup>15</sup> و شانی<sup>16</sup> قزاندیران ایسه شبه یوق
که مقصدکزك علویت<sup>17</sup> و قدسیتی<sup>18</sup> در .

عند<sup>19</sup> اهل انصافده<sup>20</sup> او اقتدارلی<sup>21</sup> شعشعهلی<sup>22</sup> قلمکزك عنوانی<sup>23</sup> "خادم
مذافع وطندر"<sup>24</sup> . نه کوزل بر عنوان مطنطندر<sup>25</sup> .

بندهکز اوته دنبری<sup>26</sup> بدایع اثار خامهکزك پرستکارلرندن<sup>27</sup> اولمغله جداً
متفخرم<sup>28</sup> . بو سببله در که ۱۱ کانون ثانی ۳۰۰ تاریخلو تحریرات<sup>29</sup> حکمت
بیناتکزده وجداور<sup>30</sup> برلذت روحپرور<sup>31</sup> بولدیغمدن انی حرز<sup>32</sup> جان ایلدم …

(1) P. *Kimetdar,* 'valuable.'—(2) *Takdir etmek,* 'to appreciate, value highly.'—
(3) A. *Ghafil,* 'negligent, ignorant.'—(4) A. *Mutéghafil,* 'pretending to be ignorant.'
—(5) P. *Hakka-ki,* 'verily, truly.'—(6) A. *Medad,* 'ink.'—(7) P. *Khamé,* 'a reed,
a pen.'—(8) A. *Katré,* 'a drop.'—(9) A. *Mizan,* 'a balance, a pair of scales.'—
(10) A. *Adl,* 'justice.'—(11) A. *Muaddel,* 'equal.'—(12) A. *Zafr,* 'victory.'—
(13) *Té'min etmek,* 'to assure.'—(14) P. *Sihr-aferin,* 'enchanting.'—(15) A. *Sheref,*
'honour.'—(16) A. *Shan,* 'glory.'—(17) A. *Ulviyyet,* 'sublimity, height.'—(18) A.
*Koudsiyyet,* 'sanctity, holiness.'—(19) *Ind,* 'the space near anything;' 'apprecia-
tion, estimation.'—(20) A. *Ehl-i-insaf,* 'people of conscience.'—(21) *Iktidarli,*
'powerful, able.'—(22) *Shashéali,* 'brilliant, flashing.'—(23) A. *Unvwan,* 'a title.'—
(24) A. *Vatn,* 'fatherland.'—(25) A. *Mutantan,* 'magnificent.'—(26) *Euté,* 'far off;'
*eutéden-beri,* 'for a long time.'—(27) P. *Perestkiar,* 'a worshipper.'—(28) A. *Mutéfa-
khir,* 'proud.'—(29) A. *Tahrirat,* 'despatches;' sometimes used in Turkish as a singular
for 'a despatch.'—(30) P. *Vejd-aver,* 'rhapsodical.'—(31) A. *Rouhperver,* 'intellectual.'—(32) A. *Hirz,* 'an amulet.'

*Translation.*

If their be anyone in the world who does not appreciate the service you have done to-day, by your valuable pen, not only to Turkey, but to the whole Muhammedan community, I maintain positively that he is ignorant, or feigns ignorance.

Verily, every drop of the ink of your pen, in the scales of justice and truth, is equal to the blood from the sword of a warrior (Ghazi).

The commander of the most complete and well-organised army cannot perhaps ensure a victory equal to your literary service to-day.

No doubt what has gained this honour and glory for your enchanting pen is the sublimity and sanctity of your purpose. Amongst righteous people your able and brilliant pen has been given the title of *" The Servant of the Interests of the Country."* What a magnificent title !

I am very proud that I have always been one of the admirers of the beauties of your works. Therefore, as I have found a rhapsodical intellectual pleasure in your philosophical letter of the 11th of January 1300 (*Anno Hijiræ*), I have made it into an amulet of the soul. . . . . . .

## DESPATCH TO THE MINISTER OF PUBLIC WORKS
## ON THE STATE OF TREBIZOND.

ممالك<sup>1</sup> محروسهٴ شاهانه<sup>2</sup> ایچنده هیچ یولی یوق بر مملکت وارسه اوده طربزون ولایتیدر دیه بیلیرم .

اندرون ولایتده معهود<sup>3</sup> ارضروم طریقندن ماعدا عربه یولی دکل عملیات<sup>4</sup> بشریه ایله وجوده کلمش دوزکونجه<sup>5</sup> عادی<sup>6</sup> بر حیوان یولی بیله یوقدر . قصبهلردن<sup>7</sup> کوپلره<sup>8</sup> و بر قصبهدن دیکر قصبهیه و هله ولایت و الویهٴ<sup>9</sup> متجاورهیه<sup>10</sup> کتمکه مجبور اولنلر دره تپه آشهرق<sup>11</sup> بر درجه زحمت و مشکلاته<sup>12</sup> دوچار<sup>13</sup> اولورلرکه کوزله کورلمدکچه تعریفی قابل دکلدر .

باخصوص طغیان<sup>14</sup> میاه اثناسنده کوپریسزلکدن طولایی یولجیلر هانکی جهتده بولنورسه محصور<sup>15</sup> کبی اواده توقفه<sup>16</sup> مجبور<sup>17</sup> اولور .

بو سببدن ناشی مملکته یول ایله کلمکه محتاج اولان ثروت<sup>18</sup> و معموریته<sup>19</sup> خلقمز متحسر<sup>20</sup> . و تزاید عمران<sup>21</sup> مملکته خدمت و دلالت ایتمک ایستیانلر هپ خائب<sup>22</sup> و خاسر<sup>23</sup> اولیور .

اورمان<sup>24</sup> و معدنلرك<sup>25</sup> کثرتی جهتیله طربزون ولایتی ممالك شاهانهنك

(1) *Memalik-i-mahrousé,* 'the well-guarded dominions;' *i. e.* the Ottoman Empire. — (2) P. *Shahané,* ' imperial.'— (3) *Mahoud,* 'well-known,' 'notorious.'— (4) A. *Amelliyat,* ' operations.'—(5) *Duzghiunjé,* ' in proper order.'—(6) A. *Adi,* 'ordinary.' — (7) A. *Kassabé,* ' a town, borough.'— (8) *Kieui,* ' a village,' ' the country.'— (9) A. *Elviyé* (pl. of لوا *liwa*), ' provinces,' ' flags.'—(10) A. *Mutejavir,* 'adjacent, neighbouring.'—(11) *Ashmak,* ' to pass over, or beyond.'—(12) A. *Mushkilat,* 'difficulties.'—(13) P. *Douchar,* 'a prey to, afflicted by.'—(14) A. *Toughyan,* 'rebellion;' ' overflowing, flooding.'—(15) A. *Mahsour,* ' besieged, shut in.'—(16) A. *Tévakkouf,* ' stopping.'—(17) A. *Mejbour,* 'forced.'—(18) A. *Servet,* ' wealth.'—(19) A. *Mamourïyyet,* ' prosperity.'— (20) A. *Mutéhasir,* 'sighing after, longing for.'— (21) A. *Umrun,* 'an inhabited place.'—(22) A. *Khaïb,* ' disappointed.'—(23) A. *Khasir,* ' disheartened.'—(24) *Orman,* 'a wood, forest.'—(25) *Maden,* ' a mine.'

اك زنكينلرندن معدود[1] اولديغى حالده مجرد[2] يولسزلق سببيله بونلردن همان هيچ استفاده[3] اولنه‌ميور .

سلطنت[4] سنيه‌نك[5] تزايد[5] وارداته[6] اك زياده محتاج اولديغى بر زمانده دخى بو مثللو منابع[7] صحيحه‌ء ثروتدن استفاده يولى ارانيلوب بولنمزسه انسانه يأس[8] كلمامك قابل دكلدر .

بو ملاحظات[9] قاصرانه‌مى[10] اولجه[11] مقام عالى‌ء نظار تبناهيلرينه[12] عرض ايتمشيدم .

شمدى‌ده ذات عالى‌ء جناب نظارتبناهيلرلرندن جمله‌نك يك بيوك اميدلرى اولدغيچون بو وجهله تكرار تصديعه[13] جرأت[14] ايلدم .

كره‌سوندن قره حصار شرقيه‌يه كيدن يوله بوندن بر قاچ سنه مقدم ايكى طرفدن باشلانوب عملياتى اپيجه ايلرولمش اولديغى حالده موخراً[15] سببسز ترك و تعطيل ايدلدى .

بونك ترك و تعطيلى مطلقا بعض عوارضه[16] اولسه كركدر . انجق بر اكر بو كبى عوارض طبيعيه و ضروريه‌نك[18] الجاآتنه تابع اولورسه‌ق مملكتمزده موسسات[19] نافعه‌دن[20] هيچ بر شيه‌ء موفق[21] اوله‌ميز .

حدم[22] اولميه‌رق بو سوزى اك صادق بر وطنپرور[23] صفتيله سويليورم اهالى كندى ثروت و سامانلرينك[24] تزايدينه خدمت ايده‌جك بو كبى عمليات نافعه‌ده نيچون بدناً[25] و مجاناً[26] خدمت ايتمسون .

---

(1) A. *Madoud*, 'counted, accounted.'— (2) A. *Mujerred*, 'mere, sole, alone;' Turkish adverb, 'merely, only.'—(3) A. *Istifadé*, 'deriving benefit.'—(4) A. *Sultaneti-seniyyé*, the 'splendid government' (the Turkish empire or government).— (5) A. *Tezayud*, 'increase.'—(6) A. *Varidat*, 'revenues.'—(7) A. *Menabi*, 'sources.' —(8) A. *Yé's*, 'despair.'—(9) *Mulahazat*, 'observations.'—(10) A. *Kasirané*, 'defective' (humble).—(11) *Evveljé*, 'previously, already.'—(12) *Nezaretpenahi*, 'the asylum of the ministry' (Your Excellency).— (13) A. *Tasdi*, 'to bother, give anyone a headache.'—(14) *Jeréet etmek*, 'to have the boldness.'—(15) A. *Mouékhkaran*, 'latterly, lately.'—(16) A. *Awariz*, 'accident, misfortune.'—(17) A. *Mebni*, 'based on, built on.'— (18) A. *Zérouri*, 'necessary, which must be.'— (19) A. *Muessesat*, 'institutions.'— (20) A. *Nafi*, 'useful.'— (21) A. *Muwafak olmak*, 'to succeed.'— (22) A. *Hadm*, 'warmth, anger.'—(23) P. *Watanperver*, 'a patriot.'—(24) P. *Saman*, 'necessary things, requirements.'—(25) A. *Beden*, 'the body;' *bedenen*, 'with one's body, bodily.'—(26) *Mejanan*, 'gratis.'

شبهه يوق كه نظام قديمى موجبنجه اهالى عمليات طرق ايله مكلف[1]
اولمزسه هيچ بر يول ياپيله‌مز .

همده خلقمز مملكته ثروت و معموريتك انجق يول ايله كيره بيله جكنى
چوقدن اكلامش . بناءً عليه ''تك''[2] همان لازم اولان يوللر ياپلسونده بزمجاناً
ايشله‌مكه راضى‌يز'' ديمكه باشلامشدر .

ايمدى خلقك تسويه طرق ايچون بو درجه ابراز[3] ايتديكى ارزو و هوسدن
بالاستفاده[5] عمليات لازمه‌نك اجراسيچون دولتجه‌ده بر از فداكارلق[6]
ايدلمليدر . . . . . . .

### Translation.

If there be one province in the Imperial Ottoman dominions without any roads, I may say it is the province of Trebizond. In the interior of the province, apart from the well-known Erzeroum road, there is not merely no carriage road, but not even an ordinary well-kept bridle-path made by man's labour. Those who are obliged to go from the towns to the villages, or from one town to another, and even to the neighbouring province or districts, passing over hill and valley, are exposed to trouble and difficulties which no one can imagine who has not seen them.

In particular, when the waters overflow, owing to the absence of bridges, travellers, wherever they may be, are blocked in, and obliged to stop there.

Owing to this, our people are deprived of the wealth and prosperity which must come by roads; and those who desire to increase and promote the cultivation and prosperity of the country are disappointed and disheartened.

Although, owing to the abundance of forests and mines in it, the province of Trebizond is accounted one of the richest in the Imperial dominions, merely owing to the absence of roads no advantage can be derived from them.

(1) A. *Mukellef*, 'responsible for, charged with.'—(2) *Tek* (*adv.*), 'only merely.'—(3) *Ibraz etmek*, 'to display.'—(4) A. *Heves* (*haves*), 'desire, inclination.' —(5) A. *Bil istifadé*, 'by taking advantage of.'—(6) *Fedakiarlik*, 'self-sacrifice.

At a time when it is extremely necessary to increase the revenues of Turkey, one cannot help regretting that some means is not sought and found to turn these real sources of wealth to account.

I have before made these observations to your office; but, as now everybody entertains great hopes from Your Excellency, I venture to trouble you again.

The road going from Kerésoun to Eastern Kara Hisar was begun at both ends a few years ago, but, after the works had pretty well progressed, they have been lately stopped and abandoned.

This stoppage and abandonment must be owing to some accidents; but if we are prevented by such natural and inevitable obstacles, we shall succeed in no useful undertakings.

Without any temper in the matter, I say this as a sincere patriot.

Why should the people not labour gratuitously, and with their own hands, at such public works, which will foster the development of their wealth and requirements ?

Undoubtedly if, in accordance with the old system, the inhabitants are not obliged to attend to the road works, no road can be made.

Our people for a long time have perceived that wealth and prosperity can only enter the country by roads, and hence they have begun to say : "We are willing to work gratuitously if the necessary roads are only made at once."

Well, the State ought to take advantage of this desire and inclination shown by the people to attend to the roads, and make a little sacrifice itself, in order to carry out the requisite works. . . . .

# APPENDIX.

---

## FACSIMILES OF MS. TURKISH LETTERS AND DOCUMENTS.

*WITH TRANSLITERATION AND TRANSLATION.*

# FACSIMILES OF MS. TURKISH LETTERS AND DOCUMENTS.

### I.

كتب عزيز و محترم

مكتوب محبت اسلوبكزى ممنونيت اخذ ومطالعه ايدم بوكونه كلنجه قدر
جوابنى ترقيم وتقديم ايده ميكده مناسف و محبوبدريمه بولى كثرت مشغلت
حل چوره حقرى مأموريد منلى جم نيه اوشتغرلبنه منا ـــــبله يد
، برابنن " سياحتى اختاربه نه وقت فرصت برلـبده جلم مجهولدر .
هرحاله عزيمى طرف عاليرنه وتنى كلنه انعار . وشوبك رعون
وانقه محبانكز رده طوجوب بيه شكروسار ايرم اقدم

حرمراهكز
عبدالحق حامد

٢٠ نور ١٤٠٤ﻫ

TRANSLITERATION.

MUHIB-I-AZIZ VÉ MOUHTEREM,

Mektoub-i-mahabet ousloubounouzou memnouniyetilé akhz vé
mutalaa etdim. Bou ghiouné kadar jawabini terkim vé takdim

*edémédiyimden muté'essif vé mahjoub isém dé bounou kesret-i-
meshgheléyé haml bouyourajakleri mé'moulilé mutéselli im. Yiné
o meshghouliyet munasebetilé bir "Braïton" seyyaheti ikhtiyariné
né vakit fursat boulu biléjéyim mejhouldour. Her haldé azimetimi
taraf-i alileriné vakiti gheliyjé ishar vé shimdilik\* davet-i-vakié-i-
muhibanénizdén dolayi béyan-i-shukr vé mésar ederim, effendim.*

*Fi* 20 *temmuz, sené* 1302.

    *Khaïrkhaniz,*

     ABD-UL-HAK HAMID.


*Translation.*

DEAR AND RESPECTED FRIEND,

    I have received your friendly letter, and considered it.
Although I am sorry and ashamed that I have not been able
until to-day to write and send an answer to it, I am consoled by
the hope that you will attribute this to my being so much occupied.
I do not know when I shall be able to find an opportunity of
making a trip to Brighton, but, in any case, when the time comes, I
will apprise you of it. For the present I merely express my thanks
and my joy at receiving your kind invitation.

Your Friend,

ABD-UL-HAK HAMID.

*July* 20, 1302.†

---

     \* Generally pronounced *shindi.*        † *Anno Hejiræ.*

## II.

\*

ه

مكتوبكزی اون طوغری

بوصباح دخی تأیسه دیجی الشمسه اوله ایکینجی مكتوبكزی مطبوعنی الدم
تركك نزجه سنه منتظم دنیا برچنی مكتوبكا تركجسنی طبع ایده جك بونا دخی
طبع ایدر

طوغریسی جوده همت بوردیكز طوغریه اینیلیز دریا یا بولو و دلیم ملته
جونكه شاشقنه التیزر الرشدی شو اجنبی جیدوده اعانه و یومعه
اولورسه كریه عصیانا شواعانه قویله بو سنه دخی طیا نمسه اولوبه
فقط شواعانه یا دیرمزرسه كریه عصیانا تمام بتر اوریب

سرمدن گجرده بوندنه تركجراك طبع اولنجه مسلمانلره هییم علیلری
تونه ملت ودولت دخی سزلیه همتلزده مرور اولدر ومأمول
ایدرم كریه مسلماندی طرفنده سزه برهدیه كلور جونكه كریه دكی
مسلمانه اهالی سائر مملكتلریزه نسبتله اوقور یازار كوزی آچیمه
وحریته مائل اصحاب فطنتدر . بنوك آی باشنه قدر بورادیم انشم

۲۷ اغسطس سنه ۲۷

سمائی

MURUVVETLU EFFENDIM,

*Bon sabah dakhi Taïmsé derj olounmoush olan ikinji mektoubou-nouzou matbououunou aldim. Turkché terjumésiné muntézirim ; zira birinji mektouboun terjumésini tab edéjéyiz bounou dakhi tab ederiz.*

*Doghrousou, chok himmet bouyourdounouz Doghroulouk etdiniz, zira, peh buyuk vé muhim meselé dir, chunki shaskin Inglizler éyer shindi shou ejnébi haïdoudleré iané veréjek oloursa Ghirid isyani shou iané kuvvetilé bou seué dakhi dayanmish olour, fakat shou iané vérmezlersé Ghirid isyani tamam bitér.*

*Shindi Mukhbirdé bounlarin turchéleri tab olounja Musulmanlerin hep maloumou oloup, bitun millet vé devlet himmetinizden mesrour olour, vé mé'moul ederim ki Ghirid musulmanleri tarafinden sizé hédiyé ghelir, chunki, ghiriddéki musulman éhali saïr memleketler-imizé nisbetilé okour yazar ghiuzu achik vé hurriyeté maïl ashab-i-fitnetdir.*

*Bendéñiz aï bashina kadar bouradé im, Effendim.*

SUAVI.

27, *Agostos*, 1868.


*Translation.*

MAGNANIMOUS SIR,

I have printed your second letter, which was inserted in the *Times*, this morning, and am waiting for the Turkish translation of it, for we shall print the Turkish of the first letter and this also.*

To speak truly, you have exerted yourself very kindly. You have done an act of justice; for this is a very great and important question: because if the English, who do not know what they are about, give assistance to the foreign banditti, the insurrection in Crete, by the aid of that assistance (subscriptions) will last this year too; but if they do not give this help the insurrection will completely end.

---

* Suavi Effendi, the writer of this letter, was the editor of the *Mukhbir*, a Turkish newspaper formerly printed and published in London.

When we print the Turkish of these letters in the *Mukhbir*, all Mussulmans will know about it, and the whole nation and the State will be pleased at your kind efforts: and I hope a present will come to you from the Mussulmans of Crete, for the Mussulman population there are better educated, more intelligent, and greater friends of liberty than those in our other dominions. I shall be here till the end of the month.

SUAVI.

*August 27th,* 1868.

III.

حضرت عاليلرينه

فضيلتلوم ومحبت فاشعايم انفم حضرتى
۱۲ ساطوقسس تاريخى واصل باردى تعظيم دتنرم اولاً كرمانه
عحيميبنرده يهزيربسيده محفنه ومنتكرفالدم او وظيفه
بكاعائد ايدرك كلده الحانيا و فوطبوعنه سبا هنده عوتى
ايحلى ابنى حففته قوهب بوارم اوننا ابشدمه كنزفدابى ناقابل
نعريفه قوهيفنه هنروك نقفيم عريضنه قوهه ايبنشه
سحفنا هوانم اركار واوصف جميلنرى ياد اتكده كروطوليفه؟
روتلوعجيما حفنرنه برعى رنه ده برقطه مفخرشنه رننشه
احننى بوليدلى بلره غرنه اوقورم اوطورنعى محل فوفان؟
حمالى بازرح قوهينى تبلووايدرمه نربنى ماوزبننه حيرم
بوقنه مرنيس مننه دب بوننه بادارك قويه واليسى ايده حهفه
برنه ديبك نيبه قوهزيه كنيس اسنبوله جيغرلكه انا رهافه
برمعوينه نيبه بوبانك ظلدايدرم يا زمحد قوهيفند بيركناره
بكا كوندريركنز حمالى كوف ديسعارنه هنكت ايده حه اوننا

مادم + + يتا ايله كوندرم دكيسنه دوسويدم
بحه اوتنه " ديدم ادوسيده د"برلوبه " يغيه بحله
' وطو ريبشره بلمه حلرله سزه كوريه ازده اين ديبلكشد
لوندره نريجكده سفينه ادغايوه ن بولديكشه يه
نيه نافه ايتيم نهواديك برتنه اول سلعات ده ايين
كوتنه حلواريدك !

بوقدجدهافده نعيح ابنيم انا ابه ينه معرفت ده غو
دكوبشيود انم اصله ١٨٨٩ ١٩١ مخلصه


TRANSLITERATION.

HUZOUR-I-ALILERINÉ,

*Fazilet-mé'abim vé muhib-i vefashiarim, Effendim, hazretleri!*

*On deurt shubat, sené bin, sekkiz yuz seksen dokkouz tarikhli vasil-i-eyyad-i-tazim vé tekrim olan keremnamé-i-alilerinizden pek ziudésilé memnoun vé mutéshekkir kaldim. O vazifé bana a'id idise dé, gechenlerdé alamanyayé vukou boulan seyyahetden avdet idéli iki hafta oloup bouraja olan ishlerimin kesreti- isé na kabil tarif oldoughoundan zérouri takdim-i-arizédé kousouroum edilmishdir. Ma huza her daïm ezkiar vé evsaf -i-jémilerini yad etmekdé ghéri douroulmamakdada devletlu Saïd Pasha hazretleriné birinji rutbéden bir kita mejidi Nishan- i-zishan ihsan bouyourouldoughou bendé ghazétade okoudoum. Otourdoughou Mahal Tophanédé, Sali-bazarindé oldoughounou bilir-idi-semdé shindiki mé'mouriyetinden khabrim yokdour. Rutbési*

*mushirdir.   Boundan evvel konia valisi idi.   Yeriné digheri ta-
yin olounarak kendisi Istambola chagirildi, ama daha henuz bir
mémouriyyeté tayin bouyouroulmadi zan ederim.   Yazajak oldou-
ghounouz tebriknamƴi bana ghieundururséniz Sali ghiunu Der-i-
Saadeté heréket edéjek olan Madam . . . . . Pasha ilé ghieundur
urum vé kendisiné suilédem.   Bash ustuna dédiler.   Adresinizi vé
Braïtona yakin bir mahalda otourdoughounouzou bilmish olsaïdi
sizi   ghieurmek   arzou   etdighini   dé   suilémishdir.   Londrayé
teshrifinizdé  séfareté  oghrayip  dé  béni  boulamadighiniza  pek
ziadé téessuf etdim.   Né olour oudou.   Bir ghiun evvel maloumat
veré-idiniz ghieurmush olour-oudouk !*

*Bou kadar kiafi dir tasdi etméyéyim.   Inshallah yiné mulakat
olour vé ghieurushulour Effendim.*

*Fi 16 Shubat,* 1889.                              MUKHLISINIZ.

### *Translation.*

My Faithful and Excellent Friend,

I am obliged and thankful to you for your kind and esteemed
letter dated the 14th of February, 1889, which has reached my
hands. It was my duty to have written, but, although it is a fortnight
since my return here from a journey in Germany I made lately, I
have been unable to write, because I cannot tell you how busy I
have been.

I also saw in the newspaper that H.E. Saïd Pasha, who is always
mentioning your good qualities, has had the Mejidiyyeh of the
First Class, in diamonds, conferred on him.   Although I know
that he resides at Tophané, at Sali-Bazar, I do not know what
office he now holds.   His rank is that of " Mushir " (Full General).
He was formerly Governor of Koniah.   Another has now been
appointed in his place, and he has been recalled to Constantinople.
As yet, I think, he has not received another appointment.   If you
send me your letter of congratulation for him, I will forward it by
Madame . . . . . Pasha, who will start for Constantinople on Tuesday.
I spoke to her about it, and she said : " Certainly ! " She said also
that if she had known that you resided near Brighton she would
have liked to have seen you. . . . .

I much regret you did not find me at the Embassy, when you visited London and called there. If you had sent word a day before we should have seen each other.

I think this is sufficient; I will not tire you. I hope we shall see each other again.

Your Sincere Friend,

HALIL.*

*February 16th,* 1889.

---

* The above letter was written by Capt. Halil Bey, now Naval Attaché at the Turkish Embassy in London, formerly a student at the Imperial Naval College at Constantinople, while I was Professor there. He distinguished himself at the College by his zeal and ability in acquiring English under myself; and he has since studied German in Germany. I have lately had the pleasure of seeing that he is most proficient both in German and English. Such linguistic ability, and other scientific talents, make him a most promising officer, of whom his country will some day be proud.—C.W.

IV.

رسنه... كايريچتشي

محترم ودقتور

كاير يچتشي نابچله ببره دست معز تراولا نمه ياتگنه
نمعه نذ رجواب باره ديتمده جدا لجوم ملنا البركيت
مشغوليت اوليغنده معذ دركه بيو يم تكريبه عفذكاوطبه
نشاباً اولدم ووريتم كناجرك ايشكله باازدخفنا ارقبرده
منونه ادوش شبقرلنك باانه بملذيفه قلغا ينم
كنلد ده نشابنله بيتله خياسه برينه باازديم مكتوبه
ملله ودرس يه ترجمة علا كناجه كوزدرمنى جباً نشدم بملوزة
كونذ ربس يه جلاء طنتكزه ايتلا ببوجم طبيب.

حامربك باذ برالا لو نذروبمحودنا تيجگنده معلم ماكن
اوديفنا بيلبو يم جلا

بودنكاذوه سعايق تشريعتبا يدربلا

كذبسبه كرد وشتوربنى ده مسدرا بدبيكلا

اميا بدبكه ماوام بترده نبوته كسباعبنا نشذ ور.

## TRANSLITERATION.

*Londra fi* 22 *Kianoun-i-evvel sené* 1889.

MOUHTEREM DOCTOR,

On deurt kianoun-i-evvel seksen dokkouz tarikhli residé-i-dest-i-mefkharetim olan tahriratinizé shindiyé kadar jawab yazamadighimdan jidden mahjoubim. Mani isé kesret-i-meshghouliyyet oldoughoundan mazour ghieurulurum fikrilé afvinizi tulabé shitaban oldoum verdighim kitablerin ishinizé yarardighini okouyarak memnoun oldoum ousedé, bashkalerinin yanimdé boulounmadighina té'essuf etdim. Gechenlerdé istambollé boulounan ahibbamdan biriné yazdighim mektoubdé mumkin oloursa bir terjumé-i-hal kitabi ghieundurmasini rija etmishdim, boulourdé ghieundururusé der hal tarafinizé isbal edéjéyim tabi dir.

Hamid Bey, beraderimiz Londraya avdet etdiyinden maloumatiniz oldoughounon biléyorim hali bir vakitinizdé sefareté teshrif edérséniz kendisilé ghieurushur bizi dé mesrour edérsiniz. Umid ederim-ki madam bitoun bitoun kesb-i-afiyyet etmishdir . . . . . Dewam-i-tévejjuhunuzu témenna ederim.

*Translation.*

*London, 22nd December, 1889.

RESPECTED DOCTOR,

I am quite ashamed that I have not until now been able to answer your esteemed letter of the 14th December. As I think I shall be excused owing to my being prevented by press of business, I hasten to ask your pardon. I was glad to hear that the books I gave you for your work were of use, and I regret that I have not

---

* The address of the writer, and the date, are usually written at the foot of the letter in Turkey. Their being written at the head of the letter is an innovation, probably made by the writer owing to his being in England.

others.   In a letter I lately wrote to a friend of mine in Constantinople, I requested him, if possible, to send a book such as you require.   If he sends it here, I will immediately forward it to you.

I know that you are aware that our " brother " (friend) Hamid Bey has returned to London.   When you have leisure, if you call at the Embassy, you can meet him, and we shall be delighted to see you.   I hope your wife has quite recovered her health.   I beg for the continuation of your favour.

HILMY.*

* I have to thank this gentleman, Hilmy Bey, for his courtesy and kindness in drawing my attention to several interesting Turkish works lately published in Constantinople.

www.ingramcontent.com/pod-product-compliance
Lightning Source LLC
Chambersburg PA
CBHW021040030726
47496CB00006B/1627